CONSTRUCTION CONTRACTING
Business and Legal Principles

Second Edition

STUART H. BARTHOLOMEW
California State University

Prentice Hall

Upper Saddle River, New Jersey
Columbus, Ohio

Library of Congress Cataloging-in-Publication Data

Bartholomew, Stuart H.
  Construction contracting : business and legal principles / Stuart H. Bartholomew.—2nd ed.
    p. cm.
  Includes bibliographical references and index.
  ISBN 0-13-091055-4
    1. Construction contracts—United States. I. Title.

KF902 .B37 2001
343.73'078624—dc21

2001018546

Editor in Chief: Stephen Helba
Executive Editor: Ed Francis
Production Editor: Christine M. Buckendahl
Production Coordination: Tim Flem, PublishWare
Design Coordinator: Robin G. Chukes
Cover Designer: Thomas Borah
Cover photo: International Stock
Production Manager: Matt Ottenweller
Marketing Manager: Jamie Van Voorhis

This book was set in TimesTen by PublishWare, and was printed and bound by
R. R. Donnelley & Sons Company. The cover was printed by Phoenix Color Corp.

Prentice-Hall International (UK) Limited, *London*
Prentice-Hall of Australia Pty. Limited, *Sydney*
Prentice-Hall Canada Inc., *Toronto*
Prentice-Hall Hispanoamericana, S.A., *Mexico*
Prentice-Hall of India Private Limited, *New Delhi*
Prentice-Hall of Japan, Inc., *Tokyo*
Pearson Education Asia Pte. Ltd.
Editora Prentice-Hall do Brasil, Ltda., *Rio de Janeiro*

10 9 8 7 6 5 4 3 2 1
ISBN: 0-13-091055-4

Foreword

After completion of my formal civil engineering training, I pursued a career as an engineer and executive employed by contractors in the heavy construction industry. Before too long, I became involved with a number of intractable disputes with a project's owner in connection with a tunnel contract I was managing. My employer suggested that I meet with our firm's lawyer to obtain guidance regarding some contract issues, and during that meeting and subsequent ones, I quickly came to realize how little I knew about some of the legal and practical aspects of construction contracts, despite having been exposed to an engineering school course on contracts. I also became aware that most of the lawyers with whom I was dealing had less than a full appreciation of the real-world challenges imposed upon those who manage construction.

I subsequently discovered that the ignorance I just described is common. Unfortunately, many, if not most, professionals involved in the construction process do not have a thorough practical understanding of the law as it applies to the contracting business. Those of us involved in the industry work in a highly complex and constantly evolving world. In addition to the obvious expertise required in engineering, construction methods, equipment, and costs, our knowledge must also encompass such other disciplines and specialties as politics, the environment, labor, finance, banking, accounting, taxes, safety, insurance, and bonding. With all of these burdens, it is not surprising that many practitioners have only a rudimentary and sometimes mistaken understanding of our construction contracts and the law that applies to them. Both owners and contractors have great sensitivity and concern with securing and protecting their rights. Many disputes would be avoided, however, if more of those involved had knowledge, greater sensitivity, and concern regarding their responsibilities as parties to the process.

Over the years, our industry has burdened the nation's courts and other resources with many disputes that the contracting parties have been unable to resolve internally. The industry has been making heroic efforts to reduce this burden with some success, but much more needs to be done. The enhancement of the parties' practical knowledge of the law will be helpful. Many disputes have at their core a lack of understanding of the law and its application to construction contracts. Construction professionals are not the only ones who are ignorant. The problem is complicated by an occasional, poorly considered, and confusing court decision that complicates and modifies long-settled legal principles.

With this background, the author presents a comprehensive overview of some of the legal principles and practices that relate to contracting for construction. While this book is designed for use as a text for a university course, students as well as practitioners employed by all of the parties will be better equipped to confidently supervise and manage the construction of our infrastructure armed with the information and wisdom contained herein. The incidence of disputes no doubt will be reduced, and our society and industry will be the beneficiary.

Norman A. Nadel, P. E.
Former Chairman & CEO, MacLean Grove & Company, Inc.
Fellow, American Society of Civil Engineers
Member, National Academy of Engineering

Preface to the Second Edition

In general, this second edition incorporates numerous changes and additions to every chapter of the first edition based on three years of the book's use as a classroom text since the publication of the first edition in 1998. Most of these changes are minor and are in response to student questions and comments. Numerous additional examples have been included to illustrate points that needed clarification.

More specifically, the material on reports of physical site conditions has been shifted from its previous location in Chapter 4 to a more appropriate place in Chapter 5 on contract "red flag" clauses. Chapter 18, on allocating responsibility for delays, has been extensively revised and expanded with new material and illustrations. Finally, a new Chapter 22 on the important subject of construction contract claims has been included before the final chapter in the book on dispute resolution, which now appears as Chapter 23.

The response from university faculty who use the book has been encouraging and my sincere thanks are due to them for the helpful comments I have received. I would also like to thank the reviewers of this second edition, who include David Bilbo, Texas A&M University; Dianne H. Kay, Southern Illinois University; and John Wiggins, New Jersey Institute of Technology. Finally, I remain grateful to Ed Francis, Executive Editor at Prentice Hall, for his continued encouragement and support; to the entire Prentice Hall editorial staff; and especially to my students at California State University, Chico, who have been immensely helpful in revising this second edition.

Stuart H. Bartholomew
Chico, California
March 2001

Preface to the First Edition

This book was written primarily as a teaching text for senior students in baccalaureate university programs in construction engineering or construction management who plan careers in the contracting or construction management segments of the industry. It should also serve as a useful reference for the younger, less-experienced person in construction contracting or construction management organizations as well as owners of small contracting firms or related businesses. The material, drawn from various sources, has been organized and presented in the light of the writer's many years in the industry and 13 years' experience in teaching construction management courses at California State University, Chico.

I am not a lawyer, and this book does not purport to offer legal advice. A competent construction attorney should always be sought for that purpose. This book does, however, furnish practical guidance for construction practitioners in typical everyday situations empirically by examination of the more common case law holdings and the customs and practices of the industry.

The field of construction law is so broad that difficult choices must be made in deciding what to include in a text primarily intended for a single three-semester-hour university course. Accordingly, I have tailored the material to those areas that, in the light of my own experience, seem most fundamental, leaving such topics as claims preparation, presentation, and defense; damages quantification; and CPM scheduling techniques, and the like to the authors of the many excellent specialized texts on these subjects available today. Similarly, I have excluded detailed discussion of mechanic lien laws and similar topics that vary widely from state to state.

The Table of Contents should provide the reader an immediate referral to topics of particular interest. The key words and concepts used and developed in each chapter are listed in the beginning of the chapter. These should prove helpful as a study guide and to test recollection as the reader completes the chapter. Also, each chapter concludes with a series of questions and problems. The questions provide a direct opportunity for testing comprehension of the material. The problems have been designed to develop the reader's understanding in the context of typical industry situations.

Many individuals have indirectly contributed to this book. They include Harvey Slocum, a legendary figure in heavy construction, who gave me my first job more than 50 years ago, and John Soult, Wallace Hunt, and Floyd Crawford (all now deceased) who furnished continual encouragement and support during my years at Fruin-Colnon Corporation. Also, extremely capable construction attorneys have skillfully guided me over the years and contributed to my understanding of legal matters. They include Harold Blasky, Esq., with both the law firms of Max E. Greenberg, Trayman, Cantor & Blasky and Schnader, Harrison, Segal & Lewis; Overton Currie, Esq., Aubrey Currie, Esq., and Tom Kellerher, Esq., all with the law firm of Smith, Currie & Hankock; John Tracy, Esq., at various times with the law firms of Lewis, Mitchell, & Moore, Gadsby & Hanna, and Thompson & Waldron; Lewis Baker, Esq., with the law firm of Watt, Tieder & Hoffer; James Hawkins, Esq., Michael Wilson, Esq., and Larry Luber, Esq., all with Greensfelder, Hemker & Gale; and William McInerney, Esq., and Robert Leslie, Esq., with the law firm of McInerney and Dillon. In addition, I would like to thank Robert Leslie, who stole many hours from his busy schedule to review an early draft of the book and offered countless helpful criticisms and suggestions for improvement.

Finally, shared construction experiences with my many friends—engineers, owners, and contractors alike—have inevitably shaped the content of this book. These individuals will have no difficulty in recognizing much of themselves in its pages.

To all who have shared and influenced my life in construction, named and not named, I am profoundly grateful. This book is my offer of thanks—by the means of passing on to young people today, with their careers ahead of them, what we collectively learned and wish we had known when we were their age.

Stuart H. Bartholomew
Chico, California
August 1996

Contents

1

Interface of the Law with the Construction Industry

Key Words and Concepts

Parties
Common law
Customs and practices of the
   construction industry
Statutes
Regulations
Contractors
Architect/engineers
Owners
Public owner
Private owner
Service and supply organizations
Labor force
Government in its regulatory capacity
General public
Construction document sequence
National Labor Relations Act

Davis-Bacon Act
Lien laws
Miller Act
License laws
Subcontractor listing laws
Equal Employment and disadvantaged
   business opportunity laws
Uniform Commercial Code
Tort law
Contract liability
Express contract provisions
Implied contract provisions
Tort liability
Statutory liability
Strict liability
Absolute liability

This book deals with the business and legal aspects of construction contracting practice from the perspective of a participating contractor. The word *legal* connotes the operation or existence of law. In what follows, *law* is meant to include federal- or state-enacted laws or **statutes,** the rules of federal and state regulatory bodies promulgated to give practical effect to enacted statutes, and the *common law.* **Common law** is that body of past court decisions, dating from the legal practice in England prior to American independence, that serves as authority or precedent governing future decisions. It can be thought of as "judge-made" law. Since judges have been, and continue to be, influenced by the **customs and practices of the construction industry,** these customs and practices in a sense are part of the law as well.

Before examining in detail the law as just defined, we should look into the various elements of the construction industry. Who is involved? Who are the players or—as one usually hears—who are the **parties** who in one way or another participate in the construction process?

THE TYPICAL PARTIES

Although others may be peripherally involved, the important parties certainly include the following major party groups.

Construction Contractors and Subcontractors

First, construction **contractors** and their subcontractors are obviously the key participants. These are the entities charged with the responsibility of actually putting construction work in place. That is, those entities who determine the means, methods, techniques, sequence, and procedures and direct the actual construction activities.

Architect/Engineers

The **architect/engineer** (A/E) who designs the work and often administers the construction phase of the project personifies the second important group of participants. These entities are the creators of the drawings and specifications for the planned construction.

Construction Owners

The construction **owners** for whom the work is done and without whom there would be no construction industry constitute the third important segment. This group is the source of the money that drives the industry. Construction contracts with private owners often operate very differently from those with public owners. For that reason, the distinction between private and public owners is important.

The **private owner** includes just about any person or entity that is not a local, state, or national governmental body. Examples include you or your neighbor who wants a home built and large commercial entities such as restaurant and retail chains, real estate developers, and the giant industrial corporations. The private sector also includes quasi-public bodies that may be regulated by state governments but are still private companies. Examples in the western United States include, among others, the Pacific Gas and Electric Company and Southern California Edison Company, which are regulated by the State of California Public Utilities Commission.

On the other hand, the **public owner** can be local, state, or federal governmental bodies. The public sector also includes entities created for specific purposes by actions of the voters, such as school districts, water supply and sewer districts, and transportation or transit authorities.

Service and Supply Organizations

A fourth segment consists of the **service and supply organizations** of the industry, such as the firms that manufacture and market construction equipment. Other examples include the producers of the basic materials of construction such as cement, concrete aggregates and other stone products, lumber and timber products, steel, petroleum products, and many other raw materials or manufactured items.

Insurance companies and sureties are service organizations. There is an important difference between the insurance and surety business, even though the same entity often engages in both, which is explained in Chapters 8 and 9.

What about banking institutions? Do you consider them to be important service organizations? If you understand the significance of the term "credit line," you know the answer. Few owners or contractors could exist without the participation of the banks, which furnish construction loans for owners and equipment loans or operating capital loans for contractors.

Finally, the service and supply group of entities includes consultants and attorneys who furnish personal services or advice. Consultants include specialty designers for such requirements as dewatering and ground support systems, management consultants, scheduling consultants, construction claims consultants, and many others. Attorneys provide legal advice to the various parties involved in construction and represent them in court as well as in many business situations.

Labor Force

Another major category of participant is the **labor force.** Without this segment, nothing would get built. *Labor force,* as used here, means not only organized labor, consisting of international and local labor unions, but also that very large group of workers in this country who comprise the open shop or merit shop segment.

Local, State, and Federal Governments

Another category of player is **local, state, and federal government,** not in the previously discussed role as a construction owner, but in their **regulatory capacity** as the promulgators of many of the rules and **regulations** governing the operation of the industry.

General Public

Finally, that broad body of persons constituting the **general public** must be included. Construction does not occur in a vacuum, and large projects, particularly those in heavily populated areas, temporarily affect the lives of many persons who are not involved in the actual construction work but who are simply living or working in the area. The general public can greatly affect construction projects in two ways. First, construction planning must consider the impact on the public during actual construction. Second, planning must cover any permanent effects on the public, including the environment, which is also "public." The provision of large programs of general liability insurance speaks to the first question, and the increasing requirements for environmental impact assessments, which take place before actual construction work is permitted, attest to the second.

RULES FOR PARTICIPANTS

The major participants or players in the construction process have just been discussed. What constitutes or defines the manner in which these participants interact or should interact?

Contracts

A primary body of rules for the conduct of the construction process is derived from the provisions of contracts and contract-related documents agreed to by participants in the industry. Figure 1-1 is a flowchart that represents the typical **construction document sequence** in which the more common contracts used in construction relate to each other.

The process typically starts with an owner who wants a project or a facility built. This person (or entity) signs a *professional service contract* with an architect/engineer to design the project and create a set of drawings and specifications. Next, the project is advertised for bids by a contract-related document called an *advertisement*. The advertisement often results in a pre-bid contract between one or more contractor bidders for the purpose of setting forth the terms of their agreement to submit a bid jointly and, if the bid is successful, to construct the project jointly. Such a contract between contractors is called a *joint venture agreement*. A contract-related offer to the owner to construct the project under stated commercial terms, submitted by a single contractor or joint venture contractor bidders, is the *bid*.

Bids are evaluated by the owner, eventually resulting in a *prime construction contract* to which the owner and the successful contractor or joint venture bidder are parties. The existence of the prime construction contract usually generates the need for *surety bonds, insurance policies, subcontract agreements, labor agreements,* and *purchase order agreements,* all of which are contracts that involve the prime contractor as a party. At this level, these secondary contracts, which flow from the existence of the prime construction contract and involve the prime contractor as a party, are called *first-tier contracts.*

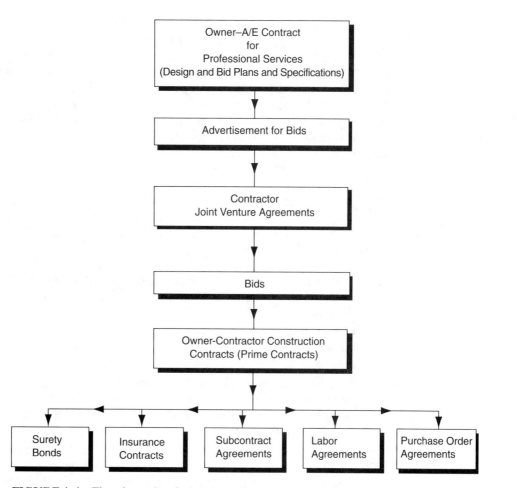

FIGURE 1–1 Flowchart of typical construction industry contract documents.

If first-tier subcontract agreements are drawn up, they may generate a new family of *second-tier* surety bonds, insurance contracts, subcontract agreements, labor agreements, and purchase order agreements. In a similar manner, it is possible that a family of *third-tier* contracts may be generated.

Laws, Statutes, and Regulations of Governmental Agencies

A second important source of rules governing the construction process consists of three separate categories of laws, statutes, and regulations of governmental agencies.

The *Federal Procurement Statutes* are the source of basic rules and authority for the contracting regulations promulgated by the executive branch of the federal government. These statutes can be found in the *United States Code* (USC).

The *Federal Regulations* are the detailed rules for contracting by the federal government. These rules are currently called the *Federal Acquisition Regulations* (FAR). In addition, most federal agencies and subagencies have supplemented the FAR, resulting in the *Department of Defense Federal Acquisition Regulation Supplement* (DFARS) and the *U.S. Army Federal Acquisition Regulation Supplement* (AFARS). Subsubagencies have also created supplements such as the *U.S. Army Corps of Engineers Federal Acquisition Regulation Supplement* (EFARS). These various regulations are published by the respective agency. Some of them are also published by commercial publishers such as the *Commercial Clearing House* (CCH), and most are published in the *Federal Register* and codified yearly in the *Code of Federal Regulations* (CFR).

State and local laws and ordinances are published and codified by the various states according to individual practices, which vary from state to state and municipality to municipality. Some of the more prominent federal and state laws include the following:

National Labor Relations Act (the Wagner Act). This federal act is the primary law in the United States governing the relations between employers and their work force.

Davis-Bacon Act. This federal act establishes minimum wage rates that must be paid on any federal project or on any project that is financed with a significant amount of federal funds.

State Mechanic's Lien Laws, the federal Miller Act, and the various state "little" Miller Acts. These state and federal laws operate to ensure that persons or entities providing labor or materials for construction projects receive the payment that they are due.

State Contractor License Laws. A number of states have enacted laws that require persons or entities to demonstrate certain minimum qualifications, post a bond, and pass a qualification examination in order to operate a construction contracting business.

State Subcontractor Listing Laws. A number of states have enacted laws to prevent "bid shopping," a practice of some prime contractors that is unfair to subcontractors and material suppliers. In California, for instance, prime contractor bidders are required by law to list in their prime bid the name of the subcontractor, the type of work, and the subcontract price for every item of work that they intend to subcontract with a subcontract value greater than one-half of one percent of the prime contract bid price. Upon award of the prime contract, the prime contractor is then compelled to subcontract the listed work to the listed subcontractor at the listed subcontract price. The prime contractor is relieved of that obligation only if the named subcontractor is unable or unwilling to enter into a subcontract agreement with substantially the same terms and conditions as the prime contract, or, alternately, the prime contractor elects to perform the listed work with his or her own forces.

Equal Employment Opportunity Laws, Disadvantaged Business, and Women-Owned Business Participation Laws, and Other Forms of "Set-Aside" Laws. These laws and the ensuing regulations at the city, state, and federal levels are intended to remedy past patterns of discrimination in employment and business opportunity based on ethnic origin or sex.

Uniform Commercial Code. This code has been adopted by statute in virtually every state. Its primary purpose is to establish fair and uniform trade practices applying to the sale of goods as distinct from the performance of construction services. Nevertheless, the code has an enormous impact on the construction industry since so many of the "nuts-and-bolts" transactions in the industry involve the sale of goods.

Tort Law

The third and final contributor to the rules governing the conduct of construction operations is a body of the common law called **tort law.** What is a tort? Broadly speaking, a tort is a civil wrong. The central concept of tort law is that in living our daily lives we cannot with impunity, either intentionally or unintentionally, conduct our affairs in a manner that will injure or damage others.

LIABILITY IN THE CONSTRUCTION PROCESS

At this point, we have discussed the participants in the construction industry and briefly examined the sources of the rules for the construction scenario. A common thread throughout is the liability involved in practically all forms of construction-related activity. This thread consists of three broad classes of liability arising in one or more separate ways.

Contract Liability

The most prominent and obvious way a participant in the construction process becomes exposed to potential liability is by becoming a party to a legal contract. This first broad class of liability is called **contract liability** and results when a party to the contract breaches the contract by failing to conform to one or more of its provisions.

There are two basic kinds of contract provisions. The first is a provision that is plainly written in the text of the contract document itself. This type of provision is called an **express contract provision.** It is stated explicitly in the contract. Most people understand provisions that are stated prominently and clearly in black letters in the text of the contract document.

The second kind of contract provision flows from the contract but is not in the form of an explicit statement. These provisions come from time-tested, commonly held understandings that are implied by the contract. Such commonly held understandings are said to be implicit in the contract and are considered **implied contract provisions**—or *implied warranties*. An example of an implied warranty is that each party when entering into a contract implicitly warrants that he or she will not act, or fail to act, in a manner that interferes with the other parties' ability to perform their duties under the contract. These commonly held understandings come both from the customs and practices of the construction industry and from past decisions of courts, known as *case law,* another term for "judge-made law" or "common law."

Examples of both kinds of contract provisions are covered in later chapters. Breach of either kind results in contract liability.

Tort Liability

The second broad class of liability flowing to persons engaged in construction is **tort liability** based on tort law. The general tort concept, discussed earlier in this chapter, is part of the common law. Tort liability does not depend on the existence of a contract. Many individuals in all segments of the industry continually incur tort liability without realizing it because they mistakenly believe their liabilities are limited to those resulting from breach of the provisions in the contracts to which they are a party.

A second mistaken notion is that tort liability arises only when a person knowingly and intentionally acts in a manner that injures or damages another. Intentional acts that injure others certainly do create tort liability, but tort liability can also be created by an act that is unintentionally committed. An intentional tort would be to damage someone else's property on purpose, whereas if the damage was caused because one was negligent, the tort would be unintentional. An *intentional tort* may constitute a criminal act in addition to a civil wrong, giving rise to criminal penalties as well as monetary damages.

Statutory Liability

The third broad class of liability is that imposed by law or statute and is called **statutory liability.** This class of liability flows directly from the provisions of enacted laws or statutes that apply in specific localities as well as from federal laws that apply throughout the United States. As is true with contract and tort liabilities, statutory liabilities may be either express or implied.

Strict Liability

Any form of liability, whether contract, tort, or statutory, is a serious matter to be avoided whenever possible. A frequently used second liability descriptor that can apply to all three broad classes of liability is **strict liability,** which means that it is not necessary to prove fault or negligence to establish that a person or entity is liable for some act or failure to act. The mere fact that the act or failure to act occurred is all that is necessary to establish the liability.

Strict liability is usually associated with tort liability situations, but it can apply to other classes of liability as well. For instance, express warranties that are frequently included in construction contracts also impose strict liability on the contractor in the event of failure to honor or make good the terms of the warranty. Such a warranty might provide, for instance, that the contractor warrants that a roof installed under the contract will not leak for a period of, say, five years, and that if it does leak within this period, the contractor will make repairs at no additional cost to the owner so that the roof will not leak. Unless the roof leaked for some reason for which the owner was directly or indirectly responsible, courts will interpret the requirements of the warranty strictly. The owner would not have to prove that the contractor was at fault or was negligent. The mere fact that the roof leaked is all that is necessary to establish the contractor's liability for the necessary repairs.

Just how strictly express warranties can be enforced is illustrated by a 1988 case in which the Iowa Supreme Court affirmed a lower court's award of foreseeable consequential damages suffered by the owner of a distillery due to a design/build contractor's failure to meet the performance guarantees stated in the contract. The contract provided that the completed plant would be capable of producing 190,000 gallons of ethanol per month and in so doing would not consume more than 36,000 BTU of heat per gallon of ethanol produced. The completed plant never met the stated output and consumed more BTUs per gallon than stated, causing the owner to lose money. The plant eventually was closed. The damages awarded the owner included the operating losses suffered during the period of plant operation plus the difference between the initial cost of the completed plant and its greatly diminished salvage value.[1]

A special kind of strict liability that applies to construction contracting is liability to third parties for damage that results from the performance of ultrahazardous construction activities such as blasting or demolition work in urban environments or liability for any activity that causes damage to a property owner's land (as distinct from damage to buildings or other improvements on the land). This particular type of liability is sometimes called **absolute liability.** The standard of care used in conducting the construction operations or the precautions taken to avoid damage are not taken into consideration. The only thing that matters is that the damage was caused by the construction activity. If it was, the contractor's liability is absolute.

CONCLUSION

This chapter briefly examined the major participants in the construction industry in the United States today, the rules by which they interact with each other, and the different kinds of liability knowingly or unknowingly assumed by participants in the industry. The emphasis here is that the first and foremost source of the rules governing the interactions of participants is the contracts into which they voluntarily enter.

---

[1]*Farm Fuel Products Corp. v. Grain Processing Corp.,* 429 N.W. 2d 153 (Iowa 1988).

Succeeding chapters continue this emphasis on the importance of contracts. Chapter 2 discusses the elements required for contract formation from a construction industry perspective leading into privity of contract and other contract relationships. The following chapters deal with the more important details of the contracts most commonly used in the construction industry.

QUESTIONS AND PROBLEMS

1. What is common law? How have the customs and practices of the construction industry influenced its evolution?

2. What are the seven main groups of participants in the construction industry? Who are typical members of each group?

3. What are the seven major statutes—or groups of statutes, laws, or regulations—that were identified in this chapter? What is each intended to accomplish?

4. What is a tort? Is tort law a part of the common law?

5. Define and suggest possible examples of the following:
   a. Contract liability
   b. Tort liability
   c. Express terms or provisions
   d. Implied terms or provisions (sometimes called implied warranties)
   e. Statutory liability
   f. Strict liability
   g. Absolute liability

6. Can certain contract liabilities also be strict liabilities? Can tort liabilities be strict liabilities? Can statutory liabilities be strict liabilities? Explain each of your answers.

7. Consider the following factual situation: The parties to a construction contract were a contractor and the U.S. Army Corps of Engineers (the Corps). The work of the contract was to construct an earth levee embankment along a river from material borrowed from a designated borrow pit shown on the contract drawings. To provide a means for the contractor to haul the borrow material from the borrow pit to the levee site, the Corps had previously obtained a 50-foot-wide easement through a landowner's property. The contract contained no provisions one way or the other concerning potential damage to the landowner's property, only that the contractor would be allowed to haul earth over the 50-foot easement previously obtained by the Corps. During the course of the contract work, construction equipment leaked crankcase oil, and a large quantity of fuel oil was inadvertently spilled by the contractor on the land within the 50-foot easement. The landowner alleged serious damage to the land and sued the contractor for damages. On the basis of these facts, answer the following questions:

a. If the damage to the land could be proved and you were the contractor, would you concentrate your legal efforts in attempting to convince the court that you had no liability or in seeking to prove that the extent of the actual damage was small? Explain your answer.

b. If the contractor had decided to contest the liability issue and the court ruled in favor of the landowner, what kind of liability would be involved: contract, tort, or statutory? Explain your answer.

c. If liability was found to exist in (b), would it flow from violation of some express provision of the contract or statutory law or from violation of an established principle founded in the common law? Explain your answer.

8. Consider these two situations:

Situation A

> A construction contract contains a provision that the contractor must guarantee that a sewer system to be installed will not be subject to groundwater infiltration of over 500 gallons per day per inch diameter of pipe per mile. Upon completion of the installation, tests reveal infiltration of 12,500 gallons per day in an 18,000-foot run of six-inch pipe.

Situation B

> A contractor encounters rock in an urban area excavation and elects to loosen it by blasting. The advice of experts was obtained, and the blasting operations were conducted with great skill and care. However, cracking occurred in the plaster walls of several houses in the immediate vicinity of the work as a result of the blasting.

Briefly discuss these two situations, stating whether either of them results in liability for the contractor and, if so, the type or kind of liability involved.

2

Contract Formation, Privity of Contract, and Other Contract Relationships

---

Key Words and Concepts

Contract formation
Offer
Acceptance
Consideration
Offering entity's standard terms and
   conditions
Conflict with the prime contract bidding
   documents
Counteroffer

Negotiation
Meeting of the minds
Subcontractor listings in bids
Nonenforceable contracts
Privity of contract
Third-party beneficiary theory
Intended v. incidental beneficiary
Multiple prime contracts

Chapter 1 discussed various sources of the rules by which the construction industry operates. One important source of these rules was found to be the actual contracts entered into by the various "players" or participating entities in the industry. The first part of this chapter will examine the concepts of **contract formation** followed by a discussion of **privity of contract** and other contract relationships.

WHAT CONSTITUTES A CONTRACT?

Since contracts are so important in defining the rules by which the construction industry operates, it should be obvious that when two parties enter into a contractural relationship, each would know and acknowledge that fact. However, this is not always the case. When one of the parties denies that a contract exists, it becomes important to understand when, and how, legally binding contracts are formed. Three elements for contract formation are necessary: an **offer,** an **acceptance,** and **consideration**.

Offer

What is an offer? What is its essential nature? One legal authority has defined an **offer** as a manifestation of interest or willingness to enter into a bargain made in such a way that the receiving party will realize that furnishing unqualified acceptance will seal the bargain.[1] If the willingness to enter into a bargain is manifested so that the person to whom it is made is aware, or should be aware, that some further manifestation of willingness will be required before an unqualified acceptance would seal the bargain, then what has transpired is not an offer.[2] For example, a house painter who declares, "I'll paint your house for a price of $3,000 during the third week of September, provided my other work will let me," or words to that effect, has not made a binding legal offer because the manifestation of willingness is qualified or "hedged."

What about the format of the offer? Is any particular format required? In the general case, no format is required as long as the offer meets reasonable standards of completeness and clarity. However, there are exceptions, the most prominent being the particular kind of offer occurring in construction that we refer to as a *bid* or a *proposal*. Bids and proposals are usually made in response to an advertised notice called an *invitation for bid* (IFB) or a *request for proposals* (RFP). Both an IFB and an RFP by their written terms usually require that the bid or proposal be in a specific format; if it is not, it is considered a "nonconforming" offer and will be rejected. Other than in situations where a format is specified, no mandatory format is required for an offer to be legally sufficient.

Does the offer have to be in writing? Generally, it does not—that is, a verbal offer that meets reasonable standards of completeness and clarity can be legally sufficient. Again, there are important exceptions. Bids and proposals made in

---

[1]Second Restatement of Contracts § 24.

[2]*Id.* § 26.

response to advertised IFB or RFP notices invariably require written submissions. Also, offers for the sale of goods are governed by the provisions of the *Uniform Commercial Code* (UCC), which requires offers of over $500 value to be in writing. Other local statutes may impose requirements on commercial transactions within the jurisdiction of the locality including, in some instances, a requirement that an offer must be in writing to be legally binding. Other than these kinds of exceptions, a valid offer can be either written or oral.

In every case, whether written or oral, a legally binding offer must be clear. It must define or describe that which is being offered. In the previous simplistic example, there is a lot of difference between

> "I'll paint your house for a price of $3,000 during the third week of September provided my other work will let me."

and

> "I'll paint your house for a price of $3,000. My price includes scraping off all existing loose, flaking paint to bare wood, priming bare wood with Sherwin-Williams exterior primer, and applying two coats of Sherwin-Williams exterior house enamel, colors of your choice, one for the body of the house and one for the trim. Glazing work or repair of downspouts and drains is not included. The work will commence the third week in September and be completed that week, weather permitting."

The second version, even if it were expressed verbally, is probably sufficiently clear and definitive to constitute a valid legal offer. The first is not, completely aside from the presence of the qualification.

Moving on, what defines the duration of an offer? Put another way, once given, for how long is an offer good? Sometimes an explicit statement in an offer clarifies that the offer will be good for only the period stated. Also, when offers or bids are made pursuant to the terms and conditions of an IFB or an RFP, the period for which the bidder may be held to the terms of his or her offer will ordinarily be explicitly stated in the IFB or RFP. Other than in exceptions such as those just given, an offer will be deemed legally valid until it is formally withdrawn. If the offer is not formally withdrawn, it will be deemed valid for a reasonable time. Unfortunately, there is no universally accepted definition of a "reasonable time." Reasonable time thus becomes what a judge or an arbitrator thinks is reasonable in a particular case should a dispute arise.

Offers can be withdrawn in at least two different ways of importance to construction practitioners. First, if the offer contains a statement establishing a fixed duration, withdrawal at the end of that stated period would be implicit. Second, an offer that does not contain a statement establishing a fixed duration can usually be unilaterally withdrawn by the person or entity making it at any time prior to acceptance.

A particular issue concerning offers commonly results in construction disputes—whether or not the **offering entity's standard terms and conditions** are deemed applicable to an offer. Another word for standard terms and conditions is *boilerplate*. That is, the fine print typically appearing on the back of vendors' sales offers that has been carefully drafted to their advantage. Obviously, if the face of the offer explicitly states that it includes the offeror's standard terms and conditions, these would apply. In addition, even though not explicitly stated on the face of the offer, the offeror's standard terms and conditions apply if it could be shown that the person to whom the offer was made knew about them through previous dealings with the offeror where such standard terms and conditions did apply. For instance, a contractor who had habitually purchased form lumber from a particular supplier and who knew about the supplier's standard terms and conditions and had accepted them in the past probably would be held to that knowledge and acceptance in regard to a new offer, even though the face of the offer did not explicitly state that it was subject to the supplier's standard terms and conditions.

Another issue unique to the construction industry is created when the subcontractor and supplier bids to prime contractors include standard terms and conditions that are in **conflict with the prime contract bidding documents.** This can occur even when these bids are stated to be in accordance with the prime contract bidding documents as illustrated in the following common bidding situation:

> A subcontractor submits a bid to a prime contractor who, in turn, is submitting a prime bid to the owner in accordance with the prime contract bidding documents. The sub-bid states prominently on its face that it is submitted "in accordance with the prime contract bidding documents" or words to that effect. However, buried in the boilerplate on the back of the subcontractor's quotation form is a statement that the sub-bid offer is good for a period of ten days and, if not accepted within this period, the subcontractor is not bound to the offer. The effective date of the sub-bid is the same as the date of the prime bid. The prime contract bidding documents require the prime bid to the owner to be held open for a period of 60 days. The prime contractor's bid is the lowest, and the prime contractor is awarded the contract 45 days after the bid date and shortly thereafter attempts to enter into a subcontract with the subcontractor. The subcontractor refuses to honor the sub-bid on the grounds that the offer expired ten days after the date of the prime bid.

Now what? Clearly, the prime contractor was in no position to contract with the subcontractor until awarded the prime contract by the owner. How would this conflict be resolved?

The sub-bid was stated to be "in accordance with the prime contract bidding documents." Thus, if it can be established that the subcontractor knew, or should have known, about the prime contract bidding provisions, those provisions would take precedence over the bidder's standard terms and conditions. Chapter 7 deals with this completely unnecessary kind of conflict between prime contractors and their subcontractors and suppliers and explains how to avoid it.

Acceptance

Moving on to the **acceptance,** the second element that must exist to form a contract, a number of points are important. Obviously, for the acceptance to have any relevance and legal meaning, it must be an acceptance of whatever was offered. A form of acceptance that changes the offer in any significant respect is not an acceptance at all but a **counteroffer.** An exchange of offers and counteroffers between two parties constitutes a **negotiation.** In a negotiation, only the final offer and acceptance matter in respect to contract formation. A contract between two parties cannot be legally binding until and unless there is **meeting of the minds**—that is, the mutual agreement is not made under duress—at the time the contract is formed. Both parties must understand and accept that they have mutually agreed to be bound by the same set of terms and conditions or, in other words, by the final offer and acceptance. The trouble starts when the parties later discover that they did not have a common understanding of the agreement. Such is the genesis of many construction contract disputes.

As in the case of the offer, the acceptance may normally be written or oral and, if written, may be in any format, providing that a true meeting of the minds results. The only exceptions are where written or specifically formatted acceptances are required by the terms of an IFB or an RFP, by local statute, or by state laws that have adopted the *Uniform Commercial Code,* which specifically requires that an acceptance be in writing.

The construction industry has also spawned a recurring dispute involving a question about acceptance found in no other line of commercial activity. The dispute arises when the advertised bidding documents require prime contractors to list the names of their subcontractors on the face of the prime bid, indicating that they have relied on those sub-bids and have incorporated them in the prime bid (see sub-bid listing laws discussed in Chapter 1). This type of requirement is fairly common and when present is ordinarily known and understood by both prime contractors and subcontractors prior to the sub-bids being given. Under these circumstances, subcontractors often contend that the prime contractor's act of incorporating the sub-bid in the prime bid and **listing the name of the subcontractor constitutes a legally binding acceptance of the sub-bid offer.** Unfortunately, from the subcontractor's point of view, courts and boards have generally held to the contrary—that is, in and of itself, the use of a sub-bid and the listing of the subcontractor by a prime contractor in the bid to an owner does not constitute a legally binding acceptance of that sub-bid. An acceptance of any offer, including sub-bids, must be communicated directly from the party to whom the offer was made to the party who made it rather than communicated indirectly through a third party (the owner). This holding may seem unfair, particularly when contrasted to the doctrine of promissory estoppel discussed in Chapter 12. Nonetheless, this has been the usual case law ruling whenever this question arises.

Consideration

The third and final element necessary for contract formation is the **consideration.** In construction, the consideration may be money, but not always. It can just as well be some other "cash good" thing, such as the discharge of an obligation that has a value. The value may not be great. The main point is that consideration for both parties to the contract must always be present in one form or another in order for a contract to be formed. One way to think of consideration is that each party must have a rational reason for entering into the contract and an expectation of receiving something of value for performing the contract satisfactorily. In a construction contract, the owner's consideration is getting the project work performed and the contractor's consideration is receiving the contract price.

Contract Must Not Be Contrary to Law—Nonenforceable Contracts

A binding contract can never be formed without the presence of the three necessary elements for contract formation explained previously. However, the undeniable presence of the offer, acceptance, and consideration does not always guarantee the existence of a binding legal contract. In addition, the contract **must not contravene the law** and, if a public contract, must not contravene or be **contrary to public policy.** For example, an otherwise valid contract to set fire to a building enabling the other party to the contract to collect the insurance would not be legally enforceable.

In a construction industry context, a more common situation arises in public work where an otherwise valid contract is entered into by a public official not legally empowered to contract for the work. Such circumstances can lead to cases where the contractor has performed the work in good faith and then been unable to secure payment.

A good illustration of normal contractual relationships being voided because the contract was illegal is afforded by an Alabama case where the contractor was not paid for extra work performed because the governor of the state had not approved the contract/change order as required by statute.[3] Another is a New York case where the contractor was not paid for work performed and was forced to pay back monies that had previously been paid, because the city commissioner who had awarded the contract was found to have been bribed.[4]

PRIVITY OF CONTRACT AND OTHER CONTRACT RELATIONSHIPS

In construction contract disputes, the threshold question is: "Does a contractual relationship exist between the parties to the dispute?" As discussed in Chapter 1, two important kinds of liability are contract liability and tort liability. Contract liabilities arise whenever the provisions of a contract, whether express or implied, are breached (broken) by one of the parties to the contract.

Privity of Contract

Contract liability flows from the existence of a contract. Without a contract, there can be no contract liability and, consequently, no sustainable legal cause of action for breach of contract. Therefore, if a party has been damaged by another and seeks redress through a lawsuit under a theory of contract liability, that party must first

---

[3]*Rainer v. Tillett Bros. Const. Co.,* 381 So. 2d (Ala. 1980).

[4]*S.T. Grand, Inc. v. City of New York,* 344 N.Y. S.2d 938 (N.Y. 1973).

establish the existence of a contract with the party who caused the damage by breaching that contract. The existence of such a contractual relationship is called **privity of contract.**

It is not uncommon for a construction contractor to sue architect/engineers or construction managers for alleged failure to properly perform their duties associated with the construction contract, although the contractor does not have a contract directly with them. Such lawsuits must be based on tort with the contractor claiming tortious interference with construction activities or negligence on the part of the architect/engineer or construction manager. In tort cases, a cause of action does not depend on the existence of a contract, so the privity of contract issue does not arise.

Third-Party Beneficiary Relationship

Contract or tort liability involving two parties is straightforward enough. However, a more complex situation sometimes arises in construction cases where lawsuits involving contract-type liabilities may be sustained against a party with whom one does not have a contract. Such lawsuits depend on the **third-party beneficiary theory.** The basic concept is that when each of two or more separate entities has a valid contract with a common third entity, they may be third-party beneficiaries of the contract between the "common" entity and the other noncommon entities. This relationship is illustrated in Figure 2–1.

In this situation, entity *A* has a valid contract with owner *C,* and entity *B* also has a valid contract with owner *C.* If the third-party beneficiary relationship is found to exist between entities *A* and *B,* *A* can sue *B* for damages suffered by *A* if *B* breaches some provision of *B*'s contract with *C.* Likewise, *B* can sue *A* for damages suffered by *B* if *A* breaches some provision of *A*'s contract with *C.*

For example, suppose that an owner *C* has a loan agreement with bank *B* to advance funds to cover monthly approved estimates for work completed on a construction project. Owner *C* also has separately contracted with contractor *A* to construct the project according to approved drawings and specifications. All goes well until bank *B* stops advancing funds without legal justification, thus breaching *B*'s contract with owner *C.* Under these hypothetical circumstances, contractor *A* could probably successfully sue bank *B* and collect full payment for work completed on the argument that *A* was an intended third-party beneficiary of the bank's contract with owner *C,* even though no contract existed between the contractor and the bank.

FIGURE 2–1   Third-party beneficiary relationship.

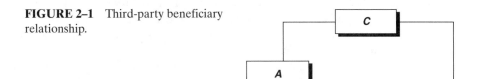

Third-Party Beneficiary Intent

The third-party beneficiary relationship illustrated in Figure 2–1 will be deemed to exist if it can be shown that the three parties had the intent to establish it when the contracts were formed. How can such an intent be shown? Obviously, if the wording of the contracts contains any explicit provisions establishing such intent, that intent would be deemed to exist.

Even though the contracts do not contain explicit language establishing intent, courts sometimes reasonably infer that the parties had that intent from the circumstances surrounding the particular contracts. In deciding whether to apply the third-party beneficiary rule, courts will make a careful distinction regarding the beneficiary relationship. It is not enough that one party may benefit from the fruits of the other's contract with the common owner. Courts will also want to know whether the **benefit was incidental or intended.** A third-party beneficiary relationship that is merely incidental is insufficient to establish rights of recovery. On the other hand, an intended third-party beneficiary relationship will establish rights of recovery.

Suppose, for instance, that in the previous example the bank loan agreement did not state the proceeds of the loan were intended to finance the construction project and did not refer to the construction project in any other way. In those circumstances, a court might conclude that the construction contractor's benefit from the loan proceeds was merely incidental rather than intended, thus denying the contractor rights of recovery.

Multiple Prime Contracts

A second common example is the **multiple prime contractor** situation. Suppose that civil works contractor *A*, mechanical contractor *B*, and electrical contractor *C* each contract directly with common owner *D* on the same project, requiring the work forces of all three contractors to be present on the site simultaneously. If the written or implied terms of each prime contract with owner *D* make little or no reference to the other prime contracts, and any one of the contractors *A*, *B*, or *C* damages one or more of the others through a breach of their individual contracts with owner *D*, the damaged contractor(s) would have no right of recovery directly against the contractor who caused the damage. The contracts with *D* do not establish an intended third-party beneficiary relationship. As discussed in Chapter 13 on contract breaches, the damaged contractor under the circumstances just described could well have a valid breach of contract cause of action against the owner for failing to manage or control the other prime contractors properly, but a lawsuit based on the third-party beneficiary rule would fail.

This principle is well illustrated by an Illinois case where the appellate court ruled that a prime contractor on a multiple-prime contract could not sue one of the other prime contractors who had allegedly caused a delay because the multiple-prime contract documents did not create an affirmative duty toward other contractors on the site. There was no intended third-party beneficiary relationship. The court ruled, however, that the damaged contractor could sue the owner for failure "to properly supervise the construction project."[5]

Years ago, the previous situation frequently occurred in projects involving multiple prime contracts. Now, owners often protect themselves from such breach of contract suits by inserting identical language in each prime contract stating that, if one of the prime contractors damages any of the others in the course of their individual contracts, the damaged contractors' only recourse is to seek recovery directly from the contractor causing the damage. In no circumstances will the owner be responsible.

An excellent example of this latter approach was the policy of the *Massachusetts Water Resources Authority* (MWRA) in administering the construction of the Boston Harbor Project, an immense sewerage collection and treatment project that is one of the largest projects of its type in the world. Approximately 30 or 40 separate prime contractors were engaged within a very confined site on Deer Island on the north end of Boston Harbor. These prime contracts contain precisely the kind of language just described, effectively insulating the MWRA from breach of contract claims from individual contractors alleging failure of the owner to properly control this virtual army of prime contractors working on the site.

The MWRA case is an example of the use of *exculpatory* clauses—or *disclaimers*—that lay off a liability that the owner would otherwise have. Under the circumstance described above, the intended third-party beneficiary relationship would be established and, if any of the prime contractors damaged any of the others through a breach of contract with the owner, the damaged contractor could directly sue the contractor causing the damage, even though privity of contract did not exist.

A Tennessee case illustrates the right of a co-prime contractor to sue another co-prime because the project bid documents provided that several prime contractors would be working on the site and that their progress schedules were to be "strictly observed." In that case, the court felt that such language was sufficient to establish the third-party beneficiary relationship, because it implied that each contractor could rely on that requirement in the other's contracts being complied with.[6]

In either of the multiple prime contract situations just described, if the behavior of the contractor causing the damage were so bad as to constitute disregard of a civil duty owed to the other primes, the damaged prime contractor would have legally sustainable grounds for suing in tort, which does not depend on privity of contract, as an alternative to the other available theories of recovery.

For example, if a civil work contractor unnecessarily and carelessly created excessive quantities of abrasive dust that interfered with a mechanical contractor's assembly and installation of permanent machinery, the mechanical contractor would probably be successful in suing the civil work contractor in tort.

---

[5]*J. F. Inc. v. S. M. Wilson & Co.,* 504 N.E.2d 1266 (Ill. App. 1987).

[6]*Moore Construction Co., Inc. v. Clarksville Department of Electricity,* 707 S.W.2d 1 (Tenn. App. 1986).

CONCLUSION

This chapter reviewed the elements necessary for contract formation from the perspective of the construction industry, the privity of contract concept, and the application of the third-party beneficiary relationship to common construction contracting situations. Chapter 3 will present an overview of prime construction-related contracts as an introduction to more detailed discussion of prime construction contracts presented in later chapters.

QUESTIONS AND PROBLEMS

1. What is an offer? Need it be in a particular format? Need it be in writing? Under what circumstances would a specific format be required? Under what circumstances would the offer have to be in writing?

2. What does the issue of clarity have to do with the legal sufficiency of an offer?

3. Must a legally sufficient offer necessarily contain an explicit statement of the time duration within which the offer may be accepted? Under what circumstances are explicit duration statements required? If a legally sufficient offer does not contain an explicit duration statement, how long would the offer be deemed to be open to acceptance?

4. In what ways may an offer be withdrawn?

5. Discuss the rules that determine when an offer in the construction industry is deemed to incorporate the offeror's standard terms and conditions. Make clear the circumstances in which such an offer would be so deemed. Explain the usual rule that courts follow when an offer purported to be in accordance with bid plans and specifications is made by an entity whose standard terms and conditions conflict with the specified bid provisions.

6. What is the fundamental requirement that a legally sufficient acceptance must meet? What is a purported acceptance that changes the terms of an offer called? Do the rules concerning the question of oral v. written form in the acceptance vary from those applying to offers?

7. Discuss the usual court holding in the case of a subcontractor's claim that a prime contractor's listing of the subcontractor in the prime's bid to the owner constitutes a legally binding acceptance by the prime of the subcontractor's offer.

8. Is the presence of consideration necessary for formation of a legally binding contract? Must the consideration be money? If not, what must it be?

9. Under what two circumstances discussed in this chapter would a contract containing legally sufficient elements of offer, acceptance, and consideration be invalid and nonenforceable?

10. What is the threshold question in breach of contract cases? What does privity of contract mean? Why is privity important?

11. What two situations discussed in this chapter would permit a sustainable lawsuit where privity of contract would not matter?

12. What rule will courts apply in deciding whether or not a claimed third-party beneficiary relationship exists?

13. An owner has entered into separate prime construction contracts with contractor *A*, contractor *B*, and contractor *C*, all on the same construction project. Each contract contains similar provisions, none of which state any benefit that *A*, *B*, and *C* have as a result of the others' contracts with the owner. None of the contracts refer to the others in any way. Although not negligent, contractor *B* falls far behind schedule in performance of the contract, which causes significant increases in the cost of performance of the separate contracts that contractors *A* and *C* have with the owner.

   a. Are contractors *A* and *C* likely to succeed in sustaining a lawsuit against *B* for damages suffered due to *B*'s failure to perform contract work in a timely manner? State the basis for your opinion.

   b. Assuming slightly different facts—namely, that *B* conducted contract operations in a grossly careless and unsafe manner that adversely affected *A*'s and *C*'s operations—respond to question (a), including the basis for your opinion.

3

The Prime Contract
An Overview

Owner–architect/engineer contract
Owner–CM contract
Owner–contractor contract
Design only
Construct only
Design-construct
Turnkey
Fast-track
Construction management
Agency relationship
Commercial terms

Risk of performance
Cost-reimbursable commercial terms
Fixed-price commercial terms
Cost plus a percentage fee
Cost plus a fixed fee
Cost plus an incentive fee
Target estimate
Guaranteed maximum price
Relationship of risk to profit
Lump sum contract
Schedule-of-bid-items contract

The prime contract is the start of the construction contract's hierarchical chain. It is from this contract that subcontracts and sub-subcontracts are derived as well as many of the related secondary contracts discussed in Chapter 1. All construction-related prime contracts are not the same, or even necessarily similar, although as pointed out in Chapter 2, they all contain the three essential elements of offer, acceptance, and consideration that are fundamental to their formation.

What are the generic types of construction-related prime contracts, and what are the major distinguishing features between them? This chapter examines these questions from the standpoint of the identity of the contracting entities, the nature of the contractual services provided, and the commercial terms under which these contracts operate.

THE PARTIES TO CONSTRUCTION-RELATED PRIME CONTRACTS

Construction-related prime contracts involve **owners, architect/engineers, construction managers,** and **construction contractors.** In each case, the owner typically contracts with one of the others, depending on the particular purpose to be accomplished by the contract.

Owner–Architect Contracts and Owner–Engineer Contracts

As discussed in Chapter 1, architect/engineers (A/Es) are entities that typically design projects, prepare drawings and specifications for the construction contract, and in some instances perform field inspection services and administration of the construction contract. Architectural firms and engineering firms provide similar types of services. The difference between them is that architects deal with residential, commercial, and institutional buildings, whereas engineering companies deal with engineered structures such as highways, dams, bridges, tunnels, and heavy industrial buildings and structures. Prime contracts between owners and architects are called **owner–architect contracts**, whereas such contracts with engineers are called **owner–engineer contracts**.

Owner–Construction Manager Contracts

Construction managers (CMs) are distinctly different entities from A/Es. Their role is to manage the construction aspects of a project on behalf of the owner, usually as the owner's agent. A prime contract between an owner and a construction manager is called an **owner–CM contract.**

Owner–Contractor Contracts

The fourth and final construction-related prime contract party is the construction contractor, the actual builder who determines the means, methods, techniques, sequence, and procedures and directs the actual construction operations. Contracts between owners and construction contractors are called **owner–contractor contracts.**

THE NATURE OF THE CONTRACTUAL SERVICES PROVIDED

Another way to separate or distinguish one prime construction-related contract from another is by the nature of the contractual services that each involves.

Design Only Services

One obvious category of services is **design only,** which pertain to owner–A/E contracts. The use of the modifier "only" distinguishes this category of contract service from another called **design-construct** (design-build). The creation of drawings and specifications is a necessary part of the design process. Thus, design only is normally understood to include the preparation of a complete set of drawings and specifications used to secure bids and to construct the project. Design only contracts may also include assisting the owner in obtaining and evaluating bids for the purpose of awarding a construction contract, providing general inspection services during construction, and providing monthly certified estimates of construction work satisfactorily performed. These estimates are the basis of monthly progress payments and final payment to the construction contractor. Such contracts seldom require continuous on-site presence of the designer during construction or exhaustive site inspections to ensure compliance with the drawings and specifications. Only such inspection services necessary to reasonably assure general compliance are normally required under a design only contract.

Construct Only Services

The second obvious kind of contractual service is **construct only,** pertaining to owner–contractor contracts. This is the typical service provided by construction contractors. It includes assuming full contractual responsibility to perform the work according to the requirements of the drawings and specifications. Again, the modifier "only" is used to distinguish pure construction contracts from design-construct contracts.

Design-Construct Services

Recently, a hybrid form of contract has become prominent, where the contractual services of design only and construct only contracts are incorporated into **design-construct** contracts, sometimes called **design-build** contracts. In this form of contract, the architectural or engineering design work, creation of the drawings and specifications, and actual construction work are all performed by a single entity. Therefore, the owner enjoys the advantage of dealing throughout with only one party that has complete responsibility. A number of companies furnish complete design-construct services using their own forces. Other companies market design-construct services as joint ventures or by using a subcontract to provide part of the required services. An A/E may form a joint venture with a construction contractor or enter into a subcontract with a construction contractor for the construction portion of the overall project. More commonly, reciprocal arrangements are made with the construction contractor in the lead role.

Design-construct contracts can be very large and complex. One such contract in the heavy engineering field was the North Fork Hydroelectric Project on the Stanislaus River in central California completed for the Calavaras County Irrigation District in the late 1980s. This $450-million project consisting of a complex of dams, tunnels, and powerhouses was built by a joint venture of two large construction contractors who entered into a subcontract with a prominent A/E to provide the extensive design engineering services required. An even larger ($1.2 billion) design-construct contract was undertaken to design and build a rapid transit system for the City of Honolulu. The contract consisted of three phases for preliminary design, final design and construction, and an initial period of system operation. The contracting parties were the City and County of Honolulu and a joint venture of four large engineering and construction companies.[1]

Turnkey and Fast-Track Design-Construct Services

The two buzzwords often used in connection with design-build contracts are *turnkey* and *fast-track*.

Turnkey refers to a type of design-construct contract in which the contractor performs virtually every task required to produce a finished, functioning facility. This includes, in addition to the normal design-construct duties, procuring all permits and licenses and procuring and delivering all permanent machinery or equipment that may be involved. It would not be unusual for an owner who had contracted on a design-construct basis for a complete hydroelectric power station to furnish the turbines, generators, transformers, and switchgear, requiring the contractor to design and construct the balance of the facility (including furnishing all other necessary equipment and materials) around this owner-procured permanent equipment. Such a contract would be a design-construct contract, but it would not be a turnkey contract. If the contractor also furnished the equipment items just listed, the design-construct contract would also be a turnkey contract. All turnkey contracts are necessarily design-construct, but many design-construct contracts are not turnkey.

A **fast-track** project is one in which the construction phase is started at a point when only limited design work has been completed. For example, site grading and structure excavation begin when foundation design work is complete, but design work for all subsequent elements of the project, although in progress, is incomplete. This approach has the obvious advantage—on paper, at least—of shortening the overall delivery period for the completed facility, as Figure 3–1 illustrates. Since "time is money," fast-track project delivery offers considerable potential savings to an owner. However, several severe risks accompany the fast-track

---

[1]Because of a change in political sentiment driven by a competition for funds and a recession economy, this project was terminated at the end of the first phase and remains uncompleted at this writing.

FIGURE 3–1 Comparison between normal project and fast-track project.

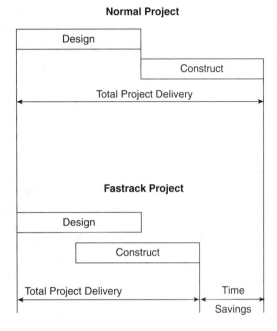

approach that can erode the potential savings. The foremost risk is that after construction is in place a problem may develop with subsequent design that requires costly and time-consuming changes to work already completed. At the very least, the owner loses the flexibility to make relatively inexpensive changes reflecting new and unexpected requirements, an advantage enjoyed throughout the design phase of a non-fast-track project.

Sometimes, the fast-track approach is used when the design and construction entities are not the same, each operating under separate contracts with the owner. This creates even greater risk for the owner, particularly if the design phase is not carefully managed. Errors, changes, or delays in design that impact construction are almost certain to result in claims from the construction contractor for additional compensation and time for contract performance.

Construction Management Services

The final type of contract service involved in construction-related contracts is **construction management,** pertaining to owner–construction manager contracts. A distinction should be made between this use of the term *construction management* as an administrative service performed for an owner and the meaning of that term as it relates to the direct management of construction operations by a construction contractor's organization. Although many of the same professional qualifications are required, the two activities are distinctly different. When services are being furnished on a construction management contract, the construction manager (CM) normally furnishes purely professional services as an agent of the owner and does not perform significant actual construction work—that is, an **agency relationship** is created between the CM and the owner. Although performing no actual construction, the CM may provide such "general conditions" items as utilities, sanitary services, trash removal, and general elevator or hoisting services for the benefit of the construction contractor or contractors. The CM's role as a provider of professional services is not unlike that of the A/E, who also provides professional services with the aim of serving the owner's interest.

CMs may be involved in the very early stages of a project, even the predesign phase, to assist the owner in planning the project and in preparing a predesign conceptual estimate of the probable project cost. This involvement may continue through the design and preparation of the contract documents phase, where the CM will provide constructability advice, evaluations of alternate designs, and assistance in obtaining and evaluating bids for the construction of the project. During construction, the CM provides general administration authority, performs inspection services to ensure compliance with the plans and specifications, and assists in closing out the contract.

A CM acting as the owner's agent is normally precluded from performing any actual construction work. However, in one form of CM contract, the agency relationship is partly replaced by the more normal owner–construction contractor relationship, where the CM's interest is separate from the owner's. Under this form of CM contract, the CM is part general contractor and does perform part of the construction work in addition to previously described CM services.

Although both entities are agents of the owner, CM and A/E services are essentially different. Figure 3–2 compares typical A/E and CM services. An A/E who has designed the project may also serve the owner as a CM. The same A/E entity may have two separate contracts with the owner, one for design services and another for CM services, or a single contract that provides for both.

COMMERCIAL TERMS

Another major difference in construction-related prime contracts centers on **commercial terms.** This part of the contract establishes the method of payment to the party providing the services and defines where the financial **risk of performance** lies. The two broad classes of commercial terms for construction-related contracts are **cost-reimbursable terms** (cost-reimbursable contracts) and **fixed-price terms** (fixed-price contracts). A cost-reimbursable contract is one performed almost entirely on the owner's funds. As the provider of the contract services incurs costs in providing the services, the owner periodically reimburses the provider for these incurred costs, usually on a monthly basis. The provider thus has little or no funds tied up in the contract and the payments received from the owner are directly dependent on the costs of the services provided. In contrast, there is no relation between the costs that the provider of services may be incurring and payment received from the owner on fixed-price contracts. The owner pays the fixed price stipulated in the contract

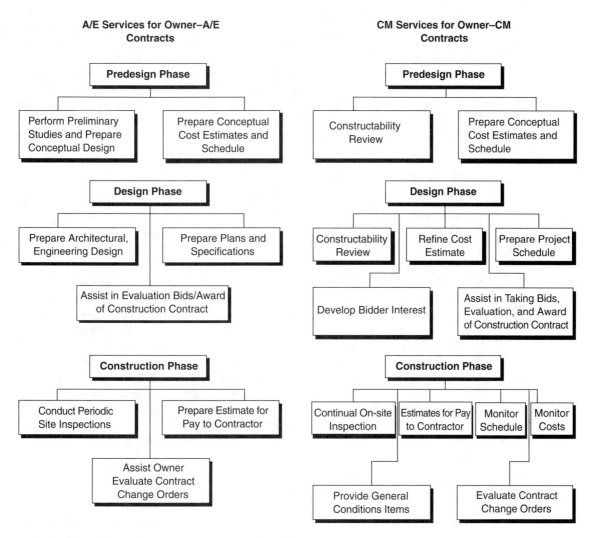

FIGURE 3–2 Comparison between A/E and CM prime contract services.

regardless of what costs the provider is incurring. The fixed price is normally paid in a series of progress payments, usually monthly, as the services are provided.

Although there is basically only one form of fixed-price commercial terms, there are a number of different forms of cost-reimbursable terms.

Cost Plus Percentage Fee Terms

The simplest form of cost-reimbursable commercial terms is the **cost plus percentage fee (CPPF)** basis of payment, sometimes referred to as a *cost plus* or a *time and materials* basis. Many owner–A/E and owner–CM contracts operate on this form as do many small construction contracts. The owner agrees to reimburse the costs incurred by the provider of the services and, in addition, to pay a fee equal to a fixed percentage of incurred costs that is stipulated in the contract. Aside from the practice of professionalism and the desire of the provider to protect his or her reputation for fair dealing in order to secure additional business, there is no incentive for the provider to control costs. Theoretically, the more money spent, the more earned. In the case of construction contracts, this form of commercial terms has a particularly great potential for abuse.

Cost Plus Fixed Fee Terms

Because of the potential for abuse of cost plus percentage fee terms, the **cost plus fixed fee (CPFF)** form of commercial terms evolved. This form of payment is often used in federal government contracts for military-related construction when war or the threat of war has created conditions where firm pricing is not feasible. It is also broadly used for owner–A/E and owner–CM contracts and for private construction contracts when for one reason or another the drawings and specifications are not definitive enough to permit firm pricing. In this form of commercial terms, the owner reimburses all of the service provider's costs and pays a fee that is fixed at the beginning of the contract. This fee will not change unless the scope of the services provided is expanded by change order to the contract. The determination of the fee is usually based on an estimate of the probable cost of the services to be provided or, sometimes in the case of owner–A/E or owner–CM contracts, on a percentage of the estimated construction cost of the project involved that is agreed to by the parties prior to entering into the contract. This form of commercial terms ensures that, if the costs overrun the original estimate without a change in scope, the provider of the services will not benefit by an increased fee as is the case under CPPF terms.

Target Estimate (Cost Plus Incentive Fee) Terms

A more sophisticated form of cost-reimbursable commercial terms is the **target estimate** form, sometimes called **cost plus incentive fee (CPIF)** terms. The target estimate is an estimate agreed upon by the parties prior to entering into the contract, as the most probable cost of providing the contemplated services. A fee as payment for the services is also agreed to, based on the magnitude of the target estimate, with the proviso that the parties will share the benefits or penalties of any underruns or overruns in the actual costs incurred in providing the services compared to the target estimate. The exact formula for the sharing of the underruns or overruns must also be agreed to at the onset and can vary widely depending on the particular contract. For instance, the formula could provide that the parties split underruns or overruns 50-50. It is not unusual for the provider of services to insist that the formula set a cap on the provider's share of any overruns, the cap usually being equal to the amount of the agreed-upon fee. In all of the previously discussed forms of commercial terms, the provider of the services bears none of the financial risk of performance. In the target estimate arrangement, however, the provider does assume part of this risk, depending on the exact formula agreed upon. Ordinarily, the target estimate approach requires that fairly definitive information about the services to be provided be known at the onset. As a result, the target estimate will be relatively more accurate than the initial estimate for a cost plus fixed-fee contract, although probably not as accurate as an estimate for a fixed-price contract.

Guaranteed Maximum Price Terms

Another form of cost-reimbursable commercial terms is the **guaranteed maximum price (GMP)** arrangement. This form is similar to the target estimate form in that the parties agree on an initial estimate for the cost of the contemplated services and on a fee for the provider based on this estimated cost. The agreed-upon estimate for the cost of providing the services and the agreed-upon fee, usually along with an allowance for contingencies, are then added together to yield the guaranteed maximum price which, as its name implies, is a price that the provider contractually guarantees will be the owner's maximum financial exposure for the services received. The owner then reimburses the provider for all costs of the services as they are incurred and makes pro rata payments of the agreed-upon fee as would be the case for CPFF and target estimate contracts. The difference is that once the owner has paid out funds equal to the GMP, no further payment is made. The provider must then continue to perform at his or her own expense until all of the agreed-upon services have been performed according to the contract terms. If a point is reached when all services have been provided according to the contract terms and the owner's financial outlay is less than the GMP, the owner receives the total benefit of the savings. The GMP form of commercial terms has gained enormous popularity in recent years, particularly for contracts in the field of residential and commercial building construction. Obviously, unless the GMP is set at an inflated level compared to a reasonable estimate of the cost of providing the services, the provider assumes a considerable risk of performance under this form of commercial terms.

Fixed-Price Contracts

All of the proceeding forms of commercial terms apply to cost-reimbursable contract situations. The one other broad class of contract is the **fixed-price contract,** also called a *firm-price* contract, or sometimes a *lump sum,* or *hard money contract.* All four terms mean that the provider will be paid an agreed fixed price for providing the contractually stipulated services. There is no relationship between the payment received from the owner and the costs incurred by the provider. The financial risk of performance is borne entirely by the provider of the services. **Fixed-price commercial terms** require a particularly definitive mutual understanding of the scope of services to be provided. In the case of construction contracts, such an understanding is difficult to attain unless a complete and accurate set of plans and specifications is available, upon which the fixed price can be determined and agreed.

In any form of contracting, there is a definite **relationship of risk to profit.** When the commercial terms of any performance contract require that the performer or provider assume the entire financial risk of performance, that performer is taking a far greater risk than under other commercial terms. It follows that the provider is entitled to greater profit than would be the case if less risk were assumed. Therefore, the profit potential in fixed-price contracting is much greater than for other forms of contracting, particularly for construction contracts. The fixed-price or hard money contract is the traditional form around which today's construction contracting industry evolved. The underlying philosophy of this form of contracting has been whimsically described by construction contractors as a matter of "what you bid and what you thought" v. "what you did and what you got."

Fixed-price contracts in construction take one of two different forms. The first is a true **lump sum contract,** where payment is made in a total fixed monetary amount called the *lump sum contract price*. Usually, a breakdown of the lump sum price agreed to by the owner and the contractor is used as the work progresses to determine the appropriate part of the lump sum price to be paid monthly for work performed that month. The sum of the monthly payments will equal the lump sum contract price. Unless the scope of the work specified in the contract is changed, the lump sum price will not change.

The second form of fixed-price contract is the **schedule-of-bid-items contract.** In this type of contract, work is broken down into a series of *bid items*, each for a discrete element of the project work. Each bid item contains a title or name that describes the particular element of work involved, an estimated quantity and unit of measurement for the units of work in the item, an agreed fixed unit price, and finally, an extension price for the bid item consisting of the product of the fixed unit price and the estimated quantity of units of work. For instance, a bid item might read

BI 21—Powerhouse Structural Excavation
10,200 cy @ $12.25 per cy = $124,950.

As the actual work progresses, the quantity of units of work performed are physically measured or counted in the field, which, when multiplied by the fixed unit price stated in the contract, determine what the contractor will be paid that month for the work of that particular bid item. Some bid items are specified by the bid form to be fixed lump sum prices. The total contract price paid to the contractor is the monetary sum of all unit price extensions and lump sum amounts for the quantities of work actually performed. Payment is usually made monthly for measured quantities of work units actually performed that month. If no changes are made in the nature of the work described in the various bid items, the fixed unit prices and fixed-bid-item lump sum prices will not change even though the quantity of work units actually performed for the unit-price-bid items may turn out to be more or less than stated in the contract.

Contracts of this type contain language to the effect that the bid item quantities are provided for bidding purposes only and are not warranted or guaranteed by the owner. Thus, the total contract price (the sum of the bid items) paid by the owner for actual contract performance may turn out to be more or less than the apparent contract price at the time the contract is signed. This can occur even when there are no changes, depending on the accuracy of the contractually stated quantities of units of work to be performed under the various bid items. Since the fixed unit and lump sum prices are determined by competitive bidding or negotiation prior to contract formation, the potential for differences between the contractually stated and the eventual measured quantities when the actual work is performed creates some interesting problems for both owner and contractor that are beyond the scope of this book.

Figure 3–3 illustrates some of the comparative consequences of previously discussed forms of commercial terms. The table is constructed around the performance of a hypothetical project with an assumed estimated cost of $15,000,000, representing the best estimate possible at the time the contract was signed. The table indicates the consequences to the contractor and to the owner for both cost underrun ($13,500,000) and cost overrun ($16,500,000) outcomes under the various forms of commercial terms illustrated.

CONCLUSION

This chapter presented a general overview of prime construction-related contracts from the standpoint of the typical parties involved, the nature of the services contracted for, and the commercial terms.

Chapter 4 will augment this general discussion by examining the format and general components of the prime construction contract between owner and general contractor for the performance of construction work. Chapter 5 will then concentrate on the content of the key clauses of such contracts.

QUESTIONS AND PROBLEMS

1. Who are the four typical parties involved in most construction-related prime contracts? What is the nature of the contract services performed for each of the three prime contract types discussed in this chapter?

2. What do the terms *turnkey* and *fast-track* mean? Discuss the relationship of each to design-construct contracts.

3. How do the services provided by a construction manager in an owner–CM contract and by a general contractor in an owner–contractor contract differ? Is it ever possible for a single construction contractor to function partly as a CM and partly as a general contractor on the same project?

4. In a typical project where the owner contracts with a CM and the work is performed by a number of individual trade construction contractors, with whom do the trade contractors contract? Who bears the financial risk of performance

THE COMPARATIVE EFFECT OF CONTRACT COMMERCIAL TERMS*

Commercial Terms	Cost Outcome At Completion	Contractor's Profit	Total Cost To Owner
CPPF @ 5% Agreed Profit	(1) Costs = $13,500,000	($13,500,000)(0.05) = $675,000	$13,500,000 + $675,000 = $14,175,000
	(2) Costs = $16,500,000	($16,500,000)(0.05) = $825,000	$16,500,000 + $825,000 = $17,325,000
CPFF @ 5% Profit on Estimated Cost	(1) Costs = $13,500,000	($15,000,000)(0.05) = $750,000	$13,500,000 + $750,000 = $14,250,000
	(2) Costs = $16,500,000	($15,000,000)(0.05) = $750,000	$16,500,000 + $750,000 = $17,250,000
CPIF @ 5% Profit. 50-50 Split on Underruns and Overruns	(1) Costs = $13,500,000	($15,000,000)(0.05) + (0.5)($15,000,000 − $13,500,000) = $750,000 + $750,000 = $1,500,000	$13,500,000 + $1,500,000 = $15,000,000
	(2) Costs = $16,500,000	($15,000,000)(0.05) − (0.5)($16,500,000 − $15,000,000) = $750,000 − $750,000 = $0	$16,500,000 + $0 = $16,500,000
GMP 5% Profit on Estimated Cost GMP = ($15,000,000)(1.05) = $15,750,000	(1) Costs = $13,500,000	($15,000,000)(0.05) = $750,000	$13,500,000 + $750,000 = $14,250,000
	(2) Costs = $16,500,000	$15,750,000 − $16,500,000 = ($750,000)	$15,750,000
Fixed Price Competitively Bid at 5% Profit on Estimate Bid = ($15,000,000)(1.05) = $15,750,000	(1) Costs = $13,500,000	$15,750,000 − $13,500,000 = $2,250,000	$15,750,000
	(2) Costs = $16,500,000	$15,750,000 − 16,500,000 = ($750,000)	$15,750,000

* Financial outcomes for a common construction project, with an estimated cost of $15,000,000, contracted for with the Owner on the basis of the five different forms of commercial terms shown.

FIGURE 3-3 The comparative effect of contract commercial terms.

for any overruns in the estimated value of the payments to the trade contractors—the CM or the owner?

5. Define each and explain the differences between CPPF, CPFF, CPIF, GMP, and fixed-price commercial terms. Discuss the allocation of the risk of performance between owner and the provider of the services for each of these commercial terms arrangements. Does the amount of profit or fee that the provider of the services can reasonably expect to receive relate to the allocation of risk of performance? How?

6. Consolidated Energy Corporation (CE) entered into a contract with the Slippery Hills Utility District (SHUD) to perform a feasibility study for a hydroelectric project on the basis that payment to CE would include actual costs of all direct salaries and expenses required for the study multiplied by a billing rate factor of 1.85. Following receipt of a favorable report (which SHUD and CE considered to complete the first contract), SHUD and CE entered into a second contract under which CE was to design completely a dam and powerhouse and, concurrently with the design work, was to start construction of the project and pursue construction to final completion. SHUD reserved to itself the task of procuring the hydraulic turbines and generators according to CE's design. CE was to be paid all costs for its work plus a fee of $5,000,000, with the provision that CE would absorb any costs in excess of a total project cost of $35,000,000 (including the $5,000,000 fee, but excluding the cost of the hydraulic turbines and generators).

   a. What kind of a contract was the first contract with respect to commercial terms?

   b. Briefly discuss the second contract, identifying the type of contract service provided, whether it was a turnkey or nonturnkey contract, and the commercial terms.

   c. Had CE agreed to perform the same contract work for the unqualified sum of $35,000,000, what kind of contract would result from the standpoint of commercial terms?

   d. Had SHUD and CE agreed to share equally any cost savings under $30,000,000 and to each pay one-half of any overruns, what kind of contract would result from the standpoint of commercial terms?

7. A contract was entered into for which an estimate of project costs (exclusive of the contractor's fee) equal to $12,250,000 was agreed to by the parties. The contractor's fee was agreed to be 4% of the estimated cost. The contract further provided that the owner would reimburse all project costs to the contractor as they were expended and pay the contractor's fee periodically as the work progressed with the proviso that the owner's obligation to pay costs and fee was limited to a total sum of $12,962,500. Any expenditure in excess of this total necessary to complete the work were to be for the account of the contractor.

   a. With respect to commercial terms, what type of contract was this?

   b. When the project was completed, the total costs, exclusive of fee, amounted to $11,275,000. How much did the owner pay for the job?

    c.   Under the circumstances in (b), how much money did the contractor gain or lose from the entire transaction?

    d.   If the total project costs had been $13,625,000, how much would the owner have paid for the job?

    e.   Under the circumstances in (d), how much money did the contractor gain or lose?

8.   A contract was entered into for which an estimate of the project costs (exclusive of the contractor's fee) equal to $22,425,000 was agreed to by the parties. The contractor's fee was agreed to be 6% of the estimated cost. The contract further provided that the owner would reimburse all project costs to the contractor as they were expended and would pay the contractor's fee periodically as the work progressed. The contract further provided that the owner and contractor would share in any cost overruns or underruns, 60% to the owner and 40% to the contractor.

    a.   With respect to commercial terms, what kind of contract was this?

    b.   When the project was completed, the total costs, exclusive of contractor's fee, amounted to $20,125,000. How much money did the owner pay for the job?

    c.   Under the circumstances in (b), how much money did the contractor gain or lose from the entire transaction?

    d.   If the total costs on project completion, exclusive of contractor's fee, had been $24,975,000, how much would the owner have paid for the job?

    e.   Under the circumstances in (d), how much money would the contractor gain or lose from the entire transaction?

4

Prime Contract
Format and Major Components

Key Words and Concepts

Owner–contractor contracts

Fixed-price, competitively bid contracts

Standard forms-of-contract

Federal government construction contract

AIA contracts

EJCDC contract

State highway department contracts

Other agency contracts

One-of-a-kind contracts

Bidding documents

General conditions

Supplementary conditions

Specifications

Drawings or plans

Reports of investigations of physical
    conditions

Continuing the overview of construction-related prime contracts presented in Chapter 3, this chapter focuses on the *particular* construction-related prime contract of interest to construction contractors—that is, **owner–contractor contracts** for construction services. This focus will be concentrated even further by confining the discussion to **fixed-price contracts arrived at by competitive bidding.**

Generally, someone who is knowledgeable and comfortable operating in the competitively bid, fixed-price contract environment usually finds little difficulty when operating under other forms of construction contracts. The reverse is not always true.

STANDARD FORMS-OF-CONTRACT

A number of **standard forms-of-contract** for fixed-price, competitively bid prime construction contracts are widely used today. A discussion of the more prominent of these follows.

Federal Government Construction Contract

Foremost among standard forms-of-contract is the **federal government construction contract.** This form of contract is normally used by all branches of the federal government for construction work. Prominent examples of different federal agencies using this contract include the General Services Administration, the Bureau of Reclamation, the U.S. Army Corps of Engineers, the U.S. Navy Facilities Engineering Command, the U.S. Bureau of Public Roads, and the National Park Service. The actual contracts, depending on the particular federal agency, all differ slightly in the wording of the basic provisions, and the titles used for the contract document divisions vary. However, the contracts are of the same type and contain the same basic provisions.

A typical instance where this form-of-contract was used is the U.S. Army Corps of Engineers Lock and Dam No. 26 project on the Mississippi River. This immense public works project, north of St. Louis, Missouri, involved a series of major contracts beginning in the early 1980s. Bids were taken for the third contract of the series on August 23, 1985, three to four months after it was advertised, so that bidding contractors would have time to prepare their fixed-price bids. The bidding documents consisted of two four-inch-thick volumes of technical specifications, four two-inch-thick volumes of drawings, and seven or eight extensive addendums, each of which made numerous changes in all of the other documents, including previously issued addendums. Obviously, preparing a fixed-price bid for this contract was a complicated matter requiring hundreds of hours. Smaller projects entail fewer documents and require less effort to prepare a bid. But regardless of the size of the federal project, the essential contract provisions under which the project is to be built will be the same. The larger, fixed-price federal contracts that contain a schedule of bid items are the most complex and offer the best example of the variety of problems that can occur. Five bids were received for this Lock and Dam No. 26 contract, ranging from a low bid of $227 million to a high of $288 million.

American Institute of Architects Contracts

A second important standard form-of-contract is the **American Institute of Architects (AIA) Standard Form of Agreement Between Owner and Contractor.** The two companion documents necessary to form the complete contract are AIA Form A-101 and AIA Form A-201. This contract is by far the most widely used form for fixed-price building construction work in both the public and private sectors, particularly the private sector. Entire texts have been written by legal scholars on this particular contract.[1]

Associated General Contractors Contracts

The *AGC Standard Form Prime Contract Between Owner and Contractor* is recommended for use by the Associated General Contractors of America (AGC). This contract is commonly used on private work and is suitable for both building construction and engineered construction projects. Its usage is less broad than that of the AIA contract.

Engineers Joint Contract Documents Committee Contract

Another form-of-contract, the **Engineers Joint Contract Document Committee (EJCDC) Contract,** is used primarily for engineered construction in the private sector. Its use has also been endorsed by the Associated General Contractors of America.

State Highway Department Contracts

Another broad class of competitively bid, fixed-price contracts consists of the **state highway department contracts** of the various states. These contracts tend to be similar in format, no doubt because the construction work within each state is similar. The influence of the Federal Highway Administration (FHWA) has forced this similarity. The format usually consists of an infrequently published "bible," which contains all general provisions and standard technical specifications of the state. Often a revision manual will be periodically published with changes. Then, in addition to the "bible" and its revision manual, each particular project will have its own set of "special provisions" that apply to that particular project. The special provisions contain site-specific provisions and information and any further changes to the "bible" as it relates to that specific project. The technical requirements of these state highway department contracts tend to be similar, even though some general provisions may vary. These contracts, like most others, are written by the owner agencies. From the standpoint of the legal rights afforded the contractor, these contracts vary considerably. Contractors who bid frequently in a particular state are aware of the provisions of that state's contract and know what to expect.

---

[1]*See* Sweet, Justin, *Sweet on Construction Industry Contracts: Major AIA Documents* (New York: John Wiley & Sons, 1987).

Other Agency Contracts

Many **other agencies** traditionally build infrastructure systems over time through a series of recurring contracts for similar construction work. Examples are the rapid transit districts and water and sewer districts of the large metropolitan centers, as well as state agencies (other than highway departments), such as the California Department of Water Resources and the California Department of Architecture. Each agency tends to create its own unique form of prime construction contract, often based on the federal government contract, which it then uses over and over. Construction contractors who frequently bid to one or more of these agencies become familiar with the terms of the particular form that each agency uses.

One-of-a-Kind Contracts

Occasionally, contracts are created for a particular project. These **one-of-a kind contracts** tend to vary widely. Little about them is standard or traditional, either in format or detailed provisions. Since contracting parties can agree to anything that is not contrary to law, these isolated, individual, one-of-a-kind contracts can take almost any hybrid form that the parties concoct. They are limited only by the imagination of the parties who draft them, each of whom attempts to secure the most favorable agreement possible from that party's point of view. Disputes that arise from one-of-a-kind contracts are usually more difficult to resolve because there is no past pattern of experience, as is the case with one of the "tried-and-true" standard forms-of-contract.

TYPICAL DOCUMENTS COMPRISING THE CONTRACT

Fixed-price, competitively bid contracts are comprised of certain, fairly typical documents. With the exception of one-of-a-kind contracts, the major categories of most contracts of this type consist of the following list:

- Bidding documents, consisting of the "Invitation to Bid," the "Instructions to Bidders," and the "Bid Form"
- General Conditions of Contract
- Supplementary Conditions of Contract
- Specifications
- Drawings
- Reports of investigations of physical conditions

Some contracts may not contain all of these categories but, with the exception of one-of-a-kind contracts, none is likely to contain material that won't logically fit into one category or another.

Bidding Documents

The first category, **bidding documents,** normally begins with an *advertisement,* originally discussed in Chapter 1. The back section of contemporary industry periodicals, such as the *Engineering News Record,* contains a plethora of bid advertisements with every new issue. The advertisement identifies the project for which bids are desired, the owner, the time and place of the bid opening, and instructions to potential bidders on how to obtain a full set of contract documents.

The second document in the bidding group is usually the *Invitation for Bids (IFB)* or, sometimes, a *Request for Proposals (RFP).* The federal government and some other owners use the IFB when bidders must strictly conform to the drawings and specifications and the RFP when bidders may propose variations for the project. Both typically include the following:

- A description of the contract work
- The identity of the owner
- The place, date, and precise time of the bid opening
- The penal sum of the required bonds (bid bond, performance bond, and labor and material payment bond)[2]
- A description of the drawings and specifications, their cost, and where they may be obtained
- The length of time after bid opening that bids will be deemed good (duration of bids)
- Rules regarding the withdrawal or modification of bids and late bids
- Information regarding any planned pre-bid conferences and pre-bid site inspections
- Particular requirements of law of which the owner wants bidders to be aware
- Any special instructions, other requirements, or other information that the owner wants to point out to bidders

In addition to the IFB or RFP, the contract documents may also contain a section called *Instructions to Bidders.* When used, this section is an adjunct to the instruction portion of the IFB or RFP. Sometimes all necessary instructions are contained within the IFB or RFP, and there is no separate Instructions to Bidders section. More logically, the Instructions to Bidders is a separate document, and the IFB or RFP contains all of the other necessary but noninstructional information that a bidder needs.

In every case, the contract documents contain the *Bid Form.* Bidders complete this document, sign, seal, and turn it in at the appointed place, prior to the deadline set for the submittal of bids. The fully executed Bid Form constitutes the "offer" element necessary for contract formation, discussed in Chapter 2. Note that the Bid Form must be completely filled out, signed, and sealed, all in accordance with the

---

[2]Bond requirements for fixed-price, competitively bid contracts are discussed in Chapter 9.

IFB or RFP and the Instructions to Bidders to constitute a responsive bid. The contents of the Bid Form usually include the following:

- *A definitive statement of the general terms and conditions of the offer.* This statement is normally unilaterally determined by the owner and is preprinted on the form.

- *The format of the commercial terms applying to the offer.* Again, this format is normally determined unilaterally by the owner either as a single lump sum total price or as a schedule of bid-item prices. In the first case, the bid form contains a single blank space in which the bidder is instructed to enter a single lump sum price for the entire project. In the second case, the form contains a numbered series of all bid items for the project, each consisting of a description of the work for discrete parts of the project and either blanks for unit prices and extensions against a preprinted quantity of work or a single blank for a lump sum price. The total bid in this case is the sum of the unit price extensions and lump sum prices. With either a single lump sum format or a schedule-of-bid-items format, the bidder fills in the blanks for defining the precise commercial terms of the bid.

- *Supplementary information that the owner may want to know about the bidder.* This usually consists of information about the bidder's financial strength and past experience.

- *Additional information for federal bids.* The bid form for federal contracts contains a number of "Certifications and Representations" in affidavit form, such as noncollusion and nonsegregated facilities affidavits, required to comply with federal law.

- *Affirmative action requirements for public projects.* Bid Forms for public projects usually require written goals and timetables for meeting the requirements of equal opportunity legislation and minority business enterprise/women business enterprise requirements.

- *Bid security.* Finally, the Bid Form must contain the required bid security, usually in the form of a bid bond issued by an approved surety. Sometimes, a certified check must be presented for the bid security.

Oddly enough, private sector bids often require much more supplementary information on the Bid Form than do public sector bids. And, among public projects, Bid Forms for federal contracts usually require less supplementary information than the average.

A final interesting point concerning bidding documents is that the AIA approach excludes the bidding documents from the contract. Article 1 of AIA A-201, General Conditions of the Contract for Construction, states:

> The Contract Documents do not include Bidding Documents such as the Advertisement or Invitation to Bid, the Instructions to Bidders, sample forms, the Contractor's Bid or portions of Addenda relating to any of these, or any other documents, unless specifically enumerated in the Owner-Contractor Agreement.

Why would the AIA wish to exclude the bidding documents from the contract? The rationale seems to be that the eventual contract is considered to be the end result of a negotiation, not the result of a binding firm-price bid. The bid is regarded as merely the starting point for the ensuing negotiation. Most other forms-of-contract include the bidding documents as part of the contract.

General Conditions of Contract

The second section of the documents that normally comprise the contract is the *General Conditions of Contract,* often referred to simply as the **General Conditions**, or sometimes, **General Provisions.** Here are found very definitive statements, clause by clause, of all general terms and conditions that govern the performance of the contract work. In the case of the federal government and other agencies that frequently contract for construction work, the general concept of this section of the documents is to include all clauses that will remain the same, contract after contract, changing very infrequently. Many of these standard clauses in federal contracts pertain to the requirements of the Federal Acquisition Regulations, which by law must be included in every federal construction contract.

Supplementary Conditions of Contract

In addition to the General Conditions or General Provisions, most construction contracts contain a section called **Supplementary Conditions** or *Special Conditions.* The idea of this section is to include clauses dealing with general matters that apply to the instant contract only—that is, those that are either site-specific or in some other way apply only to the specific contract. Such matters might better be called "project-specific" matters. Some forms of contract do not have a Special (or Supplementary) Conditions section. Instead they include all general matters, whether standard or project-specific, in the General Provisions section. It is also common to include general project-specific matters in Division 1 of the Specifications section. In the Uniform Construction Index (UCI) form of technical specifications, which is widely used, Division 1 is titled "General Requirements." Thus, to be entirely sure that nothing of a general nature has been overlooked in a particular case, it is necessary to carefully read the General Conditions, the Supplementary Conditions (if included), and Division 1 of the Technical Specifications.

One important area of the Supplementary Conditions for contracts where federal funds are involved is the Davis-Bacon Wage Determination originally discussed in Chapter 1. By federal law, wages paid the workers on any such project must be at least as high as listed in the Davis-Bacon Determination for each trade classification involved in the work. Even where federal funds are not required, many states require that prevailing wages be paid on public work. These rates are set by a commissioner on a project-to-project basis at a level he or she has determined through investigation to equal the "prevailing" wage for each classification of work in the locality of the project. This determination is obviously significant to contractors interested in submitting a bid. For example, if the determination is set at low "open-shop" rates, potential bidding contractors, bound by union labor agreements that require payment of higher rates, know that they are competing at a disadvantage and might be well advised not to bid at all. On the other hand, if the Davis-Bacon commissioner has determined the "prevailing" rates to be union labor agreement rates, all bidders are on a more equal footing. Open-shop or merit-shop contractors will have to pay the same rates as union contractors.

Specifications

The technical requirements for each division of work in the contract will be completely detailed in that section of the contract document called the **Specifications.** The format usually conforms to the Uniform Construction Index, which is understood by virtually every segment of the industry. Depending on size of contract, the Specifications can be voluminous. It is necessary that completely definitive requirements be carefully stated so that both parties to the contract have a mutual understanding of the precise technical standards the project work must meet.

Drawings

The next important section of the contract documents is the **Drawings,** which complement the Specifications. The Drawings must be sufficiently complete to adequately show exactly what is to be built. Certain features of the work may be shown in fairly general terms, with the requirement stated that the contractor must prepare detailed shop drawings that conform to and augment the general contract drawings. These must be submitted to the owner or the owner's engineer for approval prior to fabrication of the material covered by the shop drawings. For example, a contractor may supply detailed bar-bending schedules and placing drawings for reinforcing steel and structural steel fabrication and erection drawings, including the connections. However, the basic contract drawings advertised for fixed-price bids must be sufficiently clear and accurate so that, if contractors carefully conform to them, a satisfactorily constructed product will result. If either the Drawings or Specifications do not meet this standard, the owner may incur severe liability under the Spearin Doctrine, which is discussed in Chapter 13.

Reports of Investigations of Physical Conditions

An additional and final section that may or may not be included as an integral part of the contract documents consists of various **reports of investigations of physical conditions** at the project site. These reports often concern geotechnical aspects of subsurface soil or rock conditions. They usually appear in the form of written evaluations and soil boring logs describing subsurface conditions. Other examples are weather records and, in the case of projects on or near streams and rivers, stream flow hydrographs. These reports are probably the more common examples of this type of information, but basically any included information describing physical conditions at the site falls into this category. A more detailed discussion of these kinds of reports and whether or not they are considered to be part of the contract is included in Chapter 5.

CONCLUSION

This chapter focused on the format and the general contents of the major component sections of prime contracts between owners and general contractors for the performance of construction work. The prominent forms-of-contract commonly used today were also briefly discussed.

Chapter 5 will show why contractors need to understand the nature of the potential contract before they commit to any particular construction project. Also, the details of the critical or "red flag" clauses contained in such contracts will also be analyzed from the point of view of the bidding contractor.

QUESTIONS AND PROBLEMS

1. What is the historic, traditional form of contract upon which the present-day construction industry is based? What are the seven forms of contract discussed in this chapter? Why might a one-of-a-kind contract cause later trouble?

2. What major categories could you expect to find in the documents particularly related to bidding for a typical competitively bid fixed-price contract and what type of information or requirements are contained in each? Would every set of contract documents be likely to contain a General Conditions section? A Supplementary or Special Conditions section? In what three possible places in a set of typical contract documents would you look to be certain that all matters of general importance (other than technical matters and details on the drawings) were examined and noted? Which document part defines the offer element necessary for contract formation?

3. Why is the Davis-Bacon Determination important in a set of contract documents? Where would you expect to find it? Would documents for every project be expected to contain a Davis-Bacon Determination? If not, in which category of projects would you expect to find it?

4. What is the attitude concerning bidding documents held by the AIA? Do most other forms of contract reflect the AIA attitude?

Questions 5 and 6 assume that the reader has access to a set of typical federal contract documents for an actual project and to AIA Document A-201 (General Conditions of Contract).

5. With respect to the federal contract, determine the following and cite the section of the documents from which you obtained the answer (place the appropriate abbreviation from the following list in parentheses at the end of each answer):

Invitation for Bids	(IFB)
Instructions to Bidders	(ITB)
Bid Form	(BF)
Representations and Certifications	(R & C)
Davis-Bacon Determination	(DBD)
General Provisions	(GP)
Special Provisions	(SP)
List of Sections	(LOS)

    a. What is the date and time of bid opening?

    b. What is the penal sum of the required performance bond?

    c. Will there be a pre-bid conference?

    d. What is the number of days that bids must be held open for acceptance?

    e. Do bidders have to state whether they are a small business concern?

    f. Do bidders have to certify that they do not maintain segregated facilities?

    g. How many milestone completion dates are there?

    h. What is the amount of liquidated damages for each day that each milestone is late?

    i. Is there a clause pertaining to suspension of work?

    j. Does the government have the right to occupy a completed part of the work?

    k. Is there a clause dealing with variations in work quantities?

    l. What is the date of the Davis-Bacon Determination?

    m. How long does the contractor have to perform the entire project?

    n. How many bid items are there?

    o. Is there a clause pertaining to changes in the work?

    p. Is there a clause dealing with differing site conditions?

    q. How often can the contractor expect to receive progress payments?

    r. Is there a clause pertaining to default terminations and excusable delay?

    s. Is there a clause for termination of the contract for the convenience of the government?

    t. Is there a clause concerning contract disputes?

6. With respect to the AIA document A-201 (General Conditions of Contract), determine the following and indicate where in the document you obtained the answer. At the end of each answer, cite the source in the document by writing in parentheses the article and subarticle.

    a. Is the owner empowered to stop the work?

    b. Is the owner empowered to terminate the contract?

    c. Does this form of contract contemplate or imply a fixed time for completion of the work?

d. Is the contractor required to indemnify and hold harmless the owner?

e. Does this contract contemplate changes in the work?

f. Does this contract provide relief for the contractor's failure to perform due to conditions beyond the contractor's control?

g. Does this contract provide that either the owner or contractor can make a claim against the other for damages suffered?

h. Is the contractor likely to be liable to the owner for damages caused by late completion?

i. Does the contract contain the equivalent of the differing site conditions clause found in a federal contract?

j. Is the contractor required to carry insurance?

k. Does the contract imply that there could be payments made to the contractor by the owner in the event of owner-caused delays?

l. Does the contract provide for progress payments?

5

Owner-Construction Contractor Prime Contract "Red Flag" Clauses

---

Key Words and Concepts

"Red flag" clause
Dispute resolution clause
Sovereign immunity
Changes clause
Differing site conditions clause
Delays and suspensions
"No-damages-for-delay" clause
Default terminations
Convenience terminations
Time provisions
Notice to proceed provisions
"Stepped" notices to proceed
Single completion time
Milestone completion times
Liquidated damages provision
Actual damages
Availability of the site
Restrictions to site availability
Payment provisions
Payment frequency
Payment for materials and fabricated
    items

Retention
Mobilization allowance
Final payment
Exculpatory clauses
Disclaimers
Attitude of courts to disclaimers
Present trend on underground
    construction
Geotechnical design summary report
Geotechnical baseline report
Insurance requirements
Surety bond requirements
Indemnification
Basis of quantity measurement
Variation in quantities clause
Equal employment opportunity/
    disadvantaged/women-owned
    business requirements
Escalation provisions

Before preparing a cost estimate and submitting a competitive bid for a contract, a contractor must first be sure that the various sections of the contract documents are complete. Chapter 4 identified the major categories of typical contract documents and discussed the general nature of each.

Once this first step has been completed, a prudent contractor bidder will do much more before making a decision on whether to proceed. It is imperative to know what kind of a contractual situation will be encountered if a bid is submitted and the contract awarded. Will the contract be fair, or will it be heavily biased in favor of the owner? Aside from the financial "risk of performance" associated with the actual construction work, what contractual risks lie buried in the contract language?

It took a wrenching personal experience for this author to appreciate the true consequences of failure to identify properly and answer these questions at the time of bidding for a large bridge substructure project. In that instance, the fact that the owner, a state department of transportation, was shielded by the doctrine of sovereign immunity applying to all contracts with that state was not discovered until long after the project was bid, the contract entered into, and major disputes had developed in the course of the work. The eventual resolution of the contractor's claims, which was not appealable, was not obtained until 16 years after the completion of the work.

So, the lesson to be learned from this chapter is how to avoid unknowingly assuming the risks inherent in such situations.

THRESHOLD "RED FLAG" CLAUSES

An old adage states: "Do not sign a contract until you have read and understood every word." Today, literal compliance with this rule is not practical, even if one wanted to do that. Reading contract language is a tedious, sleep-inducing activity, and most people hate to do it. Also, there is an obvious difference between signing a contract and committing to the preparation of an estimate and bid. However, submittal of a bid places the contractor in a position where failure to proceed with signing the contract and completing the project according to the contract terms can become extremely costly. This is true because bid security is normally required in the case of fixed-price construction contracts. Further, the preparation of a cost estimate for a fixed-price construction project is time consuming and expensive. Although a potential bidder can always drop further consideration of a project after work on the estimate has begun, the time and money expended up to that point is lost, and failing to proceed after starting can be destructive to a construction organization's morale. So the old adage might just as well be stated: "Do not undertake a cost estimate and start bid preparation until you have read and understood the potential contract." How can one approach this ideal? One good way is to seek out, carefully examine, and understand the provisions of certain key contract clauses, often referred to as **"red flag" clauses.** Generally, these clauses tell bidding contractors the kind of contractual situation they will encounter if they are successful in securing that particular contract.

Experienced construction executives probably would agree on the choice of clauses included in this chapter even if they did not agree on the precise "pecking order" in which the clauses are listed. Each "red flag" clause will be discussed from the standpoint of what the clause typically provides and why it is important. In this discussion, clause titles are generic. Actual titles may vary from contract to contract.

Dispute Resolution and Governing Law Clause

Bidding contractors need to be aware of the contract dispute resolution provisions. If disputes arise, who will resolve them and by what set of rules?

A well-drafted **dispute resolution clause** spells out precisely what steps the contractor and owner are required take to resolve disputes between them, usually defining time limits within which various procedural steps must be initiated. Some contracts specify straightforward and reasonably simple procedures, whereas others are excessively complicated and time consuming. In extreme cases, the contract states that the architect/engineer's or owner's decision is final and binding, ostensibly leaving the contractor no recourse in the event of disagreement with that decision. Usually, such A/E and/or owner decisions will be binding on the contractor on matters having to do with the standard of acceptability of the performed contract work. Whether such decisions will be supported by the courts with respect to "questions of law" depends on whether the work is public or private and on the law of the state in which the project is located. Federal contracts do not contain clauses providing that the engineer's decisions are final and binding.

A well-drafted dispute resolution clause also states the means by which the dispute will eventually be resolved if the parties cannot come to an agreement. The normal possibilities are arbitration (usually under the auspices of the American Arbitration Association), submittal to an administrative board of the owner-agency involved, submittal to a specially appointed contract disputes review board, or a formal trial in a court-of-law. In the latter case, the contract may specify the particular court that will try the case. Of special concern from the contractor's standpoint are the contract provisions in the few states that have not waived **sovereign immunity** (see the introduction to this chapter). In these instances, the contractor may not sue the state in a court-of-law on a matter arising from the contract. The only procedure open to the contractor is referral to a claims court, controlled by the state with whom the contractor has the dispute. There is no appeal. If a monetary award is made to the contractor, the state may not be required to make payment until and unless the state legislature passes a specific bill appropriating the necessary funds.

Finally, a well-drafted clause states what legal rules will apply—that is, what the governing law will be. The federal government contract clause states that disputes will be settled in accordance with the Contract Disputes Act of 1978, a federal law. The AIA contract clause states that the law of the state where the contract is performed will apply. The importance of this clause cannot be overemphasized because the laws of different states vary considerably.

The subject of dispute resolution is more fully discussed in Chapter 23.

Changes Clause

Every construction contract today contains a **changes clause.** However, the detailed provisions of the clause vary from contract to contract. The clause generally defines the owner's right to change the contract unilaterally, places limitations on that right, establishes the contractor's duty to perform the change, and the contractor's right to be paid for performing the change. These details range from the provisions of the changes clause in the federal government contract, which are broad and even-handed, to provisions in some contracts that are grossly unfair and which place the contractor at a distinct disadvantage when the owner makes changes. Chapter 14 focuses exclusively on the detailed provisions of the changes clause.

Differing Site Conditions Clause

The **differing site conditions (DSC) clause** is probably next in importance. Not all construction contracts contain a DSC clause. Many contractors put this clause at the head of the "red flag" list and will not submit a bid if the contract documents do not include a fair and comprehensive DSC clause. This clause is sometimes called a "changed conditions" clause. In the case of the AIA contract, the clause is called "concealed conditions."

The relevance of this clause to underground construction is discussed in Chapter 4. This clause also normally applies to any physical site condition found during contract performance that materially differs from those indicated in the contract documents or from conditions normally encountered in the type of work of the contract. The detailed provisions range from the DSC clause in the federal government contract, which is comprehensive, fair, and serves as a model clause for the industry as a whole, to contracts with clauses containing less explicit language, to contracts containing no DSC clause at all. Chapter 15 is entirely devoted to the subject of differing site conditions and the operation of this clause.

Delays and Suspensions of Work

Another important "red flag" clause deals with **delays and suspensions** of work. There are several important aspects of this subject. First, construction contracts usually impose severe liabilities on the contractor because of generally stringent requirements for work to meet narrow technical standards within fixed time requirements. Such is the nature of construction contracting. However, both owners and contractors understand that certain conditions may occur under which the contractor's failure to perform within the required time limits will be excused. Such conditions are sometimes called *conditions of force majeure* and normally would include acts, or failures to act, by the owner or others and "acts of God" that delay or prevent the contractor's performance. The delays and suspension of work clause usually carefully enumerates what constitutes a reason for excusable delay for that particular contract. Bidding contractors need to know that this list is broad enough to include situations that the contractor knows from past experience may occur.

Again, the federal contract provisions are broad and fair and afford contractor's time relief for delays that are truly beyond their control. Other contracts may designate far fewer situations for which relief will be granted, and some even require the contractor to complete the work by a certain stated date, called a "date certain" under any and all circumstances—in other words, the contractor is granted no relief whatsoever.

A second question arises regarding responsibility for extra costs arising when the owner either delays or suspends the work. Who pays? The federal suspension of work clause and other similar clauses contain provisions that are complete, explicit, and generally state that the government pays if the government causes a delay that damages the contractor. Other contracts range from some that are completely silent on the subject, to those containing **"no-damages-for-delay" clauses,** which state that a contractor's relief for an owner-caused delay to the contractor's operations is limited to an extension of time only. Some contractors will not bid on contracts containing a no-damages-for-delay clause. No-damages-for-delay clauses are further discussed in Chapter 16.

Terminations and Partial Terminations

An important "red flag" clause closely related to the delay and suspension of work clause is that dealing with terminations and partial terminations. Here, we are talking about the owner's right, not to delay the work, but to unilaterally terminate all of the work of the contract or to terminate some divisible part of the work. Most construction contracts give the owner this right, usually under each of the following circumstances. First, the owner may terminate the contract when the contractor's performance is either (1) far behind a reasonable time schedule or (2) results in work that fails to meet contract quality requirements or (3) when the contractor becomes financially insolvent. Second, the owner may terminate the contract without disclosing any reason.

The first set of circumstances constitutes a default of the contract by the contractor. Most contracts give the owner broad powers in these circumstances to remove the contractor from the site, to take over the equipment and materials on the site (whether paid for or not), and to complete the work or cause it to be completed by others. If the owner's costs in completing the work exceed the unpaid portion of the original contract price, the difference must be paid by the contractor. Such terminations are called **default terminations.**

The second kind of termination is called a *termination for the convenience of the owner* or, more simply, a **convenience termination.** Contracts differ greatly in regard to this kind of termination. The difference is not in providing the right of the owner to effect such terminations (almost all present-day contracts provide for this), but in the provisions dealing with the **final payment** that the contractor receives if the owner does decide to terminate the contract or part of the contract short of completion. Many thorny questions arise. The contractor may be heavily committed to the project when suddenly, without warning, the contract is terminated. The contractor normally will have ongoing commitments in the form of purchase orders and subcontract agreements that must also be terminated and for which the contractor will incur unavoidable costs. The owner is undoubtedly due a credit for the value of the uncompleted work, but how large a credit? Is the contractor entitled to anticipated profit on the uncompleted work? Resolution of these and many similar questions never comes easily. Many contracts are completely silent on determination of a fair and equitable settlement in the event of a convenience termination, in essence leaving the parties to "fight it out." On the other hand, the federal contract and other similar contracts deal more or less effectively with this subject, depending on the particular contract. Since a convenience termination is an act completely beyond the contractor's control and must be regarded as a definite possibility, the detailed provisions dealing with payment are vitally important.

Chapter 16 deals with some of the unique problems associated with both default and convenience terminations.

OTHER IMPORTANT "RED FLAG" CLAUSES

By the time that a contractor understands the threshold "red flag" clauses just discussed, he or she will have a fairly good indication of the type of owner and type of contract involved with the project. If the contractor is still interested in submitting a bid, the balance of the "red flag" clauses provide further critical information. These clauses—some general and others highly project-specific—include the following:

- Time provisions
- Liquidated or actual damages for late completion
- Site availability and access to the site
- Payment and retention provisions
- Reports of physical site conditions
- Exculpatory clauses
- Insurance and bond provisions
- Indemnification clauses
- Measurement and payment provisions
- Variation in quantities
- Equal employment opportunity and disadvantaged business assistance requirements
- Escalation provisions

The detailed provisions of many of these clauses are complex and their potential impact on the contractor's cost of performance can be enormous. Each will be discussed in some detail.

Time Provisions

The **time provisions** are project-specific and are much broader than simply a statement of how much time that the contractor has been given to complete the work. Contractors should look for at least the following additional information:

1. What are the **notice to proceed (NTP) provisions?** Will the contractor receive NTP reasonably promptly after signing the contract, or does the owner have the right to delay giving NTP, perhaps indefinitely? In some instances, a delayed NTP may be an advantage to the contractor, but normally, once the contractor is committed to the project, starting work as soon as possible is to the contractor's advantage and delaying it is a great disadvantage. Many contracts provide that NTP will be given within a specifically stated number of calendar days from the bid date or from the date of execution of the contract, whereas others are silent on this point. Another question is whether the contract provides for more than one, or a series of "**stepped**" **NTPs,** each NTP releasing only limited parts of the project or limited activities that the contractor may perform under that particular NTP. Many difficult contractual problems can ensue when stepped NTPs are used or when the owner issues NTPs that are qualified. Both practices severely limit the contractor's flexibility.

2. What is the time period after NTP within which the contract work must be completed? The bidder should not simply assume that the time period stated in the contract is necessarily reasonable. The contractor will normally be held to that period whether it is reasonable or not, so if the stated period appears to be insufficient, the bidder had best not proceed further unless extra costs are included in the bid estimate to meet the required schedule. Otherwise, the bidder should expect to pay liquidated damages for late completion. Some contractors will not submit a bid if they believe that the time allowed for contract performance is unreasonably short.

3. Is a **single completion time** for the total project specified or is a series of "milestones" listed that must be met within specified time limits, each **milestone completion time** pertaining to a discrete part of the contract work? Contractors frequently find that they can meet the final completion deadline without undue difficulty but that intermediate milestones prove difficult and costly, particularly when very early milestone dates are specified. If milestone dates are specified, bidding contractors must take note and analyze them carefully.

Liquidated or Actual Damages for Late Completion

Closely related to the time provisions are other project-specific provisions stating the type of contractor liability that will result in the event of late completion. If the required contract work is not completed within the stated period, the contract has, in effect, been breached by the contractor, entitling the owner to be paid damages. The monetary amount will be determined in one of two very different ways.

1. Most construction contracts include a **liquidated damages provision.** This provision states that, for every day the project work remains uncompleted beyond the time allotted for contract performance, the contractor shall pay the owner a stated dollar amount. The concept of liquidated damages is that the true or **actual damages** suffered by the owner are often difficult to determine accurately. Therefore, to obviate the need for making this determination, the owner and contractor agree at the time of contract formation on a dollar amount per calendar day that will be accepted by both parties as proper and appropriate recompense for any delay in contract completion. If the contractor completes the work late, the owner does not have to prove that any damages were thereby suffered but is entitled to the liquidated damages figure stated in the contract. If the contract provides for milestone completion dates in addition to the final completion date, liquidated damages may apply separately to each milestone date, with the total liquidated damages liability of the contractor being cumulative. Obviously, the magnitude of the stated daily liquidated damage figures may be of great concern to bidding contractors. In the writer's experience, these have varied from less than $50 per day to over $50,000 per day.

2. Monetary damages due the owner in the event of late completion may also be determined by **proof of actual damages.** If the contract does not contain a liquidated damages provision, the owner is entitled by application of common law principles to be paid the actual monetary damages suffered due to late completion. Although a contractor may finish a project late but pay nothing because the owner suffered no consequential damages, the owner's damages in the event of late completion are sometimes immense and can be proven in court. Such contracts can represent a far greater financial risk to the contractor than if the contract provided for liquidated damages, depending, of course, on the stated daily liquidated damages figure. Thus, the absence of a liquidated damages provision in the contract is not necessarily beneficial from the contractor's standpoint. If a liquidated damages provision is not included, bidding contractors would be well advised to determine the potential magnitude of actual damages the owner might suffer in the event of late completion before proceeding further. Liquidated damages are discussed in further detail in Chapter 17.

Site Availability and Access to the Site

Another project-specific matter concerns the **availability of the site** to the contractor. An implied obligation of the owner in every construction contract is to make the project site and reasonable access to it available to the contractor at the time of notice to proceed without restrictions unless the contract contains provisions to the contrary. Some contracts do contain such provisions to the contrary by placing **restrictions to the site,** either on the availability of the site or on the means of access to it. The restrictions can either state that the entire site, or separate portions of the site, will be made available at a time considerably later than the date of notice to proceed and/or that the contractor must complete the work and relinquish the site or sites by stipulated dates that are earlier than the final completion date of the contract.

A large contract for rapid transit construction in Atlanta in 1968 illustrates the problems inherent in stepped or phased construction site release dates. In that case, the bid documents provided for a highly fragmented schedule of release dates for construction work areas due to difficulty encountered by the Metropolitan Atlanta Rapid Transit Authority (MARTA) in obtaining title to the property involved. Included in these stepped work area release dates were specified dates for three areas contiguous to the main underground subway station—one area for ventilation ducts and the remaining two for auxiliary entrances to the station. All three were to be released to the contractor at dates stated in the contract that were considerably later than release of work areas necessary for the construction of the main underground station itself. After construction started, MARTA's difficulties continued, delaying release of these three areas beyond the dates stated in the contract that created great uncertainty in scheduling and executing the contractor's work activities. For many months, it was not known when, or even if, these three areas would be released. After delaying station construction significantly, the area for the ventilation ducts was eventually released, but the two areas for auxiliary station entrances were never released and eventually were deleted from the contract. The end result of delay and uncertainty of release for these three areas was that the project was in a continual state of flux for a considerable period of the contract, which seriously affected the contractor's ability to schedule and carry out the underground station work. Considerable extra costs were generated which, fortunately, were eventually recognized and reimbursed by MARTA.

Another Georgia project involved the construction of 16 freeway bridges for the state department of transportation. Each bridge occupied an individual work site that the bidding documents indicated would be released to the contractor for bridge construction at stated dates. The contractor's bid was prepared in anticipation that the individual sites would be released for construction in the order and by the dates stated in the bidding documents. After submitting the low bid and entering into the contract, the contractor commenced construction according to the bid plan, which relied on the bridge site release sequence and dates stated in the contract. Only two of the 16 bridge sites were released by the dates stated, the remainder being released from one to nine months late. The contractor's planned work schedule and sequence of crew and equipment movement from site to site were totally disrupted, forcing the contractor to build the job on a continually changing schedule as first one and then another of the bridge sites were released late and out of sequence in a completely unpredictable pattern. The contractor filed claims for the greatly increased performance costs due to disruption and delay to the planned work program upon which the bid was based. The claims were denied, and the contractor sued in the Georgia courts.

Unfortunately for the contractor, the Georgia Court of Appeals reversed a trial court jury verdict that awarded the contractor substantial breach of contract damages for the state's failure to release the bridge sites as stated in the contract.[1]

---

[1] *Department of Transportation v. Fru-Con Corporation*, 426 S.E.2d 905 (Ga. App. 1992).

Apparently, in Georgia, contractors are not entitled to rely on these types of representations in bidding documents. Aside from the correctness or the incorrectness of the Georgia Court of Appeals decision, this case dramatically illustrates the risk posed to bidding contractors when the bidding documents indicate that the work site will be turned over to the contractor for construction in a piecemeal fashion.

Another form of **site availability** restriction is limiting the contractor's right to occupy the site to certain days and to certain hours of the day, often to periods in the middle of the night. Such provisions are common for contracts for work in city streets, such as underground utility work or paving work. Similar restrictions may be placed on the availability of the **means of access** to the project site or sites, even to the extreme of stating that the contractor must make their own arrangements for access to the site. Another common form of restriction is to limit the hours in the workday during which certain kinds of construction activity, such as operating heavy haulage equipment or conducting blasting work, are allowed.

These and similar restrictions can affect the contractor's cost of performance enormously. Such restrictions may not be immediately apparent when a bidder skims through a set of contract documents. However, a contractor bidding on a project must examine the documents carefully and clearly understand any restrictions to avoid later misfortune.

Payment and Retention Provisions

The *general* importance of the **payment provisions** is obvious. However, several specific aspects are somewhat less so. All large construction contracts call for successive progress payments to be made to the contractor, each based on an estimated value of the work satisfactorily completed during the progress payment time period. The important issues here are what is the duration of the progress payment period and how long after the end of the payment period can the contractor expect to receive payment? Provisions vary. A monthly period for **payment frequency** is common as is the provision that the contractor receives payment within 30 days from the date that the owner's architect or engineer certifies the correctness of the estimate of work completed. In extremely large projects, a two-week progress payment period may be stated. Less obvious provisions govern the extent to which **payment for the value of materials and fabricated products,** such as structural steel and precast concrete procured and paid for by the contractor but not yet incorporated into the work, are made. Many contracts include the value of such items in progress payments, usually at less than their full value, with the balance of the contractor's purchase price to be paid when the materials have been fully incorporated into the work. More restrictive payment terms do not recognize any value of such materials until they have been fully incorporated into the work.

A good example of the impact that payment for fabricated materials stored on site can have on a contractor's cash flow is afforded by the Bolton Hills Tunnel Contract constructed for the Maryland Mass Transit Administration in the late 1970s. That contract involved $12 million worth of fabricated steel segmented liner plate to be procured by the contractor and installed as the tunnels were excavated.

Fabrication and delivery to the site had to occur a number of months prior to payment being received for the installed plate in the tunnels. The fabricator required payment on delivery to the contractor's storage yard at the site, and the contractor would have been badly strapped for cash had the contract not provided for partial payment upon delivery of the fabricated liner plate to the job site. Had the contractor been required to carry the full investment of the value of the liner plate until payment on installation, the bid would have been higher.

Another key issue is the retained percentage provision. Retained percentage or **retention** is a deduction made from each progress payment prior to paying over the balance to the contractor. The owner holds these retained monies until after satisfactory completion of the contract and acceptance of the work to provide a fund to remedy nonconforming work that the contractor may refuse or fail to remedy, as well as to provide some protection to the owner if the contractor falls in default of the contract and/or abandons the contract. After the satisfactory completion and acceptance of all contract work by the owner, the retained funds, less any amounts used to correct defects or satisfy other unpaid obligations of the contractor to the owner, are paid over to the contractor, constituting final payment of the contract price.

A common retention percentage is 10%, meaning that the contractor will receive only 90% of the value of each progress payment. Thus, when the contractor has fully completed all contract work, the owner will hold 10% of the contract price up until the point of final payment. On many types of work, the prime contractor's markup on the estimated project cost will be less than 10%, meaning that, unless the contractor has retained 10% from all payments made to the material suppliers and subcontractors, the contractor could well be in a negative cash flow position at the completion of the contract work, even though the contract will eventually be profitable once the owner makes final payment. Under these circumstances, the point at which the final payment is made becomes increasingly important.

A more reasonable approach that has gained popularity in recent years is for the owner to retain 10% for the first 50% of the contract, then cease further retention, if the contractor is performing satisfactory work and is conforming to an agreed-upon project progress schedule. Further, at some subsequent point when most of the work has been completed, say, 90–95% of the total, and the contractor's performance continues to be satisfactory with respect to quality and schedule, the retention is reduced to 200% of the estimated value of the uncompleted work. The remainder of the retention is then paid over as the final contract payment on completion and acceptance of all the work. Another popular approach is for the owner to deposit the retainage in an escrow account for which the interest is payable to the contractor. The owner may also permit the contractor to pledge interest-bearing securities or provide an irrevocable letter of credit in lieu of retention.

The retention provisions in a particular case can have a significant effect on the contractor's cash flow, resulting in more or less investment of the contractor's own funds in the project. This becomes even more of a concern in the case of major projects for heavy engineering civil works construction, significantly affecting the amount that bidding contractors include in their cost estimates for the cost of money, which in turn affects the total cost that the owner pays for the project.

Many heavy construction projects require large investments of capital before the work of the project can begin. These early cash outlays are required for the purchase of construction equipment, freight and assembly of the equipment at the work site, and installing extensive plant facilities such as temporary utility distribution systems, batch plants, material handling systems, and heavy-duty repair facilities. If not provided for separately in some manner, these large early expenditures can only be recovered through progress payments as the permanent work of the project is put in place.

Such projects may extend over several years, resulting in large investments tied up in the project for some time before being recovered. The time value of these invested funds is considerable and raises the bid price that the owner pays for the project. Another effect is to eliminate otherwise qualified bidders who may not have the financial strength to afford the initial high investment. Even if they have the necessary funds or the credit line to borrow them, they may wish to employ these resources elsewhere. Further, large public owners frequently can borrow at lower rates of interest than contractors.

For all these reasons, projects of this type frequently contain a lump sum bid item called a **mobilization allowance,** usually fixed by the owner in the bid form at a finite number of dollars. The project specifications make clear the kinds of costs that the mobilization allowance is intended to cover, and the contractor may immediately bill these large early expenses against the mobilization bid item. This lowers the contractor's investment expense considerably and thus lowers the bid price to the owner in the same manner that favorable retention provisions and other favorable payment terms lower the bid price. Therefore, the presence or absence of the mobilization payment provision is important to bidding contractors. Otherwise, the bid must contain large interest charges as a necessary cost.

The importance of the time when **final payment** is made was previously mentioned, especially when the total retained funds are sizable. Some contracts contain straightforward procedures for contract closeout and release of final payment to the contractor. Others result in final payment months after completion and acceptance of the work. Contracts with a high retained percentage and with difficult and time-consuming closeout procedures obviously are not desirable from the contractor's standpoint and therefore usually carry a much higher bid markup.

Reports of Physical Site Conditions

As mentioned in Chapter 4, it is important to determine precisely which documents comprise the contract and whether the contract documents include reports of physical conditions at the site, particularly for projects involving underground construction.

If such reports are included, are they to be considered part of the contract documents? Practices vary. Some owners make it very clear that the material has been included for the use of bidding contractors with the understanding that bidders shall consider it accurate and rely on it in determining their bids. Under these circumstances, the information implicitly is part of the contract documents. This fact will usually also be stated explicitly.

In contrast, other owners seek to limit or to avoid completely the liability that would ordinarily flow to them if physical site conditions data they furnish proves to be incorrect. They usually do this by means of a clause stating that the data is not part of the contract documents and that the owner and the architect/engineer bear no liability for any errors or inaccuracies that may later be found. Such a clause is one example of a type of clause called a **disclaimer,** and although not generally favored, may be recognized by the courts, provided that it is prominent and unambiguous and does not conflict or fly in the face of other contract provisions. On the other hand, many courts are reluctant to give this type of disclaimer full force and effect. They reason that if the owner does not want bidding contractors to use the information and rely on it in formulating the bid, then why include the information with the contract documents? Better to let the bidders make their own investigation of the site conditions. A problem with this approach is that the bidding period is usually too short to permit bidders to make in-depth investigations of physical site conditions, particularly underground conditions.

Good examples of courts' reaction to the enforceability of disclaimers is afforded by the following two cases. In the first, a South Dakota State highway contract requiring borrow excavation contained the following disclaimer:

> The information covering the pit for the project is given to you for informational purposes only. The Department of Transportation does not guarantee the quantity or the quality of the material listed in the above information. Interested contractors should investigate the area before considering it for bidding purposes.

The successful bidder had received the bidding documents including the borrow pit data only two weeks before bids were due. The borrow pit data proved to be grossly inaccurate and, after submitting a claim which was denied, the contractor sued to recover the increased cost of performance due to the inaccurate borrow pit information. The Supreme Court of South Dakota ruled against the contractor saying:

> The unambiguous language of a contract defeats an implied warranty claim. There is no ambiguity in this case as to the parties' intentions. The burden was placed on Mooney's by expressed contract to determine the nature of the material in the pit. It appears that Mooney's would now try to escape this contractor responsibility through use of an implied warranty.

Thus, the disclaimer was enforced.[2]

The opposite ruling resulted in a Maryland case where Baltimore County took bids for underwater repairs to the concrete piers for a bridge. The contract required the contractor to build sheet pile cofferdams around the piers, then dewater and excavate the bed of the river inside the cofferdams, exposing the piers. Once the piers were exposed, the contractor was required to chip away and replace

---

[2]*Mooney's, Inc. v. South Dakota Department of Transportation,* 482 N.W. 2d 43 (S.D. 1992).

deteriorated concrete, which was represented in the bidding documents to average approximately six inches in thickness.

The bidding documents contained a disclaimer to the effect that the site data included was for information purposes only and did not purport to represent actual conditions and did not relieve bidders of the obligation to verify independently all such data before submitting a bid.

During actual construction, the river bed was found to consist of hard material that was difficult to excavate, instead of the soft material represented in the bidding documents, and it contained numerous large boulders interfering with the coffer-dam construction. The contractor incurred large cost overruns in performing the work. Further, only two inches of deteriorated concrete was found on the surface of the piers instead of the six inches stated in the bid documents. This resulted in the contractor being compensated for only 114 cubic yards of concrete removed instead of the 230 cubic yards that was calculated in the bid. The contractor sued to recover these large losses.

On appeal from an adverse lower court decision, the Court of Special Appeals of Maryland ruled for the contractor, stating that reliance on the data in the bidding documents was justified because there was no possible way that bidders could verify the data or otherwise obtain other more accurate data. The court further stated that the county's data published in the bidding documents resulted from four years of periodic underwater inspections that could not possibly be duplicated by bidding contractors in the short period allowed for bidding.[3]

A more modern view for projects involving significant **underground construction** has resulted from the work of the Technical Committee on Contracting Practices of the Underground Technology Research Council sponsored jointly by the American Society of Civil Engineers and the American Institute of Mining, Metallurgical and Petroleum Engineers.[4] This approach requires that the owner have an adequate geotechnical investigation carried out pre-bid and include the engineer's analysis of the data resulting from the investigation in the form of a geotechnical "baseline" report that the bidders may use in the preparation of their bids. Depictions of the logs of the actual soil borings and data recorded from various physical tests performed on materials at the site may or may not be included as part of the contract documents, but the engineer's geotechnical baseline report including a summary of the analysis of all the detailed data and the engineer's conclusions *will* be included as part of the contract. This engineer's geotechnical evaluation is frequently called the **geotechnical design summary report (GDSR)** or, more recently, the **geotechnical baseline report (GBR).** If geotechnical conditions actually encountered during construction are more adverse than described in the geotechnical baseline report, the contractor is afforded relief for any ensuing loss of time or money through the provisions of the differing site conditions clause of the contract. This latter clause will be examined in detail in Chapter 15.

---

[3]*Raymond International, Inc. v. Baltimore County,* 412 A. 2d 1296 (Md. App. 1980).

[4]See *Avoiding and Resolving Disputes During Construction,* published by the American Society of Civil Engineers, 345 East 47th St., New York, NY 10017-2398.

Exculpatory Clauses in General

Exculpatory clauses or disclaimers were discussed above in connection with their use in limiting the owner's liability for inaccurate or otherwise misleading reports of physical site conditions. This is but one example of such clauses. Today, many knowledgeable persons, including contractors, owners, and architect/engineers, oppose the use of this type of clause, and many courts are reluctant to enforce them. However, their use persists. Bidding contractors who encounter them in contract documents and assume they will not be enforced do so at their peril. In any contract bidding situation, all exculpatory clauses must be identified and their potential impact evaluated.

Insurance and Bond Provisions

Insurance and bond provisions, briefly mentioned in previous chapters, are of paramount importance and could probably be considered a threshold matter. Ordinarily, bidding contractors will be able to meet the **insurance requirements,** provided they are not so stringent or unusual that the required policies are not available in the insurance market. The question then becomes one of insurance premium cost. Sufficient money must be included in the bid cost estimate to pay the required policy premiums for the life of the project. The advice of insurance specialists is usually needed to assure this; therefore, the insurance requirement provisions of the documents should be reviewed pre-bid by either in-house specialists on the contractor's staff, an insurance broker, or both.

The contractor's situation with regard to the **surety bond requirements** is considerably different. Here, cost is not the only question, although the premiums for the required package of bonds can be a substantial sum that must be included in the bid cost estimate. The major question is whether the contractor will be able to obtain the bonds at all. The answer depends on the relationship between the particular contractor and the surety companies. This, in turn, depends on the contractor's financial strength and performance record on past contracts, the likely contract price for the project under consideration, and the contractor's backlog of bonded work.

The key bond is the *performance bond*. If the contractor's surety commits to furnishing the performance bond, the other normally required bonds (the bid bond and the labor and materials payment bond) will also be furnished by the surety. The surety's agreement to provide the required project bonds must be secured very early in the bid preparation process. Without this commitment, the contractor cannot sensibly proceed, unless there is reason to believe that some development occurring during the bid preparation period will cause the surety to commit to furnish the required bonds. Chapter 8 is devoted to the subject of insurance contracts and Chapter 9 to surety bonds.

Indemnification Requirements

Many construction contracts require the contractor to "indemnify and hold harmless" the owner and the architect/engineer from all losses that they may suffer arising from any act or failure to act of the contractor in the performance of the contract work. Such **indemnification** usually extends to providing the legal defense in court for the indemnified parties if they are sued by persons or entities who allege they have been damaged as a result of the contract work and, if a judgment is obtained against the indemnified parties, to pay the judgment.

An indemnification clause imposes serious potential liabilities on the contractor. Many cannot afford to accept this risk unless the risk is insurable. A serious problem arises when the indemnification requirements are unreasonably broad and the contractor finds that they cannot be covered by insurance. For instance, such requirements have sometimes gone to the extreme of requiring the contractor to indemnify the owner and architect/engineer for the self-inflicted consequences of their own negligence. Therefore, before proceeding very far in pursuit of a potential contract, it is essential that contractors find out what the indemnification requirements are and determine whether they are insurable.

The federal government has not waived sovereign immunity with respect to tort liability. Neither have many of the individual states. These entities are thus protected from lawsuits by third parties arising from any act or failure to act on the part of their contractors. Construction contracts with these entities may not contain an indemnification clause.

Measurement and Payment Provisions

In the case of schedule-of-bid-items contracts paid on the basis of unit prices for measured quantities of work put in place which are common in engineered construction, the **basis of quantity measurement** and the exact rules determining which items of work will be separately paid and which will be included in the payment for other items are very important. Usually, the answers to both questions will be found in the measurement and payment language of the specifications. Contractors may well make the decision on whether to bid or decline to bid a job on the basis of the measurement and payment provisions if they have been so unclearly or unfairly written that they impose risks on the contractor that cannot be evaluated. Although detailed discussion of this subject is beyond the scope of this text, suffice it to say here that the measurement and payment provisions must be carefully examined and understood to avoid later unpleasant surprises.

Variation in Quantities Clause

The **variation in quantities clause** is also important in contracts for heavy engineered construction paid on a unit price basis, particularly those where the estimated quantities are large and can potentially underrun or overrun. The bid unit prices on such contracts normally contain one component to cover the contractor's direct costs of performing the work and a separate component to cover the distributed portion of the contractor's total job overhead and general and administrative expense. These latter costs are more or less fixed and independent of the final quantity of work done under the various bid items. An underrun in quantity will mean that the contractor will not recover all necessary fixed costs for the job, thereby suffering a loss. On the other hand, if the quantities overrun, the contractor will recover more than the fixed costs and reap an unexpected financial gain. The contractor will also experience a loss or reap a gain separately with respect to the profit and contingency components, which are also included in the bid unit price.

One widely used form of the **variation of quantities clause** provides that the bid unit price on any bid item in the job applies for all actual measured final quantities of work that fall within 15% under or over the estimated quantity shown on the schedule of bid items (the bid quantity). If the actual measured final quantity turns out to be less than 85% of the bid quantity, the unit price will be renegotiated upward if necessary to enable the contractor to recover the distributed fixed costs that would otherwise be lost. Similarly, if the actual final quantity turns out to be over 115% of the bid quantity, the unit price will be negotiated downward if necessary to prevent the contractor from over-recovering fixed costs.

Some clauses provide that the adjustment will "be based upon any increase or decrease in costs due solely to the variations above 115% or below 85% of the estimated quantity." Under this form of the clause, the manner in which the contractor distributed the fixed general costs and profit to the various bid items is left unaltered when unit price adjustments due to quantity variations are considered. Unless the contractor's actual costs of performing the work are directly affected *solely* by the increase or decrease in the quantity of work actually performed (either over 115% or under 85% of the bid quantity, respectively), there will be no unit price adjustment.

Under either form of the clause, the actual percentage figures controlling when the clause becomes operative may vary for particular contracts, but the principles of operation remain as explained above.

Equal Employment Opportunity and Disadvantaged/ Women-Owned Business Requirements

Equal employment opportunity requirements and disadvantaged/women-owned business subcontracting requirements that are frequently included in contracts in the public sector were briefly mentioned in Chapter 1. These requirements usually take the form of specifying goals by trades for

1. The percentage of the contractor work force that should be filled by women and/or members of ethnic minorities; and
2. Specifying a percentage of the total contract price that should represent either materials purchased from, or services subcontracted with, disadvantaged person-owned enterprises (DBEs) or women-owned enterprises (WBEs).

Ordinarily, the requirement for stated percentages of women or minority employees is seldom a problem in today's contracting world, but there has been a great deal of trouble and litigation concerning the requirement for purchasing materials from, and subcontracting with, DBEs and WBEs. The issues involved are socioeconomic and often highly charged politically and emotionally. They are beyond the scope of this book. Suffice it to say that bidding contractors must know what the DBE and WBE requirements are and follow the stated instructions to the letter when submitting bids. Significant costs may be involved, which must be included in the bid price.

Escalation Provisions

Escalation provisions can be important in long-term contracts spanning a number of years. The essential idea of an escalation provision is that, in order to induce a lower bid price, the owner agrees to take the risk or part of the risk of increases in the cost of labor and key construction materials above the levels that existed at the time bids were taken.

Such contracts normally include a schedule of the labor hourly rates and the unit costs of key materials existing at the time of bid upon which the contractor's bid was based. The contractor's certified payrolls and paid invoices for all materials, maintained during contract performance, determine the actual manhours worked, labor rates paid, actual quantities of materials purchased and actual prices paid, all of which establish a basis for computing escalation costs. The contract will provide that the owner pay the contractor for all or a stated percentage of the escalation cost, in addition to the normal contract price determined by the bid.

The majority of contracts do not contain escalation provisions. However, when escalation provisions are present, the contractor is relieved of considerable risk, which will result in a lower bid price to the owner. Since the owner, not the contractor, is taking the risk, the owner will be the beneficiary of any savings when anticipated escalation does not occur, which would otherwise have been included in the bid price and thus paid by the owner even though these costs were not incurred by the contractor.

CONCLUSION

This chapter concluded the focus on prime construction contracts by first explaining why contractors must understand the implications of potential contracts for construction work by seeking out the "red flag" clauses and thereafter looking at the details of the clauses themselves.

The following chapters will shift emphasis from the prime construction contract to some of the prominent secondary contracts that are closely related to prime construction contracts, starting with Chapter 6 on the subject of labor agreements.

QUESTIONS AND PROBLEMS

1. Why is it important for bidding contractors to search out and become familiar with the "red flag" clauses discussed in this chapter? At what point in the bid preparation process should this be done?

2. Why is important for a bidding contractor to know that an owner may be protected under sovereign immunity?

3. What point does this chapter make concerning the treatment that a contractor can expect under the federal contract in contrast to other contracts with respect to disputes, changes, differing site conditions, delays, and terminations?

4. What are the five threshold "red flag" clauses discussed in this chapter?

5. What are the three separate aspects of time provisions that were discussed?

6. What are liquidated damages and actual damages? Does the contractor normally have any input to the amount of a contractually provided liquidated damages daily figure? Why or why not? Which is preferable from the contractor's standpoint—liquidated damages or actual damages? Of what significance is the contractually stipulated liquidated damages daily rate?

7. What is meant by the phrase *"conditions of force majeure"*? Cite examples. In what way is this subject of concern to bidding contractors?

8. What is the significance of site availability provisions? Discuss the several aspects of such provisions.

9. What are four important aspects of payment provisions discussed in this chapter?

10. What is the difference in the problem created for bidding contractors by the insurance provisions and the bond provisions of typical contract documents? Which is more likely to present a difficulty to a bidding contractor? Why?

11. What are the two contrasting attitudes of owners toward inclusion of reports on physical site conditions as part of the contract discussed in this chapter? What is an exculpatory clause or disclaimer? What is the attitude of the courts regarding disclaimers of the accuracy of reports of physical site conditions? What is the modern view of how owners seeking bids on underground projects should handle disclosure and intended bidder reliance on reports of geotechnical investigations? Do you think it makes sense to expand this view to other types of projects as well?

12. What is meant by indemnification? How do bidding contractors normally protect themselves from indemnification clauses? What is the general concern that may arise with indemnification requirements?

13. Why is a variation in quantities clause important? How does a typical variation in quantities clause work? Would such a clause apply to the type of contract where the contract price was bid as a single lump sum? Why or why not?

14. Which group of clauses included in equal employment opportunity or DBE/WBE requirements is likely to cause the most difficulty for contractors?

15. What are escalation provisions? How do they work? Do all contracts contain them?

6

Labor Agreements

Key Words and Concepts

Employers
Union organizations
Single-employer or multi-employer
   parties
Local and international unions
Basic and specialty crafts
Local and national agreements
Local area-wide agreements
Project agreements
Industrial work agreements
Maintenance work agreements
Single and multi-craft agreements
Single area system agreements
National trade agreements
National special purpose agreements

Union security
Union jurisdiction
Hiring hall
Grievance procedure
Work stoppage and lockout
Subcontracting clause
Wage/benefit rates
Hours worked and hours paid
Workday and workweek
Overtime
Shift work
Work rules
Manning
Stewards
Me too/most favored nation provisions

The last three chapters have discussed the distinguishing features of construction industry prime contracts in general and then focused on owner–construction contractor contracts for construction services. The "red flag" clauses that determine how individual construction contracts deal with certain critical issues were examined in detail.

The focus of this chapter is on construction labor agreements, one of a series of contracts closely related to the prime construction contract. Persons aspiring to manage construction operations should be familiar with the structure of organized construction labor in the United States and with the provisions of typical labor agreements for at least three reasons. First, managers of construction operations may be employed by union contractors who consistently work under labor agreements and are generally bound by their terms. Second, even contractors who normally work on an open- or merit-shop basis may, in particular circumstances, decide to sign and be bound by a labor agreement for a particular job. Third, both union and open- or merit-shop contractors need to know under what conditions the other will be working in order to evaluate their competitive advantages or disadvantages—in other words, to get a "handle" on the competition.

Any construction superintendent or project manager knows that the cost of labor is, by far, the most volatile, difficult to control element of total construction cost. Therefore, for the sizable segment of the industry that employs union labor, the collective bargaining, or labor agreement, governing the relationships of construction employers with their workers becomes a very important agreement indeed. It is not possible to estimate accurately the probable labor element of the cost of construction without an intimate understanding of such agreements. Simply knowing the wage rates is not enough. Large cost issues depend on the intricacies of the overtime and shift work provisions, general work rules, manning requirements, and other cost-generating provisions that are often contained in labor agreements. Further, once a construction contract has been entered into with an owner, the contractor cannot effectively manage the job or control costs without a complete understanding of these often complex provisions. Each of these considerations is discussed in this chapter.

THE PARTIES

The parties to construction labor agreements are contractor **employers** and **union organizations.** This can be represented as the beginning of a "relationship tree," as in Figure 6–1.

FIGURE 6–1   Parties to labor agreements.

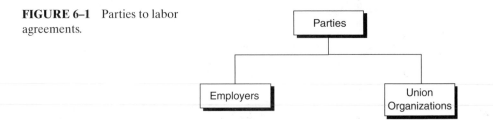

FIGURE 6–2 Employer parties.

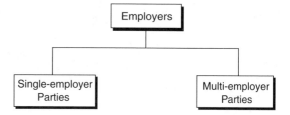

Further, the employer parties in the relationship tree can be expanded to include **single-employer** or **multi-employer parties,** as shown in Figure 6–2.

A single employer consists of one contractor, whereas a multi-employer party is a group of contractors that have banded together to form an employers' association. Examples of employer's organizations include the various state Associated General Contractors (AGC) organizations, the National Association of Home-builders, and the National Constructors Association.

Union organizations consist of either **local unions** or **international unions,** with separate unions for the basic crafts and for the specialty crafts, as shown in a further expansion of the relationship tree in Figure 6–3.

The **basic crafts** consist of operating engineers, teamsters, carpenters (including piledrivers and millwrights), ironworkers, masons (cement finishers), and (although strictly speaking, not a craft) laborers. All crafts in construction other than the basic crafts are called **specialty crafts,** which include electricians, plumbers, sheetmetal workers, tile setters, and boilermakers, to name a few.

COMMON TYPES OF LABOR AGREEMENTS

Turning from the parties to the agreement itself, we see a number of features that distinguish one labor agreement from another such as the geographical limits of the agreement. Labor agreements can be local or national in geographical scope, as indicated as the beginning of a second relationship tree in Figure 6–4.

FIGURE 6–3 Union organization parties.

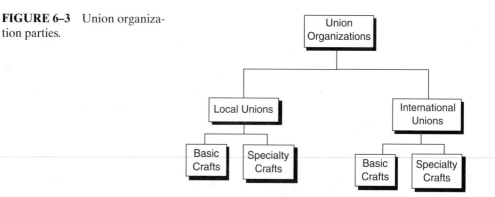

FIGURE 6–4   Geographical
scope of labor agreements.

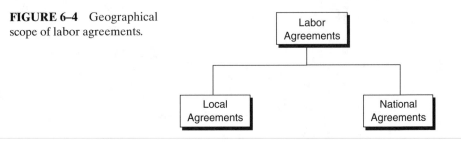

FIGURE 6–4   Geographical
scope of labor agreements.

A **local agreement** involves just one particular local union. Usually, it also involves one craft, so it is really a local **single craft agreement.** Certain local agreements can be **multi-craft agreements.** All of the local unions of a particular craft in the United States report to and are a part of a governing national body called the *international union* for that craft. If the agreement is made directly with the international union, it is binding on all of the local unions throughout the country and is called a **national agreement.**

Local agreements can be subdivided into a number of categories expanding the second relationship tree as shown in Figure 6–5.

A **local area-wide agreement** is one that applies to the full geographical limit of the particular local's territory, which might be limited to a particular county (or counties) within a state, to the entire state, or, in a few instances, to a group of several states. A **project agreement** is one that applies to a particular project named in the agreement and to no others. Some projects consist of just one construction prime contract, and a "single project" agreement would be applied to that single job only. An excellent example of this type of project agreement was one negotiated between the contractor joint venture partners who constructed the Stanislaus North Fork Project in central California a few years ago.[1] This agreement was negotiated with all of the basic crafts expected to be employed on the project and applied only

FIGURE 6–5   Local agreements.

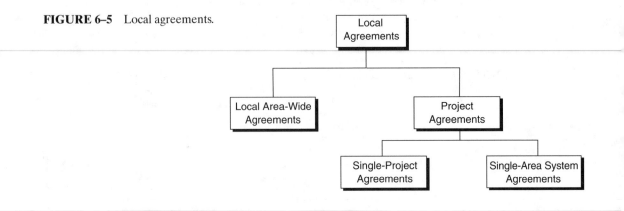

---
[1]This project is one of two projects cited in Chapter 3 as examples of very large public works design-construct projects.

to that project. The terms and conditions of the agreement were considerably more favorable to the contractor employer than other local agreements in existence in that section of California at that time. When the project work was completed, the agreement automatically terminated.

Some large projects amount to an infrastructure system built by a number of similar prime construction contracts over a number of years, and a **single-area system agreement** is an agreement that would apply to each of the separate projects within that system and to them only. The San Francisco Bay Area Rapid Transit District subway was constructed under a single-area system agreement in the late 1960s and 1970s, and the Los Angeles Area Rapid Transit District subway and the Boston Harbor Project for tunnel work and sewerage treatment plant construction in Massachusetts were both built under these types of agreements.

National agreements can be subdivided into national trade agreements and national special purpose agreements, further expanding the second relationship tree as indicated in Figure 6–6.

National trade agreements apply nationwide between the signatory employer and every local union for the particular trade, regardless of location. Currently, many contractor employers hold national trade agreements with each of the basic crafts and/or the various specialty crafts. **National special purpose agreements** are those made across the trades where all of the signatory trades are engaged in a specific common and narrowly defined type of work, such as industrial work or purely maintenance activity. The **industrial work agreement** shown in Figure 6–6 applies to

FIGURE 6–6   National agreements.

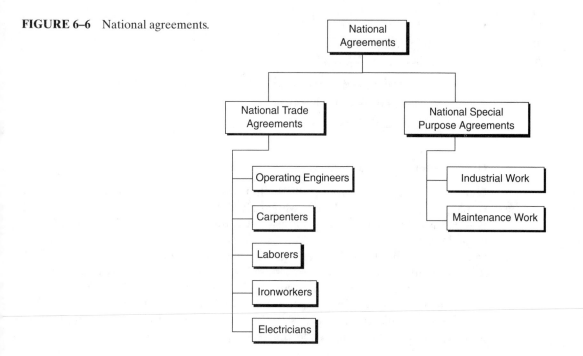

the construction of industrial facilities such as factories and plants. The **maintenance work agreement,** sometimes called the *National President's Maintenance Agreement,* applies only to the performance of maintenance work in existing industrial facilities.

Previous chapters have dealt with various aspects of construction industry contracts. Are labor agreements contracts? Chapter 2 discussed the three elements necessary for contract formation, which are the offer, the acceptance, and the consideration. Where and in what form are these elements found in the labor agreement? The offer and the acceptance occur through a long series of offers and counteroffers constituting a classic example of a negotiation. Practically everyone has heard of "labor negotiations." For unions and union employers, labor negotiations occur at regular cycles, either annually or every two or three years. The productive capacity to perform construction work on the one hand, and the wage rates and fringe benefits stated in the labor agreement constitute the necessary consideration element. So, labor agreements are very much contracts and are subject to the same laws and rules of interpretation as are other contracts.

LABOR AGREEMENT THRESHOLD "RED FLAG" PROVISIONS

As in prime construction contracts, labor agreements between contractor employers and labor unions contain "red flag" provisions. The threshold provisions include the following:

- Union security provisions
- Union jurisdiction
- Hiring hall provisions
- Grievance procedures
- Work stoppage/lockout provisions
- Subcontracting clause

Union Security Provisions

Union security provisions establish that union membership is a condition of employment. For new employees who are not already union members, a set period of time (usually a matter of days) is also established within which they must join the union in order to remain employed. It should be noted that in the several "right-to-work" states in the United States, the requirement for union membership as a condition of employment is contrary to state law and cannot be legally enforced. This does not mean that labor unions are illegal in "right-to-work" states, only that membership in a union cannot be demanded as a condition of employment.

Union jurisdiction provisions deal with the scope of the agreement, both in terms of the work performed and the geographical extent of the agreement. They list the specific kinds of work that can be performed only by the union members and specify the geographical area covered by the agreement. Union jurisdiction provisions usually differ among the various separate union craft agreements in an area. The provisions commonly conflict, with each craft reserving or claiming the same work. Employers signatory to several agreements applying to a common construction project cannot meet all of these conflicting conditions. The problem is generally resolved by the employer conducting a "mark up" meeting at the start of the project where all items of work in the project are assigned to one craft or another in accordance with the traditional work practices in the area, known as *area practice.* Unions disagreeing with such assignments can file a protest with the National Joint Board for Settlement of Jurisdictional Disputes, a national body that will hold a hearing and either support the employer's assignment or alter it. Most unions and union employer groups are stipulated to the Board, which means that they agree to abide by the Board decisions.

Hiring Hall Provisions

Labor agreements may contain a **hiring hall** provision. This is a critical provision for the contractor-employer since the specific requirements can have a significant effect on hiring flexibility. A typical hiring hall provision states that the union is the exclusive source of referrals to fill job openings. If the contractor needs to hire new employees, they must be requested from the union hiring hall. When there is no hiring hall provision, the contractor can fill job openings from other sources ("hire off the bank"), as long as the requirements of the union security provisions are met.

Significant differences can exist in the hiring hall provisions in different labor agreements. For example, some provisions give the union the right to designate foremen; in others, the employer has that right. Since foremen are the first level of management on any project, it is essential for the contractor to know who will control their selection. Also, in some hiring hall provisions, the employer has the right to bring in a specified number of key employees; in others, the contractor must rely solely on the labor force in the area of the project. Many contractors have developed a following of workers with proven skills who will move to a new area in order to maintain continuous employment. It is a significant advantage to the contractor to fill key positions with these long-term employees.

Grievance Procedures

Each labor agreement contains a set **grievance procedure** for settling disputes between the contractor and the union. This clause is analogous to the dispute resolution clause in a prime construction contract between a contractor and owner. It is obviously important to know exactly what steps will be taken at each point in this procedure as well as what will happen if initial efforts fail to produce a settlement, which leads directly to the next threshold provision: work stoppage/lockout provisions.

Work Stoppage/Lockout Provisions

Most labor agreements contain **work stoppage and lockout** provisions. These provisions provide that the union must continue work (no work stoppage) while a dispute is being settled and that the employer must continue to offer employment (no lockout). However, even if the agreement contains work stoppage and lockout provisions, the agreement may provide that the union may cease work if the workers are not being paid or if the work site is unsafe. When improperly used, this latter provision can lead to work stoppages on spurious grounds in order to pressure contractor employers during disputes. A dispute over the exact pay rate in a particular case, or similar arguments concerning the amount that the workers are paid (as long as they are being paid *some* rate provided in the agreement), does not constitute sufficient grounds for the union to engage in a work stoppage. A work stoppage on these grounds would constitute a breach of the labor agreement. In these circumstances, the proper course of action for the union would be to file a grievance.

Subcontracting Clause

The effect of a **subcontracting clause** is to bind the contractor to employ only subcontractors who agree to the terms of the contractor's labor agreement. The provisions of the clause will not necessarily require that a subcontractor actually sign a similar agreement with the union. They may only bind the subcontractor to abide by the terms and conditions of the contractor's labor agreement and to make the required fringe benefit payments into the union trust funds. Much controversy has occurred over the inclusion of such clauses in labor agreements, since the requirement to use union subcontractors can make a prime contractor's bid noncompetitive in areas where open-shop contractors are competing for the work. When the writer was managing a union contracting organization, bids were sometimes lost for this reason when open-shop competition existed.

OTHER "RED FLAG" PROVISIONS

In addition to the threshold provisions, the following "red flag" provisions, although secondary, are also important:

- Wage/benefits hourly rates
- Normal workday and workweek
- Overtime definition and pay premium
- Shift work definition and pay premium
- Work rules and manning provisions
- Steward provisions
- Me too/most favored nation provisions

Wage/Benefits Hourly Rates

The agreed-upon **wage and fringe benefit rates** obviously form the main body of the contract consideration and determine what the various crafts are to be paid. Usually, wage and fringe benefit rates are stated in terms of an amount per hour. An important point is whether the stated fringe amount per hour is to be paid on an **hours-worked** or on an **hours-paid** basis. Consider the following case:

Base rate	$ 17.50 per hour
Health and welfare	1.50 " "
Pension	0.75 " "
Vacation	0.50 " "

The question arises when a worker works overtime. For instance, if the overtime premium was time-and-a-half and the worker works 11 hours on a particular day, the respective amounts paid directly to the worker and paid into the union trust funds on an hours-worked basis would be

Worker gets: $(\$17.50)(8 + 1.5 \times 3)$
$= \$17.50 \times (12.5 \text{ hrs. paid}) = \$218.75$

Trust funds get: $(\$1.50 + 0.75 + 0.50) \times 11 \text{ hrs. worked}$
$= \$2.75 \times 11 = \$30.25$

On an hours-paid basis, the respective amounts paid to the worker and to the union trust funds would be

Worker gets: $218.75

Trust funds get: $\$2.75 \times 12.5 \text{ hrs. paid} = \$34.38$

The difference in total trust fund payments in this example of $34.38 – $30.25 = $4.13 amounts to 13.6% of the lower amount paid. A large amount of overtime on a major project can result in a considerable difference in the contractor's labor costs depending on the method labor fringes are paid.

Normal Workday and Workweek

Workday and **workweek** provisions include clauses defining the standard workday, in terms of the number of hours worked (8 hours), the consecutive number of hours worked between starting time and lunch or dinner breaks, and the minimum required hours off between consecutive shifts worked by the same worker. They may also include defining the number of hours for "show-up time" to be paid if work is canceled after a person reports to work and then is sent home due to inclement weather, the minimum number of hours that a worker must be paid after starting to work, and similar rules that result in workers being paid for more hours than they actually work.

For example, it is not uncommon for workers who actually report to work and who are then sent home without performing any work at all to be paid a minimum of two hours at the straight time rate unless they had been advised by the contractor employer before they left their homes for work not to come to work that day due to inclement weather. Similarly, in such circumstances if workers actually were put to work on arriving at the jobsite at the start of the work shift and then were sent home due to inclement weather shortly thereafter, a minimum of four hours at the straight time rate commonly is required to be paid.

These provisions also establish the number of workdays that constitute a standard workweek (5 workdays) and a range of normal or standard starting and quitting times for each standard shift during the standard workday. Some labor agreements include guaranteed 40-hour-week clauses, which provide that workers are guaranteed 40 hours' pay for the week once work is started on the first day in any one workweek. It matters not that work had to be suspended because of inclement weather or other circumstances completely beyond the control of the contractor employer. The workers still receive pay at the straight time rate for the entire week.

Overtime Definition and Pay Premium

Overtime definition and pay premium provisions establish a schedule of overtime pay rates, usually in terms of a multiple of the basic hourly pay rate (time-and-a-half, double time, or triple time). These provisions also define when the overtime rate is to be paid—for example, after so many hours worked in a day or week (8 hours per day or 40 hours per week), on weekends and holidays, or when the hours worked do not fall between normal shift starting and ending times. In special circumstances, provisions may be included that allow exceptions to what would otherwise be considered overtime work. For instance, some projects require work to be performed in the middle of the night only when no work is being performed during the other two shifts. This would be common in work performed in heavily trafficked streets in urban areas. In these circumstances, the contractor employer usually can obtain the union's agreement to pay a wage rate for this night work that is higher than the straight time rate that would be paid if the work was performed on standard day shift but considerably less than the overtime rate that otherwise would be required to be paid.

Shift Work and Pay Premium

Shift work and pay premium provisions define standard work shifts (first, second, and third shifts or "day," "swing," and "graveyard" shifts) based on the particular hours during the day that the shift works. A typical arrangement would be day shift: 8 a.m. to 4:30 p.m. with a ½ hour meal break; swing shift: 4:30 p.m. to 12:30 a.m. with a ½ hour meal break; and graveyard shift: 12:30 a.m. to 8 a.m. with a ½ hour meal break. However, a particular range of times for starting each shift is usually stated. The provisions may also contain clauses requiring that once a swing or graveyard shift is started, the workers must continue to work and be paid for a full workweek, and the union must be given a minimum notice period before shift work is to start.

This author has experienced contracts in some jurisdictions where the requirement for continued payment for workers on shift work throughout the full workweek was extremely costly. Once shift work was started in a given week, the crews involved had to be paid their shift work wages for the entire week, even though work was required to be suspended because of inclement weather or other circumstances beyond the control of the contractor employer.

The pay premium provisions for shift work are usually stated in terms of straight-time hours to be worked for eight hours' straight-time pay. For example, a day-shift worker will work eight hours and receive eight hours' pay; a swing-shift worker, seven-and-a-half hours for eight hours' pay; and a graveyard-shift worker, only seven hours for eight hours' pay.

If a day-shift worker works ten hours, he or she would be paid eight hours' straight time and two hours at the specified overtime rate. A swing-shift worker would be paid eight hours' straight time and two-and-a-half hours at the specified overtime rate. A graveyard-shift worker would receive eight hours at straight time and three hours' pay at the specified overtime rate. Such a scenario is a typical arrangement, but the specific premium pay provisions may vary from shift to shift and from agreement to agreement.

It should be clear from the preceding that such matters as overtime work and shift work must be very carefully managed when the labor agreement contains expensive provisions such as a guaranteed 40-hour-week clause, shift work clauses requiring pay for the entire week, and so on. Otherwise, costs will quickly get out of hand. Also, these provisions must be clearly understood when pricing construction work in advance of actual construction, as when formulating bids or proposals.

Work Rules and Manning Provisions

Every labor agreement will contain **work rules** and **manning provisions.** These address such issues as when foremen, general foremen, or master mechanics must be utilized; what number of workers are required for standard crews; and the requirements for employing apprentices and helpers. Some agreements are very restrictive and allow the contractor little flexibility in determining the number of workers that must be hired. Others give the contractor the right to determine crew sizes and to hire the workers as the contractor sees fit. These provisions and the presence or absence of restrictive productivity-limiting practices are of critical importance to the contractor. Construction work cannot be accurately priced or managed effectively without an intimate understanding of these matters.

The manning rules can take a number of different forms, many of which greatly limit the employer's flexibility and result in hiring additional workers who are not actually needed to get the work done. Examples of such restrictive provisions include the following:

- When equipment is broken down and being repaired in the field, the regular equipment operator is required to be present to assist the mechanic who is assigned to make repairs, rather than operate another operable unit, even though the operator is not a mechanic and is of no practical assistance.

- An equipment operator may change equipment only one time during any one shift. This requirement is particularly onerous and expensive to the contractor-employer on small jobs with several pieces of equipment that are not required to be operated continuously. For instance, a contractor doing utility work might conceivably be using a small backhoe, a front-end loader, and a small dozer intermittently where each piece of equipment is only operated a few hours during the shift. Only one operator, capable of operating any of the three pieces of equipment, is required in order to perform the required work operations.[2] Nonetheless, in some jurisdictions, the contractor would be required to employ three operators even though it would not be possible to operate all three pieces of equipment simultaneously.

- An operator must be assigned for a stated number of pumps, compressors, or welding machines on the job, regardless of whether an operator is actually needed. In one instance in the eastern United States, this work rule has resulted in contractors utilizing an inefficient jet-eductor dewatering system instead of a more efficient deep well system because the work rules applicable to the project mandated that one operator was required around the clock for every three deep wells (of which a large number were required), whereas fewer operators were required for the jet-eductor system.

- Stated crew sizes must be used, such as a minimum of four or five in a pile-driving crew when only three are actually needed to do the work.

- An oiler must be assigned to each crane over a stated size, whether or not an oiler is needed for the safe operation and maintenance of the crane. This frequently has resulted in an assignment of an oiler to a single operator center-mount crane even though an oiler is not needed and there is no place on the crane for the oiler to ride safely when the operator is driving the crane from one work location to another.

- Laborers must be assigned to assist carpenter crews at a stated number of laborers for a stated number of carpenters, regardless of how many laborers are actually needed.

- Laborers must be assigned to dewatering pumps, even when the pumps are electrically powered and automatically controlled so that they require little or no attention at all.

Steward Provisions

A labor agreement will usually contain provisions relating to the union shop **steward,** an individual appointed by the union to deal with the employer on behalf of the union employees at the site. The steward is not the same as the union business agent, who represents the union in dealing with all contractor employers within a certain area but who is not normally continually on the jobsite. The steward is employed by the contractor, ostensibly as a regular craft employee expected to do a

---

[2]Many operating engineers possess the capability to operate all three pieces of equipment.

normal day's work. The steward provisions permit the steward to engage in union activities while on the job. A danger to the contractor is that overly permissive language in the agreement permits the steward to engage in full-time union activities and perform little or no work.

Me Too/Most Favored Nation Provisions

Me too/most favored nation provisions can be very expensive to the contractor. "Me too" clauses entitle a worker to be paid the highest overtime rate of any craft actually working overtime on that day, even though the rate in the worker's union agreement is lower. Most favored nation provisions require that any clauses that are less favorable than similar clauses of subsequent agreements negotiated with another craft are replaced with the more favorable language of the later agreement with the other craft.

A telling example of the extra labor expense that can be generated by such clauses was a project in the eastern United States in which this author was involved a number of years ago. The project involved structural concrete work, requiring carpenters, operating engineers, laborers, and cement masons to be conducted simultaneously with excavation and ground support operations requiring operating engineers, piledrivers, and laborers. The labor agreements provided that all crafts on the job received overtime pay at time-and-a-half with the exception of the carpenters and piledrivers who received double time.[3] Frequently, concrete placements would run into the second shift with laborers, operating engineers, and cement masons being required for a number of hours at the overtime rate of time-and-a-half. Frequently, lagging crews, part of the ground support operation, were also required to work overtime to lag up ground that had been excavated during the day shift. This crew consisted of seven or eight laborers and one piledriver whose sole job was to cut the lagging boards to length with a chain saw so that the cut boards could be installed by the laborers. Thus, among all of the workers on overtime, sometimes totaling as many as 20, there was one piledriver. Because the piledriver was entitled to overtime at the double-time rate, each of the others was also required to be paid overtime at the double-time rate, even though their agreements called for overtime at the time-and-a-half rate.

Fortunately, for the good of the industry, such onerous provisions are antiquated today, and few labor agreements contain them. Many current labor agreements are fair and even-handed but, as the incidents just related indicate, each new agreement must be carefully read and understood to avoid unpleasant surprises.

CONCLUSION

This chapter presented a brief general survey of the types of labor agreements commonly in use in the United States today according to whom the employer and union parties are likely to be, the geographical limits of the agreements, and the general nature of the construction labor involved.

---

[3]Carpenters and piledrivers both belong to the same international union.

Also, the details of typical provisions found in labor agreements were discussed, particularly emphasizing those provisions of special importance to contractors when pricing and managing construction work.

Chapter 7 moves on to construction purchase orders and subcontract agreements. Both are additional examples of contracts closely related to the prime contract between the construction contractor and the owner.

QUESTIONS AND PROBLEMS

1. Define or explain the following relevant labor agreement terms:
   a. Single employer and multi-employer party
   b. Local and international unions
   c. Basic crafts and specialty crafts (name the six basic crafts)
   d. Local and national labor agreements
   e. Local area-wide agreements
   f. Project agreements—single project and single-area system agreements
   g. National trade agreements and national special purpose agreements
   h. Single craft and multi-craft agreements

2. Do labor agreements contain the three elements of offer, acceptance, and consideration necessary for contract formation? How do the offer and acceptance typically occur? What parts of a labor agreement comprise the consideration element?

3. What are the six threshold clauses usually found in a construction labor agreement? What is the general subject matter of each?

4. What are three important aspects of hiring that may be contained in a hiring hall clause? What does "hiring off the bank" mean when the project is operating under a labor agreement? Do workers "hired off the bank" have to be union members or agree to become union members?

5. What is a work stoppage? A lockout? What two circumstances will always be viewed by courts as justifying a union's refusal to continue work? Would a dispute over the proper rate of pay qualify as constituting one of the preceding circumstances? Would such a dispute be subject to the procedure set forth under the grievance clause?

6. What is the essential meaning of a subcontracting clause? What is the typical union position on subcontracting clauses? Why? What is the employer's position? Why?

7. What are the seven additional "red flag" clauses discussed in this chapter? What is the general subject matter of each?

8. What is the distinction between payment of union benefits on an hours-worked basis and on an hours-paid basis? Under what circumstances on a project does this distinction become important?

9. What is meant by a standard or normal workday? Standard or normal work-week? What is meant by "show-up time"? What is a shift? What does shift work mean? What is overtime? Overtime premium? How many hours of work comprise a standard (normal) straight time day shift? A swing shift? A graveyard shift? How many work shifts constitute a standard (normal) work-week? How many hours at the straight time rate are usually paid for the standard (normal) day shift? For swing shift? For graveyard shift?

10. What are work rules? Manning provisions? What are the two examples of work rules and five examples of manning provisions cited in this chapter?

11. What is a steward? A business agent? Who pays each? Does a steward perform construction work on the project?

12. What is a "me too" provision? A most favored nation provision?

13. The following question assumes that you have access to an actual construction industry labor agreement. Refer to the particular labor agreement that you have and answer the following questions:

    a. Who is the union party? The employer party?
    b. Is the employer party a single party employer or a multi-party employer?
    c. Does the union party consist of basic crafts, specialty crafts, or a mixture of basic and specialty crafts?
    d. List every "red flag" provision discussed in this chapter that you can find in the labor agreement and cite the article number for each provision that you list.

14. A project required 117,900 actual carpenter work-hours, of which 15% were performed on an overtime basis. The carpenter base pay was $27.50 per hour, and the total union fringes were $6.27 per hour. Overtime work was paid at double time. How much additional labor expense would the contractor employer incur if the union agreement called for payment of union fringes on an hours-paid basis rather than on an hours-worked basis?

15. A project cost estimate indicates that the work will require an average of six crane operators for a total of 6,494 crane operator-hours and an average of nine other heavy-equipment operators for a total of 9,720 other heavy-equipment operator-hours. The estimate was made on the basis that all work would be performed on a one-shift-per-day, five-days-per-workweek basis. The climate at the site was such that 12% of the normal workdays in the five-day workweek were expected to be lost because of inclement weather. This fact was recognized in the anticipated project schedule. How much more labor cost would have to be anticipated for crane operators and heavy-equipment operators if the labor agreement for the project provided for a guaranteed 40-hour week for these particular operating engineer classifications and provided that labor fringes were to be paid on an hours-paid rather than an hours-worked basis than if the labor agreement did not contain these two provisions? The following wage rates applied:

	Base Pay	**Fringes**
Crane operator	$32.50	$6.82
Other heavy equipment operators	$30.25	$6.82

16. Project work on a major Midwestern river was progressing on the basis of a normal eight-hour-day shift, five days per week. The owner directed the contractor to accelerate completion of a contractually mandated milestone for the project by putting the work crews on shift work, three shifts per day, five days per week. The work involved for the milestone required piledrivers and operating engineers. The labor costs per day for the total crew were $3,840 base pay and $768 union fringes per each eight-hour-day shift. The portion of the work to be accelerated would have required an additional 60 full eight-hour shifts of work or 60 × 8 = 480 crew-hours to complete. The project labor agreement provided for shift work but stated that once shift work was established at the beginning of the workweek, the crews must be paid for the entire week for each new week's work started even if work were temporarily suspended later in the week because of inclement weather or otherwise. The labor agreement further provided that union fringes were to be paid on an hours-paid basis and that the day shift was to receive eight hours' pay for eight hours' work; the swing shift eight hours' pay for seven-and-a-half hours' work; and the graveyard shift eight hours' pay for seven hours' work. The acceleration order was issued in the middle of the winter when an average of four shifts per five-day workweek (two shifts on swing shift and two shifts on graveyard shift) could be expected to be lost because of extremely cold weather. Assuming that there would be no loss of efficiency for work performed on swing and graveyard shifts, determine how many days would be required to reach the milestone required by the acceleration order and what the extra labor cost for complying with the acceleration order would be.

7

Purchase Order and Subcontract Agreements

Key Words and Concepts

Buyer
Seller
Sale of goods
Significance of labor at construction site
Uniform Commercial Code
Purchase orders for provision of services
at site
One-time/continuing supply
Maximum quantity/approximate quantity
Conflicts in boilerplate
Flow-down language
"Red flag" purchase order provisions
Rules of payment and quantity
measurement

"No pay until paid" provisions
F.O.B. point/freight/risk of loss
Sales tax
Purchase order terms and conditions
Long form/short form purchase orders
Essence of subcontracts
Flow of contract liability
Subcontract work per plans and
specifications
Incidental subcontract work
Compliance with general terms and
conditions of prime contract
"Red flag" subcontract provisions

Purchase orders and subcontracts are additional contracts that are closely related to the construction contract between owner and prime construction contractor. Although similar in some respects, they are fundamentally different in purpose.

Occasionally, a purchase order is used when a subcontract agreement would have been more appropriate and vice versa. Both are important contracts, and construction practitioners need to understand clearly the purpose and key features of each in order to decide which should be used for a particular business transaction and in order to draft them correctly.

PURCHASE ORDERS

Construction purchase orders generally are intended for transactions that involve the **sale of goods** by a **seller** and delivery of those goods to a contractor **buyer** at the site of a construction project. This purpose should be distinguished from the provision of services or the performance of work involving labor at or on the construction project site. For example, consider a transaction to provide fabricated structural or reinforcing steel to a construction jobsite. Such an undertaking clearly involves the provision of extensive quantities of labor to perform the fabrication work in addition to furnishing the basic raw material, but this labor is provided at the steel fabricator's plant or yard, not at the construction project site. The fabricator is furnishing "goods" in the form of the fabricated structural or reinforcing steel.

Goods or Provision of Services?

In settling construction contract disputes, courts occasionally struggle with the issue of whether particular transactions constitute the sale of goods or the provision of services. Resolution of this issue may determine whether the provisions of the **Uniform Commercial Code** apply that affect the seller's potential liability under the code. The issue is often resolved on the basis of whether the court believes the final product consists mostly of a manufactured material or product or mostly of on-site construction labor.

In a Florida case, a road-building contractor was sued because a passing car hit a drop-off during road-paving operations, then went out of control, killing the driver, and injuring a passenger. The suit alleged that the contractor was negligent in the "manufacture of a product." Under this theory, the contractor would be subject to strict liability for defects in the product. A trial court concluded that the contractor was a "manufacturer" and was liable for defects in the product being manufactured, which allegedly caused the accident. The Supreme Court of Florida reversed the trial court, holding instead that the construction of a public road pursuant to a Department of Transportation contract did not constitute the manufacture of a "product" and that the doctrine of strict liability could therefore not be applied.[1] In another case, the United States Court of Appeals ruled that a contractor joint venture acted in the capacity of a merchant when it purchased a tunnel-boring machine, even

---

[1] *Edward M. Chadbourne, Inc. v. Vaughn*, 491 So. 2d 551 (Fla. 1986).

though the tunnel-boring machine was intended for use on a sewer construction project, and therefore the transaction was governed by the Uniform Commercial Code.[2] In another case, a public utility contracted for the design and construction of a large reinforced concrete cooling tower for a power plant. After completion, the cooling tower exhibited a number of problems, and the utility sued the design-build contractor that had designed and constructed it. One of the utility's positions was that designing and constructing a reinforced concrete cooling tower constituted the manufacture of a "product," thus bringing the contract under the mantle of the Uniform Commercial Code, which afforded better avenues of recovery for the utility. The resolution of this kind of issue once again will depend on the determination of a court on whether the final installed product consists mostly of a manufactured material or product or mostly of on-site construction labor.

The lesson for construction practitioners is to treat all transactions involving the provision of **significant amounts of on-site construction labor** as a construction operation requiring the use of a subcontract agreement. On the other hand, transactions that do not involve the provision of significant amounts of labor at the construction site should be treated as the sale of goods. The sale of goods should be handled with a purchase order.

Use of Purchase Orders for Certain Jobsite Services

Although not appropriate for transactions involving significant amounts of labor at the construction site, **purchase orders for the provision of certain services on or at the site** that involve minimal labor are commonly used. Examples are the provision of chemical toilets, which are periodically serviced by the provider, the provision and collection of trash containers, and similar services.

Purchase Order Quantity Limitations

A purchase order can be limited to a **one-time** transaction that occurs once and is finished, or it may provide for a **continuing supply** of goods on an "as-required basis." Purchase orders for a continuing supply may be either "open-ended" as to the total quantity to be furnished, or they may be limited to some stipulated **maximum quantity** stated in the purchase order. Some purchase orders state an **approximate quantity.**

Conflicts with Seller's Sales Quotations

A "battle of the forms" may later develop when there are **conflicts in boilerplate**— that is, when the fine print on the back of preprinted vendor's sales quotation document conflicts with similar boilerplate on the back of preprinted purchase order document. Vendors naturally try to obtain the most favorable sales terms possible,

---

[2]*S & M Joint Venture v. Smith Internat'l Inc.,* 669 F.2d 1106 (6th Cir. 1982).

and the written quotations that they furnish usually contain conditions-of-sale language preprinted on the back of the quotation form aimed at achieving that result. Contractor/purchasers do likewise by using standard preprinted purchase order forms that have general conditions printed on the back, which put the contractor/buyer in the most advantageous position. To further complicate matters, buyers and sellers often negotiate "special" or "supplementary" terms and conditions applying to a particular transaction and to that particular transaction only. If any of these various terms and conditions conflict, and the conflicts are not identified and eliminated from the purchase order, future disputes between the parties are likely.

The courts' reaction to these disputes has been mixed. In one case, a contractor purchased water treatment materials from a supplier under a sales quotation that stated in the boilerplate on the back of the quotation that, among other things, the supplier disclaimed the implied warranties under the Uniform Commercial Code. The contractor's purchase order did not, by *its* terms, waive any of the contractor's warranty rights, including those contained in the UCC. The South Carolina Court of Appeals ruled that the language of the purchase order did not disclaim the specific language in the supplier's sales quotation and that the sales quotation governed.[3]

In an opposite holding, the Court of Special Appeals of Maryland held that an equipment supplier's standard terms and conditions, which contain a disclaimer of liability for failure to make timely delivery, were overridden by the contractor's purchase order that contained contradictory terms.[4]

Drafters of purchase orders should harmonize the preprinted purchase order and sales quotation language by making clear that one or the other controls. Also, it is important to make sure that the words entered on the face of the purchase order document describing the instant transaction do not conflict with the boilerplate on the back of whichever preprinted form is intended to control. Otherwise, "an argument waiting to happen" has almost certainly been created.

Flow-Down Language from Prime Contracts

When purchase orders flow from prime construction contracts, the two are closely related. Such purchase orders often contain explicit **flow-down language** intended to make all applicable provisions of the prime contract also apply to the purchase order.

Additionally, prime contractors need to specify that materials furnished by vendors for use on the project meet all requirements of the prime contract. The best way to do this is to incorporate the applicable section of the prime contract technical specifications by reference to the section and paragraph numbers when describing the material to be furnished in the purchase order.

---

[3]*Mace Industries, Inc. v. Paddock Pool Equipment Co., Inc.,* 339 S.E.2d 527 (S.C. App. 1986).

[4]*USEMCO, Inc. v. Marbro Co., Inc.,* 483 A.2d 88 (Md. App. 1984).

"RED FLAG" PURCHASE ORDER PROVISIONS

Like other contracts, certain purchase order provisions stand out because of important particulars to which the buyer and seller agreed—that is, **"red flag" purchase order provisions.** The following discussion is not all-inclusive but covers most critical provisions that usually should be included.

Necessary Identifying Information

At the onset, the purchase order should prominently identify the following on the face of the document, using correct name styles:

- Construction project for which the prime construction contract is held by the buyer
- Owner for that project
- Architect/engineer
- Contractor buyer
- Seller

Description of the Goods Purchased

An accurate and complete description of each separate item to be furnished must appear, including any appropriate references to specific sections of the prime contract plans and technical specifications where necessary. Part and parcel of this description is the quantity of each separate item to be furnished.

Shipping Instructions

Complete shipping instructions should be included, designating the exact name and address of the intended receiving party and instructions on how the goods are to be packaged and marked. This is particularly important in purchase orders for fabricated reinforcing steel to be delivered to the jobsite that is to be cut, bent, and tagged so that the individual bars are identified and in similar supply purchase orders for products such as miscellaneous metal or structural steel. Without correct definitive markings, these types of products can be extremely difficult to even locate in the contractor's lay-down area after delivery, let alone identify each piece for correct installation or erection.

When the goods purchased are susceptible to damage in shipment or when identification of individual items at the jobsite may be difficult, packaging and marking instructions are particularly important. In one case, granite facing slabs that were quarried in the southeastern United States and shipped some distance to the jobsite developed disfiguring scars after the facing slabs had been erected on the face of the building. The scars were found to have resulted from the careless use of steel banding straps during shipment to the jobsite. Great expense was incurred to remove the disfigured slabs and replace them with new slabs from the quarry. The importance of the particulars of the packaging and shipping instructions in a case like this is obvious.

Pricing and Basis of Quantity Measurement

The purchase price and the basis of quantity measurement for payment must be clearly stated. The purchase price is normally stated for each line item in the purchase order as a lump sum price or as a unit price and extension against a stated quantity. The nominal dollar amount for the entire purchase order is the sum of the lump sum prices and/or extensions for all the line items.

Just as the **rules forming the basis of quantity measurement for pay purposes** were of critical importance in prime construction contracts (refer to Chapter 5), so are these rules important for purchase orders. Is the supplier of the material to be paid on the same basis as the contractor/buyer, or on some other basis? Purchase orders often contain a flow-down provision stating that the same rules defining the basis of measurement for payment from the owner to the prime contractor in the prime construction contract will also apply to the purchase order for payment from the prime contractor buyer to the seller.

Note that even in these instances, when the rules for measurement for pay purposes are stated in the purchase order to be the same as for the prime contract, the lump sum and unit prices typically will be lower for the purchase order since only the component of the total pay item for furnishing the required material is represented in the purchase order price.

Not all purchase orders contain flow-down provisions from prime construction contracts relating to measurement and payment. Prime contractors routinely purchase many items of materials or goods for which payment will be completely unrelated to the provisions of the prime contract.

Payment and Retention Provisions

The payment and retention terms have exactly the same significance to a seller under a purchase order contract as they do to the prime contractor under the prime contract with the owner. Their positions are virtually identical, just one step apart on the payment ladder. In this respect, it is common for prime contractors to impose the same payment and retention terms on their vendors, who are the sellers under the purchase order agreements, as the owner imposes on the prime contractor in the payment and retention provisions of the prime contract.

A frequently recurring contract problem between vendors and contractor buyers is the **"no pay until paid"** dilemma. The same problem arises between prime contractors and their subcontractors when the primes are using payments from the owner as their source of funds. Purchase order and subcontract payment terms usually contain a clause stating that the prime does not have an obligation to make payment until and unless payment has been received from the owner. The provision further states that once the prime has received payment, the vendor or subcontractor must be paid within a stated period, usually ten calendar days. Such provisions are legal and enforceable up to a point. However, situations can arise where the owner never pays the prime contractor, due to insolvency, being legally prevented from paying, or some other reason. Then what? Does the prime have an enforceable liability to pay, or is the vendor or subcontractor simply out of luck?

Most courts view the "no pay until paid" clause as less than absolute—that is, it will be enforced with respect to the timing of the prime's obligation to make payment but does not excuse the prime from eventually paying. In the end, the prime, not the vendor or subcontractor, will have to pay and absorb the loss. In a few states, courts will relieve the prime from making payment if the purchase order or subcontract agreement explicitly states that receipt by the prime of payment from the owner is a "condition precedent" to any obligation of the prime to pay the vendor or subcontractor.

The following two examples illustrate the predominate court holding. In a New Jersey case, a U.S. District Court held that although the project owner's insolvency resulted in nonpayment to a prime contractor on a shopping center project for the site work required for the project, the prime contractor was still liable for payment to the subcontractor who had actually performed the work, even though the subcontract agreement provided that the prime contractor was to pay the subcontractor "within thirty (30) days after acceptance and receipt of final payment from the owner of the building." The prime contractor never received final payment for the work performed by the subcontractor from the owner but was still required to pay $101,760 to the subcontractor, the final balance due the subcontractor under the terms of the subcontractor agreement.[5]

In another example, a second-tier subcontractor remained unpaid for installation of exterior windows, walls, and doors for a building project because the prime contractor had encountered financial difficulties and had failed to pay the first-tier subcontractor for the installation work performed by the second-tier subcontractor. The subcontract agreement provided that

> Subject to the terms and conditions of this contract, final payment will be made to UPG upon final acceptance of the work by the owner, the approval thereof by the architect, and the receipt of payment in full from the general contractor.

In overturning a lower trial court decision, the Commonwealth Court of Pennsylvania said:

> The language of Article Six . . . merely addresses the time at which payment is to be made . . . Accordingly, we conclude that the trial judge erred in interpreting the language of the second paragraph of Article Six as imposing absolute conditions precedent to UPG's entitlement to MTI's final payment.[6]

An example of a case that turned on the presence of the words "condition precedent" in the payment language of the subcontract agreement is afforded by

---

[5]*Seal Tite Corp. v. Ehret, Inc.,* 589 F. Supp. 701 (D.C.M.J. 1984).
[6]*United Plate Glass Co. v. Metal Trends Industries, Inc.,* 525 A.2d 468 (Pa. Commw. 1987).

the 1991 decision by the Court of Special Appeals of Maryland. In that case, the general contractor had subcontracted exterior masonry work on a residential condominium project under a subcontract agreement that contained the following payment language:

> It is specifically understood and agreed that the payment to the trade contractor is dependent, as a condition precedent, upon the construction manager receiving contract payments, including retainer [sic] from the owner.

After receiving progress payments, the subcontractor submitted a final invoice for $283,079, which the prime contractor refused to pay because payment had not been received from the project owner, who eventually filed for bankruptcy. In absolving the prime contractor from liability for payment of the $283,079, the court said:

> In addition to providing a standard "pay-when-paid" clause, this contract further provides that payment by Carley Capital Group to Gilbane is a condition precedent to Gilbane's obligation to pay Brisk. Regardless of whether the parties discussed the prospect of owner insolvency during their negotiations, the objective meaning of the clause is clear—Gilbane, the construction manager (general contractor), is not obligated to Brisk, the trade contractor (subcontractor), unless and until Gilbane is paid by the owner, Carley Capital Group.[7]

Specified Delivery Schedule

The purchase order should carefully define the required delivery schedule for the material. This delivery requirement is equivalent to the statement of allowed contract time in a prime construction contract. In situations where the contractor/buyer is held to a tight performance period for the prime contract work, obtaining required materials from suppliers on time is obviously important.

Required Delivery Point

Another essential element is a statement defining the required point of delivery. This determines who pays the freight charges, which can be considerable, and who is responsible for the material in the event of damage or loss during shipment. Many purchase orders specify the delivery point to be the construction project jobsite. This typically would be done by stating "F.O.B. construction jobsite" (F.O.B. means "free on board"). In this case, the cost of loading the material by the seller and the delivery cost **(the freight)** is deemed to be included in the purchase price. Title does not pass to the buyer until the material reaches the jobsite where the buyer is required to unload the material. Under these circumstances, the seller would have to assume the **risk of loss** or damage during transit.

---

[7]*Gilbane Building Co. v. Brisk Waterproofing Co., Inc.*, 585 A.2d 248 (Md. App. 1991).

An alternate arrangement is for the purchase order to designate the delivery point to be "F.O.B. seller's plant or yard." In this case, title passes to the buyer when the goods are loaded by the seller onto transit vehicles supplied or arranged for by the buyer. The buyer owns and is responsible for the material from that point on. Which provision is stated in the purchase order is obviously important to both parties.

The following situation rather dramatically illustrates the importance of the preceding provisions in a purchase order. A tunnel contractor had procured a 12-foot diameter tunnel-boring machine (TBM) from a seller located some distance from the site of the tunnel project. During transport to the site, the TBM broke free of its lashings on the transport vehicle, rolled off the vehicle, bounced on the roadway shoulder, coming to rest in an adjoining farmer's field. In a case like this, the particulars of the purchase order regarding the F.O.B. point were obviously important:

- Who paid for recovering the TBM from the field, reloading it, and for any damage suffered, the tunnel contractor or the seller?
- Suppose the TBM had rolled off the opposite side of the transport vehicle onto the opposing traffic lane and had collided with an oncoming car, injuring or killing innocent third parties. Who would be liable, the tunnel contractor or the seller?

The resolution of these and similar questions can be pre-agreed by buyer and seller by designating the intended F.O.B. point.

Sales Taxes

Similarly, the purchase order should make clear that any applicable **sales taxes** either are, or are not, included in the stated purchase price. Purchase orders can be written either way.

Purchase Order General Conditions

Most construction contractor's purchase order contracts with material suppliers contain general conditions printed on the back of the purchase order form. These are usually titled **"Purchase Order Terms and Conditions."** They normally contain all of the following general clauses usually found in prime contracts (discussed in detail in Chapter 5):

- Disputes resolution
- Changes
- Termination provisions
- Provisions in the event of late delivery
- Conditions excusing late or nondelivery
- Insurance and bond requirements

- Indemnification
- Escalation

These clauses have the same significance for the contractor/buyer and the vendor/seller as they do for the owner and the contractor under the prime construction contract.

Special or Supplementary Provisions

Finally, the purchase order may contain a section titled "Special Provisions" or "Supplementary Provisions," where the buyer and seller record any special agreements or terms pertaining to that particular transaction. In the event of conflict with other provisions of the purchase order, courts give more weight to specially recorded terms than to preprinted terms. Although it concerns a conflict in a prime contract rather than in a purchase order, the following case perfectly illustrates the normal judicial treatment of the issue involved.

A pipeline company awarded a contract to a contractor to lay a 109-mile petroleum pipeline in Kansas. The contract, which in this case was typewritten, contained a broad indemnification clause, which, among other things, held the contractor responsible for all damages to the owner's property. The contractor added a handwritten clause to the typewritten contract that stated:

> Contractor shall not be liable under any circumstances or responsible to company for consequential loss or damages of any kind whatsoever including but not limited to loss of use, loss of product, loss of revenue or profit.

This handwritten addition was initialed by executives for both the contractor and owner prior to contract execution.

After completion of the project, the pipeline ruptured. The pipeline company attempted to obtain compensation for lost oil, cleanup costs, and damage to surrounding property. The contractor pointed to the handwritten clause as a defense against the claim of liability for these clearly consequential costs.

The Supreme Court of Kansas determined that the handwritten addition was in direct conflict with the typewritten indemnity clause in the contract. In resolving this conflict, the court ruled for the contractor by stating:

> The second handwritten sentence of 2.03, when given its plain and ordinary meaning, clearly limits Willbros' liability to Wood River for consequential damages. This handwritten provision controls and modifies the printed provision in 2.01 whereby Willbros agrees to pay Wood River for damages to Wood River's property.[8]

Rather than wait for the decision of a court, which may take years, the best procedure is to coordinate carefully all provisions of the purchase order, each with

---

[8]*Wood River Pipeline Co. v. Willbros Energy Services Co.,* 738 P.2d 866 (Kan. 1987).

the others, to identify and remove conflicts. This is commonly done by "lining out" conflicting preprinted language that the buyer and seller intend to delete from the agreement.

AGCC Forms of Purchase Order Agreements

Most general contractors have devised their own preprinted purchase order forms. However, for contractors who have not or in situations where vendors object to a particular company's form of agreement, standard forms of agreement promulgated by the Associated General Contractors of America (AGC) are available. Examples of such AGC forms are those published by the Associated General Contractors of California (AGCC). Form AGCC-6 **(Long Form Purchase Order)** is intended for large transactions that extend over some period of time. Form AGCC-7 **(Short Form Purchase Order)** is intended for smaller, less complicated transactions. Users of both are advised by the AGCC to consult legal counsel before using or modifying these forms.

SUBCONTRACT AGREEMENTS

A threshold point regarding subcontracts is that a prime contract between an owner and a prime construction contractor must exist before a construction subcontract can exist. The context of the previous discussion on purchase orders focused on the consideration of purchase orders that resulted from a prime construction contract. However, a contractor often will also write purchase orders for miscellaneous goods that have no relationship to a particular prime contract. In the case of subcontract agreements, however, there must be preexisting related prime contracts.

The **essence of a subcontract** transaction is that a prime contractor who holds a separate contract with an owner decides to "lay off" or subcontract a portion of the work to another contractor, called a *subcontractor*. The parties to the subcontract agreement, therefore, become the *contractor* and the *subcontractor*. It is important to realize that even when subcontracting a portion of the prime contract work to a subcontractor, the prime contractor still retains the original liability to the owner for the performance of that work according to the prime contract terms. What has occurred is the establishment of a secondary liability of the subcontractor to the prime contractor for the performance of the subcontract work in accordance with the terms of the subcontract.

Construction subcontract agreements will always involve the provision of significant amounts of labor, largely or entirely on the site of the prime construction contract. In addition, subcontract agreements may also involve the provision of materials—both materials that are permanently incorporated into the work (permanent materials) and those that are not permanently incorporated (job materials and supplies commonly called *expendable materials*). Subcontracts also may involve the use of construction equipment at the jobsite by the subcontractor for the performance of the subcontract work. In short, the subcontract involves all of the elements of work to be performed just as if the prime contractor had done the subcontracted work directly.

The **subcontract work** may be work that is directly spelled out and precisely described in the prime contract plans and specifications, or it may be work that, although related to the prime contract, is not directly spelled out and thus would be considered incidental to the contract. An example of the former is a subcontract calling for furnishing and driving precast concrete bearing piling that are clearly shown on the prime contract plans and completely described in the prime contract technical specifications. An example of **incidental subcontract work** would be a sub-contract written by an excavation contractor on an earthfill dam contract with a building subcontractor to furnish and erect a temporary shop building on the project site to be used for repairing the prime contractor's heavy earth-moving equipment. The prime contract would not ordinarily specify the construction of such a shop building as an item of required contract work so this work, although required, would be incidental to the prime contract.

Even in the case of a subcontract for work that is merely incidental, the sub-contract often imposes some of the prime contract requirements on the performance of that work. For example, in the case of the above subcontract for constructing a shop building, the subcontract agreement commonly requires the subcontractor's **compliance with the prime contract** on Davis-Bacon minimum wage rates, wage-hour laws, regulations pertaining to equal opportunity employment practices, and so on.

SUBCONTRACT "RED FLAG" PROVISIONS

Following are some of the more important "red flag" provisions of subcontract agreements.

Necessary Identifying Information

As with purchase orders, subcontract agreements should prominently provide the following identifying information using correct name styles where applicable:

- Project for the prime contract
- Owner for that project
- Architect/engineer
- Prime contractor
- Subcontractor

Description of the Subcontract Work

The work to be performed by the subcontractor must be carefully and completely described, incorporating direct references to all applicable drawings and technical specifications and all other applicable sections of the prime construction contract.

For some subcontracts, this description of the subcontract work will be relatively simple. In other cases, the description may comprise a number of pages of information and schedules of work items. When the subcontract work is exactly as specified in the prime contract, it is normal to describe the work by citing the particular drawings and sections of the technical specifications in the prime contract that define the work without reproducing them in the text of the subcontract. If pertinent portions of the prime contract general provisions are meant to apply, the subcontract should so state explicitly.

Pricing and Basis of Quantity Measurement

The subcontract price or prices and the rules to be applied to establish the basis of measurement must be clearly stated, in exactly the same manner as for purchase orders. For items of subcontract work directly lifted from the prime contract, the basis of measurement will often be exactly as stated in the prime contracts as if the work was being performed by the prime contractor. In other words, the subcontractor will be paid by the contractor in the same manner that the contractor is paid for the work by the owner, although generally not at the same price or prices. If the subcontract work is incidental to the prime contract, payment to the subcontractor is not related to the payment provisions of the prime contract.

Payment and Retention Provisions

The payment and retention provisions have exactly the same significance as they do for prime contracts and purchase orders and will not be discussed further (see the earlier discussion in this chapter on purchase orders). Also the "no pay until paid" issue arises in the same way as for purchase orders and is generally treated by the courts similarly. The clause will hold up except in cases where the owner never pays the prime contractor. Then, the prime will normally have to pay the subcontractor even though payment has not been received from the owner.

Contractor Control of Performance Time Requirements

Since the prime contractor is subject to the overall project deadlines, stringent performance time requirements can be expected to be written into all subcontracts. Generally, the prime contractor will retain the right to determine when the subcontractor is to perform the subcontract work. The subcontract will often state that "subcontractor shall perform the subcontract work on a schedule to be determined by contractor" or words to that effect. Under this arrangement, the contractor can schedule the subcontractor to perform the subcontract work in a manner that conforms to the overall project schedule, often requiring the subcontractor to move in, perform work, and move out a number of separate times.

Generally, the effect of these or similar provisions is to give the prime contractor complete control of the time requirements for the performance of the subcontractor's work. However, this control must be exercised in a reasonable manner.

Notification of when the subcontract work will be required must be furnished early enough for the subcontractor to plan and execute work efficiently. The prime contractor may not demand the impossible.

Separate cases, one in Texas and one in Idaho, illustrate how courts treat this issue. In the Texas case, a formwork subcontractor failed to staff the project at the required level of 40 to 48 manhours per day. This failure would have delayed the project by eight months if allowed to continue. The prime contractor terminated the subcontractor for default and performed the balance of the work with their own forces at an average of 68 manhours per day. The Court of Appeals of Texas ruled that the subcontractor had breached the subcontract and that the prime contractor was not required to sit by helplessly while the subcontractor fell further and further behind schedule. The default termination was upheld, and the prime contractor was allowed to recover the increased costs of completing the work from the subcontractor.[9]

In the Idaho case, when rainy weather delayed a subcontractor's performance of foundation and other concrete work on a commercial building project, the prime contractor improperly pressured the subcontractor to pour concrete under unreasonable weather conditions. When the subcontractor refused, the prime faxed a termination letter to the subcontractor without any prior notice. Further, evidence at the trial indicated that the prime's project manager directed a subordinate to "document" the subcontractor's alleged poor performance. The subordinate then went back through the contractor's daily report log, altering it by adding negative comments about the subcontractor's performance.

The subcontractor sued, alleging breach of contract. The trial court jury found for the subcontractor and awarded them payment for all of the work performed, lost profit on the unperformed work, and $25,000 in punitive damages. On appeal, the Idaho Court of Appeals affirmed the jury award stating:

> There is substantial evidence that Citadel's actions were an extreme deviation from reasonable standards of business conduct. Because punitive damages are an appropriate sanction for oppressive conduct in the marketplace, we conclude that the District Court did not err in submitting the issue of punitive damages to the jury.[10]

Some subcontracts may explicitly state the start and finish dates for the subcontractor's work. If this is the case, the subcontractor is liable for the consequences of failing to meet those deadlines, subject, of course, to any conditions of *force majeure* that are stated in the subcontract.

Damages in the Event of Late Completion

A well-drafted subcontract must deal with the subcontractor's liability for damages in the event of failure to perform in accordance with the subcontract time requirements. A flow-down clause may impose the liquidated damages liability of the

---

[9]*D.E.W., Inc. v. Depco Forms, Inc.*, 827 S.W.2d 379 (Tex. App. 1992).

[10]*Cuddy Mountain Concrete, Inc. v. Citadel Construction, Inc.*, 824 P.2d 151 (Idaho App. 1992).

prime contractor to the owner on the subcontractor to the extent that the subcontractor's failure to perform leads the owner to assess liquidated damages against the prime. In addition, the subcontract often will explicitly state the **flow of contract liability**—that is, the contract will provide that the prime contractor can recover additional damages from the subcontractor, if the prime's cost of performance was increased as a result of delays caused by the subcontractor. In this situation, the liquidated damages collected from the subcontractor (equal to what the prime had to pay the owner) constitutes just one element of the total damages suffered by the prime due to the subcontractor's failure to perform.

Subcontract Changes Clause

Most subcontracts will also give the prime contractor the right to make changes unilaterally in the subcontract work, delay or suspend the subcontract work, or terminate it in the same manner that the owner has these rights in the prime contract. Also, the subcontractor's rights and obligations are similar to those of the prime contractor in similar circumstances under the provisions of the prime contract.

Insurance and Bond Requirements

The subcontract should clearly state the insurance and bond requirements that the subcontractor must meet. The insurance requirements are generally the same as for the prime contractor with respect to work under the prime contract. The subcontract may or may not require the subcontractor to furnish a performance bond and a labor and material payment bond, depending on the requirements of the contractor who drafts the agreement. Bid bonds are normally not required.

When the prime contractor intends that the subcontractor furnish a performance bond, many contractors write the subcontract to provide that failure to furnish a performance bond constitutes a material breach of the subcontract. This enables the contractor to terminate the subcontractor for cause and engage another subcontractor in the event that the subcontractor refuses, or is unable, to furnish the bond. In these circumstances, any price increase would be for the account of the original subcontractor. Subcontractors should not bid to general contractors or sign subcontracts drawn in this manner unless they are certain that they will be able to furnish a performance bond.

Indemnification

When the prime contract contains an indemnification clause, all subcontracts should contain a similar clause, so that the prime's liability to the owner and architect/engineer for acts committed by the subcontractor is passed through to the subcontractor. Even when the prime contract does not require indemnification because the owner is protected by sovereign immunity or otherwise does not require indemnification, many subcontracts will still contain a comprehensive indemnification clause requiring the subcontractor to indemnify the prime. Although the owner is protected by sovereign immunity, the prime contractor is not and thus may require protection from the consequences of the subcontractor's acts or failures to act that is afforded by the indemnification clause.

48-Hour and 72-Hour Clauses

Any well-drawn subcontract agreement enables the contractor to compel the subcontractor to perform the subcontract work in a timely manner under the general contractor's general direction and control. This control will extend at least as far as the owner's control with respect to the contractor's performance under the prime contract and, in some cases, even further. The specific control provisions are the "48-hour" and "72-hour" clauses, present in most subcontract agreements.

The 48-hour clause pertains to the contractor's right, after directing the subcontractor to remedy some default causing a problem on the project (such as failing to pick up their construction debris from the work site), to perform the necessary corrective work with the contractor's forces for the account of the subcontractor if the subcontractor fails to remedy the default within 48 hours of receipt of the contractor's directive. The 72-hour clause permits the contractor to terminate the subcontract agreement for default, after furnishing notice that the subcontractor is in default, the particulars of the default, and the corrective action required to remedy the default. The notification must be in writing and must put the subcontractor on notice that the default must be remedied within 72 hours from the date and time of receipt of the notice. If the subcontractor does not remedy the default within 72 hours of the notice, the contractor may terminate the subcontract. In particular cases, time limits other than 48 hours and 72 hours may be specified, although these time limits are common.

Both clauses are necessary to ensure the contractor's control over the subcontractor to protect the contractor's position with the owner under the provisions of the prime contract. Both are reasonable, provided they are fairly administered. Unreasonable exercise of these clauses could constitute a material breach of the subcontract on the part of the contractor (see Chapter 13).

Union Labor Only Clause

A clause should also be included in the subcontract agreement that binds the subcontractor to the provisions of any labor agreements containing a subcontracting clause to which the prime contractor is a party (see Chapter 6). Such a clause requires the prime to subcontract work only to subcontractors who agree to sign or be bound by the terms of the prime contractor's labor agreement. The only way that the prime contractor can avoid breaching labor agreements containing such clauses is by inserting a clause in all subcontracts that ensures that the subcontractors will either sign, or at least agree to abide by, the terms of the prime's labor agreements.

AGCC Forms of Subcontract

As in the case of purchase orders, most contractors have devised their own preprinted subcontract agreement forms. In situations where such agreements are not used, the standard forms of subcontract such as those promulgated by the Associated General Contractors of California (AGCC) are available. The short form standard subcontract, Form AGCC-4, is used for relatively minor, short-term subcontract situations. The long form standard subcontract, AGCC-3, is used for more complex, long-term subcontracts. The AGCC advises users to consult legal counsel when using or modifying these forms.

CONCLUSION

This chapter emphasized the fundamental difference between construction purchase orders and subcontracts and made clear the type of transaction for which each should be used. The close relationship of both documents to the prime construction contract was also emphasized as was the necessity for drafters of these documents to avoid conflicts between boilerplate preprinted on the back of the document forms and project-specific provisions entered on the face of the documents. Finally, the reasons why the typical purchase order and subcontract "red flag" clauses are necessary were stated, and the details of such clauses were examined in detail.

Chapter 8 covers insurance contracts, another type of contract closely related to the prime construction contract.

QUESTIONS AND PROBLEMS

1. Who are the parties to a construction purchase order? What type of transaction is involved? How is this transaction distinguished from that of a subcontract? Is the provision of certain kinds of jobsite services properly handled by means of a purchase order? What kind of services?

2. With regard to purchase orders, what is the meaning of "open-ended," "one-time transaction," "maximum quantity," and "approximate quantity"?

3. How do conflicts in purchase order terms and conditions-of-sale terms arise? What is the problem? What is the solution?

4. What is flow-down language? What is the easiest way to be certain that materials furnished under a purchase order will meet the requirements of the prime construction contract?

5. What are the generic names and the typical content of the "red flag" clauses for purchase orders discussed in this chapter?

6. What typical flow-down language regarding the basis for measurement for payment is found in a purchase order? In what situation would a purchase order typically not contain flow-down language regarding measurement for payment?

7. What is the import of the typical "no-pay-until-paid" provision in purchase orders? To what extent is this provision enforeable? In what situation is it not enforceable?

8. What are two separate aspects of the declaration of the F.O.B. point in a purchase order? What do the letters F.O.B. mean? How do purchase orders handle the question of sales tax?

9. What are the eight key issues discussed in this chapter covered by the purchase order terms and conditions typically found preprinted on the back of purchase orders? Are these subjects common to prime construction contracts also? What are special provisions or supplementary provisions with respect to a purchase order?

10. What must preexist for a construction subcontract agreement to exist? Does this apply to construction purchase orders? Why or why not?

11. What is the essence of a subcontract agreement? Is the prime contractor's contract liability to the owner for work included in a subcontract changed in any way? What is the chain or flow of contract liability when a construction subcontract is created?

12. What single most important fact about a subcontract distinguishes it from a purchase order? What may be provided by the subcontractor in addition to on-site labor? Must the work of a construction subcontract necessarily be directly and completely spelled out in the prime construction contract? May it be? Cite examples.

13. Is incidental subcontract work necessarily subject to the general terms and conditions of the prime contract? Can it be? How can a prime contractor ensure that it is?

14. Are provisions concerning how the subcontractor will be paid and the basis for measurement for payment for subcontracts typically handled differently or the same as for purchase orders? How about the payment and retention provisions?

15. Describe two ways discussed in this chapter to require that the subcontract provides that the subcontractor will perform the subcontract work in a manner that conforms to the time schedule of the prime contract.

16. Under a typical subcontract agreement, what are two separate kinds of monetary damages for which subcontractors may be liable if they fail to meet the subcontract time of performance requirements? Explain the basis for each. Do conditions of *force majeure* apply to subcontract work?

17. Do typical subcontract provisions in regard to changes, delays, suspensions of work, and terminations differ, or are they the same as for prime construction

contracts? For the subcontract situation, whose position is equivalent to that of the project owner? To that of the prime contractor?

18. Are insurance and bond requirements for construction subcontracts generally the same or different than for prime contracts? How do many contractors state the requirements for the furnishing of a performance bond by the subcontractor? Why should such a clause give a subcontractor pause?

19. If a prime contract does not contain a requirement that the prime contractor indemnify the owner, should subcontracts flowing from that prime contract still contain a broad clause that the subcontractor indemnify the prime contractor? Why or why not?

20. What is the importance of the 48-hour clause? The 72-hour clause? Why are these clauses necessary?

21. How should a prime contractor signatory to labor agreements containing subcontracting clauses avoid exposure to breach of those agreements when writing subcontract agreements? What could happen if this protection is not provided?

8

Insurance Contracts

Key Words and Concepts

Insured
Carrier
Worker's compensation insurance
Employer's liability coverage
State worker's compensation commission
U.S. Longshoremen's and Harbor
   Workers' Act
Jones Act
Factors governing worker's compensation
   insurance base premiums
Modifiers
Public liability insurance
Exclusions
XCU hazards
Endorsements
Additional named insureds
Deductibles
Primary policy
Umbrella policy
Public liability insurance
Public liability premium structure
Retro insurance policies

Occurrence
P & I policies
Builder's risk insurance
Consequential damages
Proximate costs
Named peril policy
All risk policy
Error, omission, or deficiency exclusion
Losses to temporary structures
Builder's risk premium
   structure/monetary limits
Equipment floater insurance
Hull insurance
Miscellaneous construction insurance
   policies
Owner provided insurance programs
"Red flag" clauses
Policy term
Subrogation
Occurrence policies
Claims-made policies
Escalation in premiums

Thus far, the discussion in this book has covered both prime construction contracts and three examples of closely related contracts: the labor agreement, purchase order agreements, and subcontract agreements. This chapter continues with insurance contracts, a fourth category of contract closely related to prime construction contracts.

Individual companies engaged in the practice of construction contracting are exposed to many risks and liabilities besides the monetary risk of performance of the construction work itself. For example, they are responsible for the health and safety of their employees while on the job, injury or property loss to third parties, loss or damage to construction work in place but not yet accepted by the owner, and loss or damage to their construction equipment. Additionally, they bear liability stemming from indemnification clauses in prime contracts, purchase orders, and subcontracts (see Chapters 5 and 7). These risks and liabilities are so large that contractors must purchase insurance policies to protect, or partially protect, themselves. Some of these policies are required by the terms of prime contracts and subcontracts or by statute. In many respects, construction industry insurance contracts are similar to those used throughout the business world. However, these contracts also contain provisions unique to the construction industry.

The primary parties to construction-related insurance policies consist of the construction contractor (the **insured**) and an insurance company who provides the required insurance coverage (the **carrier,** sometimes referred to as "the company"). Additional parties are sometimes named as **additional named insureds.**

The following are the important individual policies for the construction industry:

- Worker's compensation and employer's liability policies
- Public (or third-party) liability policies
- Builder's risk policies
- Equipment floater policies
- Miscellaneous policies for special situations and needs

Each of these policies insures against loss from a different kind of risk or liability.

WORKER'S COMPENSATION AND EMPLOYER'S LIABILITY POLICIES

Virtually every state in the nation imposes a statutory liability on employers, including construction employers, in the event that their employees are injured or killed in the course of performing their employment duties. The liability is absolute and does not depend on the circumstances of an occurrence or who is at fault. The dollar amount of the liability to the employer for any specific occurrence is normally established by statute for the particular state involved.

The essence of the **worker's compensation** and **employer's liability** insurance contract is that the **insurer** agrees, for a price (the "premium"), to

1. Assume the liability imposed on the insured contractor employer by the worker's compensation laws of the state named in the policy when an employee is injured or killed.
2. Assume any other liability that may flow to the contractor employer related to injury or death of employees.

Worker's Compensation Section

The liability assumed by the insurer under the worker's compensation section of the policy is that liability defined by the statute for the particular state or states named in the policy. The monetary amount of this liability is the benefit level set by the **state worker's compensation commission,** a regulatory body set up by the statute. The worker's compensation commission normally sets the premium level that the contractor will pay the insurer for obtaining coverage, although this method of setting premiums is presently undergoing revision in some states, particularly in California.

Employer's Liability Section

Under this section of the policy, the insurer agrees to assume any other liability that the insured employer may have in addition to those imposed by the worker's compensation law. Under the worker's compensation statutes of the various states, the employer's liability to the employee is limited to the benefit level stated in the statute. The employer cannot be sued by the employee for additional compensation. Therefore, an injured employee or the heirs of an employee who was killed may, in addition to collecting the statutory benefits, sue the owner, architect/engineer, or construction manager for the construction project where the employee was working. In this case, an indemnification clause in the prime contract would create a liability for the contractor, which would be independent of the contractor's liability to the employee created by the worker's compensation statutes.

Such an indemnification clause requires the contractor to "indemnify and hold harmless" the owner, architect/engineer, and construction manager, which means that the contractor would have to defend all such employee lawsuits brought against these entities and, if a judgment were awarded, pay the judgment. It is this potential additional liability of the contractor that the insurance carrier assumes under the employer's liability section of the policy.

USL&HW Act and the Jones Act

Construction projects involving maritime operations on or over navigable streams and rivers come under the jurisdiction of two federal laws with substantially higher benefits than the state worker's compensation statutes. These laws are the

U.S. Longshoremen's and Harbor Workers' Act (USL&HW Act) and the **Jones Act** (for the crews of marine vessels). Workers (or their heirs) covered by these laws who are injured or killed on the job may elect to be paid benefits under the federal law rather than under the state worker's compensation statutes. Federal benefits are higher, and, therefore, the premiums for insurance coverage are also higher than for the same kinds of work not performed on or over navigable streams or rivers.

Premium Structure

Worker's compensation and employer's liability insurance **base premiums** are usually stated in terms of a percentage of payroll for each particular labor classification involved (for example, so many dollars per $100 of payroll). This is true for every state except the state of Washington, where premiums are calculated in terms of dollars per worker-hour. Except in Washington, open shop contractors, who pay generally lower wage rates, have a substantial initial competitive advantage over union contractors. The worker-hour system in the state of Washington, therefore, tends to "level the playing field" in regard to the premium costs for worker's compensation insurance.

The two **principal factors governing the worker's compensation insurance base premiums** set by the various worker's compensation commissions for each individual labor classification are:

1. The particular state where the work is being performed; and
2. The kind of work being done, which clearly bears on the likelihood of workers becoming injured or killed.

The net result is that worker's compensation base premium rates vary widely between states and between labor classifications within each state. For example, a few years ago, the premium for the classification of general carpentry in California was $13.91 per $100, whereas, in Indiana, the premium was $3.56 per $100. At the same time, the premium in Hawaii was $56.46 per $100. In each case, the premium is the amount that the contractor insured has to pay the insurer to cover the contractor's statutory liability for exactly the same kind of work.

The kind of work also affects the premium. For instance, during this same period, the rate in California for concrete sidewalk work was $6.50 per $100, whereas the rate for roofing work was $30.33 per $100, almost five times higher.

Premium Modifiers

Premiums are also affected by the rate **modifier,** a factor based on a particular employer's safety record and previous claims history. The base premium is multiplied by the modifier, which can range from about 0.75 (very good) to 1.50 (very bad), to determine the actual premium that a particular employer pays. The use of modifiers is currently undergoing revision in some states.

PUBLIC LIABILITY POLICIES

By the very nature of their work, contractors are exposed to significant potential liability for damages suffered by noncontractually-involved third parties (the general public). Depending on the nature of the project involved, these potential liabilities can be modest or of enormous magnitude. For example, building a one-story school building on the outskirts of a small country town would involve relatively little potential liability. On the other hand, performing underground utility work involving gas mains in a downtown urban location would entail great potential liability. Construction mishaps on projects of this type have resulted in explosions destroying several blocks of street, causing loss of life and millions of dollars of property damage. Construction contractors cannot afford to risk liabilities of this magnitude, so they purchase public, or third-party, liability insurance policies to protect themselves.

The essence of the **public liability insurance** contract is that the insurance company, in exchange for the premium, agrees to assume the liabilities of the insured contractor subject to a stated deductible amount, up to stated monetary limits of the policy. In addition to paying any judgment awarded in the event of third-party lawsuits against the contractor, the insurance company will furnish and pay for the legal defense in court of such suits.

It is important to understand that public liability insurance (often called *comprehensive liability insurance* or *comprehensive general liability insurance*) protects the insured contractor from the claims of third parties only, as distinct from claims of the owner who is one of the parties to the construction contract. Contractors have occasionally attempted to use comprehensive general liability insurance policies to cover the costs for making good any defective contract work performed by them or by their subcontractors. The following two court decisions demonstrate the futility of such attempts.

In the first case, a general contractor for a condominium project in Florida subcontracted the furnishing and erection of prestressed concrete. The subcontract provided that the subcontractor would be covered by a comprehensive general liability policy obtained by the general contractor. Two years after completion of the project, the owner sued the general contractor for breach of contract due to several construction defects. The general contractor settled the suit with the owner and then sued the subcontractor whose prestressed concrete work was part of the defective work. The subcontractor argued that they were protected by the comprehensive general liability policy. The District Court of Florida rejected this argument stating:

> If insurance proceeds could be used to pay for repairing and/or replacing of poorly constructed products, a contractor or subcontractor could receive initial payment for its work and then receive subsequent payment from the insurance company to repair and replace it. Equally repugnant on policy grounds is the notion that the presence of insurance obviates the obligation to perform the job initially in a workman like manner.[1]

---

[1]*Centex Homes Corp. v. Prestressed Systems, Inc.*, 444 So. 2d 66 (Fla. App. 1984).

In the second case, a Minnesota court ruled similarly but even more forcefully. The owner of a newly constructed high-rise apartment building sued the general contractor because masonry walls on the completed project were cracking and spalling. As procured by the general contractor, the comprehensive general liability policy included an endorsement that explicitly excluded coverage for property damage to work constructed by the general contractor, but a similar exclusion for work constructed by others "on behalf of" the general contractor had been deleted from the policy. The masonry work was constructed "on behalf of" the general contractor by a masonry subcontractor. Even so, the Minnesota Supreme Court ruled that the coverage of the policy did not apply to defects in the constructed work of the project, no matter by whom it was constructed.

In defense of the owner's lawsuit for breach of contract due to the defective masonry walls, the general contractor argued that although the insurance policy did not cover the defective walls if they had constructed the walls with their own forces, the deletion of the phrase "on behalf of" meant that the policy *did* cover defects in work constructed by their subcontractor. The court rejected the argument that the cost of making good any defects in the subcontractor's work was covered by the policy, concluding instead that general liability insurance polices *do not* protect contractors or subcontractors against contractually assumed business risks such as failure to complete a project properly.[2]

Clearly then, comprehensive general liability insurance policies only protect the insured against the claims of third parties who have been injured or whose property has been damaged in some way by construction activities related to the referenced project.

Normal Liabilities That Are Covered

The liabilities assumed by the insurer are limited to the risk of loss or injury to third parties only, usually caused by any or all of the following:

- Construction operations at the project site
- Ownership, operation, or use of the site itself
- Operations of the insured's subcontractors
- Automotive operations related to the work at the site

By *endorsement,* a special provision expanding coverage, the policy can be made to cover additional liabilities such as those resulting from injuries to others occurring after the project has been completed ("completed operations" coverage) and liabilities flowing to the insured because of some separate contract that is related to the prime contract.

---

[2]*Knudson Construction Co. v. St. Paul Fire and Marine Insurance Co.,* 396 N.W.2d 229 (Minn. 1986).

Exclusions, Endorsements, and Deductibles

A number of **exclusions** may apply to the coverage of the policy. Common exclusions include the **XCU hazards.** The "X" exclusion (explosion) excludes liabilities arising from the use of explosives by the contractor or from any other kind of explosion. The "C" (collapse) exclusion excludes liabilities arising from some form of structural collapse occurring as a result of insured's excavation operations, pile driving, or other foundation work activity. A structural steel frame collapse caused by a rigging accident during the structural steel erection (and thus unrelated to foundation operations) would not be a "C" exclusion. The "U" (underground) exclusion excludes liability for damage to existing underground utilities caused by the contractor's construction operations such as excavation or pile driving.

It is normally possible to obtain public liability insurance without some or all of the XCU exclusions (to be really protected, a contractor cannot accept these exclusions), but deleting the exclusions from the policy will result in higher premiums.

Endorsements are the opposite of exclusions. They are special provisions added to the policy that expand the coverage. Both endorsements and exclusions are matters of agreement between the contractor and the insurance company, not requirements of law.

A **deductible** is an amount stated in the policy that must be exceeded before the insurance company has any liability. The amount of the deductible is a matter of agreement between the contractor and the insurance company. The higher the deductible, the lower the premium that the contractor pays for the insurance.

Monetary Limits—Primary and Umbrella Policies

The contractor and the insurance company may set the monetary limits as high as they choose and agree on, although the provisions of prime contracts usually set minimum limits for the third-party liability policy that the contractor is required to carry. By custom and practice of the industry, insurance coverage involving large monetary limits is often provided through a **primary policy** tailored to meet the monetary limit requirements of the contractor's prime construction contract with the owner, whereas an excess or **"umbrella" policy** is designed to raise the monetary limits to a much higher level. Frequently, the limits required by the provisions of the prime contract, while high enough to satisfy the owner, are not high enough to satisfy a prudent contractor. Hence, the need for the umbrella policy.

Premium Structure

The **public liability premium structure** for both primary and umbrella policies can be reckoned in two distinctly different ways. The contractor may pay a premium:

1. Based on payroll dollars expended in a manner similar to that for worker's compensation insurance premiums.
2. Based on a fixed percentage of the prime contract price.

Most contractors prefer the second method since, if the estimated labor for the project should overrun, the contractor at least avoids being doubly penalized by paying more for third-party liability insurance.

Contractors can often obtain lower premium charges for public liability insurance by arranging a **"retro" insurance policy** with their insurance carrier. Under this arrangement, more favorable premium rates are offered for a low claim/loss record for previous years, whereas an unfavorable claims/loss record will cause future premiums to rise. This system is similar to the premium modifier system used on worker's compensation insurance, previously discussed.

Definition of Occurrence

The term **occurrence** has special meaning in the insurance industry. An occurrence is an event that gives rise to a claim that the insurance company must pay. Ordinarily, the occurrence is an accident from the point of view of the insured. There are some limits on the type of event that can constitute an occurrence under the terms of the policy. To constitute an occurrence, the event must be something that was neither "intended" nor "expected" by the insured. For example, a contractor who failed to take precautions against gravel spilling from trucks in a haul operation over public roads, knowing that the gravel would spill but counting on insurance to cover the cost of any broken windshields that would result, may find the insurance company refusing to pay claims for broken windshields on the grounds that the contractor "expected" the gravel to spill and, by doing nothing to prevent it, "intended" that the gravel would spill.

Along these same lines, once a particular occurrence has taken place, the insured has a duty to do everything reasonably possible to ensure that the same occurrence does not happen again. If it does reoccur and the insured cannot show that everything reasonably possible was done to prevent the reoccurrence, the insurance company is not likely to pay.

P & I Policies

Public liability policies covering marine operations are called protection and indemnity policies (**P & I policies**). They operate in essentially the same way as third-party policies covering land-based operations.

BUILDER'S RISK POLICIES

A third major type of construction insurance policy is **builder's risk insurance,** sometimes called "installation floater" insurance. According to the terms of most prime contracts, the risk of physical loss to construction work put in place by a contractor rests with the contractor until the work is completed and accepted by the owner. This risk can be enormous in dollar terms. Builder's risk insurance can be obtained to cover all or part of this risk.

The essence of a builder's risk policy is that the insurer, for a price (the premium), agrees to assume the risk of physical damage to or loss of work in place and will pay the insured contractor the value of the work that was lost or damaged, subject to any agreed deductible, up to the monetary limits of the policy.

Limitation on Policy Coverage

The insurance company's liability is limited to the value of the work that was lost up to the monetary limit of the policy, but does not include **consequential damages,** such as lost time or increased cost of performance, that the insured contractor may have suffered as a result of the loss. For example, if a fire destroys a school building project while it is under construction, the contractor's builder's risk insurance would pay for the cost of replacing the construction work lost—that is, the **proximate costs.** However, the contractor would not recover any of the extra costs that would be incurred due to the extra time required because the work had to be repeated, any increased costs due to labor and material escalation on later work, or other increased costs of that type.

Named Peril v. All Risk Policies

Builder's risk insurance can be obtained as either a **named peril** or an **all risk policy.** The named peril policy, as its name implies, insures against loss only for those risks or perils, such as fire or flood, named in the policy. The all risk policy protects against loss caused by any risk or peril, subject only to any exclusions named in the policy.

Exclusions and Deductibles

There usually will be exclusions in builder's risk policies, even in the all risk type of policy. Some of the more common exclusions include the following:

- Loss due to strikes, lockouts, war, riot, and so on
- Loss due to court orders and ordinances
- Loss due to occupancy or use by the owner
- Any portion of a loss resulting from the insured contractor's failure to take reasonable precautions to limit the extent of the loss
- Loss due to an **error, omission,** or **deficiency** in the owner's design of the project or the owner's architect/engineer's design of the project

When written in the form just stated, this last exclusion would not apply to losses due to an error, omission, or deficiency in any of the contractor's operations and would not apply to losses due to negligence of the contractor's employees. The logic behind the exclusion applying to losses caused by errors, omissions, and deficiencies in the work of the owner, or of the A/E engaged by the owner, but not to losses caused by similar failings of the contractor requires explanation.

Builder's risk insurance is basically contractor's insurance, although it is often procured by the owner. Contractors need the insurance because they cannot count on their forces being error free. However, the policy is not intended to underwrite the owner's work or the work of an A/E engaged by the owner. These entities usually purchase separate errors and omissions insurance to protect them from the consequences of faults in their work. The contractor does not need protection against faults in the owner's work because, under the terms of the prime construction contract, losses due to the fault of the owner or A/E are the owner's responsibility, not the contractor's. The loss of a completed roof structure because of a collapse caused by an error in the A/E's structural calculations would not be covered by the builder's risk policy and would be the responsibility of the owner. On the other hand, if the roof collapse was due to a rigging accident, in turn caused by the failure of the contractor to install an adequate temporary guying system, the loss would be the contractor's responsibility and would be covered by the contractor's builder's risk policy if the exclusions to the policy were stated in the form shown previously.

Of course, if the exclusions were stated in a more restrictive form with respect to the contractor's operations or those of subcontractors, the coverage of the policy would be altered considerably. An example of a more restrictive form of exclusion is afforded by a 1979 Wisconsin case in which a general contractor constructing a dormitory had purchased a builder's risk policy that contained an exclusion for "loss or damage caused by faulty materials, improper workmanship or installation, errors in design or specifications." During construction, a retaining wall constructed by a subcontractor collapsed causing extensive damage to the dormitory. When the insurance company refused to pay the general contractor's claim against the builder's risk policy, the general contractor sued, arguing that there had been no faulty workmanship on their part, and, therefore, the policy should cover the costs of repairing the damage. A trial court granted summary judgment for the insurance company—meaning that, as a matter of law in view of facts that were not in dispute, the insurance policy did not cover the occurrence, and a trial was, therefore, not necessary.

On appeal, the Wisconsin Supreme Court affirmed the trial court's decision that the policy did not cover faulty construction work no matter whether performed by the general contractor or a subcontractor but sent the case back to the trial court to determine whether faulty work on the part of the subcontractor was, in fact, the sole cause of the collapse. That question required a trial for its determination.[3]

Thus, unlike the rigging accident scenario described before, the policy in this case did not cover occurrences that were the result of faulty construction work. The exact language of the exclusions is clearly a matter of great importance.

Like public liability insurance, builder's risk insurance claim payments are usually subject to a deductible amount that must be exceeded before the insurance company has any liability. The amount of the deductible is a matter of agreement between the insurance company and the contractor. Higher deductibles result in lower premiums that the contractor pays for the insurance.

---

[3]*Kraemer Bros., Inc. v. U.S. Fire Insurance Co.*, 278 N.W.2d 857 (Wisconsin 1979).

Temporary Structures

Builder's risk policies traditionally cover **losses to the contractor's temporary structures** in addition to losses to the permanent work. The cost of replacing such structures as equipment shops, falsework, cofferdams, and access bridges or trestles in the event of their loss can be very large, and it is important to the contractor that these structures are included in the builder's risk policy. However, even though temporary structures are included in this manner, builder's risk policies do not cover the contractor's construction equipment or tools.

To put this into perspective, consider what builder's risk coverage would mean in practice after the occurrence of the following hypothetical rigging accident. Because of a rigging failure, a gang form that is being erected by a truck crane is totally destroyed after falling through an access walkway, and the falling gang form then destroys a previously poured concrete floor slab on a project under construction. The motor crane turns over and is also wrecked. Which losses would be covered by a typical builder's risk policy?

Replacement of the permanent floor slab would obviously be covered, since it is part of the permanent project being built under the construction contract. In addition, replacement of the access walkway and the gang form would be covered because they are temporary structures erected at the site by the contractor for the process of building the permanent work. However, repair of the contractor's crane would not be covered because it is a unit of construction equipment specifically excluded from coverage.

Premium Structure

Two methods are commonly used to determine the **premiums for builder's risk insurance.** The first provides for periodically increasing premium payments, with the amount of each premium payment increasing as the value of the work actually in place—and thus at risk—increases. This method is logical but more complicated than the second method, which provides for flat premium payments for the duration of the project. The flat premium payment is equivalent to the average of the periodically increasing premium payments determined by the first method. With the second method, the insured overpays with respect to the actual risk in the early stages of the project and underpays in the latter stages. The second method is the prevalent method in use in the industry. The premium is usually stated as a percentage of the full contract price.

Monetary Limits of Policy

The amount of the premium is influenced to some extent by the **monetary limits** of the policy. The policy can be written for the full contract price or for an amount less than the full contract price. The premium for coverage up to a limit less than the full contract price would be somewhat less.

Reasons for Carrying Builder's Risk Insurance

Many prime contracts require the contractor to carry builder's risk insurance with stated minimum monetary limits. In this case, the contractor has no choice and must obtain the insurance. A contractor who has the option usually evaluates the risk, compares the costs and probability of occurrence of possible losses against the certain cost of the policy premiums, and makes the decision on that basis. Obviously, the nature of the project is a major influence on the decision. A contractor whose contract consisted solely of constructing a large pedestal-type concrete foundation for a steam turbine at an open rural site would be exposed to virtually no risk of loss, but if the project consisted of a multi-story, wood, low-cost housing complex in a congested urban setting, the exposure to risk would be relatively high.

The more costly that builder's risk coverage becomes, the more it becomes a factor in competing for construction work. Wealthy companies possess the ability to "self-insure," and in cases in which the contract documents do not require the contractor to carry builder's risk insurance, these companies have a cost advantage over smaller companies who must purchase the insurance to avoid catastrophe in case of a loss.

EQUIPMENT FLOATER POLICIES

The fact that builder's risk policies exclude construction equipment leads to the fourth major kind of construction insurance called **equipment floater insurance.** This type of policy protects the contractor against physical damage or loss to tools and construction equipment (including theft). On many kinds of construction projects, the contractor's tools and equipment can be exposed to considerable risk of loss or damage. In this type of insurance contract, the insurance company agrees to make good any loss or damage to the contractor's equipment subject to any agreed deductible up to the policy limits. Equipment floater policies, like builder's risk policies, can be all risk policies or may insure only against certain named perils. All risk policies are more common.

Method of Determining Loss

The policy stipulates the method of determining the value of a total loss to the contractor's equipment. Commonly used methods include the following:

- Under the *replacement value* method, the insurer will pay the cost of replacing the lost unit with an equivalent new unit.
- Under the *book value* method, the insurer will pay only the depreciated value of the unit on the contractor's books at the time of the loss.
- Under the *pre-agreed value* method, the insurer will pay a value pre-agreed by the parties and stated in the policy for each unit of equipment insured.

The book value method is more common.

Premium Structure

Equipment floater insurance premiums are usually reckoned as a percentage of the value of the covered equipment per year (usually the book value). As the equipment depreciates, the book value is less, and the premiums decline.

Equipment Floater Insurance for Marine Equipment Operations

Equipment floater insurance is called **hull insurance** when it covers permanently floating marine equipment, such as barges, tugs, and dredges. When land-based equipment is working from barges on water—for example, a crawler crane working from crane mats on a barge deck—the equipment on the barge is normally insured under the equipment floater policy, but at a higher premium for the time that the equipment is on the water. The barge would be covered by a separate hull insurance policy.

Evaluating the Need for Equipment Floater Insurance

A final point on equipment floater insurance concerns the need for the insurance. The chances of damage or loss for certain kinds of equipment may be relatively high, whereas, for others, it is virtually nil. For example, contrast the previously mentioned example of the crawler crane operating on crane mats on a flat-decked work barge on a river bridge crossing with a service crane in the contractor's home-base shop or yard complex. The former certainly would be insured, whereas the latter probably would not. The need for insurance is highly project-specific and use-specific. When the purchase of new equipment is financed by pledging the equipment as collateral for the loan, the lending institution will insist that the equipment be insured to its full value.

MISCELLANEOUS POLICIES FOR SPECIAL SITUATIONS

A final construction insurance category consists of the **miscellaneous construction insurance policies** that are sometimes obtained by construction contractors. Chief among these are:

- Railroad protective insurance (usually required when working over or near a railroad right-of-way), in which the railroad is insured against loss caused by contractor's operations.
- Transit insurance, which covers loss or damage when items are being transported (refer, for instance, to the TBM incident related in Chapter 7).
- Business interruption insurance, which is intended to cover the costs incurred by a contractor when normal business is interrupted by some event beyond the contractor's control. This type of insurance is seldom purchased because it is so expensive.

- Fidelity and forgery insurance, which is intended to replace losses due to malfeasance in the office place by a contractor's own employees, such as theft or forgery—that is, so-called "white collar" crime.

OWNER-PROVIDED INSURANCE PROGRAMS

Owner-provided insurance programs sometimes provide all or part of the insurance policies required for a project free of charge to the contractor. The project bidding documents will include the scope of the insurance coverage provided. For instance, the AIA form of contract provides that the owner will provide builder's risk insurance for the full value of the contract work. It is not uncommon for large public owners to provide a complete package consisting of worker's compensation insurance, major public liability insurance, and builder's risk insurance. This latter arrangement is often called a "wrap-up" insurance program.

Under this arrangement, the contractor excludes from the bid all premium costs for the insurance designated to be provided by the owner, including premium monies only for insurance policies required by law or by the terms of the contract that the owner is not providing. The bid may also include the premium costs for any additional insurance that the contractor considers necessary on and above that provided by the wrap-up program.

Contractors generally do not favor owner-provided wrap-up insurance. They prefer to control the insurance procurement process so they can benefit from the bargaining power derived from a favorable claims/loss history and their past relationships with a particular insurance company. Under owner-provided wrap-up insurance arrangements, contractors with low claims or loss experience lose the benefit of their superior past performance.

"RED FLAG" INSURANCE PROVISIONS

As with all contracts, insurance policies contain certain provisions that are particularly important to both construction contractors and their insurance carriers. An adequate comprehension of the protection actually provided by the policy is impossible unless these provisions are completely understood; hence, the following discussion of the principal **"red flag" clauses.**

Named Exclusions

Probably the most important of all of the "red flag" provisions is the named exclusion section of the contract. This section includes a clear statement of the particular risks and hazards that are excluded from the coverage of the policy; however, insureds sometimes overlook important exclusions simply because they do not read the policy carefully.

Additional Named Insureds

An insurance policy may, by endorsement, add other insured parties in addition to the insured contractor. These other insured parties are called **additional named insureds.** The named parties then have the same insurance coverage as the insured contractor. Adding additional named insureds increases the risk that the insurer is assuming, and thus also increases the premium paid by the insured.

As previously discussed, the indemnification clause in prime construction contracts states that the contractor promises to indemnify and hold harmless the owner, the architect/engineer (and, sometimes, the construction manager as well) from the claims of third parties arising out of any act or failure to act of the contractor. Most contractors cannot afford to accept the risk that this clause imposes on them and must obtain insurance coverage. By naming the owner, the architect/engineer, and construction manager as additional named insureds in the public liability insurance contract, the contractor obtains this necessary protection.

As discussed earlier in this chapter, the contractor meets the requirements of the prime contract indemnification clause with respect to claims against the owner and A/E by contractor's employees who become injured on the job (or by the heirs of workers who are killed) through the employer's liability section of the worker's compensation policy.

Deductibles

A deductible is an amount stated in the policy that, in the event of a loss, the contractor must pay or absorb "off the top," leaving the balance of the loss for the insurance company's account. If the amount of the loss is less than the deductible, the insurance company has no liability. This provision is common in the insurance industry and results in lower premiums than if the entire loss was paid by the insurance company. However, the insured should be aware of the magnitude of the deductible in a particular case in relation to the premium paid for the insurance.

Policy Term

An additional important clause deals with the time period, or term, that the insurance policy is in effect. This **policy term** is stated in the policy either in the form of fixed dates between which the coverage is in effect or, alternately, until the prime contract work is completed and accepted by the owner. Thus, the periods during which the coverage is in effect may be very different if delays occur and the work takes longer than the contractor planned when the insurance coverage was placed, depending on which way the term is stated. If the policy term is stated in the fixed date form and expires before the project is finished, the contractor must renew the policy to continue the insurance coverage. If the contractor should inadvertently fail to renew, the result could be catastrophic. When the policy is renewed, the contractor has to pay an additional premium. On the other hand, if the policy is written to remain in effect until the project is completed and accepted, the contractor is fully protected for the original premium, even if there are delays.

Subrogation

Another "red flag" clause concerns **subrogation.** An insurer who has been granted subrogation rights literally "stands in the insured's shoes" with regard to any right or remedy that the insured may have against the party who was at fault causing claims to be made. This means that once the insurance company has paid a claim or judgment entered against the insured, they are free to attempt to recover the money paid by suing (in the name of the insured) the original party at fault. They have this right whether the insured wants its name to appear in such a lawsuit or not. Contractors may not want to be named as plaintiffs in lawsuits in which they no longer have a direct interest. If this is the case, it is important when they consider a potential insurance contract to note whether or not the insurance company has been granted subrogation rights.

Policy Cancellations

Finally, insurance policies normally contain provisions establishing the right of the insurance company to unilaterally cancel the policy prior to the expiration of the normal term. The contractor must be sure this clause also requires the insurance company to give adequate notice before canceling so the contractor will have a reasonable opportunity to canvas the market and replace the insurance at a reasonable premium.

RECENT TRENDS IN THE CONSTRUCTION INSURANCE INDUSTRY

The insurance industry has changed significantly in recent years. Two examples occurring in the mid-1980s were the emergence of the claims-made policy and a dramatic increase in premium levels coupled with reduced coverage. Fortunately, from the construction contractor's point of view, both trends were decreasing by the mid-1990s.

Claims-Made v. Occurrence Policies

The traditional form of insurance policy is the **occurrence policy.** The insured is covered if the occurrence giving rise to the loss takes place within the term of the policy, even though the claim with respect to the loss is made after the expiration of the policy. Claims or lawsuits commonly are initiated several years after the event causing the loss occurred, often after the project has been completed and the policy has expired. Occurrence policies cover this situation, as long as the event giving rise to the loss and to the claim occurred during the policy period.

In the mid-1980s, the insurance industry aggressively promoted a different type of policy called a **claims-made policy.** In this form of coverage, the insurer is liable only when both the event giving rise to the claim and the claim itself occur during the policy term. If the actual claim is not made during the policy period, the policy will not cover it, even though the event giving rise to the claim occurred during the policy period. Contractors have no way to control when third parties may decide to file claims and are thus at considerable risk under this type of policy.

Under a claims-made policy, contractors cannot meet prime contract indemnification requirements without putting their entire companies on the line. Although the trend toward claims-made policies is currently on the wane, contractors should be alert to their existence and note this aspect of policy coverage provisions carefully.

Premium Escalation and Diminished Coverage

The mid-1980s also saw a marked **escalation in insurance premiums.** The increases far exceeded price increases generally, and many smaller contractors were driven out of business. Even some larger companies experienced severe difficulties. For example, prior to 1985, one large contractor bought public liability insurance in a combined policy covering all of its projects for a premium of about 0.6% of the company's total annual labor exposure (the total yearly labor cost expenditure for all of the company's projects). The total annual labor exposure was about $15,000,000, so the annual premium was $90,000 ($15,000,000 times 0.006). The limit of the third-party liability coverage was an aggregate amount of $30,000,000.

By 1987, the same company paid 5% of its total labor exposure for only one-third the coverage. This meant that the annual premium increased to $750,000 ($15,000,000 times 0.05), and coverage decreased to an aggregate amount of $10,000,000. Builder's risk insurance premiums increased about the same. Fortunately, insurance premiums have since abated.

CONCLUSION

This chapter discussed the general need for construction contractors to protect themselves from various kinds of losses by purchasing insurance policies. The common insurance policies in use in the construction industry today were listed, followed by a discussion of the kinds of protection provided by each policy and details of how the policy generally operates. The principal "red flag" clauses pertaining to insurance policies in general were briefly discussed, followed by a brief examination of some recent trends in the construction insurance field.

Chapter 9, on the subject of surety bonds, will round out this book's discussion of closely related contracts that arise or result from the existence of prime construction contracts.

QUESTIONS AND PROBLEMS

1. What are the five general categories of insurance contracts discussed in this chapter?

2. What is the essence of a worker's compensation and employer's liability insurance contract? Can a worker who has been injured on the job sue the employer for damages? Who can be sued? Explain the two separate kinds of liability involved. Which of these liabilities is statutory, and which is contractual?

3. What is the function of a state worker's compensation commission?

4. What is the general import of the Longshoremen's and Harbor Worker's Act? The Jones Act? Are these state or federal laws? What is their relationship to state worker's compensation laws? Which is more favorable to the worker? In what way? Can a worker receive benefits under the Longshoremen's and Harbor Worker's Act and state worker's compensation laws simultaneously? Are the insurance premiums under the Longshoremen's and Harbor Worker's Act and the Jones Act higher or lower than those for coverage under most state worker's compensation laws?

5. How are premium payments for worker's compensation and employer's liability policies usually reckoned? How is this done in the state of Washington? Which is better from the standpoint of a contractor employing union labor in a high wage rate area? Why? What two factors influence how high the basic premium (before application of a rate modifier) will be? Are the differences in premiums that could result from the first factor great or small? How great? How about the premium differences resulting from the second factor? What is a rate modifier? Can it have a significant effect on a contractor's competitive position? How?

6. Hypothetical contractor A performs an annual construction volume of work containing a labor component of $15,000,000 at the base pay level—that is, excluding union fringes and all forms of insurance premiums and taxes. Their average worker's compensation insurance premium is $19.00 per $100 of payroll (calculated on base pay). Their experience modifier is 0.72.

   Hypothetical contractor B performs the same annual volume with the same labor component and same average worker's compensation insurance premium rate, but their experience modifier is 1.45.

   What is the dollar difference in annual total worker's compensation insurance premiums paid by contractors A and B?

7. What is the essence of a public liability or third-party liability insurance policy? Who are the beneficiaries under this kind of insurance? Do risks covered by this kind of insurance vary much from project to project? What were the two extreme examples discussed in this chapter? Can you think of other greatly contrasting risks that might be encountered? What about a contract for the disposal of toxic wastes from a construction site?

8. What is completed operations coverage? How may it be included in the policy? What are exclusions? What are the XCU hazards? Can they be excluded? Are they always excluded? If they are not excluded, what is the effect on the premium? What are deductibles? What relation do they have to the premium?

9. Are the monetary limits and inclusion or absence of exclusions in public liability insurance policies governed by law, or are they matters of agreement between the contractor and insurance company? What is a primary policy?

An umbrella policy? What are the two different ways in which the premium for public liability insurance is reckoned? Which is the most favorable from the contractor's standpoint? Why?

10. What is an occurrence? What is the significance of the phrase "neither intended or expected"? What duty does the contractor have with regard to the reoccurrence of an event that has resulted in a claim against the policy?

11. What is P & I insurance?

12. What is the essence of a builder's risk policy? Does the need for builder's risk insurance apply equally to all construction contracts? What two contrasting examples were discussed in this chapter?

13. What kind of losses are typically covered under a builder's risk policy? What is the difference between consequential damages and proximate damages associated with a causal event? Does a builder's risk policy respond to both? To either? If so, to which?

14. What is the difference between a named peril builder's risk policy and an all risk policy? Can exclusions still apply to an all risk policy? If so, what are some of the common ones that might apply?

15. What is the distinction between how the errors, omissions, or deficiencies exclusion of a builder's risk policy may be applied (depending on the wording of the exclusion language in the policy) to the insured contractor's operations and to those of the designer when a project or portion of project is lost or destroyed during construction due to an error, omission, or deficiency? Explain the logic of this distinction.

16. What are the two ways of reckoning builder's risk premiums discussed in this chapter? How is the premium usually stated in an insurance broker's quotation to a contractor?

17. Is the need for builder's risk insurance the same for different types of projects? What would be an example of a project that does not justify it? A project that does? Is builder's risk insurance ever contractually required? Do some contractor's "self-insure"? Which ones?

18. What is the essence of an equipment floater policy? What three methods are discussed in this chapter for determining what the policy will pay in the event of a loss? Can equipment floater insurance be a named peril or an all risk policy?

19. What is hull insurance? How is equipment floater insurance handled under one policy with respect to equipment such as crawler cranes operating from mats on floating barges as well as on dry land? Is the need for equipment floater insurance a variable, depending on the piece of construction equipment involved and the project involved? Cite some examples to illustrate your answer.

20. What are some of the types of miscellaneous insurance policies discussed in this chapter? What are the risks against which they insure?

21. What is an additional named insured? What is the relationship of additional named insureds on a public liability policy to the indemnification requirements in a prime construction contract?

22. What does right of subrogation mean with respect to an insurance contract? What is a common contractor attitude regarding an insurance company's rights of subrogation?

23. What is an occurrence policy? A claims-made policy? Why is a claims-made policy not responsive to the needs of a construction contractor? What trends occurred in the 1980–1990 period in the insurance industry with regard to the level of premiums charged?

9

Surety Bonds

Key Words and Concepts

Hired guarantees
Surety
Principal
Obligee
Guarantee
Penal sum
Premium
Indemnitor
Indemnity agreement
Differences between surety bonds and
  insurance contracts
Requirements for serving as surety
Surety belief in principal
Bid bond
Performance bond
Determination of surety obligation
Common owner misconception about
  performance bonds

Effect of excess early contract payments
Contractor's protection of bonding
  capacity
Labor and material payment bonds
Mechanic's liens
Claimants
Used or reasonably required in
  performance of construction contract
Work guarantee bonds
Lien discharge bonds
Second-tier bonds
Third-tier bonds
Subcontract performance bonds
Labor and material payment bonds
Material supplier bonds

Surety bonds are unique examples of important construction industry documents that flow from prime construction contracts. Essentially, they are **hired guarantees.** Guarantees of what? Who makes them and to whom? On whose behalf are the guarantees made? Why are the guarantees required? What happens when demands are made that the guarantees be made good? This chapter deals with these issues.

RELEVANT PARTIES AND SURETY BOND TERMS

To understand the purpose and operation of the various construction industry **surety bonds,** you should become familiar with the following commonly used terms:

- Surety
- Principal
- Obligee
- Guarantee
- Penal sum
- Premium
- Indemnitor

Surety

The **surety** (sometimes called the *obligor* or the *bonding company*) is a financial institution possessing great wealth and stability. Sureties will be required to furnish convincing evidence of their financial strength and are often required by the terms of prime construction contracts to be registered as *approved sureties* and to appear as such on a published list maintained by the U.S. government.

Principal

The entity that actually furnishes the bond is called the **principal.** The surety is the entity that furnishes the guarantee that the bond promises.

Obligee

The guarantee promised by the bond is made to an entity called the **obligee.** In the case of bid bonds and performance bonds furnished by the prime construction contractor, the owner of the project being constructed is the obligee. In the case of labor and material payment bonds furnished by the prime contractor, the owner is usually the obligee for the use and benefit of subcontractors and material suppliers.

In some jurisdictions, the subcontractors and material suppliers themselves are considered to be the obligees. When performance bonds are furnished by a subcontractor, the prime contractor is the obligee.

Guarantee

The **guarantee** is a promise made by the surety to the obligee that, if the principal should fail to carry out fully and faithfully whatever particular duty to the obligee is stated in the bond, the surety steps in and either performs that duty or causes it to be performed by others. The exact nature of the guarantee varies, depending on the type of surety bond involved. This concept is different from that of an insurance policy where the insurer agrees to pay for a loss resulting from some unexpected catastrophe or from claims made by third parties to the construction contract. Essentially, the guarantee is a case of the surety underwriting the performance of the principal.

Penal Sum

Although the surety guarantees the performance of the principal, there is a monetary limit to the guarantee called the **penal sum** of the bond. The amount of the penal sum is stated in different ways, depending on the type of bond. For example, the penal sum of one type of surety bond, called a *bid bond,* is usually 10% of the amount of the bid, whereas the penal sum of performance bonds and labor and material payment bonds is usually 100% of the contract price. The penal sum is the upper limit of the surety's potential financial liability to the obligee.

Premium

The **premium** is the fee that the principal pays to the surety in exchange for providing the guarantee to the obligee. Before 1985, bond premiums on large contracts for well-established contractors ranged from ½ to ¾% of the total contract price for a package consisting of the bid, performance, and labor and materials payment bonds. The cost of the same bond package in the small contract market was between 1½ and 2% of the construction contract price. Bond premiums have escalated, then stabilized somewhat, since that time.

Indemnitor

An **indemnitor** is a person or entity who promises to pay the surety back for any cost that the surety incurs if called upon to make good the guarantee. The principal always is an indemnitor. A surety often also requires personal indemnification from the officers or owners of the entity that is the principal. This concept of personal indemnification is the origin of the oft-repeated expression "going on the line." If the principal is a subsidiary company of some other entity, the surety generally wants indemnification from the parent company as well as from the subsidiary. In other words, the surety makes sure that it is indemnified by the entity "where the money is" and from which the assets cannot be transferred by accounting manipulations in the face of an impending claim against the bond.

HOW DO SURETY BONDS WORK?

The potential liability assumed by a surety greatly exceeds the premium charged for underwriting the performance of the principal. In part, the surety is operating on an actuarial basis, but additional considerations lie behind the willingness of the surety to assume the liability involved. These other considerations are explained in this section.

Indemnity Agreement

The surety bond proper is a legal instrument that results from a separate contract between the surety and the principal, in which the surety agrees, for a price (the premium), to guarantee the principal's performance with respect to some obligation to the obligee that the principal has assumed. In this sense, the bond is the evidence that the obligee wants to see that this separate contract exists. The separate contract, which the obligee never sees directly, is called an **indemnity agreement.** In addition to specifying that the surety will provide the required guarantee to the obligee, the indemnity agreement will provide that the principal and all other named indemnitors who may be a party to the agreement will pay the surety back for any losses that the surety incurs in making good the guarantee.

Surety Bonds v. Insurance Contracts

What are the **differences between surety bonds and insurance contracts?** Under an insurance contract, the insurer agrees, for the premium, to pay damages or replace something that has been lost or destroyed as a result of the occurrence of a covered event, such as an accident or a fire (including claims made against the insured by third parties arising from these occurrences). Surety bonds are very different. In the event of a call against a surety bond, the surety's obligations are not triggered by an event such as an accident or fire. Instead, the call against the surety's guarantee is made as a result of some kind of alleged failure of the principal to perform.

How Good Is the Guarantee?

The guarantee is as good as the financial resources and integrity of the surety. The main **requirement for serving as surety** is that the entity must be perceived as having great financial strength with a history and reputation of living up to its obligations. The obligee would not have confidence in the guarantee unless these requirements were met.

Surety's Belief in the Contractor's Ability to Perform

The potential cost to the surety in the event of a call on its guarantee can be enormous. (The penal sum of the performance bond for the Lock and Dam No. 26 contract discussed in Chapter 4 was the full contract price of $227 million.) Insurance contracts may also involve large risks, but there is a key difference. In providing insurance to a contractor, the insurer is betting that it can predict the likelihood of losses on an actuarial basis accurately enough so that it makes money on the average. The competence and financial strength of the contractor are not key factors in the insurer's decision-making process.

The surety bond case is very different. Since it is the performance of the principal that is being guaranteed, the **surety has to believe in the principal** and be convinced that the principal has the intention, the resources, and the ability to perform. Even though protected, at least on paper, by the terms of the indemnity agreement, sureties simply will not furnish bonds to construction contractors if they have any doubt about the contractor's ability to perform.

BID BONDS

An important element of the bidding process is that owners have the assurance that the bidding contractor who is awarded the contract will accept and sign it and will furnish all insurance policies and additional surety bonds required by the bid documents. If the successful bidder refuses to sign the contract, the owner must accept a higher price for the work or rebid the project. Neither alternative is desirable. Even though the owner can sue the low bidder for damages, the project will be delayed, and it may not be possible to recover all of the costs. The **bid bond** protects the interests of the owner against this potential loss.

Bid Bond Guarantee

The guarantee of the bid bond is twofold:

1. The surety guarantees to the obligee (the project owner) that the principal will enter into the contract in the event of an award; and

2. The principal will furnish the performance bond and insurance policies required by the contract.

Bid Bond Penal Sum

The penal sum for bid bonds can be expressed in one of two distinctly different ways:

1. As either a fixed amount of money or as a percentage of the bid total, which serves as liquidated damages for failure to enter into the contract. According to the terms of the bond, the obligee does not have to prove actual damages but must merely show that the principal failed to enter into the contract

and/or failed to furnish the required insurance policies and other required bonds.

2. The penal sum can be stated in the form of actual damages suffered, up to a stated limit. Here, the obligee must prove the extent of actual damages before the surety will pay on the guarantee.

The first method is more common, and 10% of the total bid is usually the stated amount. However, even though the bond is written in this form, courts sometimes limit the owner's recovery to actual damages.

Some bid documents provide that bidders furnish a certified check in the amount of 10% of the bid price instead of a bid bond. The checks are returned to all unsuccessful bidders the day following the bid opening—and to the successful bidder when the signed contract and the required insurance policies and bonds are received by the owner.

PERFORMANCE BONDS

Owners naturally want assurance that, once they have awarded a contract, the contractor will perform according to the contract's terms. This assurance is provided by the **performance bond.**

Performance Bond Guarantee

The guarantee is the surety's promise to fulfill the principal's obligations to perform the separate contract that the principal has made with the obligee if the principal is unwilling or unable to perform. Before a call against the guarantee can be legally sustained, the obligee must clearly establish that the principal is in default of the terms of the contract. It is sometimes unclear whether the contractor principal is truly in default or if the principal's performance or lack of performance has been caused by an act or failure to act of the owner obligee or has been the result of some other condition of *force majeure*. Under these circumstances, establishing a *de facto* (actual) default can be a complicated matter, which often is settled only in court following protracted litigation.

Surety's Options to Make Good the Guarantee

Once convinced that the principal is truly in default, the surety has three options for making good the guarantee to the obligee:

1. Assist the principal to remedy the default. Ordinarily this would be accomplished by advancing funds to the principal but not taking control of the contract.

2. Take control of contract performance and complete the work by engaging another contractor or by retaining the principal and subsidizing project operations and actively directing the work.

3. Allow the obligee to complete the contract by engaging another contractor and, when the work has been completed, pay money to the obligee for any excess costs incurred in completing the work.

The second and third methods are more common.

Penal Sum—How Much Does the Surety Pay?

The penal sum for performance bonds is usually 100% of the contract price, the upper limit of that surety's monetary exposure in the event of a default. **Determination of surety obligations** can be reached in various ways. One method is for the surety and the obligee to negotiate a fixed amount to discharge the guarantee (up to the penal sum limit) to be paid by the surety "up front" before the balance of the work is completed. If the actual costs incurred by the obligee in completing the work exceed this amount, the surety pays nothing further. If the actual costs are less than the agreed-upon amount, the obligee keeps the difference. This method amounts to the surety buying their way out of the liability.

A second more common procedure is for the surety to agree to pay the obligee's actual costs to complete the contract work, less any unpaid contract balance, plus any liquidated damages that may be due under the contract. The amount that the surety must pay is limited to the penal sum of the performance bond. The way that the surety's payment is calculated under the second method is illustrated with the following hypothetical example:

> A contractor defaults on a $5,000,000 construction contract after beginning work and receiving a total of $1,500,000 in progress payments for work completed prior to the default. The contractor has furnished the owner with a performance bond with a penal sum equal to the full contract price. The surety agrees that the owner (obligee) should complete the work, which costs the owner $4,750,000. In addition, the project is finally finished well after the required completion date of the original contract and, under the terms of that contract, $300,000 in liquidated damages are due.

$$\text{Unpaid Balance} = \$5,000,000 - \$1,500,000 = \$3,500,000$$

$$\text{Surety's Obligation} = \$4,750,000 - \$3,500,000 + \$300,000 = \$1,550,000$$

If it had cost the owner $5,750,000 to complete the work, the surety's obligation would increase to $2,550,000. However, if the owner had spent $8,750,000 to finish the work, the surety would have to pay only $5,000,000, the amount of the penal sum of the bond, not the $5,550,000 that would otherwise be calculated.

Owner's Misconception About Performance Bonds

A common **misconception about performance bonds by owners** is that they sometimes mistakenly feel that they have absolute power over the contractor because they hold a performance bond. They believe that the surety will immediately respond to complaints and force the contractor to do whatever the owner wants done. This expectation is not likely to be fulfilled for a number of reasons.

First, the surety will not act until and unless they believe that the principal is truly in default and will not or cannot cure the default. The surety is even less inclined to act if the principal is financially strong. The principal has indemnified the surety. If the principal has substantial assets, the surety knows that it will recover any money that it might have to pay if the owner sues to enforce performance of the bond guarantee and if the decision of the court supports the owner's position. Therefore, there is less incentive for the surety to act immediately.

A second factor may motivate the surety not to act on the guarantee in questionable cases. Under the legal theory of subrogation, the surety has all of the contractual rights of the principal and is not likely to remedy an alleged default until all viable legal defenses to the owner's claim of default have been investigated and found to be of no avail. If the surety should pay the obligee when there is a viable legal defense to the claim of default, it may be legally found to be a volunteer and be unable to recover the money paid to the obligee from the principal and other indemnitors.

Thus, the owner/obligee may be surprised to find that the surety sides with the contractor/principal when faced with a call on the guarantee. To collect eventually on the performance bond guarantee, the obligee must be legally correct on the facts of the alleged default, or both the principal and surety will be excused from their obligations. However, if the allegation of default is legally correct, the obligee eventually is made whole, but only up to the penal sum limit of the bond.

Excess Early Contract Payments

It has previously been mentioned that the obligee's recovery is limited to the penal sum of the bond. However, the obligee may recover less than the excess costs required to complete a defaulted contract even though the penal sum of the performance bond has not been exceeded. Suppose that at the time of the default, the owner had overpaid the contractor for work completed in terms of the actual cost of the work completed relative to the actual cost of the work remaining.

Under these circumstances, the **effect of excess early contract payments** is that the owner/obligee may be unable to collect the full cost to complete the work less the unpaid balance of the contract, even if that total is less than the penal sum of the performance bond. The surety will contest its obligation to pay the full amount by showing that the owner improperly overpaid the contractor for the work actually performed. This will reduce the unpaid contract balance at the time of the default and increase the amount that the owner is asking the surety to pay. If the surety can prove overpayment to the contractor, it will reduce the amount to be paid to the obligee accordingly. This is a real danger to the owner in paying out on contracts where payment schedules have been heavily front-end loaded—that is, payment heavily unbalanced in favor of work items scheduled to be performed early in the contract.

Contractor Protection of Bonding Capacity

It may appear from the preceding discussion that the performance bond provides little protection for the obligee after all. This would be more true if it were not for the necessity of contractor/principals to **protect their bonding capacity.** Since so much construction work is bonded, contractors must maintain their ability to obtain performance bonds. Smaller contractors particularly do not want their surety to receive complaints about their performance, jeopardizing their ability to secure bonds for future projects. For this reason, they are more likely to respond to owners' demands when complaints over performance arise.

If being declared in default looms as a real possibility, contractors generally do everything possible to avoid the surety taking over their contracts for two main reasons:

1. If the surety should take a loss, the contractor will find it difficult to ever get another bond.

2. Since the surety is indemnified, the contractor loses control of expenditures in the event of a takeover but not the legal obligation to pay the surety back for them. As long as they can maintain operations, contractors naturally prefer to spend their money themselves rather than have the surety or the owner spend it for them.

LABOR AND MATERIAL PAYMENT BONDS

Private construction contracts are subject to **mechanic's lien** laws, which enable subcontractors or suppliers to file liens, or legal claims, against the project property if they are not paid by the owner's contractor for their services or furnished materials. Payment bonds assure that such persons or entities are paid by the surety if the contractor/principals refuse or are unable to pay. If there is no bond and liens are perfected—where, through a lawsuit, liability to pay the amount of the lien is established by a court—owners have to pay the claimant to avoid having their property sold to satisfy the lien. For this reason, private owners want payment bonds.

A mechanic's lien cannot be placed against federal government or other public property. However, at the federal level, and in most states, public policy demands that subcontractors and suppliers on public projects be paid for their work. Thus, Congress has enacted the Miller Act, and many of the state legislatures have enacted "Little Miller Acts," both of which, among other things, require labor and material payment bonds on public construction contracts, federal and state respectively.

Labor and Material Payment Bond Guarantee and Claimants

The guarantee of a **labor and material payment bond** is the surety's promise that it pays claimants if the principal is unable or refuses to pay them. To understand the guarantee depends on understanding the definition of a **claimant.** For a person or entity to be a proper claimant, a number of conditions must be met.

First, a construction contract between the principal and the obligee must exist, and this contract must be referenced in the bond. The bond then defines claimants as those persons or entities who have contracts with the principal to perform services or furnish materials on the project pursuant to the principal's construction contract with the obligee. Thus, someone who wants to collect on a payment bond must first be sure that this requirement is satisfied—that is, that the claimant has a contract with the principal who, in turn, has a contract with the obligee. Some payment bonds go further, including as claimants those persons or entities who have contracts with other entities that, in turn, have contracts with the principal.

In the case of federal contracts for which a Miller Act bond is required, sub-subcontractors and material suppliers to subcontractors of the principal are also treated as claimants. So are material suppliers to sub-subcontractors. Material suppliers to the principal are always considered to be claimants. However, second-tier material suppliers to first-tier material suppliers who hold a purchase order contract with the principal do not qualify.

The federal practice is mirrored in the laws of some states, as the following Kansas case illustrates. The City of Wichita awarded a prime contract to a general contractor for construction of a sewage digester. The general contractor (Penta) then awarded a contract to Wells Products Corp. for furnishing the digester floating cover and gas compressor system. Penta also furnished a public works payment and performance bond in accordance with the Kansas "Little Miller Act" statute. Wells Products Corp. failed to pay J. W. Thompson Co., one of its suppliers, who then brought a claim against the prime contract payment bond. As in federal contracts, Kansas public works payment bonds protect only suppliers to subcontractors, not suppliers to suppliers. It, therefore, became important for the trial court to decide whether Wells Products Corp. functioned as a subcontractor or as a supplier to Penta. J. W. Thompson Co., who was, in effect, a second-tier supplier, argued that Wells Products Corp. had furnished personnel on site for the purpose of assisting in adjusting and starting up the equipment and, therefore, was functioning as a subcontractor. The prime contractor claimed that the agreement with Wells Products Corp. was a sales agreement since the actual contract evidenced all of the "trappings" of a sales agreement and contained none of the clauses usually found in subcontracts. The trial court concluded that Wells Products Corp. was a subcontractor, making J. W. Thompson Co. a proper claimant under the prime contract labor and material payment bond. The Kansas Supreme Court reversed the trial court, deciding instead that Wells was a material supplier, not a subcontractor. The Kansas Supreme Court stated:

> Modern conditions frequently demand a high degree of specialization in manufacturers and suppliers. The facts that Wells had the duties to inspect Penta's installation of the components purchased from Wells, to be present at the start up, and to instruct the City of Wichita employees on the use of the gas compressor system were key factors in the trial court's conclusion that Wells was in fact a subcontractor. But it is clear that such activities are common in the construction of sophisticated systems.

Since J. W. Thompson Co. was determined by the Kansas Supreme Court to be a supplier to a supplier, they could not recover against the payment bond.[1]

This case illustrates that, in claims against labor and material payment bonds, the determination of who qualifies as a claimant and who doesn't can become a very complicated matter that will be decided based on the specific facts in each case and on the statutes that apply in the particular jurisdiction involved. The specific wording of the bond itself is also very important in defining who may qualify as a claimant.

Claimant status, in and of itself, does not guarantee the right to recovery under the bond. Although the wording of individual bonds may differ, most generally require that additional tests be met. Claimants must prove that they have not been paid within a period of time stated in the bond after completing services or furnishing materials and that the services or the materials they furnished were **used or reasonably required in the performance of the construction contract.** The phrase "used or reasonably required" originally meant literally "bricks and mortar in place at the site of the work," and courts would exclude such items as the delivery costs of materials because they were not incurred on the work site. Modern courts tend to construe the meaning of the phrase more broadly, but many cost items are still excluded. For example, the overhead expense of a home office, expense of estimating material and subcontract quotations, and cost of negotiating and preparing purchase orders and subcontract agreements are ordinarily excluded.

OTHER FIRST-TIER BONDS

A number of less common first-tier bonds are also used in the construction industry.

Work Guarantee Bonds

In a **work guarantee bond,** the surety guarantees that the completed construction work of the principal will meet the requirements of a warranty contained in the contract. A roofing bond, for example, could be written with respect to an explicit warranty stated in the contract that the completed roof will not leak or require replacement for a minimum of five years after it is accepted by the owner. Such contracts sometimes permit the owner to hold part of the retention until the end of the warranty period. By putting up a bond, the contractor can secure the release of the retained funds. The specific guarantee of this bond is that, if the roof leaks and the contractor either cannot or will not return and repair it, the surety will pay the cost of repairs.

---

[1] *J. W. Thompson Co. v. Wells Products Corp.,* 758 P.2d 738 (Kan. 1988).

Lien Discharge Bonds

In a **lien discharge bond,** the surety guarantees that the principal pays the obligee in the event that the obligee is compelled at some future date to satisfy a lien placed on the facility constructed by the project because the principal had not paid the lien claimant. A prime contractor who refused payment to a supplier or subcontractor who had filed a lien because of a dispute over that party's performance would obtain a lien discharge bond. This bond protects the owner against a possible adverse judgment on the lien placed on the owner's property by the subcontractor or supplier. Therefore, the owner need not withhold money from the final payment to the prime contractor to protect its interests. If the contractor had previously furnished a payment bond, the owner already has that guarantee and would not require an additional lien discharge bond.

SUBCONTRACT BONDS AND MATERIAL SUPPLIER BONDS

All of the bonds previously discussed have been first-tier bonds. Many possible lower levels, or tiers, of contracts can relate to the same project. For example, the prime contractor's subcontractor may subcontract a portion of the subcontract work to yet another entity. This situation gives rise to the need for subcontract **second-tier bonds** and sub-subcontract **third-tier bonds.**

Typically, the first-tier bonds that can be obtained for lower tiers are **subcontract performance bonds** and **subcontract labor and material payment bonds**. Each serves the same purposes and operates in the same general manner for lower tiers as for the first tier. Essentially, the parties simply change seats and shift down one tier. For example, in the case of a subcontract performance bond, the contractor becomes the obligee instead of the owner, the subcontractor becomes the principal instead of the contractor, and so on. The surety position would remain the same as for a first-tier bond. The wording of lower-tier bonds differs slightly from that of first-tier bonds, but they operate the same way.

Material supplier bonds are another example of lower-tier bonds that are available. Generally, they are intended to cover claims from a subcontractor (or material supplier) against a material supplier holding a material supply contract with the prime contractor. If such material suppliers fail to pay their own material suppliers or subcontractors, the surety would respond.

Determining the need for lower-tier bonds requires business judgment as well as legal advice from attorneys knowledgeable in the bonding field.

CONCLUSION

This chapter explained that surety bonds are very different than insurance policies in that they are essentially hired guarantees rather than protection from the consequences of some physical catastrophe. Relevant surety bond terms and the way in which surety bonds work were then discussed. The details of operation of the bonds in common construction industry use followed, including subcontract and material supplier bonds.

The following Chapter 10, on construction joint-venture agreements, concludes the examination of the normal industry contracts that are closely related to the prime construction contract.

QUESTIONS AND PROBLEMS

1. What is a surety? Who is a principal? An obligee? What is the general nature of a surety bond guarantee? What is a penal sum? The premium? Who is an indemnitor?

2. How do surety bonds work? What is the essence of a surety bond? What is an indemnity agreement?

3. How do surety bonds differ from insurance contracts?

4. What is the primary requirement for an entity to serve as a surety? What belief must a surety hold with regard to a principal before the surety will furnish a bond?

5. What is the purpose of a bid bond? What does the guarantee of the bond promise? What are the two parts of a bid bond guarantee? What are two ways of stating the penal sum for bid bonds? Which way is more common?

6. What is the purpose of a performance bond? What does the guarantee of the bond promise? What fact must be clearly established before a surety can properly be expected to make good on the guarantee?

7. What three options does a surety normally have once it becomes convinced that the principal is in default? Which options are more commonly utilized? When the surety agrees to pay money to the obligee, what two alternate means are used to determine the surety's obligation? Which of these latter two methods is the more common? What is the top limit of the surety's obligation in any case?

8. What is the misconception that owners sometimes hold about performance bonds? Is the surety as likely to act to cure an alleged default if the principal is financially strong and has the means to cure the default? Why not? What is another factor that a surety will carefully consider in making the decision on whether to cure an alleged default? If an owner is legally correct in alleging that the principal is in default, will recovery under the bond ultimately be realized?

9. Even when the surety agrees to cure a default by paying the owner/obligee money, under what two circumstances could the owner be paid less money than the excess costs expended in completing the contract?

10. What is a typical construction contractor's mindset in regard to bonding capacity? Why will contractors at all costs try to avoid a surety's taking over performance of their contract?

11. What is the reason that labor and materials payment bonds are required by owners on projects subject to mechanic's lien laws? Why are they required on public contracts that are not lienable? What are the Miller Act and "Little Miller Acts"? What do they provide with regard to payment bonds?

12. What is the guarantee of a labor and materials payment bond? Who is a claimant? What does an entity who has not been paid have to establish in order to be considered a claimant?

13. Payment can be claimed for what kind of things under a payment bond? What did the words "used or reasonably required" originally mean to courts? What do the words mean today?

14. What is a work guarantee bond? How is it used? What is the guarantee? Answer the same three questions with respect to a lien discharge bond. What are second-tier bonds? What are the shifts in position of the various parties from first-tier bonds to second-tier bonds?

15. A contractor entered into a $6,755,000 subcontract with a subcontractor, who furnished a performance bond of 100% of the subcontract price. After the contractor paid the subcontractor $5,252,000 for work completed, the subcontractor became bankrupt, and the contractor terminated the subcontract for default. With the agreement of the surety, the contractor engaged another subcontractor who completed the work of the original subcontract for a total additional cost to the contractor of $3,927,000. The work was completed 185 calendar days later than the subcontractor was contractually bound to complete the original subcontract. The liquidated damages for the original subcontract were $1,500 per calendar day.

    The subcontractor's surety refused to pay the amount of its normal obligation on the grounds that the contractor had grossly overpaid the subcontractor for work completed. The contractor sued the surety. At the trial, the court determined that the contractor had, in fact, overpaid the subcontractor prior to the default by $1,403,000.

    a. What is the actual unpaid balance of the subcontract in dollars at the time of the default?

    b. What should the unpaid balance have been in dollars at the time of the default according to the ruling of the court?

    c. What would the surety's monetary liability in dollars have been if the court had ruled that there had been no overpayment to the subcontractor prior to the default?

    d. What was the surety's monetary liability in dollars in view of the court's actual decision?

10

Joint-Venture Agreements

Key Words and Concepts

Joint and several liability
Conventional joint ventures
Item joint ventures
Formation and termination of joint
   ventures
Agreement on terms of bid
Participation formula
General management matters
Managing partner
Management fees
Management committee
Working capital

Capital calls
Failure to meet capital calls
Return of capital
Investment of excess funds
Accounting matters
Bond and indemnification matters
Insurance
Bankruptcy of a partner
Equipment acquisition provisions
Item/conventional joint-venture
   similarities and differences

Two or more construction contractors sometimes compete for a particular project as a joint venture by pooling their resources and sharing the risk and potential profit. Several factors make this practice attractive. Joint venturing may make it possible for a single contractor to participate in a bid on a project that would otherwise be too large a risk. Since each partner in a construction joint venture usually prepares an independent cost estimate for the performance of the project, risk is reduced by basing the joint-venture bid on more than a single cost estimate—that is, two (or more) heads are better than one.

To submit a joint-venture bid, two or more contractors form a new and separate legal entity to submit the bid and, if the joint-venture bid is successful, this entity then executes the ensuing construction contract. The concept is not unlike that of a partnership between individuals, except that entire companies are involved as partners.

When a joint-venture entity submits a successful bid, a series of issues are created that affect both the owner of the project and the joint-venture partner companies. For instance, who is responsible to the owner for contract performance? Who is liable in the event of a default? The partners, in turn, need to decide how liability as well as profits are to be shared between them, where they get their working capital, who will direct the day-by-day activities on the job, who will own the joint venture's assets, and what will happen if an individual partner cannot or will not meet its obligations to the other partners.

The subject of this chapter—the joint-venture agreement—is the construction industry document that addresses these concerns. This agreement is a contractor's contract. Although it refers to the owner and the prime construction contract to which the joint-venture entity and the owner are the parties, it is not a flow-down agreement. Usually, the joint-venture agreement will predate the prime contract.

JOINT AND SEVERAL LIABILITY

The fundamental principle behind joint-venture agreements is that the partners agree to be jointly and severally liable with respect to the duties, obligations, and liabilities of the joint venture. **Joint and several liability** means to each partner company that, if the other partners are unable or unwilling to meet their share of joint-venture obligations, each partner company can be held liable, not only for that partner's share but also for the other partners' shares as well—for the joint venture's total obligation. Without joint and several liability, owners would not award construction contracts to joint ventures.

CONVENTIONAL V. ITEM JOINT VENTURES

Two basic types of joint-venture arrangements are common in the construction industry: **conventional joint ventures** and **item joint ventures.** In a conventional joint venture, the partners (two or more in number) agree to share benefits and liabilities according to a participation formula, with each partner accepting its specified share of each according to the formula (subject to the previously explained principle of joint and several liability). Usually, in a conventional joint venture, the actual on-site construction work will be performed by the field forces of just one of the partners. The cost of providing the field forces and other costs of actual construction are charged to the joint venture. In item joint ventures, each partner (usually only two) agrees to be responsible for a separate physical part of the contract work. Each partner constructs that separate part with their own individual field forces according to the contract specifications, incurs separate costs, and retains payment for that part of the work from the owner. One partner may profit while the other suffers a loss. The partners do not mutually share the risks and benefits of the total contract. Rather, each accepts the risks and benefits accruing to each separate part of the contract. The aforesaid arrangements are internal between the partners. There is still only one joint-venture entity responsible to the owner for the total project, and there is still joint and several liability.

A common example where item joint ventures are used is a highway construction contract that contains heavy grading and paving work and bridge work. A grading and paving contractor who does not do bridge work may form an item joint venture with a bridge builder who does not do heavy grading and paving. If the joint-venture bid is successful, the grading and paving contractor will perform the grading and paving work, while the bridge contractor performs the bridge work. This arrangement permits bidding without depending on subcontract bids and can result in certain advantages.

CONVENTIONAL JOINT VENTURES

The mode of operation of a conventional joint venture is that of a single independent entity, with its own assets, bank accounts, books of account, and management structure. The joint-venture agreement should contain the following key provisions, which define this mode of operation.

Formation and Termination Matters

The **formation** section of the agreement normally states that the joint venture is formed for the purpose of submitting a bid for some specific project named in the agreement and, if the bid is successful, to enter into a contract for the project with the owner and construct the project according to the terms of the contract. It should be made clear that the agreement is limited to the single project stated in the agreement and that the agreement expires when the project is completed and all of the terms of the joint-venture agreement have been fulfilled. In other words, the agreement does not create a permanent marriage between the partners, nor is the agreement intended to place any limitation on other business of any of the partners.

The agreement also normally states that each partner in the joint venture is responsible for that partner's pre-bid expense incurred in investigating the project and preparing an independent cost estimate on which to base the bid.

The agreement provides that no bid shall be submitted until and unless all the partners **agree on the terms of the bid.** Further, the agreement provides that if a partner disagrees with the terms of the bid, they may withdraw from the joint venture at that point, permitting the remaining partners to continue with the bid.

Once the agreement has been signed and the partners start preparing their bid for the project, a partner who decides to withdraw is precluded by the terms of the agreement from either submitting a separate individual bid for the named project or from becoming a member of another joint venture that submits a separate bid for the same project.

The joint venture created as a result of the agreement constitutes a completely separate legal entity that will exist throughout the entire life of the agreement. That entity must have a legal name-style in order to do business, and the agreement includes this agreed-upon name-style.

The agreement states the **termination provisions** applying to the joint venture. The purpose of these provisions is to establish what happens after the joint venture submits its bid if the bid is not successful and, alternatively, what happens if the bid is successful and a construction contract is awarded to the joint venture. The agreement normally provides that, if no contract is awarded, the agreement expires and has no further force and effect. In the event of a contract award, the agreement remains in effect until each and every provision of that contract has been carried out. Provisions are also included that apply after completion of the construction contract, such as those dealing with disposition of the assets of the joint venture.

The provisions dealing with the assets of the joint venture usually state that no partner will accrue any right to any of the joint-venture assets until the construction contract with the owner has been fully completed according to its terms. The agreement then details the specifics for the division of assets among the partners when the construction contract has been completed. These normally provide that the liquid assets will be distributed to the partners according to the participation formula stated elsewhere in the agreement and that nonliquid assets be sold at auction and the proceeds similarly distributed. Any remaining nonliquid assets are then usually distributed to the partners as the partners may agree at that time.

Participation Percentages

A conventional joint-venture agreement must establish how partners share the assets and liabilities of the joint venture. A **participation formula** must be stated defining the proportional share of each partner in percentages, which total 100% for all of the partners.

Since partners are jointly and severally bound to the owner, if one or more partners should refuse or be unable to meet their proportional share of any liability that the joint venture may have, the remaining partners are required to make up the delinquent partner's share as well as meet their own obligation. Because of this possibility, the agreement provides for cross-indemnification for losses, wherein each partner furnishes indemnification to the other partners for any losses suffered by any of them because that partner failed to meet its full share of any liabilities. This indemnification permits partners who had to pay more than their proportionate shares of a loss, because of another partner's failure to pay, to get their money back eventually, as long as the delinquent partner has any assets or later comes into any assets.

General Management Matters

Another major section of a conventional joint-venture agreement deals with **general management matters,** which include at least five separate general management areas:

1. The agreement must provide the name of the **managing partner.** Usually, the managing partner is the partner company that has the largest participation percentage and provides the field organization that performs the actual construction work of the contract.

2. The agreement defines the authority of the managing partner. This authority gives the managing partner the ability to legally obligate the joint-venture entity and to designate the individual who will occupy the position of project manager. The project manager usually is a proven member of the managing partner's permanent organization but can be any person satisfactory to the managing partner.

3. The agreement should deal with the often contentious subject of a **management fee** to be paid to the managing partner (on and above their share of the joint-venture profit) for furnishing the field forces and managing the project. Some agreements provide that the managing partner will not receive a fee. Others may provide that the managing partner receive a fixed fee stated in the agreement, regardless of whether the joint venture makes a profit. This latter arrangement, where the fee is unrelated to profit, is not popular since many contractors feel that it is inequitable for the managing partner to be paid a fee when the joint venture fails to make a profit (or incurs a loss). Consequently, a more common method is for the management fee to be dependent on the profit earned by the joint venture. Under this arrangement, the managing partner is paid a fee equal to a stated percentage of the total joint-venture profit prior to the distribution of the remaining profit to the partners according to the participation formula. For instance, consider the following specific case:

$$\text{Partner} \quad A \text{ (managing partner)} \quad 60\% \text{ participation}$$
$$B \quad 25\% \text{ participation}$$
$$C \quad 15\% \text{ participation}$$

The management fee for the managing partner is 10%. The total joint-venture profit = \$3,500,000. This would result in the following profit distribution:

A's share: $0.10 \times \$3,500,000 + 0.60 \times (0.90 \times \$3,500,000)$

$\qquad = \$350,000 + \$1,890,000 \qquad = \$2,240,000$

B's share: $0.25 \times (0.90 \times \$3,500,000) \qquad = \qquad \$787,500$

C's share: $0.15 \times (0.90 \times \$3,500,000) \qquad = \qquad \$472,500$

Total: $\qquad \$3,500,000$

Obviously, the greater the joint-venture profit, the greater the management fee taken off the top prior to the distribution of the balance. If no profit or a loss results, there will be no management fee.

4. The agreement normally establishes a **management committee** to set joint-venture policy for the guidance of the project manager. The authority of the committee, the committee's meeting schedule, and the voting rights of the partners in making committee decisions will generally be set forth.

5. Joint-venture agreements sometimes delineate specific tasks or services to be performed by a partner for the benefit of the joint venture for which the partner will be paid directly. Such payments are considered to be normal costs of the joint venture. Common examples include data-processing services performed in the managing partner's home office or design engineering services for project temporary structures performed in the home office of one of the partners. In these cases, the agreement may also state the dollar value of the compensation to be paid for such services.

Some agreements provide that each partner bill the joint venture each month for an amount equal to their proportionate share of 10% of the revenue received by the joint venture from the owner for that month and that these amounts be paid out to each partner as compensation for that partner's home office general and administrative effort chargeable to the joint venture. Such a provision in the joint-venture agreement is then advanced as support for a 10% charge on all construction contract change orders to meet the expenses of each partners' home office general and administrative management effort.

Working Capital Matters

Three main points dealing with **working capital** should be addressed in a conventional joint-venture agreement. The first, the **capital call,** is a request made from time to time by the managing partner for each partner to contribute funds to the joint venture for operating capital. The partners are required to respond to capital calls by contributing their proportionate share of the total call. When a call is made, a date is set by which all contributions must be received.

The second point deals with the consequences of a partner's refusal or **failure to meet a capital call.** Specific agreements vary but generally provide that from that point onward the delinquent partner loses all voting rights and all rights to a share of the joint-venture profits until the delinquency is made up. Under some agreements, delinquent partners lose all rights permanently. However, delinquent partners are not relieved of their share of the joint-venture's full liabilities. These potential liabilities flow to the partners as result of each partner signing the joint-venture agreement and, if such joint-venture liabilities eventually occur, they can only be discharged by partners paying their proportionate shares.

The third point deals with the **return of capital** to the partners. Conventional joint-venture agreements typically provide that the joint venture only retain funds sufficient to guarantee the ability to meet all future liabilities. In other words, the joint-venture management will not retain funds in excess of reasonable needs. A prudent joint-venture management committee will construe this provision very conservatively, particularly in situations where, because of front-end loading, the joint venture's earnings from contract work are disproportionally high in relation to the cost of the work performed. Unanticipated costs later in the job may require the expenditure of those funds, and an imprudent partner may have committed them elsewhere and be unable to respond to the capital call asking for their return. For this reason, some joint-venture agreements specify that no excess funds be distributed until the project work is completed. This latter provision is viewed by some as overly conservative and is less frequently used than simply providing for distribution of funds in "excess of reasonable needs." Additional provisions in this section typically deal with such matters as how the joint venture will report income for tax purposes, where options are permitted by the tax laws, conditions under which a partner may borrow from the joint venture against its share of equity, and requirements **for the prudent and conservative investment of excess funds** in interest-bearing securities, pending eventual distribution to the partners.

Accounting Matters

A conventional joint-venture agreement must also deal with at least six separate **accounting matters:**

1. The partners must agree on the bank or banks where the joint-venture bank accounts are to be established. The joint-venture agreement should either list the banks or provide a means for their selection.

2. The agreement should provide that separate books of account be set up for all necessary joint-venture accounting records and that joint-venture accounts must not intermingle with the accounts of any other business entity, particularly those of any of the partners.

3. The agreement should state the required frequency of financial reports to the partners, normally monthly.

4. The tax reporting declaration, where there is an option, should be stated in the agreement.

5. The agreement should contain a fiscal year declaration fixing the starting and ending dates of the particular fiscal year for the joint venture agreed on by the partners.

6. If a home office charge by the managing partner for the provision of data-processing and accounting services is intended, in addition to the management fee, the agreement should so provide.

Bond and Indemnification Matters

A number of provisions in conventional joint-venture agreements deal with **bond and indemnification matters.** Three main points are of interest:

1. Usually only one package of bonds is put up by the joint venture, in which the agreed-upon name-style of the joint venture appears as principal. The sureties of the several partners, through internal indemnification agreements among themselves, arrange for one of the sureties to furnish the necessary guarantees on the bonds and to sign the bonds as surety. For all of this to occur, each partner has to indemnify its individual surety for its proportionate share of the contract. Such indemnifications may involve personal indemnifications by the owners and/or officers of the individual contractor partners.

2. When personal indemnifications are required by a partner's surety, a prudent joint-venture partner will insist that similar personal indemnifications be furnished to all of the other partners as well. Therefore, many joint-venture agreements provide that such "like indemnifications" be given by each partner to each of the others.

3. Bond brokerage fees on large contracts can be sizeable. Since the brokers of all of the partners are usually involved to some degree, the total brokerage commission is sometimes split among them in proportion to the partners' participation percentages. Some joint-venture agreements provide for this.

Insurance Matters

Conventional joint-venture agreements also contain provisions regarding **insurance.** Since the joint venture is going to be a separate, independent operating entity, the joint venture name-style appears as the insured on all the normal insurance policies discussed in Chapter 8. The joint-venture agreement insurance provisions deal with five main points:

1. All partners in the joint venture should be named as additional named insureds on all joint-venture insurance policies. Otherwise, partners can be sued individually regarding a joint-venture matter and required to defend such suits and pay any judgments that are entered against them without any joint-venture insurance protection.

2. Many joint-venture partner companies do not want the insurance company to have subrogation rights. (See discussion of subrogation in Chapter 8.) If this is the case, the joint-venture agreement should require that the insurance company's subrogation rights be waived.

3. The added protection of a completed operations endorsement with third-party liability insurance was discussed in Chapter 8. The joint-venture agreement should require that this endorsement be included with the joint-venture's third-party liability policy.

4. When the prime construction contract requires the joint venture to indemnify the owner and architect/engineer, the joint-venture agreement should provide that the joint-venture's third-party liability insurance policy be written with

the owner and architect/engineer named as additional named insureds for the reason explained in Chapter 8.

5. Joint-venture insurance policies should be written to cover the use of partner-furnished construction equipment rented to the joint venture so that the individual partners who actually own the equipment are protected.

Partner Bankruptcy Provisions

The typical conventional joint-venture agreement also contains provisions dealing with the unhappy event of the **bankruptcy of one or more of the partners.** First, the agreement normally provides that bankrupt partners will immediately lose rights to all further profit and all management committee rights but are not relieved of their share of liability.

The agreement also provides that surviving partners assume the bankrupt partner's share of any further joint-venture profits, pro rata to the surviving partner's original shares, and then complete the construction contract according to its terms.

Construction Equipment Acquisition and Disposal

Comprehensive conventional joint-venture agreements deal with the problems of how, and from where, the joint venture will obtain the necessary construction equipment to construct the project through its **equipment acquisition provisions.** The value of the necessary equipment acquisitions can run to many millions of dollars for large projects.

A comprehensive agreement provides for acquisition of the equipment as determined by the management committee in one of three basic ways:

1. The partners may contribute the necessary cash for the joint venture to purchase new or used equipment outright from third parties.
2. Some or all of the equipment may be purchased from one or more of the partners at sale prices to be mutually agreed upon. An alternate form of purchase from a partner includes a guaranteed buy-back agreement at the end of the project. With this arrangement, it is often also specified that the original sale price and the buy-back price be determined by an independent equipment appraiser.
3. The equipment may be rented, either from one or more of the partners or from third parties at rental rates to be approved by the joint-venture management committee. A related provision is that when equipment rented from one of the partners is damaged when in use by the joint venture, such damage will be repaired at the expense of the joint venture, normal wear and tear excepted.

ITEM JOINT VENTURES

The mode of operation for item joint ventures (usually only two partners) is that each partner operates as a separate company. The partners have little in common except a common name-style and common contract bonds furnished to the owner. Each partner has separate assets, bank accounts, books of account, and profits or losses. The item joint-venture agreement provides the specifics of the key arrangements between the partners.

Comparisons with Conventional Joint-Venture Agreements

Item joint ventures are similar to conventional joint ventures in the following ways:

- The partners of item joint ventures are jointly and severally bound to the owner under common contract bonds.
- There will be a single management interface with the owner, and the item joint-venture agreement indicates which joint-venture partner will provide this interface.
- The purpose of the item joint-venture agreement states that the agreement is for the purpose of submitting a bid and performing the resulting construction contract if it is awarded.
- The item joint-venture agreement contains provisions similar to conventional joint-venture agreements in dealing with termination in case no contract is awarded, as well as when a contract is awarded.
- The agreement specifies the agreed-upon name-style for the joint venture.
- The provisions of the item joint-venture agreement in regard to pre-bid expense are the same as for conventional joint-venture agreements. Both agreements call for each partner to bear their own pre-bid expense.

Although item joint-venture agreements have many of the same features as conventional joint venture agreements, many other features are different:

- Item joint-venture agreements contain no requirement for common **agreement on terms of the bid.** Instead, the agreement provides that each partner controls the portion of the schedule of bid items pertaining to its own work but has no control of portions of the schedule that pertains to the other partner's work.
- There is no joint-ownership-of-assets provisions in an item joint-venture agreement since each partner maintains full ownership of individual partner assets.
- No common participation in profits or losses is provided for in an item joint-venture agreement. Partners benefit or suffer separately on their own section of the job.

- The item joint-venture agreement provides that the managing partner will control affairs of the other partner only in respect to the necessary interface with the owner and serve only as a necessary administrative conduit. The managing partner is not given the power to bind the other partner legally to anything.

- The item agreement does not provide for a management fee, except for costs of the administrative interface services performed by the managing partner on behalf of the other partner.

- The item joint-venture agreement does not provide for a management committee.

- No common working capital or common books of account, bank accounts, tax returns, or insurance policies are provided for in an item joint-venture agreement. Partners maintain their own.

CONCLUSION

This chapter concluded the discussion of common construction industry contracts by examining construction joint-venture agreements. It explained why contractors enter into joint-venture agreements and introduced the principle of joint and several liability, without which joint ventures could not exist. The chapter examined typical provisions of both conventional and item joint-venture agreements in detail and concluded with a discussion of the similarities and differences between these two types of joint-venture arrangements.

The following two chapters on the subject of the bidding process in the construction industry shift emphasis from the contract documents themselves to how the customs and practices of the industry and past decisions of courts have influenced contract operation and interpretation.

QUESTIONS AND PROBLEMS

1. What reasons for the formation of construction contractor joint ventures were discussed in this chapter? What does "jointly and severally bound" mean? Why is it important with respect to construction joint ventures?

2. What are the two major types of construction joint ventures? What are the distinguishing features of each?

3. With respect to conventional joint-venture agreements, what are the seven aspects of formation and termination matters that were discussed?

4. What is a participation formula for a conventional joint venture? What does cross-indemnification for losses mean? Why is it important?

5. What is meant by the term *managing partner*? What are two important powers normally bestowed on the managing partner by a conventional joint-venture agreement?

6. Discuss two alternate arrangements for the payment of a management fee to the managing partner. Which is generally favored by contractors? Why?

7. What is a joint-venture management committee? How does it usually work? What is its primary function? Is it intended to control the day-by-day management of the work?

8. What are some of the home office services for which a managing partner might reasonably bill the joint venture in addition to any management fee? Why do some joint ventures follow the practice of having each partner bill the joint venture each month for its proportionate share of 10% of the joint-venture revenue for that month?

9. What is a capital call? Is notice generally required? What normally happens if a partner fails to meet a capital call?

10. What is the reason for a joint venture's management committee to be very conservative in returning funds in excess of immediate needs? Why is conservatism in this respect particularly important when a job's payment schedule has been front-end-loaded? What should be done with such excess capital?

11. What are six separate issues regarding accounting matters for conventional joint ventures that should be addressed by a comprehensive joint-venture agreement?

12. What are the three separate aspects of bond and indemnification matters that were discussed in this chapter with regard to conventional joint-venture agreements?

13. What were the five main points made with regard to insurance matters?

14. What two consequences will follow the bankruptcy of a conventional joint-venture partner?

15. What are three ways for a conventional joint venture to obtain construction equipment?

16. What are six similarities between conventional joint-venture agreements and item joint-venture agreements? What are seven differences between the two kinds of agreements?

17. Contractor *A*, contractor *B*, and contractor *C* are in a conventional joint venture with shares of 55%, 25%, and 20%, respectively. Contractor *A* is the sponsor with a management fee equal to 7½% of any profits of the joint venture. All capital calls are met by all partners. On completion, the job has made a $2,750,000 profit prior to any distributions.

   a. What is the total amount that each partner will receive from the job?
   b. If contractor *B* failed to respond to any capital calls, what would be the total amount that each partner would receive from the job?
   c. If contractor *B* failed to respond to any capital calls and, instead of making a profit of $2,750,000, the job incurred a loss of $200,000, what is each partner's liability for the loss?

11

Bids and Proposals

Key Words and Concepts

Public/private sectors
Difference in bid rules
Bidding statutes
Bid document addendum
Purpose of bidding statutes
Influence of the federal policy
Requirements of the United States Code
Public owner's compliance with bidding
   rules
Material impropriety
Factual determination of low bid
Unit prices
Written price extensions

Bid total
Alternate bids
Responsive bidder
Responsible bidder
Late bids
Rejection of all bids
Irregularities and informalities
Bidder's property right to the contract
Bid protests
Status
Timeliness
Successful protests
Right to reject all bids not absolute

The first ten chapters of this book deal with specific types of contracts that are widely used in the industry. From here on, the focus will be on the customs and practices of the industry and with past decisions of our courts that govern how these contracts operate and how they are interpreted. Chapter 11 is the first of two chapters on the subject of bids and proposals.

PUBLIC AND PRIVATE SECTOR BIDDING

Bidding practices of the **public** and **private sectors** of the industry differ tremendously. The term *public* in this context means that the construction work is financed by public funds in the form of tax dollars or the proceeds from the sale of municipal, state, or federal bonds.

Public and private work have **different bid rules.** Public construction contracts are advertised and let in accordance with the **bidding statutes** and other legislatively mandated rules of the particular governmental entity that is paying for the construction work. For instance, when the work is financed with federal funds, the laws and regulations promulgated by federal agencies and bodies govern the process of advertising and awarding construction contracts. Similarly, state, county, and municipal governments have statutes and regulations that govern when their funds are used to pay for the cost of the work. In addition, special governmental or quasi-governmental bodies such as sewer or rapid transit districts are often established by special enabling legislation. The enabling legislation usually provides definitive rules for advertising and awarding the construction contracts required to carry out the mission of the particular special body involved.

Unlike public owners, private owners can establish whatever rules that they want. They also can change the rules at will with the result that these rules are not necessarily observed. Although the public owner has the ability to set particular rules and to change them by issuing an addendum to the bidding documents, this power is severely regulated. A **bid document addendum** is a modification to the bidding documents formally issued by the owner to all holders of bidding documents before bids are received. In the public sector, there must be a reasonable time period from the issue date of the last addendum issued and the date of the bid opening to ensure that all bidders have sufficient time to reflect properly the import of the addendum in their bids. Bidders are required to list on the bid form all addenda received for their bids to be considered responsive. Failure to list addenda may result in the bid being rejected.

In the private sector anything can happen, whereas in the public sector the result will usually be that the job will be awarded to the lowest "responsive" and "responsible" bidder. These terms have important special meanings that will be discussed later in this chapter.

PUBLIC BIDDING STATUTES

The requirements of the federal, state, and local bidding statutes and resulting regulations make the outcome of the bidding process in the public sector very predictable compared to the private sector. The **purposes of public bidding statutes** are:

1. To protect public funds. In other words, bidding statues are designed to ensure that the public pays the minimum possible price for construction work determined by open competitive bidding.

2. To protect and ensure a continuation of the free enterprise system upon which the political and economic structure of the United States is founded.

The public bidding statutes are stringently written and enforced to ensure that public sector construction contracting remains honest. Increasingly, those who violate the rules find themselves subject to both civil and criminal liability. Errant construction companies have been assessed large fines and their owners or officers sent to prison along with the corrupt public officials who have been caught, tried, and convicted of violating the public trust.

Federal Construction Contract Procurement Policy

Because numerous separate statutes regulate the public bidding and contract award process for different public owners, a discussion of specific rules that may apply in a particular case is not practical. However, examining the federal construction contract procurement policy, which is broadly reflected throughout all public construction work in the United States today, will help in understanding the basic principles behind most bidding statutes. The **influence of the federal government policy** has been enormous, and the federal contracting rules serve as a model for the rest of the public sector. Therefore, understanding the major federal rules will aid in understanding the general requirements of public sector bidding and contract award at most other levels.

The federal rules set forth in the *United States Code* include the following five broad requirements:

1. There must be sufficient advertising time between the first advertisement of the bid and the bid opening so that prospective bidders know about the project and have sufficient opportunity to prepare their bids.

2. The bidding documents must be sufficiently clear and detailed to assure free and open competition. The purpose of this requirement is to assure that each bid received represents a price tendered by each individual bidder to construct the identical project.

3. There must be a public bid opening and a public reading of all bids received at the date, time, and place stated in the bid advertisement. This requirement ensures that every person present at the bid opening has the opportunity to hear the bid prices tendered by the various bidders. It follows from this requirement that the contents of all the bids received and opened become public knowledge and that any bid received may be examined by any person with a legitimate interest in doing so.

It should be noted in connection with this rule that a procurement procedure leading to a negotiated contract is also permitted by the federal rules and is occasionally employed for certain projects. In these cases, there is no public bid opening, and the government does not publicly divulge the contents of the various proposals received. The procedure requiring a public bid opening and a public reading of all bids received and opened is far more common.

4. The contract must be awarded to the lowest responsive and responsible bidder whose bid is in the best interest of the government. For contracts other than those awarded on a negotiated basis, this requirement will usually be satisfied by the lowest bid received from a responsible bidder that is fully responsive to the terms and conditions of the bidding documents. The requirement also applies to contracts that are negotiated in that the government is required to award the contract to the bidder whose proposal is determined (price and other factors considered) to be in the best interest of the government.

5. All bids may be rejected when rejection is determined to be in the best interest of the government.

When these federal rules are applied to public sector bidding, the usual result will be that the contract is awarded to the lowest responsive, responsible bidder. It matters not that this bidder has no past relationship with the public owner or that the public owner might prefer that another bidder had won the contract. All that matters is that the bidder to whom the job is awarded be the lowest responsible bidder whose bid is responsive to the terms and conditions stated in the bidding documents.

PUBLIC OWNERS' ACTIONS AFTER BIDS RECEIVED

To comply with the basic principles just stated, a public owner will normally take a number of separate actions once bids or proposals have been received for a construction project.

Material Improprieties

A public owner must determine whether there is any **material impropriety** that would preclude award of a public contract. A material impropriety can be anything that is not proper in either the bidding documents or the bidding process. Examples include such acts as bribery, bid rigging, or offering private clarification of bid document requirements to selected bidders, or anything else that would impugn the integrity of the bidding process. A material impropriety can also include unfair or improper resolution of errors or ambiguities in the bidding documents or in the bids received that make it impossible to be certain that each bid is for exactly the same intended work.

Factual Determination of the Low Bid

A public owner must make a **factual determination of the low bid.** This is more complicated than simply noting and recording which bid submitted has the lowest dollar figure written in the space for the total bid price. The public owner must also make certain that the bids received include no arithmetic mistakes or discrepancies, or, if such mistakes or discrepancies are found, that the apparent low bid remains low when they are corrected.

The rules governing the determination of the low bid may be set forth in the bidding statutes applying to the project and are usually stated in the bidding documents themselves. One common question is whether the **unit price** or the **written price extension** determines the intended bid price for a bid item in a schedule-of-bid-items bid when there is a discrepancy between them. Typically, the rules state that the unit price governs. Also, when the price extensions and lump sum prices in a schedule-of-bid-items bid are totaled, they sometimes do not equal the written **bid total.** The normal rule in this situation is that the correct total be substituted for the figure written in the bid form and be considered the bidder's intended bid.

The preceding rules are illustrated by an Alaska case where the State Department of Transportation took bids for grading and drainage work. This project was advertised as a schedule-of-bid-items contract by the Alaska State Department of Transportation. The apparent low bidder was announced at the bid opening, but it was later discovered when the bids were checked that the sixth bidder had made an arithmetical mistake when summing the total of the bid-item extensions. This resulted in an apparent bid total higher than the arithmetical total of all of the bid-item extensions. The Department of Transportation corrected the sixth bidder's arithmetical mistake, making them the low bidder. Over the original low bidder's protest, the contract was awarded to the sixth bidder on the basis of the corrected bid. The low bidder filed suit to set aside the award.

The standard specifications governing the bid provided that, in case of discrepancies between prices written in words and those written in figures, the prices written in words would govern and that, in case of discrepancy between unit bid prices and extensions, unit prices would govern. The original low bidder argued that these provisions did not apply since there was no discrepancy in the sixth bidder's bid between the unit prices written in words or numbers or between the unit prices and the bid-item extensions. The error occurred in the addition of the extensions. The State Department of Transportation argued that if the specifications permitted correcting unit price extensions, the State clearly had the power to correct the addition error in totaling the extensions. The Supreme Court of Alaska agreed that, if the State Department of Transportation was empowered to correct arithmetic errors in bid-item extensions, it was implicitly empowered to correct the arithmetic total of those extensions. Additionally, the court noted that the bid specifications provided that the total of the bid-item extensions was merely for informational and comparative purposes at the bid opening. The unit prices controlled, and the downward correction of the sixth bidder's bid total was proper.[1]

Alternate bids will be considered in making the factual determination of the low bid if the bid documents provide for alternate bids and include the rules for evaluating alternates. These rules must be such that the determination of which bid is low will be a factual and objective process wherein all bidders are treated equally.

---

[1]*Vintage Constr., Inc. v. State Dept. of Transp.,* 713 P.2d 1213 (Alaska 1986).

A final point is that the low bid determination cannot be made on a basis different from that indicated in the bid documents. That is, the public owner cannot change the basis expressly stated or implied by the bid documents for determining the low bid and then make a determination on this changed basis. For instance, if after the bids are opened, the owner alters the bid quantities on a schedule-of-bid-items bid to quantities different from the quantities stated in the bid documents, the order of bidders, low to high, may be drastically altered. Such a practice is strictly prohibited.

The preceding point was convincingly demonstrated to this author in the mid-1970s when a division of his company was the low bidder by a narrow margin on a contract for driving eight 20 ft. diameter tunnels through a railroad embankment. Each tunnel was approximately 300 feet long, and payment was to be made on the basis of a unit price per foot of tunnel actually driven and measured for payment. The bid quantity for the tunnel excavation bid item was stated to be approximately 2,400 feet.

The bid schedule contained one lump sum bid item for mobilization and seven other unit-price bid items, all of them for minor work except for the tunnel excavation bid item, which constituted more than 95% of the work of the project. The specified contract duration was two years. The contract stated that after the expiration of one year, the owner, a medium-sized city, could elect to delete one of the eight tunnels from the contract even though bids were to be submitted for constructing all eight tunnels. This fact resulted in individual bidders distributing fixed indirect costs and anticipated job profit to the individual bid items in a highly variable manner.

At a meeting the day after the bid opening attended by the city engineer, the city attorney, and the author, the city engineer announced that he had determined that, if the city decided after the first year of construction to delete one of the tunnels, which the city engineer considered to be likely, the author's company would become the third bidder on the basis of seven tunnels even though we were the low bidder on the basis of the as-advertised eight tunnels. The city engineer then indicated his inclination to award the construction contract on the basis of the seven-tunnel scenario. Before I had an opportunity to voice my objection, the city attorney interrupted, advising the city engineer in no uncertain terms that such an act on the city's part would be illegal and would not receive the support of the city attorney's office. The matter was thereupon immediately dropped, and the discussion shifted to details germane to award of the contract on the basis of our bid. Bids for public work must be evaluated on the basis advertised in the bid documents, not on some other basis.

Responsive and Responsible Bidders

The public owner must make a separate determination that the low bidder is both a *responsive bidder* and a *responsible bidder*. These terms sound like much the same thing but are, in fact, very different.

A **responsive bidder** is one who has filled out and signed the bid forms in accordance with the bidding instructions and who has submitted an unqualified bid in full conformance with the requirements of the bid documents. There may be no additions or alterations of any kind.

A **responsible bidder** is one who possesses sufficient financial resources to undertake the project and, in addition, has the necessary experience and a track record indicating the ability to execute successfully the work of the contract.

A public contract cannot be properly awarded to a bidder who has not been determined by the public owner to be both responsive and responsible. Bid responsiveness is determined by examination of the bid itself, which cannot be altered by the bidder once it is submitted and opened. On the other hand, bidder responsibility is a matter that the public owner can determine after the bid opening. Both bid responsiveness and bidder responsibility must be conclusively demonstrated to the public owner's satisfaction prior to the award of the contract.

Three federal contract decisions by the Comptroller General of the United States are good examples where low bids were rejected on the grounds that they were nonresponsive. In the first case, the low bidder had submitted a preprinted bid bond that differed materially from the terms of the required bid bond for government contracts.[2]

In the second case, the apparent low bidder submitted a bid bond that contained the following notation:

> If this contract includes the removal of asbestos materials, then this bond is to be null and void.

Removal of asbestos materials was, in fact, required by the contract. Post-bid-opening assurances by the low bidder's bonding company that they would waive the restriction noted in the bond were to no avail in persuading the Comptroller General to consider the bid responsive, since determination of bidder responsiveness is a matter that must be based entirely on the bid as it appeared at the time of the bid opening.[3]

In the third case, the low bid had been declared nonresponsive by the Army Corps of Engineers because the bidder "clarified" the specifications by adding the following statement to the bid:

> Bid based on Army furnishing four voice-grade phone lines to building 9370.

The Comptroller General supported the Corps' determination of nonresponsiveness stating:

> By qualifying its bid, Howard has attempted to shield itself from responsibilities from which other bidders would not be similarly protected. Since the phone lines at issue will be required under the contract, Howard's clarification has the effect of shifting these costs to the Army. We therefore find that Howard's bid was properly rejected as nonresponsive.[4]

[2]Matter of *Allgood Electric Co.* Comp. Gen. No. B-235171 (July 18, 1989).

[3]Matter of *Star Brite Construction Co., Inc.* Comp. Gen. No. B-255206 (February 8, 1994).

[4]Matter of *Howard Electrical & Mechanical, Inc.* Comp. Gen. No. B-228356 (January 6, 1988).

A case where the low bidder was denied the contract on the grounds that they failed to meet the bidder responsibility requirements occurred in New Jersey where the Army Corps of Engineers took bids for a hazardous waste remediation project. The Corps asked the low bidder to provide references as part of the pre-award survey. They then contacted the references provided as well as reviewed internal government records regarding prior projects performed by the bidder. Considerable negative information emerged, including a prior project owner's complaint that the bidder had refused to honor a warranty, an allegation that on a prior contract the bidder had allowed the release of contaminated water and gas, and an incident where the bidder's personnel had been indicted and convicted for submitting false payment requests. Additionally, the low bidder's proposed project manager appeared to lack adequate experience on similar projects. When the government contracting officer determined that the low bidder was a nonresponsible bidder and ineligible for contract award, the low bidder went to court arguing that it had been improperly debarred from government contracting without due process of law. The U.S. District Court for the District of Columbia determined that a rational basis for the government's nonresponsibility determination existed and refused to disturb the contracting officer's finding.[5]

In another case, however, the Comptroller General allowed a bidder to furnish information after the bid opening demonstrating that its proposed subcontractor possessed the required specialized experience. The low bidder had submitted a list of projects performed by its proposed subcontractor, but this list did not meet the five-year experience period required by the specifications. When questioned by the contracting officer after the bid, the low bidder supplied additional information showing earlier projects and was awarded the contract. The second low bidder protested that the low bidder's bid should have been rejected as nonresponsive because complete information had not been supplied with the bid. In rejecting the second bidder's protest, the Comptroller General stated:

> Even though the solicitation provided that a bidder's failure to submit with its bid evidence of compliance with this requirement would render the bid nonresponsive, such a solicitation provision is not effective to convert a matter of responsibility into one of responsiveness. Information concerning a prospective contractor's responsibility may be submitted any time prior to award.[6]

Rejection of Late Bids

A public owner normally must reject bids received after the time specified in the bid documents for submitting bids. The only exception might be when a bidder can show that the lateness in submitting the bid is due to circumstances totally beyond that bidder's control and that accepting the bid would not prejudice the position of

---

[5]*Geo-Con, Inc.,* 853 F.Supp. 537 (D.D.C. 1994).

[6]Matter of *BBC Brown Boveri, Inc.,* Comp. Gen. No. B-227903 (September 28, 1987).

other bidders whose bids were submitted within the time limit. In other words, for a **late bid** to be accepted, it must be determined that the late bidder gained no advantage over competitors as a result of submitting the bid late, such as receiving a last-minute price cut in a major subcontract quotation.

In practice, late bids are usually rejected, but not always. For instance, a New Jersey court permitted the acceptance of a late bid where the bidder had phoned in shortly before the bid opening, advising that it was being delayed by inclement weather and would arrive shortly. The bidder submitted the bid two minutes late, but before any bids had been opened. Under these circumstances, the court judged that permitting the acceptance of the bid and awarding the contract to the late bidder was proper.[7] Similarly, the Comptroller General permitted the acceptance of a late bid because a government representative had directed the bidder to the wrong room. The bidder arrived at the designated place for the bid opening about a minute early. A government representative mistakenly gave the bidder inaccurate information on where the bids were being received. In this case, the tardiness was caused by improper government action, no bids had been opened when the bid was received, and the Comptroller General ruled that the acceptance of the bid and award of the contract was proper.[8]

In spite of occasional exceptions, bidders should assume that bids will be rejected if submitted late.

Rejection of All Bids

Public owners may **reject all bids** upon a determination that rejection is in the public interest. However, once a public owner has rejected all bids, the contract cannot be awarded later unless the entire advertising and bidding process is repeated and entirely new bids are received. Once bids are rejected, they remain rejected.

BID IRREGULARITIES/INFORMALITIES

As previously pointed out, one form of a material impropriety precluding award of a public contract is error or ambiguity in the bids received that make it impossible to determine that each bid is for exactly the same work. Such error and/or ambiguity are known as **bid irregularities** or **informalities.** If a public owner awards a contract on the basis of a bid containing an irregularity or informality, the other bidders may sue to prevent the award of the contract or, if it has already been awarded, to set aside the award. Therefore, it is important to understand what these terms mean and when their presence may disqualify a bid.

---

[7]*William M. Young & Co., Inc. v. West Orange Redeveloping Agency,* 311 A.2d 390 (N.J. Super. A.D. 1973).

[8]Matter of *Baeten Construction Co.*, Comp. Gen. No. B-210681 (August 12, 1983).

Major and Minor Irregularities/Informalities

The terms *bid irregularity* and *bid informality* mean the same thing; both have to do with bidder responsiveness. Essentially, they refer to a deviation from the literal requirements of the bidding instructions in the format and content of a submitted bid. A bid with an irregularity or informality is, by definition, not fully responsive, so the question becomes one of deciding whether the deviation is significant enough to cause the bid to be rejected.

A *major* irregularity or informality means one that has an important effect on the terms of the bid, whereas a *minor* irregularity or informality is one of less significance. A bid containing a major irregularity is required to be rejected, whereas a minor irregularity may be waived by the owner.

Rule for Determining Major or Minor Irregularities

How does the public owner determine whether an irregularity is major or minor? Although there are no universally accepted rules, there *is* one very practical guide that serves to identify a major irregularity or informality. If the irregularity or informality is such that it could reasonably relieve the bidder of the contractual obligations that they assumed by submitting the bid, the irregularity or informality should be deemed major. An obvious example of this type of irregularity or informality is the submittal of an unsigned bid. Since a bidder usually cannot be legally held to the terms of an unsigned bid, this irregularity would probably be considered major, requiring the bid to be rejected even though the bidder may want the owner to accept the bid and award the contract. Other examples of major irregularities are the failure to list subcontractors when such a listing is required by bidding statutes or the failure to include a signed bid bond in the required form with the bid.

An example where a minor informality was waived is afforded by a federal case where the Comptroller General ruled that the low bidder's failure to acknowledge receipt of a bid addendum extending the contract performance time could be waived as a minor informality. The addendum in question changed the contract performance time on a river channel project from 100 calendar days to 130 calendar days. The low bidder failed to acknowledge receipt of the amendment in its bid. The Army Corps of Engineers waived this irregularity and awarded the contract, and the second lowest bidder filed a protest. The Comptroller General noted that failure to acknowledge all addendums usually renders a bid nonresponsive; but when the effect of an addendum is to make the contract requirements less stringent rather than more stringent, failure to acknowledge may be waived as a minor informality.[9]

In another case, however, the Comptroller General ruled that failure of the low bidder to acknowledge receipt of an addendum altering a Davis-Bacon wage rate determination may not be waived and rendered the bid nonresponsive. The low bidder argued that its collective bargaining agreement obligated it to pay Davis-Bacon wages and that its low bid would remain unchanged, with or without the addendum. Therefore, the government should have waived this minor informality.

---

[9]Matter of *Patterson Enterprises Limited,* Comp. Gen. No. B-207105 (August 16, 1982).

The Comptroller General disagreed, stating that Davis-Bacon wage rate determinations exist for the protection of the contractor's employees and their rights may not be waived under any circumstances. Therefore, the low bidder's failure to acknowledge the correction to the Davis-Bacon wage determination was an informality that rendered the bid nonresponsive.[10]

Similarly, the Delaware Supreme Court ruled that subcontractor listing requirements must be strictly followed when receiving bids. On a project for improvements to sewage treatment facilities, the low bidder failed to list the subcontractors that it intended to employ on the project. The Delaware statutes required bidders on state projects to list all subcontractors that would be used. The low bidder had indicated "none" in the space provided for listing the electrical subcontractor. When the State Department of Natural Resources and Environmental Control rejected the bid, the low bidder went to court to have the decision reversed. In upholding the rejection of the bid, the Delaware Supreme Court acknowledged that rejection of the low bid would result in higher costs to the taxpayers but, nonetheless, stated that the state statute reflected a clear legislative intent to prevent "bid shopping and the evils which are said to arise from such a practice." Therefore, the statute must be strictly enforced despite the increased expenditure of public funds.[11]

BIDDER'S PROPERTY RIGHT TO THE CONTRACT

The usual result of the public bidding process, as just described, is that the lowest responsive and responsible bidder is awarded the contract. However, there is no **property right to the potential construction contract** established by the mere fact that a bidder is the low bidder. We have already seen that a bidder must be determined by the public owner to also be responsive and responsible before the contract can be awarded. Even when the low bidder is determined to be both responsive and responsible, the bidder still does not acquire a property right in the potential contract because the owner may reject all of the bids if such an action is in the public interest. Only when the public owner decides to award the contract can the lowest responsive and responsible bidder be thought to have a property right to the contract.

BID PROTESTS

Bid protests are formal objections filed by a bidder to some aspect of the bidding process. They may be objections to the bid document terms and conditions, in which case they should be filed before the bid opening date. Bid protests can also be filed after the bids have been opened to challenge the award of a contract to a low bidder if the protester believed that bid was irregular or improper.

---

[10]Matter of *Bin Construction Co., Inc.*, Comp. Gen. No. B-206526 (June 30, 1982).

[11]*George & Lynch, Inc. v. Division of Parks and Recreation*, 465 A.2d 345 (Del. 1983).

Status to File Bid Protests

Not just anyone has the **status** (standing) to file a bid protest. Who does? Generally, this right is vested in any potential bidder when the protest is lodged prior to the bid opening. Similarly, any actual bidder has status to file a bid protest after the bid opening. There may also be others, but those just cited are always considered to have status.

Timeliness

The **timeliness** of the protest affects its chance of success. Protests concerning the terms and conditions of the bid documents should be made before rather than after the bid opening. Those lodged after the bid opening will probably be to no avail. The further in advance of the bid opening date that such a protest is made, the better chance it will have.

A bid protest regarding the award of the contract should be made as soon as possible after the bid opening and/or the owner's declared intention to make the award.

Protest to Whom?

Bid protests can be directed to the administrative bodies overseeing the particular office of the public owner who is taking bids. Such bodies can be expected to investigate and intervene if the protest is meritorious. Alternatively, bid protests may be directed to a court of law having jurisdiction in the locality where the bids are taken. In that case, the bid protester would seek injunctive action by the court. Also, bid protests may be simultaneously directed to both the agency administrative body and the courts. Typically, the court's decision will prevail—that is, the court may support the protest and order relief with respect to a bid protest that has been previously rejected by the administrative agency involved.

What Can Be Gained by a Bid Protest?

Successful protests depend on both the timing and nature of the protest. For example, when the protest concerns the terms and conditions of the bid documents, a successful protest can result in an injunction issued by a court or administration action on the part of the public owner's parent agency that prevents bids from being taken until the objectionable terms in the bid documents are changed. On the other hand, when the protest concerns the awarding of the contract, a successful protest can result in injunctive or administrative action to prevent the public owner from awarding the contract or to compel cancellation of the original award and re-award of the contract to a named alternative bidder.

A number of years ago, the author's company and another general contractor were each individually certified by a major city to have met all bidder prequalification requirements for a sewer tunnel project funded by the federal Environmental

Protection Agency (EPA). Bidder prequalification was required as a condition for bidding. As frequently happens, the two companies decided during the bidding period to bid together as a joint venture and asked the city to furnish a registered set of bidding documents in the name of the agreed joint venture. The city arrogantly refused to certify the joint venture as meeting prequalification requirements, even though each partner was individually prequalified, and refused to issue the registered set of bid documents that would permit the joint venture to bid.

Such an egregious, arbitrary action clearly has the effect of limiting free and open competition. We therefore immediately lodged an administrative protest with the EPA office disbursing federal funds for the project. After conducting a fact-finding hearing, the EPA froze the funding for the project, delaying the bid opening for over a month. To restore the federal funding, the city was required to rescind their previous action, permitting our joint venture to bid. This result came about only because of the strong protest lodged with the EPA.

The chances of securing the preceding results are much improved by a timely filing of the bid protest. However, it sometimes happens that, due to the time required to resolve the issue, all that can be gained is a "paper victory" or, at best, a recovery of the costs of bid preparation and submittal. For example, if a contract award protest is not resolved until after the contract has been awarded and the work started, a court is not likely to force the owner to cancel the existing contract in midstream and award the balance of the work to the bidder filing the protest. The court may, however, award the protesting bidder damages equal to the bid preparation and submittal costs.

REJECTION OF ALL BIDS IN THE PUBLIC INTEREST

As previously stated, a public owner has the right to reject all bids. However, this **right is not absolute.** There are limitations.

The first limitation is that bids may be properly rejected only after a formal determination or finding that such rejection is in the public interest. This determination cannot be arbitrary and must be based on reasonably compelling grounds. Examples of reasonably compelling grounds would include discovery of major irregularities or informalities in the bidding documents or in the bids received, the low bid exceeding available funds (or, even if within available funds, exceeding the architect's or engineer's estimate), some demonstrable last-minute change in the immediate or ultimate need for the project work, and so on.

For instance, in a New Jersey bid protest case, a court ruled that economic considerations, including the prospect of a more favorable bidding climate, justified the owner's rejection of all bids. The Township of Belleville took bids for a street and utility improvement contract. The apparent low bidder had omitted the bid bond and was allowed to go to its office, retrieve the bond, and return to the bid opening 20 minutes later with the bond. The township then accepted the low bid. The second low bidder protested that the bid submitted without the bond at the time of bid opening was nonresponsive and had to be rejected. A trial court agreed with this second bidder. However, rather than award the contract to the second bidder, the township then elected to reject all bids and resolicit at a later date. The second bidder challenged this decision. The Superior Court of New Jersey ruled in favor of the township, stating that, although a public project owner is not allowed unfettered discretion in rejecting all bids, they are allowed to take economics into consideration. In the opinion of the court, the township made a good-faith decision that the best interest of the public would be served by a rebid.[12]

The second limitation is that if the public owner rejects all bids and cannot justify the determination that the rejection of the bids was in the public interest, the bid rejection is subject to court challenge and reversal. Although the outcome of such a case is uncertain and the benefit of any doubt will probably be given to the public owner, reversal is possible.

A Louisiana court ruled that when a public owner rejects all bids, it must inform the bidders of the cause for the rejection. The State of Louisiana Legislative Budgetary Control Consul took bids for renovation on the state capitol building. All bids were rejected and the project put out to bid again. One of the original bidders demanded to know the reasons for all bids being rejected and went to court to compel an answer. The Consul argued that they were not expressly required to divulge the reason for the rejection of the bids.

The Court of Appeals of Louisiana agreed that the state statute authorizing public owners to reject all bids did not expressly require divulgence of the cause for the rejection but said that divulgence was an implicit requirement if the statute was to serve its intended purpose. The court said:

> If only the public entity knows the reason for the rejection of bids, but yet refuses to divulge the reason for the rejection, then what safeguard is there that the rejection was for just cause? To conclude otherwise is to make a mockery of the law. We are of the opinion that the bidder in the instant case has a right to know the reason for the rejection, and the legislature has imposed a duty on the public entity to inform a requesting bidder of the reason for the rejection.[13]

All bids received will normally not be rejected, and the outcome of the bid opening will be that the construction contract will be awarded to the lowest responsive and responsible bidder.

CONCLUSION

This chapter emphasized the great difference in bidding practices of the public and private sectors of the construction industry, the importance of public bidding statutes, and the tremendous influence of the federal bidding policy as set forth in the *United States Code*. The actions that should be taken by a public owner after taking bids were discussed as well as the general subjects of bidder responsiveness

---

[12]*Marvec Construction Corp. v. Township of Belleville,* 603 A.2d 184 (N.J. Super. L. 1992).

[13]*Milton J. Womac, Inc. v. Legislative Budgetary Control Consul,* 470 So.2d 460 (La. App. 1985).

and responsibility, bid irregularities and informalities, late bids, bid protests, and rejection of all bids in the public's best interest. Chapter 12 deals with the important subject of mistakes in bids.

QUESTIONS AND PROBLEMS

1. What is the fundamental difference between public and private bidding? What are two examples mentioned in this chapter illustrating the freedom that private owners have in setting bidding terms and conditions? Can the public owner set its own rules? Can a public owner change the rules once a set of bid documents has been issued? What is an addendum?

2. What are two main purposes served by public bidding statutes? Who creates these statutes? What three sources of bidding statutes were discussed?

3. What are the five main requirements of the federal bidding policy as set forth in the *United States Code?*

4. Is the federal policy very influential? Must all federal contracts be awarded to the lowest responsive and responsible bidder?

5. What is a material impropriety? When an extension for a unit-price bid item on a schedule-of-bid-items bid conflicts with the unit price that was bid, which usually governs? When the sum of the lump sum items and the extensions of the unit-price items on a schedule-of-bid-items bid form is incorrectly added and entered as the bid total, what will be taken to be the bidder's intended bid—the total written in or the correct total?

6. Can alternate bids be considered in making a determination of the low bid? Under what conditions? Can a public owner change the basis for determination of the low bid from that explicitly or implicitly stated in the published bid documents?

7. What does bidder responsiveness mean? What does bidder responsibility mean? At what point in time must bidder responsiveness be demonstrated? How about bidder responsibility?

8. What are bid irregularities or informalities? Explain the two broad classes of bid irregularities and informalities discussed in this chapter. What is the rule discussed in this chapter as a practical test to distinguish one class from the other? What three examples of major irregularities were mentioned?

9. Does a bidder necessarily have a property right to a contract on which it was the lowest bidder? To a contract on which it was the lowest responsive and responsible bidder? Does a bidder ever have a property right to a contract? Under what circumstances?

10. Who has status to file a bid protest prior to bids being opened? How about following bid opening? When should protests concerning bidding terms and conditions be filed? When should protests of the award of the contract to a particular bidder be filed?

11. What can a protester hope to gain from a bid protest concerning bidding terms and conditions? A protest concerning award to a particular bidder? A protest to contract award to a particular bidder once the job is well under way?

12. What are the two kinds of bodies to which a bid protest can be made? Can the protest be made to both simultaneously? In case of differing decisions, which body's decision governs?

13. What must a public owner do prior to rejecting all bids received? What may happen if the public owner fails to perform this step or does so without having reasonably compelling grounds? Is the outcome certain in these cases? What are three examples of reasonably compelling grounds?

12

Mistakes in Bids

Key Words and Concepts

Firm bid rule
Doctrine of mistake
Meeting of the minds
Right of bidder to withdraw
Rescinded contract
Six tests for right to withdraw a bid
Importance of timeliness in declaring a
  mistake
Proof of mistake

Duty of owner to request bid verification
Contract reformation
Required conditions for reformation
Sub-bids and material price quotations
Promissory estoppel
Required elements to establish liability
Reliance
Reasonable reliance

In the previous chapter, the bidding and contract award process was extensively discussed. The point was made that this process is consistent and predictable for the public sector of the industry, but not for the private sector. This chapter deals with an additional aspect of the bidding process applying to the public sector: mistakes in bids.

FIRM BID RULE AND DOCTRINE OF MISTAKE

Clearly, public owners are subject to many restrictions in the advertising, bidding, and contract award process as illustrated by federal law and the federal construction procurement policy. Similarly, these same procurement rules impose an important requirement on bidders called the **firm bid rule.**

The firm bid rule is not limited to federal government contracts but is a consistent feature of all public procurements. Under this rule, a submitted bid is understood and required to be firm. The price is fixed, not subject to negotiation, and the only terms and conditions of the bid are those established by the owner's bid documents. Once the construction contract is awarded, the bidder is legally bound to perform the contract according to those terms and conditions. An exception to this in the federal practice are those instances when the government calls for proposals leading to a negotiated contract. Under these circumstances, the bidder's proposal would be subject to further discussion under rules determined in advance by the government and stated in the request for proposals.

Not only are public bids required to be firm, but public owners also require that bid security be provided to guarantee that the low responsive and responsible bidder will enter into a contract and furnish the required bonds. As discussed in Chapter 9, this security will usually be a bid bond or a certified check in the amount of 10% of the bid price. When used, certified checks are returned uncashed to the unsuccessful bidders, usually the day following the bid opening. The check is returned to the successful bidder when the required bonds and insurance policies are furnished and the contract signed. If the successful bidder then fails to sign the contract and furnish the required bonds and insurance policies, the bid security is forfeited.

Since the terms and conditions of the contractor's bid, except for the pricing, are entirely determined by the owner, the firm bid rule imposes immense liability on public bidders. For the bid price, they undertake a firm obligation to perform the contract work strictly in accordance with the owner's terms and conditions, typically consisting of section after section of highly technical specifications. Not only that, the bidder must perform all of the contract work within fixed time limitations that are often very restrictive.

The severe implications of the firm bid rule raise the question of what happens when a low bidder makes a mistake and submits a bid with a price lower than intended. Under the **doctrine of mistake,** the bidder on federal contracts and in most states may be relieved of the duty to perform the contract and, in certain circumstances, may be allowed to correct the bid and still be awarded the contract. Several logical reasons underlie this concept.

First, from the standpoint of equity, one party to a contract should not be permitted to profit unconscionably because of a mistake of the other party. A corollary point is that a bid containing a mistake does not represent the intent of the bidder, and a contract based on such a bid cannot represent a **meeting of the minds.** Without such a meeting of the minds with respect to the three elements required for contract formation—offer, acceptance, and consideration—there can be no proper, legally binding contract.

The doctrine of mistake, as it has been applied by our courts, usually has resulted in bidders who make a mistake in their bids on federal contracts (and other public contracts following the federal policy) being allowed to withdraw. In this case, the potential contract would be said to be a **rescinded contract.** When the contract has been rescinded, both the bidder and the bidder's surety are released from the normal obligations guaranteed by the bid bond.

GENERALIZED RULES FOR WITHDRAWAL

If low bidders were indiscriminately released from the obligations of their bids whenever they claimed that they had made a mistake, the integrity of the public bidding process would be undermined. Bidders who were low by large margins could avoid performing the contract by the simple expedient of claiming that they had made a mistake. Therefore, the kinds of mistakes that permit bidders to withdraw are strictly limited, and our courts have defined narrow generalized grounds for withdrawal. The following six separate **tests for withdrawing a bid** must be met by a bidder who has made a mistake in a bid:

1. The claimed mistake must be *material*—that is, it must make a significant difference in the total bid price.

2. The claimed mistake must be subject to *objective determination.* This means that the nature and magnitude of the mistake must be clearly demonstrable by examining the bid or bid preparation documents.

3. The claimed mistake must be clerical in nature as opposed to a mistake in judgment. An example of a clerical mistake would be a mistaken total for a column of figures or some other demonstrable arithmetic mistake. An example of a mistake in judgment would be overestimating the productivity of a pile driving crew, resulting in an estimated cost for that work that was far too low.

   In an Iowa case, a contractor was relieved of its bid because of a bid error attributed to a last-minute recording of a subcontractor's price as $22,000 instead of the correct price of $220,000. The contractor had requested bid withdrawal immediately after the bid opening.[1]

   Similarly, in a New York case, a contractor who had intended to make a last-minute price reduction of $21,300 inadvertently transposed this reduction to

---

[1]*M. J. McGough Co. v. Jane Lamb Memorial Hospital,* 302 F. Supp. 482 (D.C.S.D. Iowa 1969).

the final bid papers as $213,000. The contractor informed the owner immediately of the mistake and requested withdrawal of its bid. When the owner refused to allow the contractor to withdraw and awarded the contract, the contractor refused to perform, and the owner sued for monetary damages and for forfeiture of the contractor's bid bond. The contractor and surety moved to have the alleged contract rescinded. The court ruled for the contractor stating:

> There was never any meeting of the minds of the parties which could give rise to a contract since the bidder never submitted its real bid but instead, an erroneous one not at all expressing its intent.[2]

However, in a case where the bid involved the construction of bridge decking over the Mississippi River between Missouri and Tennessee, the Missouri Supreme Court refused to excuse a bidder who had claimed two separate mistakes, one involving the use of incorrect labor rates and the second involving the omission of state sales tax. The court concluded that both mistakes were judgmental, not clerical. The court also concluded that the bidder conducted a poor pre-bid investigative analysis of the local conditions affecting its bid.[3]

These cases illustrate the distinction that courts make between judgmental and clerical errors.

4. It must be clear that the owner would unconscionably profit from the mistake if the bidder were not allowed to withdraw. This is really an extension of the first test mentioned, that of materiality.

5. The position of the owner must not be prejudiced except for the *loss of bargain* resulting from allowing the bidder to withdraw. If the bidder who submitted a bid that was too low as the result of a mistake is allowed to withdraw, the owner obviously loses the benefit of the bargain that otherwise would have been enjoyed. This consequence of bidder withdrawal is inevitable. However, the owner should lose nothing else. This test is usually associated with the **timeliness of the bidder's claim of mistake.** If the bidder waited for a considerable period before calling an obvious mistake to the owner's attention, the owner will lose a great deal of valuable time in addition to the obvious loss of the bargain of the low price.

6. The bidder's mistake should not have resulted from a failure to perform some positive legal duty or from *gross or culpable negligence.* In other words, if the bidder made no effort to ascertain the local laws and regulations that clearly affect the contract work or prepared the bid in a haphazard and careless way that indicated gross negligence, relief may not be granted.

---

[2]*City of Syracuse v. Sarkisian Bros., Inc.,* 451 N.Y. S.2d 945 (App. Div. 1982).
[3]*State of Missouri v. Hensel Phelps Constr. Co.,* 634 S.W.2d 168 (Mo. 1982).

Timeliness in Reporting Mistakes

Timeliness in reporting a bid mistake as soon as possible is a key element in gaining relief from the consequences of the mistake. Failure to do so could very well preclude the bidder's right of withdrawal because of the requirement that the owner's position not be prejudiced beyond loss of bargain. Delay in declaring the mistake could easily result in such prejudice.

PROOF OF MISTAKE

Before the bidder and bidder's surety are released from the obligations of the bid, **proof of the mistake** is required. The burden of proof is on the bidder, and the proof must be clear.

The best evidence to prove a mistake is the written bid preparation "papers," which can include anything written, ranging from the formal bid preparation sheets on the bidder's stationery, to computer printouts, to even such things as notations on telephone memo pads or scraps of paper such as the back of an envelope. Finalizing a bid is often a stressful and frenetic affair resulting in many opportunities for making mistakes. A bidder who has made a mistake cannot afford to be shy and must be prepared to explain exactly how the mistake occurred.

DUTY TO VERIFY A LOW BID

Not only do bidders for public construction contracts have certain rights when they discover a bid mistake, but some public owners also have a duty to verify the low bid when a mistake is suspected. There are three important points in connection with this **duty to request bid verification.**

1. The federal practice requires the government to seek verification of the low bid when a mistake is suspected or should have been suspected. The government normally does this by promptly requesting the low bidder to check the bid and confirm in writing that it is correct and represents the intent of the bidder. The government request for verification should be made in writing.

2. The fact that a low bid is substantially lower than the next lowest bid or substantially lower than the government estimate is in and of itself cause to suspect that a mistake was made.

3. When a specific mistake is suspected, it is not enough that the government merely seek general verification of the bid. In these circumstances, the government should direct the bidder's attention to the specific area of the bid where the mistake is suspected and request confirmation of the bidder's intent with respect to that specific area of the bid.

The following cases illustrate this point. In the first case, a public utility in Oregon took bids for a project in which the specifications stated that concrete-encased duct banks were to be used under railroads or roadways in filled areas. The electrical drawings did not show any railroads or roadways or any other clear indications of duct banks extending under these kinds of surface features. Even after the issue of an addendum consisting of additional drawings, the presence of duct banks under railroads or roadways was unclear. When the bids were opened, the owner's consulting engineer suspected that most bidders had failed to provide for concrete-encased duct banks under road areas and recommended that the owner contact the low bidder before the contract award and ascertain that they had included the cost of concrete encasements for the duct banks under roads in their bid. The owner did contact the low bidder but only inquired whether they were satisfied with their bid. The inquiry did not mention the particular mistake that was suspected by the engineer. The low bidder rechecked the bid, did not discover the mistake, and confirmed the bid and executed the contract.

Once the contract was underway, the owner sent the contractor a set of drawings clearly indicating the requirement for concrete encasement around the duct banks and the location of duct banks under various roads. The contractor immediately informed the owner that the duct bank encasement work on the new drawings constituted a constructive change to the contract and would require additional compensation. A dispute ensued that eventually wound up in court.

The Court of Appeals of Oregon was not persuaded by the owner's contention that they had warned the contractor by requesting them to recheck the bid prior to award of the contract, ruling instead that when the owner had reason to know the low bidder had likely made a mistake and strongly suspected where the potential mistake lay, the so-called warning was completely insufficient. The court further ruled that the concrete encasement requirement constituted a change to the contract and that the contractor was entitled to additional payment.[4]

In a federal case, the U.S. Claims Court (now the United States Court of Federal Claims) ruled that the government improperly accepted a bid knowing that the bid contained a mistake and knowing the general area where the mistake was made. Bids were taken for the construction for a health center in Utah where the bidders were given approximately a seven-week period in which to prepare their bids. The project required a modular storage system (MSS), which the specifications indicated must be manufactured as a unit by a single manufacturer. The bid documents indicated that a separate addendum would be issued prior to the bid date listing those firms qualified to manufacture the MSS.

The specifications made continuous reference to a particular manufacturer for the MSS system. The addendum that was to have been issued no less than 72 hours prior to the bid opening was never issued. The trial testimony indicated that the government architect had discussed the addendum with the government but was told that there was insufficient time to issue it. The architect's proposed addendum indicated only one manufacturer qualified to supply the system, and that manufacturer was different than the one referenced in the specifications.

---

[4]*Ace Electric Co. v. Portland General Elec. Co.*, 637 P.2d 1366 (Or. App. 1981).

The low bidder, whose bid was considerably below the government's estimate, orally advised the government on the day of the bid opening that their bid did not contain any costs for the MSS. Later, in response to an oral inquiry from the government for confirmation of its bid, the low bidder confirmed its bid in writing, believing (according to the trial evidence) that the nonissue of the addendum meant that no costs were intended by the government to be included for the MSS. The oral "inquiry" from the government consisted of a telephone call from a government representative to the contractor's office leaving a message with a person who answered the phone that only requested bid confirmation. There was no reference of any kind to the costs for the MSS system. In ruling for the contractor, who eventually went to court after the contract was awarded, the court noted that the government had actual knowledge that the low bid did not include costs for the MSS because they had been so advised orally at the bid opening. Under these circumstances, a request for bid verification that did not specifically refer to this problem was judged to be insufficient. The court said:

> Such failure, in light of the defendant's actual knowledge that D & D was misreading the specifications, i.e., believing that receipt of the Addendum was a condition precedent to including bidding costs on the MSS, indicates at the very minimum of bad faith on the government's part, and ordinarily would entitle plaintiff to an equitable adjustment.

The court concluded that the contractor was entitled to an equitable adjustment for costs of the MSS system that had been omitted from the bid.[5]

The owner's request for verification for a low bid can produce a completely different result. A number of years ago, the author's company had submitted a bid for a subway project that was 20% below the second low bid and the owner's estimate. The bid had been based on our interruption of the requirements for support of the underground openings required by the project. We received both an oral and written notification that our bid was very low along with the request that we confirm our bid in writing. After checking the bid for errors and finding none, we carefully explained by letter our interpretation of the ground support specifications upon which our bid was based, and that, based on that interpretation, our bid was correct. Upon receipt of our letter, the owner, a major rapid transit district, advised that our interpretation of their specifications was erroneous and construction of the project according to our interpretation and by our intended methods would not be acceptable to them. Following an extended series of conferences, the owner finally agreed that our interpretation of their specifications was possible, although not what they had intended. All bids were rejected, and the project readvertised for bids with revised drawings and specifications making clear exactly what the owner required. The author's company was once again the low bidder, although at a considerably higher figure. Had there not been a requirement for bid verification on the part of the owner, this misunderstanding regarding the ground support requirements for the job would have not surfaced until after the contract had been entered into, probably resulting in a major dispute.

---

[5] *Derrick & Dana Contracting, Inc. v. United States,* 7 Cl. Ct. 627 (1985).

Possible Outcomes on Mistake Verification

A number of outcomes are possible under federal rules when a bid mistake has been discovered and verified. The usual result is that the mistaken bidder withdraws the bid, and the potential contract is rescinded. However, that is not always the case.

First, if the lowest responsive, responsible bidder who has made a bid mistake is willing to waive the right of relief, the discovery of the bid mistake will not matter, and the bidder will be awarded the contract at the original bid price. If the magnitude of the error is not too great, many bidders will elect this option. In most cases, waiver of the bidder's right of relief will be effected by the bidder's simply remaining silent after the mistake is discovered—that is, not informing the owner that a mistake was made.

Second, in some circumstances, a better result for the bidder on a federal government contract may be obtained with a **contract reformation.** The bidder may be allowed to correct the mistake resulting in the contract being reformed rather than rescinded, as when a mistaken bid is withdrawn. In this case, the reformed contract price will be the original bid price corrected upward by the amount of the mistake. Such a correction is allowed only when the correction does not alter the order of bidders in terms of lowest bid price to highest.

Formerly, the government would permit this option only when it could be conclusively shown on the face of the bid itself what the dollar amount of the intended bid would have been without the mistake. In effect, this is what occurs when the government makes upward corrections in erroneous unit price extensions and errors in the addition of the total of the individual bid items in a schedule-of-bid-items bid. More recently, bidders have been allowed to make upward corrections to the contract price based on demonstration of a mistake in the bid work papers as well, as distinct from a mistake demonstrable on the face of the bid, provided that reference to the bid papers clearly establishes the amount of the intended bid. For instance, the Comptroller General of the United States supported a government contracting officer's decision allowing a bidder who had misplaced a decimal point when transposing the cost of subcontracted electrical work to correct its bid, raising the bid total to within one percent of the second low bidder. When the second low bidder filed a protest, the Comptroller General ruled that it was proper to allow bid correction because the bidder submitted clear evidence of both the existence of a mistake and the intended bid price. The bidder's worksheets indicated not only the misplaced decimal point but also the intended markup to be applied to the subcontract work. Therefore, it was possible to determine the intended bid price with precision.[6]

The Comptroller General acted similarly over the objection of the second low bidder in another case by allowing the low bidder to increase its bid by the amount of omitted home office overhead cost. The bid preparation worksheets indicated that the bidder intended to include home office overhead costs of $370,000, but because of a decimal point mistake, included only $37,000. The low bid was corrected upward

---

[6]Matter of *Guardian Construction,* Comp. Gen. No. B-220982 (March 6, 1986).

by $333,000, still leaving it low. The correction was allowed because the low bidder's worksheets furnished convincing evidence of the intended bid price.[7]

However, the Comptroller General refused to reverse a contracting officer's determination that a low bidder not be allowed to increase its bid when the bidder claimed that they had mishandled the interrelationship between their base bid and certain option items. When the contracting officer examined the low bidder's bid preparation papers, he discovered that it was possible to arrive at two different bid prices. The Comptroller General said that a mistaken bid can be raised only when the bidder can provide clear evidence of the intended bid amount and that when examination of the bid papers indicated that it was possible to arrive at two different bid prices, this standard had not been met. The bidder was allowed to withdraw its bid but was not allowed to make an upward correction.[8]

A third point is that contract reformation is possible even when the bid mistake is not discovered until after the contract has been entered into. However, the reformed contract total can never exceed the price of the next higher bid.

Finally, if the correction of a mistake would result in the contract price increasing to a figure higher than that of the second lowest bid, the only remedy available to the bidder is the withdrawal of the mistaken bid and rescission of the contract. If the contract has already been entered into, the only possible remedy would be cancellation of the contract.

PROMISSORY ESTOPPEL

General contractors commonly rely on price quotations from subcontractors and material suppliers to competitively and accurately determine their costs for significant portions of their work. Very few can efficiently execute all of the work required by the typical prime construction contract, and most tend to build organizations that focus on performing particular kinds of work only. In addition, few prime contractors are also construction material suppliers. Therefore, general contractors bidding for prime construction contracts depend on price quotations received from subcontractors and material suppliers, the lowest of which will be included in the general contractor's bid to the owner.

The **subcontractors' and material suppliers' price quotations** are based on the drawings and specifications that are part of the bidding documents prepared by the owner for each project. These are the same documents upon which the general contractor relies, and it is presumed that the general contractors, subcontractors, and material suppliers all have the same understanding of the requirements of the project drawings and specifications when the price quotations are offered and received. Further, when subcontractors and material suppliers tender their price quotations to general contractors, they understand that the general contractors will rely on these

---

[7]Matter of *Lash Corporation*, Comp. Gen. No. B-233041 (February 6, 1989).
[8]Matter of *H. A. Lewis, Inc.*, Comp. Gen. No. B-249368 (November 16, 1992).

quotations and consider them to be in strict conformance with the project drawings and specifications unless advised otherwise. The subcontract and material supply price quotations are typically received only a short time before the prime contract bids are due.

If the subcontractor or material supplier should then refuse or otherwise fail to honor the quotation, the general contractor who is determined to be the low bidder and awarded the prime contract usually is forced to obtain the subcontract work or materials from others whose price quotation was higher. Since the price differential would not have been included in the prime contract bid to the owner, the general contractor has been damaged. These damages can be recovered under the doctrine of **promissory estoppel.**

Concept of Promissory Estoppel

Promissory estoppel is based on the concept of equity and requires that one who has placed another in a changed and untenable position by promising a certain performance is "estopped" from denying the performance. One who denies performance must make good the damage caused by failure to perform as promised. Although involving the common law principle of damages for breach of contract, promissory estoppel does not depend on the existence of a contract between the general contractor and the subcontractor or material supplier. In the bidding situation just described, a contract between the general contractor and the subcontractor or material supplier has not yet come into being. It is the refusal or failure of the subcontractor or material supplier to enter into a contract based on the price quotation that triggers the application of promissory estoppel.

Elements Necessary to Establish Liability

The subcontractor or supplier who refuses to honor a price quotation to a general contractor is liable for the resulting damages if the general contractor can prove the following **elements that establish liability:**

1. The general contractor must establish that a clear and definite offer was made by the subcontractor or material supplier.

2. The general contractor must establish that at the time the offer was made the subcontractors or material supplier knew that the general contractor would rely on the offer. This condition of **reliance** is satisfied if the subcontractor or material supplier knew that the purpose for which the general contractor was receiving quotations was to use the lowest of the quotations received in the prime bid to the owner.

3. The general contractor must have relied on the offer in the prime bid to the owner, and the reliance must be considered to be **reasonable;** that is, the price quotation must not be so much lower than others received that the general contractor would have reason to suspect a mistake in the quotation or a misunderstanding regarding the scope of work included and specifications that apply.

4. Before the subcontractor or material supplier can be held liable, the fact that
the general contractor has or will be damaged by the failure to perform and
the extent of the damages must be established.

The following cases illustrate the application of the preceding rules. In an Alaska
case, the low bidder had relied on an electrical quotation received prior to its bid to
the owner. Two days after the bid opening, the electrical contractor informed the
prime contractor that it had omitted certain work from its subcontract bid and
would be unable to perform the electrical work at the quoted price. Following the
prime contract award, the prime contractor awarded the electrical subcontract to
the second low electrical bid and sued the low electrical bidder for the price differential. The low electrical bidder defended the suit, arguing that its quotation was
nothing more than an offer to enter into a subcontract and that no binding subcontract was formed since the prime had never formally accepted the offer.

In ruling that the original electrical subcontractor was liable on the basis of
promissory estoppel, the Supreme Court of Alaska indicated that the subcontractor would be held to its bid if it was foreseeable that the prime contractor would
act in reliance on the bid by incorporating it into the prime contract. The court further said:

> It is industry custom for subcontractors to submit bids at the last moment. This trade
> practice has evolved because of the industry demands for firm, current prices. The cus-
> tom is facilitated by the ease with which a bid can be placed without the formalities of
> a contract. However, if the contractor is to deliver a set price to an owner, these bids
> must be binding for a reasonable time.[9]

In a federal case, the U.S. Court of Appeals also ruled that a subcontractor
was bound to its quotation to a prime contractor submitting a bid to an owner. In a
contract for the construction of a storage reservoir, the prime contractor informally
requested bids from subcontractors for earthwork and piping. The low subcontract
bidder submitted their quotation and, at the prime's request, confirmed it with a
detailed written breakdown. After award of the contract to the prime contractor,
the subcontractor advised that they would be unable to perform the subcontract
work on the project due to "changes in our workload and other developments."
The prime contractor awarded the subcontract for the work to the next lowest subcontractor available and sued the original low bidder for the $155,056 price differ-
ential. The U.S. District Court held that the subcontractor was liable for the price
differential based on the doctrine of promissory estoppel. The U.S. Court of
Appeals affirmed.[10]

On the other hand, an Illinois court refused to hold a subcontractor liable on
the grounds that the prime contractor was unable to prove that its reliance on the
sub-bid offer was reasonable and justifiable. The court found that there was such a
great disparity in bids received from subcontractors for the same work that the

---

[9]*Alaska Bussell Electric Co. v. Vern Hickel Construction Co.,* 688 P.2d 576 (Alaska, 1984).
[10]*Preload Technology, Inc. v. A. B.& J. Construction Co., Inc.,* 696 F.2d 1080 (5th Cir. 1983).

prime contractor should not have relied on the low bid without verification. The court said:

> We hold that the trial court properly refused to apply the Doctrine of Promissory Estoppel because Nielsen knew, or should have known of the obviously mistaken bid by National. Consequently, such reliance as Nielsen claims it placed on National's bid was as a matter of law not reasonable.[11]

Although the preceding discussion has been framed in terms of price quotations to general contractors in a bidding situation, the doctrine of promissory estoppel is a general legal principle that can be applied to other situations in construction as well. Construction owners, for instance, can have an expectation induced as well when receiving bids from contractors. When a bid bond or other form of bid security is required, however, the owner's interest is protected without resort to the doctrine of promissory estoppel.

CONCLUSION

This chapter concluded an examination of construction industry bidding practices with a brief discussion of the firm bid rule, the doctrine of mistake, bid rescission and reformation, and promissory estoppel. The next seven chapters focus on the operation and interpretation of the contracts that result from the bidding and award process.

QUESTIONS AND PROBLEMS

1. What is the import of the firm bid rule? Does it apply to all federal projects? To most? To what type of project does it not apply? What is the import of the doctrine of mistake? Why is it so important to contractors bidding competitively today?

2. Why doesn't a contract based on a bid containing a mistake represent a meeting of the minds? Could a meeting of the minds result if the contractor elected to waive the normal right to relief?

3. What does "rescinded" mean in the context of a contract based on a bid containing a mistake? What are the six tests that must be met in order for the potential contract to be rescinded when a bidder declares a mistake in the bid?

4. Does a bidder who has made a mistake in the bid have to prove the existence of the mistake before being allowed to withdraw the bid? What is the best way to prove the existence of the mistake? What are bidding "papers"? What do they include?

---

[11]*S. M. Nielsen Co. v. National Heat & Power Co., Inc.,* 337 N.E.2d 387 (Ill. App. 1975).

5. What three points does this chapter make about a public owner's duty to verify a suspected bid mistake?

6. Once a bidder has proved the existence of a mistake and has established grounds for withdrawal of the bid, what are the three possible outcomes under federal rules? What is a reformed contract? In the recent past, what two requirements had to be met for a federal contract that had not been awarded to be reformed on account of a bid mistake? How have these requirements changed?

7. Why is timeliness so important with respect to declaring a bid mistake? What does "loss of bargain" mean in this connection? Is it affected by the timing of the declaration of a bid mistake? What is affected?

8. Does the doctrine of promissory estoppel depend on the existence of a contract? What is the central idea of the doctrine? What are the four aspects of today's competitive bidding situation discussed in this chapter that make the doctrine so important? Does the doctrine apply to other situations in construction?

9. What are the four necessary elements that must be proved to recover damages under the doctrine of promissory estoppel? Distinguish between reliance and reasonable reliance with reference to the doctrine. Give an example of this distinction in the typical sub-bid/prime bid situation.

10. A material supplier gives a clear, firm quote to a contractor, who is bidding a well-publicized construction job. The supplier knows the contractor is bidding the job as a prime contractor when the quote is given. The price quoted was reasonable compared to other quotes that the contractor received for the same material. The contractor uses the supplier's quote in the prime bid, is the low bidder, and is awarded the prime contract. The supplier then refuses to furnish the material, and the contractor has to spend an additional $200,000 over the amount of the supplier's quote to obtain the same material from another supplier.

    a. Is the contractor likely to get a judgment for the $200,000 by suing the supplier? Why or why not?

    b. If, at the time the quote was given, the supplier did not know that the contractor was bidding the job as a prime contractor and did not know why the contractor wanted the quote, would the contractor be likely to get a judgment for the $200,000? Why or why not?

    c. If the supplier's price was 40% of the next lowest bid and, without further contact with the supplier, the contractor used the price in the bid, would the contractor be likely to get a judgment? Why or why not?

    d. If the contractor had received the supplier's price so late that it could not be used in the prime bid to the owner but took the price over the phone anyway, and the supplier then refused to furnish the material for that price, would the contractor be likely to get a judgment? Why or why not?

13

Breach of Contract

Key Words and Concepts

Breach of contract
Privity of contract
Proof of breach
Materiality of the contract breach
Protest and reservation of rights
Waiver of rights
Written notice of protest
Effect of disclaimers
Anticipatory breach of contract
Express contract provisions

Implied warranties
Failure to make payment
Interference with contractual
  performance
The Spearin Doctrine
Misrepresentation
Nondisclosure of superior knowledge
Improper termination of contract
Uncompleted punch list work

Up to this point, we have dealt in general terms with construction prime contracts, contracts closely related to prime contracts, and the bidding and contract award process, including the subject of mistakes in bids. This chapter covers issues connected with breach of contract. Following chapters concern the actual operation of contracts in practice.

Consider the following scenarios:

A contract between a prime contractor and an owner provides that the owner will make monthly progress payments within 30 calendar days from the engineer's approval of the contractor's estimate of work performed the previous month, subject to a 10% retention requirement. The owner, however, consistently does not pay until an average of 60 days after the engineer's approval and in some instances as late as 90 days after monthly estimate approval. Or suppose that the owner states at some point that all future progress payments will be withheld until the contractor agrees to withdraw a claim filed on a previously disputed contract matter.

Consider a subcontract situation in which a prime contractor treats a subcontractor as the owner treated the contractor in the situation described in the previous paragraph. Or suppose a subcontractor refuses to continue subcontract performance and walks off the job because of a dispute over the proper amount of payment for a subcontract work item previously performed. Suppose that after having entered into a subcontract agreement with a subcontractor, the prime contractor arbitrarily terminates the subcontractor in favor of another subcontractor who offers to perform the subcontract work for a lower price.

All of these situations have one thing in common—each constitutes a breach of contract entitling the nonbreaching party to recover monetary damages resulting from the breach.

BREACH OF CONTRACT AND MATERIALITY OF BREACH

Breach of Contract

A **breach of contract** is a default of a contract obligation, or, in other words, a refusal or a failure by a party to a contract to meet some duty required by the contract. The failure can be either a failure of omission or commission. There can be no breach of contract unless **privity of contract** exists (see Chapter 2).

Once privity of contract has been established, two additional elements must be proven to show that a contract breach has occurred. First, it must be proven that the contract imposed a specific duty on one party or the other or on all parties to the contract. This duty may be either a requirement to perform certain acts or duties or to refrain from certain acts. Second, it must be proven that there was a failure to meet that duty.

Materiality of the Breach

The concept of materiality previously discussed with respect to bidding irregularities and mistakes in bids (see Chapters 11 and 12) also applies to contract breaches.

Because of the complexity of construction contract terms and conditions and technical specifications in today's world, few contracts are performed to completion without a variety of breaches by both owner and contractor parties to the contract. The question then becomes how important is a particular contract breach—or, what is the **materiality of the contract breach?**

The more "material" the breach, the greater the rights and remedies that accrue to the nonbreaching party or parties. Minor breaches may not give rise to any remedy at all, whereas a major or material breach of contract may relieve the nonbreaching party from any obligation to continue performance of the contract. This means, in theory, that an owner has the right to terminate the contract in the case of a material breach by the contractor and the contractor may refuse further performance and abandon the contract in the case of a material breach by the owner. Of course, just how serious or major a breach has to be to constitute a "material" breach is an important legal question requiring advice of competent counsel. Hasty or precipitous action should never be taken on the grounds of a perceived material breach of contract by the other party. The legal consequences of later being found incorrect are extremely serious.

Having a means to judge how important a particular breach is would be highly desirable. Unfortunately, there are only a few recognized rules to help resolve this question. First, look to the wording of the contract itself, which may make it apparent that some matters are much more important than others. For instance, strongly worded explicit provisions that are prominent, clear, and not in conflict with other provisions of the contract are given great weight.

Second, consider the response of the nonbreaching party at the time of the breach. This response generally indicates how the nonbreaching party viewed the seriousness of the breach when it occurred. Courts usually consider the response to be an indication of the materiality of the breach. For example, the party who immediately sends a written **protest and reservation of rights** to the breaching party clearly has notified that party that a breach has occurred, that damages will result, and that the nonbreaching party expects to be compensated for those damages. A message has been sent that something important has occurred. Contrast the preceding described reaction to a case where the nonbreaching party takes no action at all following the breach. Such a failure to call notice to the breach may constitute a complete **waiver of rights** and remedies or, at the very least, may reduce the materiality that a court may later attach to the breach, thus reducing the nonbreaching party's rights and remedies.

The following cases illustrate what can happen when a party acquiesces to the other party's breach without protest. In one case, the owner and contractor had a disagreement over the handling of a subcontractor's payment during the construction of a residence. At that point, the owner took over all project accounting and made payments directly to subcontractors and suppliers, telling the contractor that it should consider itself a volunteer if it continued work. Nonetheless, the contractor did continue work for five additional months, at which point the owner ordered the contractor off the job. When the contractor filed a lien to secure payment for work performed, a trial court found that the owner had breached the contract by preventing the contractor from continuing performance but that the contractor could not recover damages because the contract had been rescinded. The Court of Appeals of Indiana upheld the trial court, stating that by failing to demand modification or termination, the contractor had consented to rescission of the contract.[1]

In another case, the Supreme Court of Arkansas held that a contractor who performed extra work directed by the owner on a shopping center without demanding a change order for the work, by acquiescence, agreed that the contract should be interpreted to have included that work. The owner had demanded the removal of unsuitable soils and replacement with more easily compacted soils beneath the paving sections of the project, and the contractor performed the work without protest or demand for a change order. When the contractor later filed a claim for payment for the work, the owner refused to pay. In ruling for the owner, the court held that

> Where a contract is ambiguous, the court will accord considerable weight to the construction the parties themselves give to it, evidenced by subsequent statements, acts, and conduct. This record reflects that throughout the performance of the contract, Coney did all the undercutting that was required. Not only were there no claims for extra work, there is virtually nothing in the record to indicate that undercutting was of any serious concern to Coney prior to this litigation.[2]

This case illustrates that the contractor's failure to protest and demand a change order not only barred recovery for the extra work performed but resulted in the court believing that the extra work was intended to be in the contract in the first place.

Written Notice of Protest

Since the rights and remedies available to the nonbreaching party are proportional to the materiality of the breach, it is extremely important that the nonbreaching party immediately sends a **written notice of protest** and reservation of rights when any breach occurs unless the matter is extremely minor. What appears to be a relatively minor matter may turn out to have serious consequences. A businesslike written protest and reservation of rights protects the nonbreaching party's interests.

Contractors naturally wish to avoid being considered "claim happy," and some fear retribution as a result of putting the owner on notice of alleged breaches. However, the contractor ultimately is judged by overall performance and the degree of professionalism exhibited. In the long run, a reasonable owner respects the contractor for making contractual positions clear from the beginning, as long as the contractor behaves reasonably. If the owner is not reasonable when advised of a breach, the contractor is better off discovering this fact earlier rather than later in the course of performing the work of the contract.

---

[1]*Glen Gilbert Construction Co., Inc. v. Garbish,* 432 N.E.2d 455 (Ind. App. 1982).

[2]*RAD-Razorback Limited Partnership v. B. G. Coney Co.,* 713 S.W.2d 462 (Ark. 1986).

Effect of Disclaimers or Exculpatory Clauses

Consideration of contract breaches often involves the matter of disclaimers or exculpatory clauses (see Chapters 4 and 5). These clauses may govern whether a contract breach has occurred.

First, recall that a **disclaimer** or exculpatory clause is a clause in the contract stating that a party to the contract, usually the owner, is not liable for the consequences of some act or failure to act that otherwise would have been a breach of contract. The mere presence of a disclaimer in a contract does not necessarily mean that it will be enforced by the courts. Some courts are disinclined to give certain types of disclaimers full force and effect. However, if the disclaimer is prominent and clear and does not conflict with any other provision of the contract, it probably will be enforced. A disclaimer that conflicts with other contract provisions generally is not enforced, particularly in federal government contracts. Courts reason, using an old adage, that the left hand cannot properly take away what the right hand has bestowed.

ANTICIPATORY BREACHES OF CONTRACT

A threat by a party to a construction contract to take a course of action or to refuse to perform some duty required by the contract that would constitute a breach if actually carried out can, in and of itself, constitute a contract breach. The breach resulting from this type of situation is called an **anticipatory breach of contract.** As an example, consider a contract in which the owner controls and is contractually required to provide the means of access to the project. If the owner advised the contractor at some point during contract performance that the contractor's access would be shut off in two weeks, such advice would constitute an anticipatory breach.

Because the nonbreaching party can be damaged by the threat alone, it is not necessary to wait until the threatened action actually occurs to accrue rights of relief. For instance, in the previous example, the contractor faced with the access closure might immediately expend monies to procure or construct an alternate means of access in anticipation of losing the contractually provided access. Once the money has been spent, the damages have been incurred, even if the owner should later relent on the threatened closure. The contractor has accrued the right to be compensated for the money spent. The breach is created by the threat itself.

In such situations, the nonbreaching party should file a written protest and reservation of rights in anticipation of the threatened event after ascertaining that the breaching party really means to carry the threat out. There must be evidence of the clear intent to commit the threatened act or the clear intent not to act, as the case may be. Such intent is usually established by the words and acts of the breaching party at the time. "Words and acts of a party" means their written or oral communications and general behavior.

An anticipatory breach can also arise from an announced intention not to act when the contract requires some action to be taken.

EXPRESS OBLIGATIONS AND IMPLIED WARRANTIES

As discussed in Chapter 1, there are two types of contract provisions: **express contract provisions** and implied provisions (or **implied warranties**). Both types result in contract obligations or duties.

Express Obligations

Express obligations result directly from the clear meaning of the written words in the contract. The possibilities for breaches of express contract obligations are virtually endless since there is no limit to the different provisions that parties may expressly insert into the contract.

Implied Obligations (Implied Warranties)

Implied obligations are not expressly stated in the contract. Rather, they are the result of widely shared and well-understood implications of the contract. Frequently referred to as *implied warranties,* implied obligations are much more limited in number than express obligations and are frequently repeated from one contract to another.

FREQUENT BREACH OF CONTRACT SITUATIONS

In practice, most common contract breaches are breaches of implied warranties. Far fewer common breaches involve express contract obligations. Of the following breach situations, all but the first are breaches of an implied warranty.

Failure to Make Payment for Completed Work

The obligation to make payment for completed work is always expressly stated in the contract (see Chapter 5). The obligation would be implied even if it were not expressly stated. **Failure to make payment** is a "material breach" and excuses the nonbreaching party from further performance—that is, courts will support the right of a contractor or a subcontractor who is not being paid to stop work and abandon the project or the right of a material supplier to abandon a purchase order contract and cease supplying material. This particular breach by an owner—or contractor in subcontract and purchase order situations—invariably excuses further performance of the contract. A party who is not being paid cannot be expected to continue to perform.

In a leading case on this issue, the U.S. Supreme Court stated in 1919 that

> In a building or construction contract like the one in question, calling for the performing of labor and furnishing of materials covering a long period of time and involving large expenditures, a stipulation for payments on account to be paid from time to time during the progress of the work must be deemed so material that a substantial failure to pay would justify the contractor in declining to proceed. . . . [3]

The failure to pay must be "substantial" to justify a contractor abandoning the work. In a Kansas case, a subcontract for concrete work to be performed for a general contractor provided that the subcontractor was to submit invoices by the 25th of each month and the prime contractor would forward the invoices to the owner for approval and payment. The subcontract also provided that the prime contractor was under no obligation to pay the subcontractor for work performed until the prime contractor had been paid for the work by the owner. During performance, the turnaround time between the subcontractor's invoice submittal and receipt of payment ran 36 to 38 days. The subcontractor walked off the job and sued the prime contractor for breach of contract, stating that lack of prompt payment prevented them from meeting their payroll. In reversing a trial court decision in favor of the subcontractor, the Supreme Court of Kansas determined that the subcontract did not require the prime contractor to make payment within 30 days as the subcontractor alleged and that, even if it did, a delay of six to eight days was not enough to justify the subcontractor's abandonment of the work. [4]

Although courts will support contractors walking off the job when failure to pay reaches substantial proportions, stopping work and abandoning the contract under other breach situations is an extremely risky course for any contractor or subcontractor to take and can result in the contractor or subcontractor being held to have materially breached the contract.

As discussed in Chapter 7, contractors often include clauses making payment to the material supplier or subcontractor conditional upon being paid by the owner. Also, courts have usually held such clauses enforceable only with regard to the timing of the prime contractor's payment to the material supplier or subcontractor. Such clauses permit delay in making payment when the owner has not paid the contractor for the work in question, but if the contractor continues to withhold payment from the subcontractor after it has become clear that the owner will never pay, the contractor will be in breach of contract. Extremely strong, clear, and prominent contract language is required to establish the contractor's right to withhold payment altogether from a material supplier or subcontractor who has properly performed the contract when the owner does not pay. Even then, courts may refuse to enforce the right because they strongly support the proposition that a material supplier or subcontractor that has performed according to the contract is entitled to be paid.

---

[3] *Guerini Stone Co. v. Carlin Constr. Co.,* 248 U.S. 334 (1919).

[4] *Havens v. Safeway Stores,* 678 P.2d 625 (Kan. 1984).

Interference with Contractual Performance

Every contract includes an implied warranty that no party shall act or fail to act in a manner that impedes or interferes with the other party's ability to perform the contract work. There is an implied duty of cooperation.

Frequently encountered examples of breaches caused by **interference with contractual performance** include the owner's failure to coordinate properly the work of multiple prime contractors, taking unreasonable time to check and approve shop drawings, or failing to make the site or access to it available to the contractor. Another frequent claim of contract breach arises from a prime contractor's failure to coordinate properly the work of subcontractors, so that one subcontractor's work interferes with another's.

The following cases illustrate incidents in which courts found breaches of contract due to interference. In Illinois, an electrical contractor on a multiple prime project recovered lost labor productivity because of the owner's failure to coordinate properly the various prime contractors on the site. The electrical contractor's progress was hampered by the general building contractor's failure to complete rough-in work. The electrical contractor was also forced to perform work in a start-and-stop, out-of-sequence manner because the general building contractor was frequently moving its crews about the site. In ruling for the electrical contractor, the Appellate Court of Illinois said:

> Although we agree the District's duty to keep the project in the state of forwardness is not tantamount to a warranty guaranteeing that no delays will occur, if the District either actively created or passively permitted to continue a condition over which it had control which made performance of the contract more difficult or expensive, it may be held to have breached an implied contractual duty for which it must respond in damages.[5]

In a Florida case involving construction of a shopping center, the District Court of Appeals of Florida ruled that the owner's lateness in providing necessary drawings and specifications and in executing required change orders amounted to active interference in the work.[6]

In another case, during performance of a government contract requiring the installation of meters in apartments housing naval personnel, the contractor encountered recurring problems with noncooperative occupants. The U.S. Court of Appeals determined that the Navy had breached the contract by failing to provide reasonable access for the performance of the work. In reversing an earlier decision by the Armed Services Board of Contract Appeals, the court held:

> After the contractor notified the project manager that the contractor's reasonable efforts had not resulted in gaining entry to certain apartments, the Navy was under an implied obligation to provide such access so that the contractor could complete the contract within the time required by its terms. Consequently, if any part of the contractor's work was thereafter delayed for an unreasonable period of time because of the

---

[5]*Amp-Rite Electric Co., Inc. v. Wheaton Sanitary District,* 580 N.E.2d 622 (Ill. App. 1991).

[6]*Newberry Square Development Corp. v. Southern Landmark, Inc.,* 578 So. 2d 750 (Fla. App. 1991).

Navy's failure to provide access to the apartments, the contractor is, under the "Suspension of Work" clause entitled to an increase in the cost of performing the contract.[7]

The preceding cases are illustrative only. Abundant case law decisions support many other forms of breaches of contract caused by interference.

The Spearin Doctrine

Perhaps the most important and well-known implied construction contract warranty is the **Spearin Doctrine,** which refers to the owner's implied warranty of the accuracy and sufficiency of the drawings and specifications. The Spearin Doctrine resulted from a landmark case decided in 1918 by the U.S. Court of Claims (now the United States Court of Federal Claims). Spearin had a contract with the government to construct a dry dock project that contained a large sewer. Spearin performed the contract work strictly in accordance with the government's drawings and specifications. During contract performance, a storm occurred, and the completed sewer burst, destroying itself and causing considerable damage to the balance of the other work in progress. The government took the position that the possibility of damage to the work during the life of the project was a risk that Spearin as the contractor had assumed. Spearin disagreed. The Court of Claims decision in this case has proven to be the Magna Carta of rights for construction contractors. In ruling for the contractor, the court said:

> If the contractor is bound to build according to plans and specifications prepared by the owner, the contractor will not be responsible for the consequences of defects in the plans and specifications.[8]

Simply stated, the Spearin Doctrine says that the owner warrants the accuracy and sufficiency of the drawings and specifications that are for the contractor's use in performing the contract work. The basic principle involved applies to owners, prime contractors, or anyone who contracts with and furnishes drawings and specifications for the use of the party actually doing the work. This means that if the drawings and specifications are precisely followed and the result is not satisfactory, the responsibility rests with the entity that furnished the drawings and specifications. Additionally, the responsibility for the consequences of errors and omissions lies with the furnisher of the drawings and specifications. This responsibility extends to the cost of attempting to comply with defective drawings and specifications, including the costs of all delays involved, such as time needed for the drawings and specifications to be corrected.

An exception to the applicability of the Spearin Doctrine is the situation when the specifications are of the *performance* type. Performance specifications are those that simply define the requirements that the finished product must meet, leaving it to the contractor to devise the design, means, methods, and materials required to

---

[7]*Blinderman Construction Co., Inc. v. United States,* 695 F.2d 552 (Fed. Cir. 1982).

[8]*United States v. Spearin,* 248 U.S. 132, 39 S. Ct. 59, 63, L. Ed. 166 (1918).

meet the specified requirements. Here, if the finished product does not meet project requirements, the contractor bears the liability.

A number of other implied warranties are similar in principle to the Spearin Doctrine:

- Architect/engineers impliedly warrant that their design work is competently performed and conforms to the normal standards of the profession.

- When the contract calls for owner-furnished materials or equipment, owners impliedly warrant that the materials or equipment that they furnish are proper and suitable for their intended purpose.

- When a contract requires the contractor to follow a specified erection procedure or construction sequence, the owner impliedly warrants that the contractually specified construction method or procedure will work and produce the desired result. If it does not, the responsibility for both the poor result and the costs associated with attempting to comply with the specified method or procedure lie with the owner.

- When architect/engineers, construction managers, or contractors provide cost estimates to owners, they impliedly warrant that these cost estimates are reasonably accurate.

- Contractors who perform construction work for laypersons who are relying on the contractor's skill and expertise impliedly warrant that such construction work will be done properly and will result in a product generally satisfactory for the intended purpose.

In all of these situations, the entity that impliedly furnishes the particular warranty involved is responsible for the damages suffered by the other party to the contract if the warranted promise is not fulfilled.

Misrepresentation

In a sense, **misrepresentation** can be considered a breach of an implied warranty that representations in the contract documents are accurate. If such representations turn out to be materially different from indicated in the contract documents, a misrepresentation breach of the contract has occurred, entitling the nonbreaching party to damages consisting of the costs and delays resulting from reliance on the representation.

The representation in the contract documents need not necessarily be explicit. It may be implied or suggested by the information that is provided. A Missouri contractor on a highway grading project recovered damages from the Missouri Highway Commission after discovering that the cuts and fills on the project were not balanced, even though the contract documents did not explicitly state that they would be balanced. The Missouri Court of Appeals held that other information in the contract had the effect of representing to the contractor that the cuts and fills were balanced.[9]

[9]*Idecker, Inc. v. Missouri State Highway Commission,* 654 S.W.2d 617 (Mo. App. 1983).

Misrepresentation can be either intentional or nonintentional. Nonintentional misrepresentation is more common. When misrepresentation can be shown to have been intentional, it is also a *tort*. Tortious misrepresentation subjects the wrongdoer to punitive damages in addition to the actual damages resulting from the misrepresentation.

Three essential elements must be proven to establish misrepresentation. First, there must have been a positive representation, either expressed or implied by other expressed representations in the contract documents. Second, the representation must subsequently be found to be either untrue or incorrect. Finally, the nonbreaching party must have both relied on the representation and suffered damage as a result of that reliance.

Nondisclosure of Superior Knowledge

Another important breach of a contract implied warranty is the **nondisclosure of superior knowledge.** This concerns a situation in which some material condition or circumstance emerges during the course of contract performance that makes performance more difficult and costly, about which the contract documents are totally silent. If it can be proven that the owner or, in the case of a subcontract, the prime contractor, was aware of the condition or circumstance and either deliberately concealed or failed to disclose it, such nondisclosure constitutes a breach of the contract. The nonbreaching party is then entitled to damages amounting to the extra cost in dealing with the nondisclosed condition or circumstance as well as the cost of any resulting delays.

In a sense, nondisclosure of superior knowledge is a form of negative misrepresentation. Both parties to the contract are commonly understood to warrant that they have made available to the other party all information or data that they possess that might affect the other party's performance of the contract work.

The doctrine of nondisclosure of superior knowledge has evolved from a long line of court cases. In the leading case, an industrial manufacturer had a contract to manufacture a product for the federal government. The government failed to disclose the fact that it was necessary to grind a new disinfectant prior to blending it in with the other ingredients. The government had sponsored research on the development of the product and was aware that the grinding process would be required to meet the product's specifications. The U.S. Court of Claims (now the United States Court of Federal Claims) determined that the government breached the contract by not disclosing its superior knowledge. The court said:

> Where the "balance of knowledge" favors the government, it must disclose its knowledge, less by silence it "betray a contractor into a ruinous course of action."[10]

In a later classic construction case, the U.S. Navy contracted with a joint-venture contractor to construct very tall radio towers on the northwest coast of Australia. The contractor's performance was adversely affected by a destructive

---

[10]*Helene Curtis Industries, Inc. v. United States,* 312 F.2d 774 (Ct. Cl. 1963).

pattern of high winds and dangerous offshore currents. The court found that the Navy knew about the winds and the currents but did not disclose this superior knowledge to prospective bidders by including the known data in the bid documents or otherwise making this superior knowledge known. The court, in finding for the contractor and awarding the resulting extra costs, stated that under these circumstances "the government cannot remain silent with impunity."[11]

This principle can apply to any contractual relationship in which one party possesses superior knowledge affecting the other party's burden of performance and does not disclose it prior to entering into the contract. Also, the duty to disclose superior knowledge continues after award of the contract throughout contract performance.

Improper Termination of Contract

Another breach situation that occasionally arises is **improper termination of the contract.** This breach is really a form of interference with contractual performance, discussed earlier in this chapter. If an owner or, in the case of a subcontract, a contractor, improperly terminates the contract, the contractor or subcontractor has been prevented from performing.

Most construction contracts contain express provisions for termination for default (see Chapter 5 on "red flag" clauses). However, when these provisions are improperly or unjustly invoked, the party invoking them has committed a material breach of contract. In other words, the party terminating the contract must be certain that the other party actually was in default.

If the terminating party is not correct and a court later finds the termination improper, the act of terminating the contract may itself be declared a material breach of the contract, entitling the terminated party to all damages flowing from the improper termination. These can include damage to a contractor's reputation, loss of bonding capacity, and in some cases the bankruptcy of the company. The monetary damages are usually very substantial.

For example, the writer was involved as an expert witness in a case where a private contract had been signed for the renovation of an existing structure to convert it to a large central office facility. The owner terminated the design-build contractor at approximately the 95% completion point, alleging that the contractor was behind schedule and was producing shoddy work. The owner then entered into a contract with another contractor for the completion of the original work plus a number of changes and additions. Substantial monies were due the original contractor at the time of termination for a number of months of contract work that had been performed, consisting primarily of work performed by a large number of subcontractors, all of whom remained unpaid. A board of arbitrators first ruled that all of the subcontractors were entitled to be paid in full and directed the design-build contractor to immediately pay them. The board then ruled that the design-build contractor be paid by the owner for all payments made to subcontractors plus their own costs and

---

[11]*Hardeman-Monier-Hutcheson v. United States,* 458 F.2d 1364, 198 Ct. Cl. 472 (1972).

a reasonable profit thereon. Additionally, the arbitrators were so offended by the circumstances of the termination, which they determined to be totally unjustified, that they took the unusual step of ordering that the owner pay all costs of the arbitration proceedings.

Owners and contractors administering subcontracts are often under the mistaken impression that they can properly terminate a construction contract (or subcontract) for default because the contractor or subcontractor fails to complete promptly minor defects, called "punch list" items, after the contract work is substantially complete. **Uncompleted punch list items** do not constitute a breach. The contract cannot be properly terminated on this account.

For instance, the Corps of Engineers Board of Contract Appeals determined that a road construction contractor who had achieved substantial completion, but who had not performed punch list items, was improperly terminated for default by the government. They concluded that once it had the use of the project for its intended purpose, the government must pay for contract performance. The board said:

> Failure to correct minor deficiencies in a substantially completed contract is not a default; it is a constructive, deductive change . . . to declare a contract in default under such circumstances would work a forfeiture—a result the law abhors.[12]

In this situation, the contractor or subcontractor is entitled to be paid the balance of the contract price, less the actual cost to remedy any punch list items that the owner actually remedies, or engages others to remedy, less any diminished value to the completed project for punch list items that either are not remedied by choice or that are impossible to remedy.

CONCLUSION

Any discussion of possible breach of contract situations can be virtually endless, particularly if one attempted to elaborate on breaches of express contract obligations. This chapter is merely a brief look at this important subject. The next chapter examines some important provisions and ramifications of contract changes clauses.

QUESTIONS AND PROBLEMS

1. What is a contract breach? What two elements (in addition to privity of contract) are necessary to prove a contract breach? Do breaches involve acts of commission, acts of omission, or both?

2. Are all breaches equally material? Why is the degree of materiality important? What should the nonbreaching party do when the contract has been breached? Why are some contractors reluctant to put the owner on notice

---

[12]*Appeal of Wolfe Construction Co.,* Eng. BCA No. 3610 (June 29, 1984).

that the contract has been breached? Why should a contractor's actions in a breach situation not be governed by this concern?

3. What two means might a court employ to determine the materiality of a breach?

4. What is the significance of a disclaimer with respect to contract breaches? What two conditions must exist for a disclaimer to be given full force and effect?

5. What is an anticipatory breach? How may a party be damaged by a threat of something that is not carried out? How can the nonbreaching party judge whether the threat posed in an anticipatory breach is likely to be carried out?

6. Must the obligation element of a contract breach be expressed, implied, or can it be either? What type of contract breach tends to recur in similar ways more frequently?

7. What is the single breach of an express contract obligation discussed in this chapter? Can this breach be a material breach excusing continued performance by the nonbreaching party?

8. Explain the breach of interference. What implied warranty is involved? What single example of a contractor-committed interference breach and what three examples of owner-committed interference breaches were discussed in this chapter?

9. What is misrepresentation? What implied warranty is involved? What three elements are necessary to prove misrepresentation?

10. How did the Spearin Doctrine originate? What is the implied warranty involved? Describe five implied warranties that are similar to the Spearin Doctrine.

11. What is the doctrine of nondisclosure of superior knowledge? Give the names and the details of the cases mentioned in this chapter that illustrate the principle of this doctrine. What is the central implied warranty?

12. Why is improper contract termination a form of interference? Is this breach a material breach? If the terminating party is wrong, what is a court of law likely to decide?

13. Do uncompleted punch list items constitute a material breach that justifies termination of the contract? How is final payment to the contractor reckoned when all of the contract work is complete except for punch list items that the contractor either cannot or will not remedy?

14. Indicate whether each of the following occurrences during the performance of a federal construction contract is (a) a breach of an express condition of the contract, (b) a breach of an implied warranty of the contract, or (c) not a breach but an occurrence contemplated by the contract and dealt with by one or more of the standard clauses of the contract. Refer to Chapter 5 on standard ("red flag") clauses.

    a. Contractor encounters a differing site condition.

    b. Government refuses to grant a timely, fully justified, and documented request for an extension of time.

    c. Government suspends work on a portion of the project.

    d. Government does not disclose to bidders or to the successful contractor important information affecting the contractor's cost of performance.

    e. Government fails to pay properly submitted monthly progress payment requests in a timely manner.

    f. Government orders acceleration.

    g. Government terminates contract without stating any reason.

    h. A government-specified construction method proves completely unsatisfactory when the contractor follows it.

    i. Government changes the specified manner in which the work is to be performed.

    j. The plans contain a number of serious errors.

14

Contract Changes

Key Words and Concepts

Three questions central to the changes concept

Federal contract changes clause

Respects in which contract cannot be unilaterally changed

General scope of the contract

Change order, change directive, change notice

Formal change to the contract

Equitable price adjustment

No pay without signed change order

Two-part change to the contract

Oral change orders

Constructive changes

Change element

Order element

Constructive change notice requirement

Cardinal changes

Forward-priced changes

Retrospectively priced changes

Force account

Extended contract performance situations

Breach damages not limited by changes clause

Impact costs

Time-related impacts

Loss-of-efficiency impacts

Change order payment disputes

Current judicial attitude to payment disputes

Conditions likely to result in payment for changes

Proper contractor reaction to oral or written directives

Think back for a moment to some trip that you had planned. Did the undertaking unfold exactly as envisioned? Probably not. Now suppose that you had been compelled to carry out the plan exactly as originally conceived, regardless of the circumstances encountered, the additional expense, and the impracticality of adhering to the original plan. Such a situation would obviously be far from desirable, especially if a flight were canceled or a bridge washed out!

This analogy can be applied to construction contracting in which *change is virtually inevitable.* Even small, simple projects normally involve necessary or at least desirable changes, whereas large, complex projects sometimes involve thousands of changes. Without an agreed-upon, orderly **procedure for making changes to the contract** that are desired or necessary, a construction owner would be placed in a similar situation as you were on your trip.

CONTRACT CHANGE PROCEDURE

After accepting the reality that changes are inevitable in construction contracts and procedures for handling such changes are necessary, those drafting construction contracts must consider these central questions:

- Will the owner have the right to unilaterally make changes to the work?
- Will the contractor be compelled to carry out changes made by the owner?
- After performing changed work directed by the owner, will the contractor be entitled to payment for the additional costs incurred?

From a contractual point of view, answers to these questions cannot be implied. They must be clearly stated in the written contract. A well-drafted changes clause explicitly answers each question in the affirmative and provides detailed language defining the entire contract change procedure.

FEDERAL CONTRACT CHANGES CLAUSE

A changes clause is not an exculpatory clause excusing the owner from liability for changes. Rather, the clause provides for a structured way for the owner to direct changes and for the contractor to perform them and be properly compensated. The **federal contract changes clause** states:

(a)   The Contracting Officer may, at any time, without notice to the sureties, by written order designated or indicated to be a change order, make changes in the work within the general scope of the contract, including changes

   (1)   In the specifications (including drawings and designs);

    (2)   In the method or manner of performance of the work;

    (3)   In the Government-furnished facilities, equipment, materials, services, or site; or

    (4)   Directing acceleration in the performance of the work.

(b)   Any other written order or an oral order (which, as used in this paragraph (b), includes direction, instruction, interpretation, or determination) from the Contracting Officer, that causes a change shall be treated as a change order under this clause, *provided,* that the Contractor gives the Contracting Officer written notice stating (1) the date, circumstances, and source of the order and (2) that the Contractor regards the order as a change order.

(c)   Except as provided in this clause, no order, statement, or conduct of the Contracting Officer shall be treated as a change under this clause or entitle the Contractor to an equitable adjustment.

(d)   If any change under this clause causes an increase or decrease in the Contractor's cost of, or the time required for, the performance of any part of the work under this contract, whether or not changed by any order, the Contracting Officer shall make an equitable adjustment and modify the contract in writing. However, except for an adjustment based on defective specifications, no adjustment for any change under paragraph (b) of this clause shall be made for any costs incurred more than 20 days before the Contractor gives written notice as required. In the case of defective specifications for which the Government is responsible, the equitable adjustment shall include any increased cost reasonably incurred by the Contractor in attempting to comply with the defective specifications.

(e)   The Contractor must assert its right to an adjustment under this clause within 30 days after (1) receipt of the written change order under paragraph (a) of this clause or (2) the furnishing of a written notice under paragraph (b) of this clause, by submitting to the Contracting Officer a written statement describing the general nature and amount of proposal, unless this period is extended by the Government. The statement of proposal for adjustment may be included in the notice under paragraph (b) above.

(f)   No proposal by the Contractor for an equitable adjustment shall be allowed if asserted after final payment under this contract.[1]

The words *change order* as used in the federal clause mean a directive from the contracting officer (the owner) or designated representative to make a change in the work within the general scope of the contract, including

- Changing the details of original work
- Adding new work
- Deleting original work
- Changing the method or manner of performance of the original work, which could mean changing the times in the day, or days in the week, month, or year, during which work may be performed

---

[1] F.A.R. 52.243-4 48 C.F.R. 52.243-4 (Nov. 1996).

- Shortening the time period allowed for completion of the work (acceleration)
- Slowing the rate at which the work may be performed
- Changing the commitments of the government with respect to materials, facilities, equipment, services, or the site conditions to be furnished to the contractor

Although this list of potential changes is very broad, **federal contracts cannot be changed in two respects.** The government cannot unilaterally change any of the general conditions ("General Provisions" in the federal contract) and cannot unilaterally make changes that are beyond the general scope of the contract.

For instance, clauses such as the differing site conditions clause, the suspension of work clause, or the changes clauses itself cannot be unilaterally changed or deleted.

The **general scope of the contract** means the size, type of construction work, and the intended purpose of the work to be contracted for, as contemplated by the government and the contractor when the contract was signed. Changes outside this intended general scope are not permitted. For instance, adding the construction of a boiler house for a steam heating system to an original contract for the grading and paving of a parking lot would be a change beyond the scope of the contract, whereas simply changing the configuration of the parking lot on the same site would not be. Adding quantities of paving would not normally be a change beyond the scope of the contract, nor would changing design details for the paving. However, if such changes were made in quantities that doubled or tripled the contract price, the general scope of the contract would probably be judged to have been exceeded.

SPECIFICS IN CHANGES CLAUSES

The federal contract changes clause is broadly regarded as the model clause in the industry. It is comprehensive, fair, and has stood the test of time. Although the federal clause has been widely copied, clauses in other contracts vary. Following are some important points to note when examining an unfamiliar changes clause.

Distinctions Between Contract Change Terms

There is an important distinction between the terms *change order* as previously discussed and *formal change to the contract*, which does not even appear in the federal clause. **Change order** means a directive from the owner or designated representative to the contractor to make some change (see the preceding examples). **Formal change to the contract** means the written modification to the contract which describes the change and states the increase, or decrease in the case of a deletion, in total contract price and total time for contract performance. Formal changes to the contract are written legal documents executed by the owner and contractor at some time after the change order has been issued. Other terms often used in lieu of change order are *change directive* and *change notice*.

Who Is Empowered to Make Changes?

The changes clause addresses the issue of who can make changes in different ways, depending on the contract. The specific language in the contract must be carefully read to obtain a definitive answer. Note that the federal clause mentions only the "contracting officer," a person defined in the federal acquisition regulations. After the contract has been awarded, the contractor is always formally advised of the name of the contracting officer. In practice, the contracting officer frequently designates others as authorized representatives to issue change orders to the contractor.

Contractors who perform changes ordered by persons without authority under the contract run the risk of not being paid for the change. For instance, a contractor providing construction services to the government under a fixed-price contract discovered that payment would not be made for the extra work of attending meetings, performing inspections, and providing other services not included in the contract that had been directed by a government official bearing the title of "project coordinator." The role and authority of the project coordinator were not defined in the contract. The Veterans Administration Board of Contract Appeals ruled that, although the contractor had performed the work in good faith, the contract provisions requiring authorization of changes by the contracting officer would be strictly enforced. In the Board's words:

> It is long been a tenet of Federal contract law that employees without actual authority cannot bind the government. . . . It is the duty of the contractor, when ordered by an unauthorized Government employee to perform work obviously beyond the contract requirements, to promptly register a protest with the Contracting Officer.[2]

Similarly, a contractor constructing a building for the Postal Service found that specification relaxations approved by the government inspector were not binding on the government. The inspector believed he had authority to approve "minor changes," and the contracting officer did not learn what had occurred until after the work had been completed, at which point he refused to ratify the change. The Postal Service Board of Contract Appeals ruled that, although there may have been an honest misunderstanding, the inspector could not alter the contract. The Board said:

> Although Mr. Hale agreed to relax the specifications, his agreement was not binding on the government, as he lacked authority to change the specifications. The notice to proceed, after designating the Contracting Officer Representative, gave notice to Appellants that changes were reserved to the Contracting Officer. Mr. Hale's misrepresentation as to his authority did not create any right in Appellants to avoid the contract's express terms.[3]

[2] *Appeal of Bud Rho Energy Systems, Inc.*, VABCA No. 2208 (December 31, 1985).

[3] *Appeal of Henry Burge and Alvin White*, PSBCA No. 2431 (May 19, 1989).

A more difficult question arises when the person ordering the change has "apparent authority." This apparent authority can be created by previous actions of the owner, such as readily paying for previous changes ordered by that person, which create the impression that the owner intended that person to have such authority. The point is illustrated by a North Carolina case where the issue became the apparent authority of the prime contractor's field superintendent. A subcontract agreement for excavation and grading work provided that the subcontractor would be paid extra for rock excavated, the quantity to be measured by the general contractor's engineer. During contract performance, representatives of the subcontractor and the prime contractor's field superintendent agreed that rock measurements would no longer be required to be made by the prime contractor's engineer. Rather, other prime contractor on-site personnel could take the measurements. This agreement was confirmed in writing by the subcontractor in a letter to the prime contractor. Subsequently, the prime contractor refused to make payment because their engineer had not performed the measurements for the rock quantity excavated. At that point, the subcontractor abandoned work and sued the prime contractor, alleging breach of contract. The prime contractor countersued for the extra cost of obtaining another subcontractor to complete the work. A trial court ruled in favor of the subcontractor. In affirming the trial court decision, the Court of Appeals of North Carolina said that the "dominant question" was whether the prime contractor field superintendent "had authority to modify the contract with subcontractor by dispensing with the requirement that ADC's engineers measure the rock. . . . " Trial evidence indicated that there were other occasions when the prime contractor's field superintendent had orally ordered additional work to be performed as changes to the contract, all of which were subsequently paid. Evidence also indicated that substantial quantities of rock were excavated on the project without the prime contractor's engineers being sent to the site to do the measuring and that the prime contractor knew that the measuring was being done by other site personnel and initially continued to pay the subcontractor's invoices. For these reasons, the Court of Appeals concluded that the prime contractor's field superintendent had authority to orally modify the written subcontract.[4]

When the changes clause makes clear where the authority lies, problems such as those just described are more easily avoided.

Who Is Empowered to Make Formal Changes to the Contract?

Executing a formal change to the contract on behalf of the owner is different from ordering the change to be made. Both should be formalized in writing, with a clear, unambiguous description of the change, and the formal change to the contract should also include the agreed-upon change in contract price and contract time extension (if any). A person possessing authority to act for the owner in increasing the contract price and the time allowed for contract performance always possesses

---

[4]*Son-Shine Grading, Inc. v. ADC Constr. Co.,* 315 S.E.2d 346 (N.C. App. 1984).

the authority to order changes, but the reverse is often not true—that is, the person with authority to order the change may not possess the authority to change the contract price or the time for performance. It is, therefore, helpful if the changes clause makes clear which representative of the owner possesses the authority to perform each separate function. In some jurisdictions, defining respective functions and designating who is empowered to perform them is governed by statute.

How Are Price and Time Adjustments Determined?

Interestingly, this is one area where the changes clause in the federal contract is silent, saying only that there shall be an **equitable adjustment** to the contract price and time. Changes clauses in other contracts usually state precisely how the change in price will be determined, often specifying several alternate methods. If the owner and contractor do not agree on the price change, the changes clause usually prescribes that payment will be made by the **force account method**, the details of which are spelled out in the clause. The force account method of payment is more fully discussed later in this chapter.

"No Pay Without Signed Change Order" Language

Most changes clauses contain language intended to strictly limit the contractor's right to payment to only those changes authorized by the owner prior to the change being undertaken. Usually, the clause will require that the authorization be in writing.

Some especially restrictive clauses require that the actual formal change to the contract, stating the agreed price and time for performance, be executed prior to performance of the change. Such provisions are unworkable today. Even in the most efficient owner's organization, it takes too long administratively after the change has been ordered to agree on price and time and to prepare an appropriate formal change to the contract. The project would grind to a halt in the meantime. The problem is exacerbated because large jobs commonly involve several hundred or even several thousand changes.

It is a different matter when the changes clause merely says there shall be **no payment without a signed change order** (also called *change notice* or *change directive*) in hand prior to performance of the change. This at least permits the work to be completed while the price and time changes are negotiated and the formal change to the contract prepared, although this procedure requires the contractor to carry the financial burden of performing the change in the interim. To solve this problem, some contracts provide for a **two-part change to the contract**, in which the contractor is promptly paid demonstrable costs under a Part I change to the contract prior to finalization of the change under a later Part II change to the contract.

Sometimes, change orders are written on a "price not to exceed" basis. Under this arrangement, the contractor is assured payment up to the not-to-exceed limit, although payment normally is not received until a formal change to the contract has been executed by both parties.

In practice, contractors are given many **oral change orders** (the federal contract mentions the words "oral order"). After the contractor has performed the changed work, owners sometimes refuse to make payment, claiming that the work was not authorized by a written change order. Sometimes the refusal to pay is based on a claim that the person who issued the oral order was not authorized to do so or that person will deny that he or she issued the order. The attitude of our courts toward payment disputes of this type is discussed later in this chapter.

Constructive Changes

A **constructive change** is a change that is not acknowledged by the owner as such when it occurs, but which nonetheless is a change. In this situation, the owner takes the position that whatever the contractor is directed to do or is prevented from doing is not a change, but rather is required or prohibited by the original contract, as the case may be. In these situations, the contractor is required to proceed according to the owner's instructions but is free to assert and later attempt to prove that the owner's instructions constituted a change order. If the contractor is correct, courts will deem that a constructive change has occurred, and the contractor will be awarded the costs incurred plus a reasonable profit thereon.

Two elements must be proved to establish a constructive change. First, the **change element** must be proved. Proof hinges on the facts of each particular case. The court must be convinced that a true change occurred in the work or requirements of the contract. Second, the **order element** must be proved. This is established entirely by the owner's acts or words, both written or oral. It is not sufficient that the owner made a "suggestion" that something be done or an "observation" that something might be a "good idea." There must have been an actual order or directive to the contractor or a course of conduct by the owner that had the practical effect of such an order or directive.

The following cases illustrate court determination of three different types of constructive change. In the first case, a contractor constructing an underground parking garage for the federal government recovered extra costs when earlier permission to alter excavated slopes was rescinded by the government after the majority of the slopes had been excavated. The project specifications required slopes for the exterior berms to be excavated at a one-foot vertical to two-foot horizontal slope and also required an excavation bracing system. During performance, the contractor requested and received permission to cut the slopes at the steeper ratio of 1 to 1.5. After most of the slopes had been cut and a new bracing system designed based on the steeper slopes, the government rescinded its earlier approval of the steeper slopes. The contractor asserted a constructive change for the extra costs of reverting to the original system. The government argued that it had the right to rescind earlier permission and to insist on compliance with the excavation slopes specified in the contract. The U.S. Claims Court (now the United States Court of

Federal Claims) agreed that the government could rescind its earlier approval but ruled that the contractor was entitled to an equitable adjustment for the extra costs caused by the rescission. The equitable adjustment awarded the contractor not only the additional construction costs of revising the slopes back to one-foot vertical on two-foot horizontal but also included the costs incurred for redesigning the bracing system to accommodate the originally specified slopes.[5]

In the second case, the Armed Services Board of Contract Appeals ruled that a government contracting officer's refusal to allow the contractor to use its intended method of performance was a constructive change. The contract work involved installing a telephone switching system at an Army ocean terminal. New cable was to be installed along three miles of wharves, but the contract documents did not indicate where or how the cable was to be attached to the wharves. The contractor had planned to strap the cable to the guardrails, but the contracting officer required that the cables be installed underneath the wharves, which required drilling 15,000 bolt holes through reinforced concrete. When the contractor appealed the contracting officer's denial of the contractor's claim for a constructive change, the board ruled for the contractor, holding that:

> By disapproving appellant's proposed method, the Government required appellant to employ a more expensive and time-consuming method of installing the cable on the wharves and thereby constructively changed the terms of the contract. The appellant is entitled to additional compensation and performance time for that constructive change.[6]

In the third case, the federal government had awarded a contract for construction of a new auto repair shop at a naval air station. The contract specified that the new shop was to be built during the first phase of the project, during which time the existing shop on the site was to remain in operation. The second phase of the contract consisted of demolishing the original shop. The contractor intended to grade and pave the entire site around the existing shop during the first phase and so indicated this intention on their critical path method (CPM) schedule which the government approved. When the government refused to give the contractor access to the entire site to perform the intended grading, the contractor asserted this refusal was a constructive change. The Armed Services Board of Contract Appeals concluded that the contractor's interpretation of the contract was reasonable, in that, although the contract required existing shop to remain operational, it placed no restrictions on access to the site. Further, the board said that the government's approval of the contractor's CPM schedule was evidence of the reasonableness of the contractor's expectation. Since the contractor had incurred considerable additional costs and delay due to performing the site work in two separate phases, the board ruled that the contractor was entitled to an equitable adjustment for a constructive change to the contract.[7]

---

[5]*Baltimore Contractors, Inc. v. United States,* 12 Cl. Ct. 328 (1987).

[6]*Appeal of Communications International, Inc.,* ASBCA No. 30976 (October 23, 1987).

[7]*Appeal of West Coast General Corporation,* ASBCA No. 35900 (April 14, 1988).

Constructive Change Notice Requirements

A contractor who believes a constructive change has occurred must give **prompt written notice of the constructive change** to the owner. Notice is crucial to preserve the contractor's rights of recovery for the additional costs and extra contract time associated with the change. Without such notice, it can later be argued (rightly or wrongly) that the owner was unaware that the contractor regarded the owner's instructions to constitute a change to the contract for which the contractor expected payment.

It should be noted that the federal contract changes clause refers directly to the constructive change situation and to the importance of notice in the second full paragraph of the clause.

CARDINAL CHANGES

A **cardinal change** is a change to the contract that, because of its size or the nature of the changed work, is clearly beyond the general scope of the contract. It is beyond the reasonable contemplation of the owner and contractor at the time of contract formation. Additive cardinal changes are illegal on public contracts, even if both owner and contractor agree to the change, because such a large addition of work violates public bidding statutes guaranteeing free and open competition. On private work, such a change is not illegal and not improper if both owner and contractor agree to the change. However, even in private work, a cardinal change cannot be forced upon the contractor.

These principles are illustrated by a recent decision of the United States Court of Federal Claims. The Department of Energy had awarded a performance specification contract for the construction of a fabric filter particle collection system (that is, a "baghouse") of an open-end design to accommodate potentially explosive conditions. Among other performance specifications, one specification called for an inlet gas operating range of 0.6 to 1.6 psi. The contractor interpreted this specification to mean that gas entering the baghouse would exert a pressure of 0.6 to 1.6 psi at an imaginary line separating the inlet pipe from the baghouse, whereas the government insisted that a constant internal operating pressure must be maintained throughout the baghouse within that range. During construction, the contracting officer demanded written assurances from the contractor that the baghouse would maintain a constant internal operating pressure in the range of 0.6 to 1.6 psi. The contractor refused on the grounds that, given the government's open-end design, it was impossible to comply with the contracting officer's demand. The government terminated the contractor for default.

The court found that the government's insistence on a constant internal operating pressure of 0.6 to 1.6 psi was a constructive change to the contract because the specifications did not stipulate any particular internal operating pressure. Further, the court ruled that the government's directive constituted a cardinal change to the contract. In converting the default termination to a termination for the convenience of the government, the court said:

If the requirements that the government imposed on Airprep, in this case, were in the general scope of the contract, then Airprep was obligated to perform, even if the government misinterpreted the contract. A contractor has no right to stop work if the project to be constructed is fundamentally the same as the one contracted to build. A contractor is not, however, obligated to undertake "cardinal changes"—drastic modifications beyond the scope of the contract work . . . changes that alter the nature of the thing to be constructed.[8]

No universal standards exist to determine precisely how large or how unusual the change must be to constitute a cardinal change. In some cases, courts have ruled that an extraordinary number of changes, each of which was not excessive in itself, amounted to a cardinal change. In one such case, a private owner awarded a guaranteed maximum price (GMP) contract for the modernization of a paper mill. Once contract performance started, the owner issued a steady stream of drawing revisions, in most instances ignoring the contract requirement for written change orders. More than 16,000 manhours of redesign effort were expended by the owner, resulting in such an excessive number of changes that the California Court of Appeals determined that the degree of change was far beyond the contemplation of the parties at the time the contract was entered into and that by issuing excessive revisions and radically altering the scope of the work, the owner had abandoned the original contract. In the court's words:

> When an owner imposes upon the contractor an excessive number of changes such that it can fairly be said that the scope of the work under the original contract has been altered, an abandonment of contract properly may be found. In these cases, the contractor, with the full approval and expectation of the owner, may complete the project. Although the *contract* may be abandoned, the *work* is not.

> Since the work performed benefitted the owner and was performed with their approval, the contractor was entitled to recover its total direct costs plus a reasonable overhead and profit.[9]

Fortunately, relatively few contracts result in such massive change.

As a general operating principle, a contractor should refuse to perform a change believed to be a cardinal change, except under the threat of being placed in default of the contract by the owner. Even then, the contractor should proceed only after notifying the owner in writing that the directive to perform the work is a cardinal change and that performance is being compelled under protest. This principle holds on both public and private contracts, unless the contractor on private work is willing to perform the cardinal change.

An architect/engineer or construction manager who compels a contractor to perform a cardinal change on either public or private work has committed a tortious act and may be sued in tort (see Chapter 1) even though privity of contract does not exist. This would be in addition to whatever contractual remedies that the contractor has with respect to the owner.

---

[8] *Airprep Technology, Inc. v. United States*, 30 Fed. Cl. Ct. 488 (1994).
[9] *C. Norman Peterson Co. v. Container Corporation of America*, 218 Cal. Rptr. 592 (Cal. App. 1985).

PRICE AND TIME ADJUSTMENTS FOR CONTRACT CHANGES

Forward Pricing

If the contractor and owner agree on the price and time requirement for the changed or additional work before starting performance of the change, the change is said to be **forward priced.** Under fixed-price contracts, the contractor assumes the full financial risk of performance in the same manner as for the original contract when changes are forward priced. For this reason, the adjustment to contract price and time should include, in addition to a reasonable profit, an allowance to cover the risk that the contractor is assuming. Depending on the nature of the change, the price and time adjustment to the contract will be greater than if the owner were assuming the risk.

Once agreement has been reached on a forward-priced change order, the payment terms may not be altered. This principle is illustrated by a Corps of Engineer Board of Contract Appeals decision on a mass transit contract. The contractor had negotiated a forward-priced lump sum change order with the resident engineer whom the contract documents had designated as the authorized representative of the contracting officer. Following the contractor's completion of the work covered by the change order, the contracting officer would not agree to the negotiated price, demanding instead that the contractor provide proof of the actual costs incurred. The court ruled that since the resident engineer, acting within the scope of his contractual authority, had negotiated the forward-priced change with the contractor and the contractor had performed the change in good faith, the contracting officer could not require an after-the-fact accounting of actual costs.[10]

Retrospective Pricing

When price and time adjustments to the contract are not determined until after the changed or additional work has been completed, the change has been **retrospectively priced.** In this situation, the basis of the price and time adjustment normally will be job records maintained by the contractor or owner, or both. If the contractor and owner cannot agree on the proper price and time adjustments, the dispute must be resolved under the dispute resolution provisions of the contract. In any event, the price and time adjustment is determined retrospectively, either by the contractor and owner, or by others.

Force Account

Force account is a particular form of retrospective pricing in which the contract spells out a specific procedure for arriving at the price adjustment when the contractor and the owner fail to agree on the price by forward pricing. Force account is also widely used to determine price adjustments for miscellaneous minor added work.

---

[10]*Appeal of Excavation Construction, Inc.,* ENGBCA No. 4106 (December 27, 1985).

When force account is used, daily records are kept of labor, material, and equipment usage expended on the changed work by the general contractor and all subcontractors involved. The records are agreed upon daily and signed by representatives of both owner and contractor. When the work has been completed, the records are used as the basis for computing the direct costs associated with the change. The force account provisions then state fixed percentages of labor, materials, equipment operation, and subcontract costs that are allowed for overhead and profit markups, regardless of what the contractor's actual overhead costs may be.

Application of Force Account Provisions to Extended Performance Situations

If the force account markup percentages are too low compared to the contractor's actual overhead costs, the contractor will receive less than an equitable cost adjustment. This is particularly true when **the contract performance time has been extended** because of changes directed by the owner or, as frequently occurs, because the contractor encounters differing site conditions (see Chapter 15). In these situations, the contract time and price adjustments are more equitably determined using the force account records as the best evidence of the time of contract performance change as well as for the direct cost portion of the contract price change. Then, the indirect cost portion of the contract price change is also determined on the basis of the contractor's actual indirect costs which take the extension of contract performance time into consideration. In addition, the contractor is allowed a reasonable profit.

Use of Force Account Records in Determining Breach of Contract Damages

The provisions of the changes clause, including the force account provisions, are contractually prescribed procedures that parties to a contract should follow for matters falling within the purview of the contract. However, when the contract has been breached, the proper determination of the monetary **value of the breach damages is not limited by the changes clause** in the contract. For instance, if the owner has breached the contract, the contractor is entitled to be paid *all* costs resulting from the breach, both direct and indirect, plus a reasonable profit. If force account records have been kept, they are the best possible evidence of the contractor's direct costs. However, the contractor's *actual* indirect costs should be paid in lieu of the force account markup percentages, and a reasonable profit on both direct and indirect costs should be added to make the contractor whole. This is true whether the contract performance time has been extended by the breach or not.

Impact Costs

Costs flowing from the change in addition to the *proximate costs* (meaning the direct labor, materials, and so on, actually incurred at the time of performing the change) are **impact costs.** These consist of (1) the time-related costs that flow from the change and (2) the effect that the change may have on the efficiency of performance of the original unchanged work.

The **time-related costs** usually consist of extended job overhead and extended home office overhead costs because the project took longer to complete as a result of the change. They also frequently include labor and material escalation costs and the higher cost of performing work in inclement weather. All of these kinds of costs are associated with the original work on the project being performed later than it would have been if the change had not occurred.

For instance, suppose the project was scheduled to be completed in a northern city by mid-September and was proceeding on schedule when a large quantity of extra work was directed to be performed in April of the project's final year. The extra work extended the completion of all following original work four months past September into a severe winter. Also, ready-mix concrete prices and craft labor rates both increased on October 1. Clearly, additional costs would be incurred for winter protection, concrete cost increases, and increases in craft wages.

Loss-of-efficiency costs in the performance of the unchanged work are additional costs incurred to complete part or all of the original unchanged work on the project due to the disruptive effect of changes made to the changed work. This is particularly important when a large number of changes must be dealt with on a continuing basis. Numerous studies indicate such situations can have a devastating effect on construction costs for a number of reasons, such as crowding of the trades, frequent moving of crews with associated starts and stops, frequent requirements for overtime, the necessity of going through a learning curve more times than would otherwise be necessary, and the general effect on morale due to continual changes and delays.

The National Association of Electrical Contractors has conducted studies to assist in quantifying the loss of efficiency due to these effects. Also, the Business Roundtable has published data illustrating the loss of labor efficiency when excessive overtime is worked on an extended basis.

When the forward-priced method of pricing changes is used, impacts can be included on an estimated basis along with the proximate costs. Otherwise, they and the proximate costs will be determined retrospectively.

Change Order Payment Disputes

Change order payment disputes frequently arise between owners and contractors and between contractors and subcontractors. At least three separate root causes are responsible:

- The owner or, in the case of a subcontract, the contractor, claims that the work was not authorized in advance by a signed change order.
- The person alleged to have directed the work denies directing it, or the owner or, in the case of a subcontract, the contractor, claims that person did not have authority to order the work performed.

■ The contractor or subcontractor alleges that the direction received from the owner or contractor respectively constitutes a constructive change to the contract.

Judicial Attitude to Payment Disputes

In some cases, changed work has been performed by the contractor in good faith, and courts have denied payment on the grounds of the absence of a signed change order or other proper advance authorization. However, the **current judicial attitude** is toward equitable principles to avoid unjust enrichment of the owner in the owner-contractor relationship or of the contractor in the contractor-subcontractor relationship. Courts are heavily influenced by the contemporaneous words, acts, and conduct of the parties and by their past patterns of behavior. *Contemporaneous words, acts, and conduct* refer to how the parties behaved when changes in the contract work were actually performed. *Earlier patterns of behavior* means the way in which the parties handled similar changes earlier in the contract. For instance, suppose an owner had consistently paid the contractor for changed or additional work orally directed by the resident engineer throughout contract performance and then refused to pay for a particularly large later change that the contractor performed on the resident engineer's oral direction. Even if the changes clause said there would be no pay for work performed without a signed change order, a court today would probably hold that the contractual provision had been waived by the owner's earlier behavior.

The following cases illustrate situations in which the contractor was not paid for performing extra work because the work was performed in the absence of a signed change order. In a 1984 Ohio case, an excavation contractor on a bridge improvement project encountered Brea sandstone in an excavation represented in the contract to contain no rock. Brea sandstone is extremely hard. The county engineer acknowledged that the material excavated was not as represented in the contract and directed the contractor to blast and remove the rock and to keep track of costs for payment purposes. The county engineer witnessed the performance of the work. However, the county commission refused to pay for all but a small portion of the extra work on the grounds that Ohio law requires extra work be authorized in writing and approved by the county commission. When the contractor sued for the balance, a trial court ordered payment but was reversed by the Court of Appeals of Ohio.[11]

Similarly, a contractor in Florida on an airport project failed to secure payment for extra work directed by the owner. The contract contained a changes clause requiring advance written authorization for any extra work. During construction, the owner revised the plans for the underground drainage system, resulting in considerable extra work. No change order was ever issued. When the contractor presented an itemized claim for the extra work after completion of construction, the owner refused to pay. Despite the fact that the owner had ordered the extra work

---

[11]*Cleveland Trinidad Paving Co. v. Board of County of Commissioners of Cuyahoga County,* 472 N.E.2d 753 (Ohio App. 1984).

and it was satisfactorily performed, the District Court of Appeals of Florida supported the owner's position. The contractor was not paid for the work.[12]

However, the following cases illustrate the current trend in judicial attitude. In a 1993 Arkansas case involving the construction of a residence, the topographical information furnished by the owner proved to be inaccurate, which required a large number of changes to be made by the construction contractor due to inaccurate ground elevations. The owner orally directed the changes and paid progress payments systematically for a number of them. Eventually, the owner refused to make a progress payment, alleging that changes had been made without written authorization as required by the General Conditions of the construction contract. The Supreme Court of Arkansas ruled in favor of the contractor on the grounds that the owner was aware of the changes, orally assented to them, made progress payments, and continued to approve changes orally. The owner could not behave in this manner and then rely on the "no pay without written change order" language as grounds for refusing to make payment.[13]

In a Wyoming case involving a guaranteed maximum price (GMP) contract for the conversion of an existing building to a restaurant, the contract required changes in the work to be authorized in writing by the owner as a condition for adding their value to the guaranteed maximum price. To meet the owner's schedule, the contractor was repeatedly asked to make renovations that were beyond the scope of the original contract. All extra work performed was by oral direction of the owner. When the owner refused to increase the guaranteed maximum price by the value of the extra work, the contractor sued. In ruling for the contractor, the Wyoming Supreme Court held that

> The habitual disregard of a provision which requires that change orders for extras be in writing, if determinable as a matter of fact, can amount to a waiver of the contractual requirement. It is apparent from the record that the parties ignored the writing requirement and frequently orally agreed to "extras." The record also clearly demonstrates that the provision requiring written approval of all changes in the work was waived by the words and conduct of the parties.[14]

A 1994 Missouri case resulted in the same holding. The framing subcontractor on a large apartment complex in Kansas City assisted the concrete and plumbing subcontractors at the prime contractor's request in order to expedite the work and were paid for this extra work. At that point, the general contractor instructed the subcontractor not to include extra work in future payment requests because it created a problem with the owner and construction lender. The subcontractor was directed just to keep track of the extra work which was to be paid separately. When the subcontractor continued to perform extra work orally directed by the prime contractor and separately billed for it, the general contractor paid for part of the work, but not all. The subcontractor eventually filed a mechanic's lien on the project

---

[12]*Southern Roadbuilders, Inc. v. Lee County*, 495 So.2d 189 (Fla. App. 1986).

[13]*Hempel v. Bragg*, 856 S.W.2d 293 (Ark. 1993).

[14]*Huang International, Inc. v. Foose Construction Co.*, 734 P.2d 975 (Wyo. 1987).

for the value of the unpaid extra work. The project owner and general contractor then argued that, in the absence of written change orders, the subcontractor was not entitled to payment and should not be allowed to maintain a lien. The Missouri Court of Appeals found that the general contractor, through the words and deeds of its site representatives, had waived the written change order requirement. The court said:

> All of the extra work performed and the extra materials supplied for buildings 12 through 17 were furnished either at the direction or under the supervision of Mr. Ryan or the agents of Ryan's Construction. Based on the action of Ryan Construction concerning the extra work performed by Henley on buildings 12 through 17, the general contractor's conduct concerning extras in general, and the large scale of the extra work, the trial court could reasonably infer that Ryan Construction either expressly or by acquiescence waived the written change order requirement with regards to the claim for extras on buildings 12 through 17. The trial court did not err in including these extras in the mechanic's lien.[15]

As the preceding cases indicate, waiver of a contractual right occurs when the parties' behavior is inconsistent with the enforcement of that right.

Orders for Payment of Disputed Changes

Regardless of the literal wording of the changes clause, the following conditions usually result in a court's **order for payment for changes:**

- The owner, or contractor in the case of a subcontract, approves the work being done;
- The owner or contractor authorizes or allows the work to proceed; and
- The owner or contractor knows that the contractor or subcontractor respectively expects to be paid for the work.

Proper Contractor Reaction to Oral or Written Directives

When oral or written instructions or directives are received from the owner that the contractor believes constitute a change order, the proper reaction is as follows:

- Promptly request a written change order.
- If a change order is not received, proceed only after written advice to the owner that the instruction or directive received constitutes a change to the contract and that the work is being undertaken in expectation that payment will be made for the change.
- If the owner maintains that the directed work is not a change, but, at the same time, insists that the instruction or directive be carried out, the contractor must proceed with the work. However, this should be done only

---

[15]*T. D. Industries, Inc. v. The Lakes Project Investors,* 883 S.W.2d 44 (Mo. App. 1994).

after advising the owner in writing that the work is being performed under protest and that all rights under the contract or subcontract are reserved.

- File a claim for the costs and time involved in performing the changed work and proceed under the disputes resolution provisions of the contract.

If the contractor's position is contractually proper, the chances of eventual recovery of costs and time for performing the work according to oral or written directives is greatly enhanced by following this procedure.

CONCLUSION

This chapter highlighted the concept and operation of contract changes clauses. One reason that construction contracts, particularly heavy construction contracts, undergo changes is because the contractor encounters differing site conditions, the subject of the following chapter.

QUESTIONS AND PROBLEMS

1. What three interrelated rights and/or obligations are central to the concept of contract changes? What would happen in today's contracting world if construction contracts did not contain changes clauses? Is a changes clause an exculpatory clause? If not, what is the purpose of the clause?

2. Are all changes clauses more or less the same, or are they different? What seven broad kinds of changes provided for by the federal changes clause were listed in this chapter?

3. What is the difference between a change order (change directive, change notice) and a formal change to the contract?

4. Explain the differences in legal empowerment required by an individual in the owner's organization to order changes and to authorize formal changes to the contract.

5. Why is it important that a contractor who has been directed to perform a change be certain that the person from whom he received the order had proper authority to order changes? What is apparent authority? How can it be created?

6. What does the federal contract changes clause have to say about the change in contract price resulting from changes? What are some other methods for determining change order pricing?

7. What is the intent of the "no pay without signed change order" language? What would be the effect in today's construction world of a clause providing that a formal change to the contract be signed before actual work on the change could begin?

8. Explain the concept of two-part formal changes to the contract, including why such a procedure is often utilized.

9. What is the danger to the contractor in performing added or changed work on the basis of an oral change order?

10. What is a constructive change? Explain the nature of the two necessary elements to establish that a constructive change has occurred.

11. Explain the importance of the contractor giving prompt written notice of constructive change. What argument might the owner later make if notice is not given?

12. What is a cardinal change? Why are cardinal changes illegal in public work? Can a contractor properly be forced to perform a cardinal change in private work? Do universally accepted precise standards exist to define when a cardinal change has occurred?

13. Explain the difference between forward-priced changes and retrospectively priced changes.

14. What is force account? Explain typical force account provisions.

15. Explain how application of force account provisions might result in the contractor receiving less than an equitable adjustment in contract price after performing changed work. How is this possibility of inequitable payment affected when the changed work extends the period of contract performance?

16. Explain why the provisions of the changes clause, including the force account provisions, do not apply when determining breach-of-contract damages. Explain how force account records can still be helpful when determining such damages.

17. What are impact costs? Name three separate examples of time-related impact costs.

18. What are loss-of-efficiency impact costs? Name five general causes for these kinds of extra costs.

19. What is the current judicial tendency in dealing with change order payment disputes?

20. Why are words, acts, and conduct of the parties to the contract and their earlier patterns of behavior important when a court seeks to resolve a change order payment dispute?

21. What three conditions, when met, will usually result in a court ordering that payment be made in cases involving change order payment disputes?

    What four-step procedure was outlined in this chapter that a contractor (or subcontractor) should follow to ensure eventual payment for changed work when the owner (or contractor) denies that his (or her) directive constitutes a change to the contract but insists that the directive be carried out?

15

Differing Site Conditions

The differing site condition clause has an interesting history. Today many contractors refuse to submit bids on projects where unknown site conditions could result in surprises and the contract does not contain a differing site conditions clause. This was not always the case.

In the past, the risk of encountering adverse physical conditions at the site that were unknown when the contract was entered into was borne by the contractor. For instance, if excavation work that was expected to be entirely in soil turned out to be in rock below a certain depth, the contractor was bound to complete the contract without any adjustment whatsoever. In addition to absorbing the additional costs of excavating rock instead of soil, the contractor could also be required to pay liquidated damages if, due to encountering the rock, the time allowed for performance of the contract was exceeded. In other words, the contractor, not the owner, bore the entire risk of cost and time performance regardless of what was encountered.

Recognizing this considerable risk exposure, prudent contractors included substantial cost contingencies in their bids to protect themselves if unknown adverse site conditions were encountered. The contingencies were, therefore, also included in the contract price. Thus, if these conditions were actually encountered, the owner, in effect, had already paid the cost to deal with them. However, this practice also resulted in the owner paying costs to overcome unknown adverse conditions whether such conditions actually were encountered or not, frequently producing a windfall for the contractor.

The federal government eventually realized that considerable savings in federal contract dollars were possible by the government assuming the risk of unknown adverse site conditions rather than imposing this risk on the contractor. This was the genesis of the current *differing site conditions clause*. This clause provides that, if unknown conditions are encountered during performance of the work that differ materially from the conditions represented in the contract or those ordinarily encountered in the work of the contract, the contract price and time for performance will be increased accordingly. Under this arrangement, the government pays and allows extra contract time only for conditions that are actually encountered. Contractors do not include cost contingencies in their bids for unknown adverse site conditions and reap no "windfall" if such conditions are not encountered.

THE FEDERAL DIFFERING SITE CONDITIONS CLAUSE

The federal contract differing site conditions clause reads as follows:

DIFFERING SITE CONDITIONS

(a)   The Contractor shall promptly, and before such conditions are disturbed, give a written notice to the Contracting Officer of (1) subsurface or latent physical conditions at the site which differ materially from those indicated in this contract, or (2) unknown physical conditions at the site, of an unusual nature, which differ materially from those ordinarily encountered and generally recognized as inhering in work of the character provided for in this contract.

(b) The Contracting Officer shall investigate the site conditions promptly after receiving the notice. If the conditions do materially so differ and cause an increase or decrease in the Contractor's cost of, or the time required for, performing any part of the work under this contract, whether or not changed as a result of the conditions, an equitable adjustment shall be made under this contract and the contract modified in writing accordingly.

(c) No request by the Contractor for an equitable adjustment to the contract under this clause shall be allowed, unless the Contractor has given the written notice required; *provided,* that the time prescribed in (a) above for giving written notice may be extended by the Contracting Officer.

(d) No request by the Contractor for an equitable adjustment to the contract for differing site conditions shall be allowed if made after final payment under this contract.[1]

Type I Differing Site Conditions

The first of the two differing site condition types described in the federal clause refers to any physical condition encountered in the work of the contract that differs materially from a condition indicated in the contract documents. In other words, the condition must be indicated a certain way in the contract documents and, when encountered during actual performance, must be found to be materially different. Such a condition is commonly called a **type I** or **Category I condition.** It is not necessary that the indication in the contract be explicit. In other words, conditions implied by the drawings and specifications taken as a whole, as well as conditions that are expressly stated, are considered by a court to be "indications" of the contract.

Two facts must exist to establish a type I differing site condition. First, the contract documents must have indicated a physical condition in a certain way. Second, when the condition was encountered during actual performance, it was found to be materially different. A simple example of a type I differing site condition is finding wet, sticky clay at a location in an excavation where the soil boring logs, which were stated to be part of the contract documents, indicated that the material would be damp sand. In the absence of a differing site condition clause in the contract, this situation constitutes misrepresentation on the part of the owner. Without the clause, a contractor who encounters such a condition has no means of relief except to sue the government for breach of contract and prove in court the necessary elements to establish a misrepresentation breach (see Chapter 13).

Type II Differing Site Conditions

The second type of differing site condition referred to in the federal contract is called a **type II** or **Category II condition.** This refers to a physical condition encountered during contract performance that differs materially from conditions normally expected in the type of construction work in the contract involved. In this case, the

---

[1]F.A.R. 52.236-2 48 C.F.R. 52.236-2 (Nov. 1996).

difference is not between an encountered condition and a condition shown or indicated a certain way in the drawings or other parts of the contract documents, but rather is a difference between the conditions encountered and the conditions considered normal or usual for the type of construction work being done. In other words, the condition encountered must be of such an unusual nature that it could not have been reasonably anticipated for the type of project at hand. To establish a type II differing site condition, a contractor must prove that the condition encountered is truly unusual and thus not anticipated when the contract was signed.

An example of a type II differing site condition is finding a material in an excavation that, even though identified correctly on the soil boring logs, behaves in a manner materially different from the material's usual behavior—that is, exhibits some abnormal physical property that could not have been reasonably anticipated by an experienced contractor. Without the differing site conditions clause, the contractor has no other means of relief unless it can be established that the government knew about the abnormal behavior of the material and did not disclose this superior knowledge prior to contract formation.

An excellent illustration of a type II differing site condition occurred on one of the tunnels for the Boston Harbor Project in Massachusetts. The tunnel was founded in massive competent argillite, and the specifications required that it be excavated by use of a tunnel-boring machine (TBM). The spoil, or "muck," produced by a TBM normally consists of small rock chips no larger than two to three inches maximum dimension grading on down to sand size. When handled by the TBM discharge conveyors and muck haulage equipment, the material usually behaves much like sand and gravel. Instead, in a limited section of the Boston tunnel, the TBM produced muck that resembled wet flowing concrete that was difficult to handle on the tunnel muck conveyors and haulage equipment. The material was correctly described geologically in the contract documents, but its behavior was highly unusual and could not have been expected in the work of the contract at hand.

Duty of Contractor to Give Notice

Note that the federal clause requires the contractor to promptly notify the government whenever either type I or type II differing site conditions are encountered and "before such conditions are disturbed." The purpose of this **duty of the contractor to give notice** is to provide an opportunity for the government to view and investigate the condition to verify that the condition is, in fact, a differing site condition. If the condition is disturbed or obliterated, it may be difficult or impossible to do this, which could effectively bar recovery under the clause.

A secondary purpose for giving notice promptly is to provide the government the opportunity to direct the actions to be taken by the contractor in dealing with the differing site condition. Since the government is paying the costs, it clearly has the right to direct the manner in which the condition is dealt with in the field when a choice is available. Also, some encounters with differing site conditions make it necessary to redesign all or part of the project, a function obviously controlled by the government in its capacity as owner.

Duty of Government to Promptly Investigate

The federal clause provides that, once notified, the government has a positive **duty to investigate the condition and make a determination** that it is or is not a differing site condition. Failure to investigate promptly and make a determination in good faith is a breach of contract.

The significance of this point was illustrated in a contract for the construction of an immigration processing center where the contract documents contained detailed representations of the subsurface soil conditions. During performance, the contractor encountered organic muck that was not indicated in the soil information included with the contract documents. The presence of this material made it impossible to construct the building's concrete foundations in the manner described in the contract. Although the contractor promptly informed the government's site representatives when the muck was encountered and requested instructions, three months passed before the government finally acknowledged a differing site condition and directed the contractor to remove the muck. The contracting officer agreed to pay the direct costs for removing the muck but refused to pay delay damages or other impact costs caused by the three months' delay. When the contractor sued, the U.S. Court of Claims (now the United States Court for Federal Claims) held that the government's slow response had brought the contract work to a complete halt and that under these circumstances the government must pay the contractor not only its direct costs but all increased costs of contract performance including delay damages.[2]

If the government determines that the condition is not a differing site condition, the contractor may accept the decision or, as with any other contracting officer's decision, dispute the determination under the provisions of the disputes resolution clause in the contract.

Equitable Adjustment Provided

The federal clause makes clear that if the contracting officer finds that the condition is a differing site condition that increases or decreases the cost or time for performance of the work, an **equitable adjustment** will be made to the contract price and time. This promise is unequivocal and cannot be overridden by any other provision of the contract. Most, if not all, encounters with differing site conditions result in upward adjustments in contract price and time.

Differing Site Conditions and Government Liability

The federal differing site conditions clause is **not an exculpatory clause.** It is true that, in the case of a type I differing site condition, the clause does partially exculpate or remove the stigma of fault or blame associated with a breach of contract by the government, but it does not operate to relieve the government of liability. Rather, it has the reverse effect of explicitly establishing the government's liability

---

[2]*Beauchamp Construction Co., Inc. v. United States,* 14 Cl. Ct. 430 (1988).

for costs and contract time to overcome the condition and provides an orderly process by which the contractor may claim and recover these costs through an equitable adjustment to the contract.

Thus, the clause provides a contract remedy as distinct from a breach remedy—that is, the contractor's right to relief is based on a specific provision of the contract that promises relief. Without this contractual remedy, the contractor's only avenue for relief is to sue the government for breach of contract, alleging misrepresentation in the case of a type I condition or failure of the government to disclose superior knowledge in a type II condition.

OTHER DIFFERING SITE CONDITIONS CLAUSES

The right to relief based on differing site conditions is **not an implied right** of the contract. There is no right of relief unless the contract contains a differing site conditions clause promising relief. In a typical case on this point, a U.S. District Court ruled that the absence of a differing site condition clause in the contract placed the risk of subsurface conditions squarely with the contractor.[3] Inexperienced contractors sometimes make the mistake of assuming that they will automatically receive cost and time adjustments for encountering conditions different than they expected.

Although many public contracts, and even many in the private sector, contain the federal differing site conditions clause verbatim or nearly verbatim, many others do not. In some contracts, the analogous clause is titled "Changed Conditions" or "Concealed Conditions." If the federal clause is not used, it is important to read the alternate clause carefully to see what it does and does not provide.

Does the Clause Cover Both Type I and Type II Conditions?

The wording of the clause is particularly important in determining whether both type I and type II differing site conditions are included. Type I conditions will generally always be included, but some differing site conditions clauses do not include type II conditions. There will be no relief under clauses providing only for type I differing site conditions unless the condition that is actually encountered has been indicated differently in the contract documents. It makes no difference how unusual the condition actually was.

Does the Contract Contain Conflicting Exculpatory Clauses?

Some contracts contain **conflicting exculpatory clauses**—that is, they conflict directly with a differing site conditions clause contained in the same contract. For instance, if the contract contains soil boring logs and a differing site conditions clause, the contractor is clearly protected if adverse soil conditions different from those indicated in the boring logs are encountered. However, if the contract also

---

[3]*Pinkerton and Laws Co., Inc. v. Roadway Express, Inc.,* 650 F.Supp. 1138 (N.D. Ga. 1986).

contains a clause stating that the owner will not be responsible for the accuracy of the soil boring logs, an obvious conflict has been created.

Court decisions resolving this conflict have been mixed. The current judicial and administrative trend is to favor the differing site conditions clause over the exculpatory clause, often on the basis of a "precedence of contract documents clause" that gives precedence to general conditions clauses over clauses in other parts of the contract. The following cases illustrate this point.

A subcontract for performance of excavation work in Illinois contained a differing site condition clause allowing additional compensation for "subsurface and/or latent conditions at the site materially differing from those shown on the Drawings or indicated in the Specifications." When the excavation subcontractor encountered pockets of peat which were not indicated on the boring logs and which substantially increased the costs of excavation, they submitted a claim under the differing site condition clause. The general contractor would not pay, claiming that the subcontractor was not entitled to rely on the boring logs because the specifications expressly disclaimed responsibility for their accuracy. A trial court ruled for the subcontractor, holding that when a contract contains both a differing site condition clause and a disclaimer of site condition data, the differing site condition clause takes precedence. The Appellant Court of Illinois affirmed on the grounds that the subcontract contained an "order of precedence" clause establishing the precedence of the general conditions over the specifications.[4]

In a similar case, an excavating subcontractor in Idaho encountered subsurface water in the soil that was so serious that its trucks were mired in up to the wheel hubs. A pre-bid site inspection had revealed only a dry cracked surface. The standard AGC form of subcontract agreement had been used that incorporated a differing site conditions clause. However, the contract also contained a disclaimer assigning to the subcontractor the risk for

> All loss or damage arising out of the nature of the work aforesaid, or from action of the elements, or from unforeseen difficulties or obstructions which may be encountered in the prosecution of the work until its acceptance by the Principal, and for all risks of every description connected with the work.

When the subcontractor filed a claim for the extra expense in dealing with the muddy conditions, the general contractor refused to pay, arguing that the subcontract agreement imposed that risk on the subcontractor.

In spite of the disclaimer, the Idaho Supreme Court held that the subcontractor had encountered site conditions differing from those indicated in the contract documents and that could not be seen during a reasonable pre-bid site inspection. The subcontractor was awarded additional compensation.[5]

In an earlier federal case, the Engineer Board of Contract Appeals found that a contractor was entitled to extra compensation under the differing site condition

---

[4]*Roy Strom Excavating & Grading Co., Inc. v. Miller-Davis Co.*, 501 N.E.2d 717 (Ill. App. 1986).
[5]*Beco Corp. v. Roberts & Sons Construction Co., Inc.*, 760 P.2d 1120 (Idaho, 1988).

clause when it was discovered that a government-approved quarry could not produce acceptable stone when commercially feasible construction methods were employed, even though the government had disclaimed in the contract any knowledge of whether the approved quarry contained acceptable material.

A general contractor had entered into a contract for the construction of a perimeter dike in Lake Huron, Michigan, and had subcontracted the production of stone from the government-approved quarry. The subcontractor was able to produce stone from the quarry only by the use of commercially infeasible and costly procedures. The general contractor was forced to switch to an alternate source 100 miles farther from the jobsite. When the contractor filed a claim for the extra costs involved, the government cited the disclaimer, arguing that designation of the original quarry as an approved source of stone did not amount to a representation regarding the cost of production or of the suitability of the material removed. However, the Board held that the inability to produce satisfactory material from the quarry using normal commercial construction methods amounted to an "unforeseen condition" within the meaning of the differing site condition clause, entitling the contractor to compensation for the additional costs involved in obtaining the stone from the alternate source.[6]

Without the presence of a differing site condition clause, exculpatory language in the contract disclaiming responsibility for the accuracy of the site conditions represented poses a great risk to the contractor. Courts generally will enforce these disclaimers unless it can be shown that the owner withheld site information in their possession from bidding contractors.

A 1987 decision of the New Jersey Supreme Court underscores this point. A highway contractor for the Department of Transportation (DOT) encountered soft soil conditions in saturated clay that greatly increased excavation costs. Nothing in the contract documents indicated that such conditions would be encountered, but the contract did not contain a differing site condition clause. The contract did contain a clause disclaiming the DOT's responsibility for the accuracy or completeness of site condition data and said that the contractor would not be entitled to a price increase due to differing site conditions. When the contractor sued for additional compensation, they were able to show at the trial that, prior to taking bids, the DOT had received a letter from a consultant warning of difficult work conditions that would be caused by the saturated soil. This letter was never made available, or in any way disclosed, to bidders. In ruling for the contractor, the court stated that, although the DOT could not be held liable for failing to depict site conditions accurately, it must disclose all relevant information in its possession to bidders. The court further said that there was no doubt that the letter contained information that would have assisted bidders in pricing and planning the contract work. For this reason, the contractual disclaimer was unenforceable, and the contractor was entitled to recover its increased costs.[7]

---

[6]*Appeal of Construction Aggregates Corporation*, ENGBCA No. 4242 (Dec. 31, 1980).

[7]*P. T. & L. Construction Co. v. State of New Jersey Department of Transportation,* 531 A.2d 1330 (N.J. 1987).

What Are the Notice Requirements?

The federal clause provides that the contractor notify the government promptly when differing site conditions have been encountered and "before such conditions have been disturbed." The reasons for this requirement were discussed earlier in this chapter. Under the federal contract, the contractor's failure to furnish notice in accordance with the requirements of the clause is not necessarily fatal to the success of a differing site conditions claim. If it can be demonstrated that the **lack of notice did not prejudice the rights of the government** in any way, recovery under the clause will usually not be barred. Prejudice to the government's rights could be caused by both denying the opportunity to make an investigation to verify the condition before it was disturbed and by precluding the opportunity to direct and control the course of action to be taken to deal with the condition. For this reason, when notice has not been given, the contractor must be able to show that the owner was not placed at a disadvantage (or prejudiced) in either of these ways to recover under a differing site conditions claim. The contractor must clearly establish that lack of notice could not possibly have made any difference—that is, where there is no doubt that the condition was a differing site condition and that the contractor had taken the only possible course of action, or at least a course of action that was no more costly and equally preferable from the government's standpoint to any other course that might have been taken.

The notice requirements in the differing site conditions clause in other contracts can be considerably more restrictive than in the federal clause, particularly in clauses stating that the prompt furnishing of notice is a *condition precedent* to recovery under the clause. Courts will be more inclined to give full force and effect to the literal interpretation of clauses containing such language rather than applying the *no prejudice to the rights of the owner* standard.

What Are the Owner's Responsibilities Under the Clause?

The government's contractual duty under the federal clause to investigate and determine whether the conditions encountered by the contractor are differing site conditions was discussed earlier in this chapter. The contractor has a legitimate right to know whether the owner agrees that the conditions encountered constitute differing site conditions under the contract and whether a cost and time adjustment to the contract will be forthcoming. The importance of the cost adjustment is obvious. The time adjustment is also important when significant time is involved since the contractor bears the burden of completing the project within the contractually stipulated time allowance. This increase in time allowance should be equal to the additional time needed to complete the project because of differing site conditions. The contractor is entitled to know whether the completion date will be extended by the owner in order to realistically and economically schedule the remaining contract work.

If a time extension is not forthcoming when significant time has been lost, usually the only way the project can be completed by the original completion date is by accelerating the rate of performance of the remaining work, a costly undertaking.

Thus, it is important for the contractor to receive the results of the owner's determination promptly.

Once the owner's determination has been obtained, the contractor at least knows the owner's position. If the owner determines that the encountered conditions do not constitute differing site conditions under the contract, the contractor must either accept the determination or dispute it under the dispute resolution provisions of the contract. In either case, the contractor must absorb the extra costs involved (temporarily, at least) and attempt to complete the unextended contract on time by accelerating performance or risk being held in default by the owner. Clearly, the contractor cannot properly explore available options without knowing the owner's position. The federal clause imposes the duty of making a prompt investigation and determination on the government. Clauses in other contracts may or may not impose a similar duty on the owner. If the clause does not impose this contractual duty, the contractor is placed in a very disadvantageous position when differing site conditions are encountered.

REASONS FOR DENYING DIFFERING SITE CONDITION CLAIMS

Once the contractor has claimed differing site conditions, the owner may deny the claim. Common reasons for denial follow.

Lack of Notice

As discussed earlier, most differing site conditions clauses require the contractor to furnish prompt notice, sometimes (as in the federal clause) before the conditions are disturbed. **Lack of notice can bar an otherwise valid claim** if prejudice to the owner's interests can be shown. Some courts interpret the notice clause so strictly that a valid claim will be disallowed even when it is shown that the lack of notice did not prejudice the owner's interests.

The following cases illustrate how courts deal with the lack of notice issue. In the first case, a government contractor removing and stockpiling riprap from a government quarry encountered explosive charges in the rock left by a previous government contractor. Although the contractor did not provide prompt written notice as required by the federal differing site conditions clause, they later submitted a claim for lost productivity because of the explosive charges found in the quarry. When the contracting officer failed to pay, the contractor filed an appeal with the Interior Board of Contract Appeals. The board held that the contractor's failure to give notice was prejudicial to the government because the contracting officer did not know about the conditions encountered by the contractor. Having this knowledge would have enabled the contracting officer to elect to terminate the contract for the convenience of the government rather than pay the increased costs involved in dealing with the explosives. The contractor's appeal was denied.[8]

In the second case, a contractor for a federal contract for the construction of a post office building encountered soft clay not indicated on the soil boring logs when

---

[8] *Appeal of M. D. Activities,* IBCA No. 2113 (Dec. 7, 1987).

excavating the site. They removed the clay without putting the government on notice after calling in a consultant who advised that there was no reasonable alternative. By the time the government's architect learned of the situation, the contractor had removed the clay and was backfilling the area. The contracting officer denied the contractor's differing site condition claim because of failure to comply with the notice requirement providing the government an opportunity to investigate and control the fix. The contractor appealed.

The Postal Service Board of Contract Appeals found that a differing site conditions claim can be denied because of lack of notice but only when the government can show that its options were limited by the lack of notice. This was not true in this case, and the government had suffered no prejudice. The board said:

> There is sufficient reliable evidence to conclude that a differing site condition existed in the southwest corner of the site. The government, however, has not demonstrated there was a reasonable alternative to the method adopted by the contractor to deal with the problem which would have been more efficient or less costly. Accordingly, the contractor may recover the costs of removing and replacing 1,794 cubic yards of soil in the southwest corner of the post office site.[9]

Difference Not Material

The owner may deny a contractor's claim on the basis that the condition is not different, or not sufficiently different, from the condition indicated in the contract (Type I differing site condition) or from the conditions normally encountered (Type II differing site condition). To qualify as either a Type I or Type II differing site condition, the **condition difference must be material.** Marginal differences are not sufficient.

For instance, the Armed Services Board of Contract Appeals was not convinced that an 18-inch difference between the depth of an existing sewer line shown on contract drawings and the actual depth of the sewer line encountered during contract performance was a "material" difference under the meaning of the differing site conditions clause. The drawings indicated that the invert of the sewer line was 10 feet below the ground surface. The contractor asserted that the 18-inch lower depth of the sewer required working below the watertable, necessitating more expensive construction techniques. In ruling that the 18-inch difference was not a material difference, the board said:

> We are simply not persuaded on the evidence that had the sewer line been 18 inches higher, none of this would have happened and instead, the 8 foot section of pipe could have been replaced with the rubber tire backhoes without the shoring, a trench box, or dewatering.[10]

Unfortunately, there are no generally accepted rules for deciding whether a particular difference is significant enough to be material. The question often rests on judicial determination.

[9]*Appeal of M & M Builders, Inc.,* PSBCA No. 2886 (May 29, 1991).

[10]*Appeal of H. V. Allen Co., Inc.,* ASBCA No. 40645 (Oct. 4, 1990).

Failure to Conduct an Adequate Pre-Bid Site Inspection

Frequently, owners deny contractor's differing site conditions claims based on the owner's contention that, if the contractor had conducted a reasonable and proper site inspection prior to contract formation, the condition would have been discovered and the contractor would have included additional costs in the bid to deal with it. Most bid documents strongly suggest or even require that the contractor make such a site inspection prior to submitting a bid. A bidding contractor who had knowledge prior to the bid that an actual physical condition at the site was more severe than indicated in the contract documents and who had then bid only an amount to cover the less severe condition indicated in the contract cannot reasonably expect relief under the differing site conditions clause. For this reason, the argument that the **contractor's failure to make an adequate pre-bid site inspection** can be effective in barring the contractor's differing site conditions claim.

On the other hand, the contractor will not be held to a *standard of clairvoyance*—that is, that the requirement for a reasonable pre-bid site inspection does not mean that the contractor will be held responsible for the discovery of latent conditions or be held responsible for failing to make "a skeptical analysis of the plans and specifications." This means that unless there are specific instructions to verify certain measurements or to determine certain quantities of work to be done, the contractor is entitled to take the drawings and specifications at face value and to rely on them.

The application of this general concept to differing site conditions is illustrated by the words of the U.S. Court of Claims (now the United States Court of Federal Claims) in a related case:

> Contractors are businessmen, and in the business of bidding on Government contracts, they are usually pressed for time and are consciously seeking to underbid a number of competitors. Consequently, they estimate only those costs which they feel the contract terms will permit the Government to insist upon in the way of performance. They are obligated to bring to the Government's attention major discrepancies of errors which they detect in the specifications or drawings, or else fail to do so at their peril. But they are not expected to exercise clairvoyance in spotting hidden ambiguities in the bid documents, and they are protected if they innocently construe in their own favor an ambiguity equally susceptible to another construction.[11]

A **latent condition** is one that is hidden or not obvious, whereas a **patent condition** is obvious. Generally speaking, bidding contractors are only expected to note patent conditions in pre-bid site inspections. If a condition is not patent, a bidding contractor's failure to discover it during a pre-bid site inspection will not bar a later claim for a type I condition under the differing site conditions clause.

The following cases illustrate how our courts have dealt with the site inspection issue. In the first case, the contractor was denied a differing site conditions claim because it failed to conduct any pre-bid site inspection at all. The contract required renovation of dormitories at a military base, and many of the contract

---

[11]*Blount Bros. Construction Co. v. United States,* 346 F.2d 962 (Ct. Cl. 1965).

drawings bore the notation for the contractor to "verify in field" many of the building dimensions. The government provided bidders an opportunity to inspect the building prior to submitting bids. During performance, the contractor encountered a number of discrepancies in various building dimensions from those indicated on the drawings and asserted a differing site conditions claim. The Armed Services Board of Contract Appeals denied the claim on the grounds that the discrepancies could have been detected during a reasonable pre-bid site inspection. The contract called for the renovation of an old building, and the drawings specifically required field verification. The board said:

> The contractor certainly knew that this was a renovation contract which included demolition from the invitation to bid. There were two scheduled walk-through site investigations where the type of construction and likelihood of irregular dimensions could be uncovered. Unfortunately, the contractor chose not to look at the subject of its bid. It chose to rely on what because of the nature of the undertaking were less than perfect drawings, definitively labeled as such by the terms "verify" and "verify in field."[12]

In the next case, the contractor conducted a pre-bid site inspection, but the General Services Administration Board of Contract Appeals concluded that the inspection was inadequate. The contract required the renovation of a ten-story building including the replacement of the flooring. During performance, the contractor found that the north wall of the building was out of square with the other walls, which increased the total square footage of each floor. They asserted this was a differing site condition. The board concluded that the drawings strongly suggested that the walls were out of square and that the contract documents required the contractor to conduct a pre-bid site inspection and verify the dimensions shown on the drawings. The board felt that if the contractor had complied with these requirements, it would have known the exact floor area of the building. In denying the contractor's claim, the board opined:

> The contract drawings gave ample indication that a problem possibly existed regarding the angles at which the east and west walls intersected with the north wall. The effect of uneven angle of intersection on the calculations of surface areas is obvious, and the significance of this fact is only enhanced by the fact that we are dealing here with a 10-story building. When, in making the site inspection, the party ignores such data in contract drawings and makes no measurements for purposes of verification, we can not conclude that the inspection is reasonably adequate.[13]

In another case, the Armed Services Board of Contract Appeals supported a contractor's differing site condition claim, holding that the contractor had no obligation to pretest soil samples to determine whether subsurface conditions were suitable for the proper bedding of pipe. In a contract to replace sewer lines at an Air Force base, the contract documents expressly represented that the material to be excavated would be sand and that no hard material would be encountered. Pipe was required to be set on a bedding of sand or gravel. The contractor priced its bid

---

[12]*Appeal of Zenith Construction,* ASBCA No. 33576 (Mar. 11, 1989).

[13]*Appeal of J. S. Alberici Construction Co., Inc.,* GSBCA No. 9897 (Aug. 31, 1989).

on the basis that it could bed the pipe on the native material but instead encountered hardpan sandstone that had to be removed and replaced to bed the pipe properly. The contracting officer denied the contractor's differing site conditions claim, asserting that a more thorough pre-bid site inspection would have revealed the presence of the hardpan. The board ruled that the pre-bid site inspection requirement did not impose a duty on the contractor to test subsurface materials. The contractor was entitled to rely on the affirmative representations in the contract documents, and the removal and replacement of the hardpan constituted a differing site condition.[14]

DEALING WITH DIFFERING SITE CONDITIONS

The following course of action will greatly enhance the chances of an equitable contract cost and time adjustment being granted when differing site conditions are encountered.

Prompt Written Notice

The **importance of prompt written notice** to the owner that differing site conditions have been encountered cannot be overemphasized. The notice should be given before the conditions are disturbed. Although **constructive notice** may have occurred, written notice is far preferable. An example of constructive notice would be a contractor encountering a differing site condition during excavation operations when the owner's inspector was present, observed the condition, and thus was aware of it.

The written notice should also request the owner to investigate promptly the encountered conditions and to issue a determination that differing site conditions have been encountered.

Request for Owner's Instructions

The contractor should also **request the owner's instructions or directive** on how to deal with the encountered conditions, unless there is only one possible course of action. Further, the contractor should advise that contract performance will be delayed due to lack of instructions if instructions or a directive from the owner is not received within a reasonable period of time.

Failure to Receive Determination or Receipt of Adverse Determination

If the owner either fails to make a determination within a reasonable period of time or determines that the encountered condition does not constitute a differing site condition, the contractor must assume that no cost or time adjustment to the contract is

---

[14]*Appeal of Tenaya Construction*, ASBCA No. 27799 (Nov. 5, 1986).

immediately forthcoming. Unless the contractor is prepared to concede the matter, the owner should be advised in writing that the contractor disagrees with the determination and is **reserving all rights** under the contract. **A claim should then be filed** in accordance with the disputes resolution provisions of the contract for later adjudication by others. In the interim, contract work must be continued according to the owner's instructions or directive with no guarantee that an equitable contract cost or time adjustment will ever be received. Although placed in a very disadvantageous position, the contractor has no alternative but to proceed on this basis. If the encountered condition is truly a differing site condition under the contract, the contractor usually will eventually be made whole through the disputes resolution provisions of the contract.

DETERMINATION OF THE EQUITABLE ADJUSTMENT

The adjustment in contract price and time may be determined by **agreement between contractor and owner** or, if the owner and contractor are unable to agree, the **equitable adjustment may be determined by others** under the dispute resolution provisions of the contract. In either case, the **contractor must prove cost and time impacts**—that is, the performance cost increases and impact of the overall contract performance time extension as a basis for the equitable adjustment.

As a general rule, the same principles that govern determination of contract price and time adjustments resulting from contract changes apply (see Chapter 14). In fact, the differing site conditions clause in many contracts provides that the **price and time adjustment be determined by the provisions of the changes clause,** although the federal clause and the clauses in some other contracts are silent on this point. If force account provisions under a changes clause are used to determine differing site conditions cost and time adjustments, the difficulty discussed in Chapter 14 arises when the force account indirect cost markups are not high enough to meet the contractor's actual costs when project performance time has been extended. In this case, the contractor would receive less than an equitable adjustment. Therefore, when the contract has been extended due to differing site conditions, **force account provisions** can be considered equitable for direct costs only. Indirect costs should be determined on the basis of the contractor's provable actual costs and a reasonable profit should be added.

CONCLUSION

Differing site conditions, contract changes, and breach of contract situations usually result in delay to the project. In the following chapters, we turn to the general subject of delay and how it is handled in a contractual sense.

QUESTIONS AND PROBLEMS

1. Explain the reason why differing site conditions clauses are included in construction contracts.

2. Without a differing site conditions clause in the contract, what must the contractor do to obtain relief if conditions are encountered that are different from those indicated in the contract documents?

3. What is a type I differing site condition? A type II? Does the federal differing site conditions clause include both?

4. What does the federal clause provide regarding the contractor's duty to notify the government when a differing site condition has been encountered? What does the clause state that the contracting officer must do when notified that a differing site condition has been encountered?

5. Explain why the federal clause is not an exculpatory clause.

6. Can the rights provided by differing site conditions clauses ever be considered to be implied by the contract?

7. What four specific points should you look for when reading the differing site conditions clause in contracts other than the federal contract?

8. List the three common reasons discussed in this chapter that owners deny contractor differing site conditions claims.

9. What is constructive notice? Is constructive notice an adequate substitute for written notice? What request should a contractor make to the owner as part of a written notice that a differing site condition has been encountered? What should the contractor do when the owner does not respond within a reasonable period of time?

10. What two actions should the contractor take after receiving the owner's determination regarding previous notice of encountering a differing site condition when the contractor disagrees with the determination?

11. By what two avenues mentioned in this chapter can the amount of differing site conditions cost and time adjustments to the contract be determined? What does the contractor have to prove regardless of which avenue is used?

12. What other prominent contract clause provisions are frequently used to make the equitable adjustment resulting from encountering a differing site condition? What restrictions should be placed on the use of force account provisions to ensure that an equitable adjustment is reached?

16

Delays, Suspensions, and Terminations

Key Words and Concepts

Time is of the essence
Suspension of work
Delay
Increases in direct/time related costs
Inefficiency due to interruptions of performance
Excusable delay
Compensable delay
Contractual provisions for compensable delay
The federal contract suspension of work clause
No-damages-for-delay clauses
Attitude of courts toward no-damages-for-delay clauses
Contracts that are silent on delay

Delay in early completion situations
Root causes of delay and suspensions of work
Importance of the notice requirement
Constructive notice
Difference of terminations from delays or suspensions of work
Federal contract default termination clause
Federal contract termination-for-convenience clause
Genesis of termination-for-convenience clause
Abuse of discretion
Termination-for-convenience clause in other contracts

DELAYS AND SUSPENSIONS OF WORK

Delays in construction contracting can be both psychologically and financially destructive, just as they are in everyday life. Whether the delay results from an act of God, breach of contract by one of the parties, or differing site conditions, its impact on construction contracts is often catastrophic. The old adage "time is money" is definitely true in these situations.

Time Is of the Essence

Construction prime contracts and subcontracts often contain a statement that **"time is of the essence."** These words appear to mean that contract performance be started promptly and continue without interruption until completion within the specified time period. Taken absolutely literally, the words mean that the contractor or subcontractor has an absolute duty to perform all contract requirements with no delay whatsoever and is in breach of the contract for failing to complete the contract work within the contractually specified time. Similarly, these words also suggest that an owner who does not promptly review and approve shop drawings or promptly perform other contractually specified duties has breached the contract.

The common judicial view is not quite so stringent. Courts usually apply the time-is-of-the-essence concept only to delays in performance that are unreasonable. In this view, construction contracts by their very nature are so fraught with the possibility of delay that some delay is almost inevitable. Also, the clause is sometimes interpreted to mean that the contractor or subcontractor is required to meet time deadlines, but the owner or prime contractor in subcontract situations is not—that is, it is a "one-way street." However, contractors, subcontractors, and owners would be well advised to act as though time-is-of-the-essence requirements will be strictly enforced with respect to their commitments to others. They would equally be wise not to count too heavily on reciprocal commitments made by others being strictly enforced.

Delays v. Suspensions of Work

Interruptions to work can result in either a delay or a suspension of work. A **suspension of work** results from a written directive of the owner to stop performance of all or part of the contract work. When this occurs, work on the entire project or on some discrete part of the project ceases entirely until the owner lifts the suspension. A **delay** differs from a suspension in two ways: First, a delay may be only a slowing down or a temporary interruption of the work without stopping it entirely. Second, whether a slowing down or a temporary interruption of work, a delay is triggered by something other than a formal directive from the owner to stop work. As with suspensions, delays can affect the entire project or only a discrete portion of it. Suspensions of work and delays can be caused by a variety of conditions—bad weather, strikes, equipment breakdowns, shortages of materials, changes, differing site conditions, or some act, or failure to act, of the owner separate from a directive to the contractor to stop work. Regardless of the cause, and whether within the control of the parties to the contract or not, suspensions and delays can be devastating for both parties to the contract.

The distinction between a suspension of work and a delay is a technical one. In the following discussion, the word *delay* indicates a loss of time, whether caused by a suspension of work or by some other delaying factor. Such delays result in **increases to direct and indirect time-related costs** for both the contractor and owner, with the magnitude of the cost increases depending on the extent of the suspension or delay. In addition to these increases in time-related costs, the contractor often experiences increases in direct costs due to **inefficiencies caused by the interruption of performance.**

The owner's cost increases usually involve additional project administration costs since supervisory staff is on the job longer as well as consequential cost increases due to the project going on line later than anticipated. As any cost estimator knows, time-related costs have a tremendous impact on the overall cost of performance. The potential magnitude of these costs makes interruption in the performance of the work a very serious matter for both owner and contractor. There is no doubt that time *is* money in the construction contracting world.

Compensable v. Excusable Delay

Once contract time has been lost, a threshold question is whether the delay is compensable or excusable—that is, whether the contractor will be paid, or made whole, for the extra costs incurred as a result of the delay or whether only an extension of contract time will be granted.

An **excusable delay** is a noncompensable loss of time for which the contractor will receive an extension of time but no additional payment. Excusable delays are not the fault of either party to the contract. Although given an extension of time, the contractor must bear the costs associated with the delay. Since they are also absorbing time-related costs, the owner is also bearing the consequences of the delay. Thus, each party bears its own share of the costs of an excusable delay. Common examples of excusable delays include strikes, unless caused by the contractor's breach of a labor contract or some act contrary to reasonable labor management and inclement weather over and above the normal inclement weather experienced at the project's location.

A **compensable delay** entitles the contractor to both a time extension and to compensation for the extra costs caused by the delay. Unless the contract contains an enforceable no-damages-for-delay clause, an owner-caused delay is a compensable delay. It is also possible that some delays that would normally be excusable only may become compensable if they flow from an earlier compensable delay. An example is a case where an owner-caused delay resulted in follow-on work to be performed at a time in the year when normal weather-related delays are likely to occur, and when that work would have been completed before the inclement weather had the owner-caused delay not occurred. In this situation, the extra costs resulting from performing in the normal inclement weather, although ordinarily not compensable, become compensable.

Contractual Provisions for Compensable Delay

A contractor cannot reasonably expect to be paid for delays that are self-inflicted. On the other hand, one would expect that the contractor be compensated when the delay is caused by the owner. The extent to which the contractor is entitled to compensation for extra costs resulting from delays and suspensions varies according to the **contractual provisions for compensable delay.** Reading and understanding these provisions is critical to protection of the interests of both contractor and owner.

THE FEDERAL SUSPENSION OF WORK CLAUSE

The **federal contract suspension of work clause** reads as follows:

SUSPENSION OF WORK

(a)   The Contracting Officer may order the Contractor, in writing, to suspend, delay, or interrupt all or any part of the work of this contract for the period of time that the Contracting Officer determines appropriate for the convenience of the Government.

(b)   If the performance of all or any part of the work is, for an unreasonable period of time, suspended, delayed, or interrupted (1) by an act of the Contracting Officer in the administration of this contract, or (2) by the Contracting Officer's failure to act within the time specified in this contract (or within a reasonable time if not specified), an adjustment shall be made for any increase in the cost of performance of this contract (excluding profit) necessarily caused by the unreasonable suspension, delay, or interruption and the contract modified in writing accordingly. However, no adjustment shall be made under this clause for any suspension, delay, or interruption to the extent that performance would have been so suspended, delayed, or interrupted by any other cause, including the fault or negligence of the Contractor or for which an equitable adjustment is provided for or excluded under any other term or condition of this contract.

(c)   A claim under this clause shall not be allowed (1) for any costs incurred more than 20 days before the Contractor shall have notified the Contracting Officer in writing of the act or failure to act involved (but this requirement shall not apply as to a claim resulting from a suspension order), and (2) unless the claim, in an amount stated, is asserted in writing as soon as practicable after the termination of the suspension, delay, or interruption, but not later than the date of final payment under the contract.[1]

Note that the clause first establishes the authority of the contracting officer to order the contractor to "suspend, delay, or interrupt all or part of the work. . . . " Then, it promises that, if the performance of all or any part of the work is suspended, delayed, or interrupted for an "unreasonable" period of time by an act or failure to act of the contracting officer, an adjustment will be made for any increase in the cost of contract performance excluding profit.

---

[1]F.A.R. 52.242-14 48 C.F.R. 52.242-14 (Nov. 1996).

A separate clause in the federal contract provides that the contracting officer will "extend the time for completing the work" for justifiable cause, which includes delay due to acts or failure to act of the government. The contractor must notify the contracting officer of the cause of the delay within ten days of its occurrence or within such further period of time before the date of final payment under the contract that may be granted by the contracting officer.

Thus, the federal contract provides that the contractor receive both the costs and an appropriate extension of contract time for delay caused by any government act or failure to act administratively in respect to contract changes, constructive changes, differing site conditions, and so on. Therefore, delays of this type are compensable delays under the terms of the federal contract.

DELAYS AND SUSPENSIONS IN OTHER CONTRACTS

Although many federal contract provisions are widely copied throughout the industry, the federal delay provisions are often not contained in other contracts. The federal contract approach could be said to be at one end of the spectrum and contracts containing no-damages-for-delay clauses at the opposite end.

No-Damages-for-Delay Clauses

A typical **no-damages-for-delay clause** reads as follows:

NO DAMAGES FOR DELAY

The Contractor (Subcontractor) expressly agrees not to make, and hereby waives, any claim for damages on account of any delay, obstruction or hindrance for any cause whatsoever, including but not limited to the aforesaid causes, and agrees that its sole right and remedy in the case of any delay . . . shall be an extension of the time fixed for completion of the Work.

Under these provisions, the contractor's or subcontractor's relief in the event of delay "for any cause whatsoever" is limited to an extension of contract time for whatever period the delay can be shown to have extended overall contract performance. There is no cost adjustment. Taken literally, this clause means that the contractor receives no relief other than a time extension even in instances where the owner's acts or failure to act, including the owner's negligence, caused the delay. This provision is a classic example of an exculpatory clause.

Judicial Attitudes on No-Damages-for-Delay Clauses

Individual judicial response to no-damages-for-delay clauses has been mixed. Courts in some states are loath to enforce the clause because the contract documents are drafted by the owner and advertised on a "take it or leave it" basis, compelling the contractor to accept the clause or refrain from bidding. Contracts resulting from such bidding documents are called *contracts of adhesion*. Many feel that such contracts are bargains unfairly struck, particularly when the potential delay may be caused by some act or failure to act on the part of the owner. When the owner's acts or omissions have been particularly egregious, courts often refuse to enforce the clause. However, this is not universally true. In the state of New York, for example, courts generally enforce no-damages-for-delay clauses on the reasoning that the bidding contractors were aware of the risks imposed by the clause and should have included sufficient contingencies in the bid to cover them. This mindset is totally opposite the thinking behind the differing site conditions clause and similar clauses where owners try to eliminate large bid contingencies by creating even-handed bidding conditions.

The following cases illustrate the courts' uneven treatment of this issue. For example, the highest court of the state of New York held that a no-damages-for-delay clause prevented contractor recovery of even those damages caused by the owner's active interference with the contractor's work. The contractor completed its contract 28 months later than originally scheduled and attributed the delay to the city's failure to coordinate its prime contractors and to interference with the sequence in timing of the contractor's work. A trial court, hearing the contractor's suit for $3.3 million, instructed the jury that the contractor could not recover unless the city's active interference resulted from bad faith or deliberate intent, and the jury denied recovery. The Court of Appeals of New York upheld the trial court's instructions, describing the no-damages-for-delay clause as "a perfectly common and acceptable business practice" that "clearly, directly and absolutely, barred recovery of delay damages."[2]

Courts in Illinois and Iowa have ruled similarly. In the Illinois case, when the contractor received notice to proceed with construction of a new high school, the site was not ready. After the site became available, the owner began to issue a barrage of change orders that eventually totaled more than $2.1 million. In a lawsuit filed by the contractor to collect delay damages, an official of the owner testified that in order to avoid cost escalation, the contract had been awarded before all design decisions had been finalized. The architect's field representatives testified that, although this was new construction, it resembled a remodeling job before it was completed. Nonetheless, the trial court denied recovery of delay damages. In affirming the trial court, the Appellant Court of Illinois held, "If the contract expressly provides for delay or if the right of recovery is expressly limited or precluded, then these provisions will control." The court further opined:

> Lombard's experience with public construction projects should have enabled it to protect itself from risks by either increasing its bid or negotiating the deletion of this contractual provision. . . . In any event, the Commission bargained for the right to delay with the insertion of the no-damage provision.[3]

In the Iowa case, a contractor installing lighting and signs on a new interstate highway was not permitted to start work until two years after the contract was

---

[2]*Kalisch-Jarcho, Inc. v. City of New York,* 448 N.E.2d 413 (N.Y. 1983).

[3]*M.A. Lombard & Son Co. v. Public Building Commission of Chicago,* 428 N.E.2d 889 (Ill. App. 1981).

awarded because of delays by others in the construction of the highway. The Iowa Department of Transportation paid for cost escalation on certain materials but refused to compensate the contractor for the delay, relying on a no-damages-for-delay clause in the contract. The trial court directed a verdict for the Transportation Department, and the Supreme Court of Iowa upheld the directed verdict. Incredibly, the Supreme Court said:

> There was no evidence that 2-year delays were unknown or even that they were uncommon in highway construction.[4]

Other courts have taken a more lenient view. In Missouri, a contract was awarded for the alteration of the superstructures of two bridges. Separate prime contracts had been let for the construction of the bridges' substructures. The superstructure contractor received notice to proceed eight months before scheduled completion of the substructures, and to comply with the superstructure schedule, the contractor immediately placed mill orders and began steel fabrication. Because of a differing site condition problem, the substructure completion was delayed, and the superstructure contractor was forced to start field work 175 days behind schedule. The owner granted a 175-day time extension but refused to pay additional compensation, relying on a no-damages-for-delay clause included in the contract. At the subsequent trial, it was found that when the notice to proceed was issued, the owner was aware of the differing site condition problem and the likelihood that the substructure contractor would be delayed. A federal district court awarded the superstructure contractor substantial delay damages, and the U.S. Court of Appeals affirmed. Both courts held that active interference is a recognized exception to the enforceability of no-damages-for-delay provisions. The U.S. Court of Appeals further stated that active interference requires a willful bad faith act by the owner, which in this case had occurred because the owner knew that a delay by the substructure contractor was likely but nonetheless issued a notice to proceed to the superstructure contractor.[5]

In a Florida case, the contractor for the construction of a shopping center was delayed because the owner was late in providing necessary drawings and specifications and delayed executing change orders, even though written change authorization was required before the contractor could proceed with the work. The contract contained a no-damages-for-delay clause. The contract was completed behind schedule, and when the owner withheld final payment, the contractor sued for the contract balance plus damages incurred because of the owner-caused delay. In ruling for the contractor, the District Court of Appeal of Florida held that active interference by the project owner is a well-recognized exception to the enforceability of no-damages-for-delay clauses and that the owner's unreasonable delay in issuing drawings and specifications and executing change orders amounted to active interference.[6]

---

[4]*Dickinson Co., Inc. v. Iowa State Dept. of Trans.,* 300 N.W.2d 112 (Iowa 1981).

[5]*United States Steel Corp. v. Missouri Pacific Railroad Co.,* 668 F.2d 435 (8th Cir. 1982).

[6]*Newberry Square Development Corp. v. Southern Landmark, Inc.,* 578 So.2d 750 (Fla. App. 1991).

CONTRACTS WITH NO PROVISIONS FOR DELAYS

Some **contracts are silent on the issue of damages for delay.** They contain no express language that either establishes or denies the contractor's right to be paid for the extra costs associated with owner-caused delays. Under these circumstances, the only way the contractor can recover the costs and lost time associated with owner-caused delays is through a lawsuit proving breach of contract on the part of the owner. The particular breach that would have to be proved would be the breach of the owner's implied warranty not to impede or interfere with the contractor's performance (see Chapter 13). Although a heavy burden, this is a far better situation for the contractor than if the contract contained a no-damages-for-delay clause. Of course, for the contractor, the best contract contains fair and equitable provisions promising compensation for costs and time extension for delays caused by the owner.

DELAY IN EARLY COMPLETION SITUATIONS

Occasionally, a contractor makes a claim for recovery of extra costs resulting from a suspension, delay, or interruption of work by the owner even though all the contract work is completed by or before the contractually specified completion date. In **delay in early completion situations,** is the contractor entitled to be paid delay costs?

This question can be illustrated by comparing this situation to one in which the delay causes the contract to be completed after the specified contract completion date (see Figure 16–1). In the first case, after working for 14 months at a pace

FIGURE 16–1   Early completion delay claims.

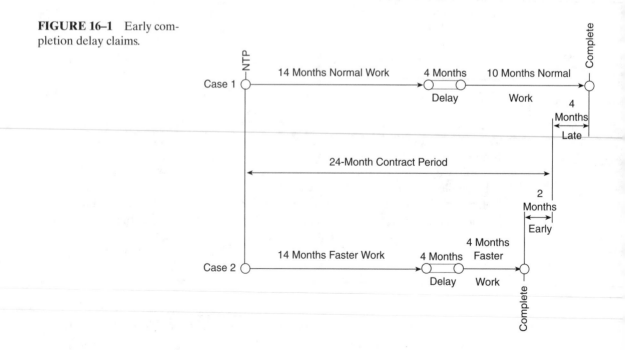

sufficient to meet contract requirements, the contractor was delayed for four months. Performance then continued at the predelay pace, and the project was completed four months late. Without the delay, the project would have been completed on time. If the delay was caused by the owner and the contract does not contain a no-damages-for-delay clause, the contractor is entitled to the extra costs for the four-month delay as well as a four-month time extension.

In the second case, the contractor worked 14 months at a pace faster than that required to meet the 24-month contractual requirement when the four-month delay occurred. Following the delay, the contractor progressed at this same pace for four additional months and finished the contract in 22 months, two months early. In this situation, it is more difficult for the contractor to sustain a claim for damages. Many owners take the position that, since the contractor finished the contract early, there was no damage caused by the delay, and, thus, the contractor is not entitled to either a time extension or extra costs. Presumably, these owners consider that the contractor's bid was based, or should have been based, on taking the full allowable time for contract completion and, since performance was not delayed beyond the time allowed for completion, the contractor is due nothing.

The weakness of this position is that the contractor accepted all risk of performance of the contract and, in the absence of an owner-caused delay, would be liable for all extra time-related costs if the contract was not finished on time as well as for any contractually mandated liquidated damages. It cannot then reasonably be argued that the contractor should not also be entitled to save costs by finishing the work earlier than required by the contract if able to do so. Therefore, the owner causing a four-month delay is liable for the resulting extra costs to the contractor even though the contractor finishes the contract work early.

In this case, the contractor also should have been given a four-month extension of time at the conclusion of the delay, extending the time allowed for contract performance to 28 months after notice to proceed. Had the contract been extended in this manner, the contractor finished six months early, just as would have been the case if there had been no owner-caused delay. If not prohibited from doing so by explicit contract language, the contractor has the right to complete the contract early and, if prevented from doing so by an owner-caused four-month delay, as in this case, is entitled to be paid any extra incurred costs due to the delay.

Federal case law and most state law is highly supportive of the preceding principle. The Armed Services Board of Contract Appeals ruled in a 1982 case that a contractor had the right to complete the contract ahead of schedule and the government was liable for preventing or hindering early completion. A contract for the renovation of military buildings provided that the government was to arrange access to the individual buildings within two weeks of the contractor's request for access. The government failed to provide access within the time specified for several of the buildings. Even though completing the project in less than the contractually stipulated time, the contractor submitted a claim for delay damages. The board said:

> Barring express restrictions in the contract to the contrary, the construction contractor has the right to proceed according to his own job capabilities at a better rate of

progress than represented by his own schedule. The government may not hinder or prevent earlier completion without incurring liability.[7]

In another federal case, an excavation contractor had submitted a schedule showing project completion in February, indicating the intention to work under winter conditions. However, the contractor's in-house schedule, based on more optimistic production, indicated much earlier project completion. The contractor was achieving its in-house schedule, but when the quantity of unclassified material to be excavated overran the estimated bid quantity by 41%, the contractor was prevented from completing excavation before the winter season, forcing them to shutdown until spring. The government denied the contractor's claim for delay damages on the grounds that the submitted schedule indicated working under winter conditions. The U.S. Court of Claims (now the United States Court of Federal Claims) held that it did not matter that the contractor had not informed the government of its intended schedule. The court stated:

> There is no incentive for a contractor to submit projections reflecting an early completion date. The government bases its progress payments on the amount of work completed each month, relative to the contractor's proposed progress charts. A contractor which submits proposed progress charts using all the time in the contract, and which demonstrates that work is moving along ahead of schedule will receive full and timely payments. If such a contractor falls behind its true intended schedule, i.e., its accelerated schedule, it will still receive full and timely progress payments, so long as it does not fall behind the progress schedule which it submitted to the government.
>
> On the other hand, if a contractor which intended to finish early reflected such intention in its proposed progress charts, it would have to meet that accelerated schedule in order to receive full and timely progress payments; any slowdown might deprive the contractor of such payments even if the contractor is performing efficiently enough to finish within the time allotted in the contract. In short, a contractor can not lose when it projects that it will use all the time allowed, but it can be hurt by projecting early completion.[8]

Owners have more difficulty understanding their liability when they are not aware that the contractor intends to finish the work early. Contractors are therefore well advised to put the owner on notice formally whenever they are planning to complete the contract work earlier than required by the contract even though, as the preceding Court of Claims decision demonstrates, there is no contractual requirement to do so. Although not stated in the court decision, even if the contractor informs the owner that they intend to finish early, they retain the contractual right to revert to the original completion date if future events should force a change in plan.

There are exceptions to these rules. Some contracts contain explicit provisions that, although not prohibiting early completion, make clear that the owner will only

---

[7]*Appeal of CWC, Inc.,* ASBCA No. 26432 (June 29, 1982).

[8]*Weaver-Bailey Contractors, Inc. v. United States,* 19 Cl. Ct. 474 (1990).

be responsible for otherwise compensable delay costs or time extensions for delays that extend contract performance beyond the contractually stipulated date. For instance, contracts for subway construction in Los Angeles and a tunnel contract on the Boston Harbor Project in Massachusetts contain contract provisions to this effect. The language in the Boston Harbor Project reads as follows:

> An adjustment in Contract Time will be based solely upon net increases in the time required for the performance for completion of parts of the Work controlling achievement of the corresponding Contract Time(s) (Critical Path). However, even if the time required for the performance for completion of controlling parts of the Work is extended, an extension in Contract Time will not be granted until all of the available Total Float is consumed and performance for completion of controlling Work necessarily extends beyond the Contract Time.[9]

The contract separately provided that without an extension of contract time, there would be no extra payment for time-related costs.

When provisions of this kind are included in the contract, they will be enforced and the contractor will receive no compensation for delay damages when completing the contract early.

CAUSES FOR DELAYS AND SUSPENSIONS OF WORK

What are the **root causes of delays and suspensions of work**? What causal events seem to occur again and again? The following are typical examples:

Defective Specifications

One of the most common causes of delay is defective specifications resulting from the application of the Spearin Doctrine. When the drawings and specifications contain errors or omissions, costly delays often result—first, in attempting to comply with the erroneous drawings and specifications and, second, in waiting for the errors to be corrected and revised drawings and specifications to be issued.

Site Availability Problems

Another common cause of delay is lack of site availability at the time the notice to proceed is issued. Unless the contract provides otherwise, the contractor is entitled to the full use of the site at the time of notice to proceed. If the site is not available at that time, the contractor may be delayed. Also, an owner's failure to provide a reasonable means of access to the work or interruption of access previously provided may delay the contractor.

---

[9]*MWRA Contract CP-151,* General Conditions Article 11.12.1.

Changes and Differing Site Conditions

Delays are also caused by changes directed by the owner, including changes because of problems associated with encountering differing site conditions. Just the requirement to perform added work may delay completion of the contract, and additional time is often lost waiting for the architect or engineer to revise the drawings and specifications when changes are required. This is particularly true when differing site conditions are encountered.

Owner's Failure to Act Administratively

The owner may delay the contractor by failing to act or by acting in a dilatory manner administratively. The contractor is entitled to expect reasonable promptness in performance of contractual acts required of the owner, such as approvals of shop drawings and so on. If the owner does not cooperate, the contractor is delayed. Problems also arise when the contractor needs additional information, instructions, or a directive to proceed in connection with changes or differing site conditions, and the owner either refuses or is unreasonably slow in providing the needed information, thus delaying the contractor.

Case law decisions previously cited in Chapters 13, 14, and 15 illustrate the courts' handling of such causes of delay.

NOTICE REQUIREMENTS

The federal suspension of work clause and the clauses in most other construction contracts that promise relief for the contractor in the event of suspensions, delays, or interruptions contain a **stringent notice requirement.** Several aspects of this requirement are important.

Purpose of the Notice Requirement

Usually the contractor is required to furnish written notice to the owner within a stated period of time following any event that the contractor contends has caused or will cause a delay. Without such notice, the owner may not know that some act or failure to act is delaying the contractor. The requirement is reasonable, and failure on the contractor's part to comply with it may result in waiver of entitlement to relief.

A secondary reason for notice is to establish a start date for the delay. This reason applies to all delays, both compensable delays caused by the owner and excusable delays. Although not appreciated at the time, in case of dispute, the time extent of many delays may have to be decided by a court or arbitrator years after the event, and a record establishing the start date can be invaluable.

Case law decisions denying contractors' recovery due to lack of notice are legend. For instance, the U.S. Court of Appeals denied any recovery for extra costs when a contractor encountered more subsurface rock than indicated in the contract documents because they failed to notify the owner within five days of any event that could give rise to a claim for additional compensation or an extension of time, as the contract required. The contractor's claim, without prior notice of claim, was filed three months after completion of the work where the rock was encountered.[10]

Similarly, the Armed Services Board of Contract Appeals denied a contractor's claim for extra compensation due to the poor condition of exterior surfaces on Navy housing units that were being painted. The claim was not raised until after the contractor had applied primer and finished coats to the surfaces. Once the surface had been primed and painted, there was no way for the government to evaluate or verify the contractor's allegations.[11]

Constructive Notice

In some circumstances, the owner may be held to have received **constructive notice** of delay. For instance, if an act of God shuts down the work or the owner issues a written directive to suspend all work, the owner is presumed to be aware of the associated delay. Constructive notice means that, even though not specifically notified formally, the owner knows that the work is being delayed.

In Ohio, a contractor on a sewer construction project failed to give the owner notice when differing site conditions were encountered. The contractor had bid the project on the basis that it would be possible to bore a tunnel and jack the sewer pipe into place for most of the job, which would have been possible according to the soil boring logs contained in the contract documents. During the work, saturated silty sand was encountered, which had not been indicated in the boring logs, preventing the contractor from using the jacked-pipe method of construction. A far more expensive open-cut method was required. The owner's representatives were present at the site throughout performance and were aware of the soil conditions encountered. Additionally, many meetings were held to discuss the problem, and extensive written correspondence passed between the contractor and the owner.

When the contractor submitted the claim under the differing site condition clause, the owner denied the claim on the grounds that timely notice had not been given as required by the contract. The Court of Appeals of Ohio ruled that the contractor's claim was not barred by failure to give written notice because the owner through its on-site representatives knew of the conditions, which served as constructive notice of the situation. In the words of the court:

> There is no reason to deny the claim for lack of written notice if the District was aware of differing soil conditions throughout the job and had a proper opportunity to investigate and act on its knowledge, as a purpose of formal notice would thereby have been fulfilled.[12]

---

[10]*Galien Corp. v. MCI Telecommunications Corp.*, 12 F.3d.465 (5th Cir. 1994).

[11]*Appeal of Lamar Construction Co., Inc.*, ASBCA No. 39593 (Feb. 6, 1992).

[12]*Roger J. Au & Son, Inc. v. Northeast Ohio Region Sewer District*, 504 N.E.2d 1209 (Ohio App. 1986).

Although most courts would probably rule as the Ohio court did in similar circumstances, the contractor should always promptly give written notice of a delay to the owner.

TERMINATIONS

There is an obvious **difference between terminations and suspensions or delays.** Suspensions or delays mean a slowing of work or a cessation of work that is temporary in nature. However, terminations mean the cessation is permanent. Some construction contracts contain provisions where, under circumstances stated in the contract, both the owner and the contractor may terminate the contract, but the following discussion refers only to situations in which the contract is unilaterally terminated by the owner.

Requirement for an Enabling Clause

The owner's right to terminate the contract depends on the existence of a specific clause in the contract giving the owner that right. Practically all construction contracts contain clauses permitting the owner to terminate the contract when the contractor is not meeting the contract requirements. Such terminations are called *default terminations.* Today, most contracts also contain a clause permitting termination *for the convenience of the owner.* In both cases, specific contract clauses establish the owner's right to take the termination action.

Default Terminations

The federal contract default termination clause provides in pertinent part:

> **DEFAULT (FIXED-PRICE CONSTRUCTION)**
>
> **(a)**   If the Contractor refuses or fails to prosecute the work or any separable part, with the diligence that will insure its completion within the time specified in this contract including any extension, or fails to complete the work within this time, the Government may, by written notice to the Contractor, terminate the right to proceed with the work (or the separable part of the work) that has been delayed. In this event, the Government may take over the work and complete it by contract or otherwise, and may take possession of and use any materials, appliances, and plant on the work site necessary for completing the work. The Contractor and its sureties shall be liable for any damage to the Government resulting from the Contractor's refusal or failure to complete the work within the specified time, whether or not the Contractor's right to proceed with the work is terminated. This liability includes any increased costs incurred by the Government in completing the work....[13]

This contract language provides very strong rights to the government in order to protect the public interest when a contractor fails to meet the obligations

---

[13]F.A.R. 52.249-10 48 C.F.R. 52.249-10 (Nov. 1996).

of the contract. The contractor loses any further right to proceed and, together with the surety, is liable for all excess costs that the government may incur in completing the contract. Default termination language in other contracts contains similar provisions.

The consequences of default terminations are so severe that this step should be taken only in extreme situations. The attitude of our federal courts on this point is clear in the following citations from typical case law:

> Termination for default is a drastic action which should only be imposed on the basis of solid evidence.[14]

> It should be observed that terminations for default are a harsh measure and being a species of forfeiture, they are strictly construed.[15]

Convenience Terminations

The federal fixed-priced contract termination-for-convenience clause reads as follows:

TERMINATION FOR CONVENIENCE OF THE GOVERNMENT (FIXED-PRICE)

(a) The Government may terminate performance of work under this contract in whole or, from time to time, in part if the Contracting Officer determines that a termination is in the Government's interest. The Contracting Officer shall terminate by delivering to the Contractor a Notice of Termination specifying the extent of termination and the effective date.

(b) After receipt of a Notice of Termination, and except as directed by the Contracting Officer, the Contractor shall immediately proceed with the following obligations, regardless of any delay in determining or adjusting any amounts due under this clause:

    (1) Stop work as specified in the notice.

    (2) Place no further subcontracts or orders (referred to as subcontracts in this clause) for materials, services, or facilities, except as necessary to complete the continued portion of the contract.

    (3) Terminate all subcontracts to the extent they relate to the work terminated.

    (4) Assign to the Government, as directed by the Contracting Officer, all right, title, and interest of the Contractor under the subcontracts terminated, in which case the Government shall have the right to settle or to pay any termination settlement proposal arising out of those terminations.

    (5) With approval or ratification to the extent required by the Contracting Officer, settle all outstanding liabilities and termination settlement proposals arising from the termination of subcontracts; the approval or ratification will be final for purposes of this clause.

---

[14]*Mega Construction Co., Inc. v. United States,* 29 Fed. Ct. 396 414 (1993).

[15]*Composite Laminates v. United States,* 27 Fed. Ct. 310 (1992).

(6) As directed by the Contracting Officer, transfer title and deliver to the Government (i) the fabricated or unfabricated parts, work in process, completed work, supplies, and other material produced or acquired for the work terminated, and (ii) the completed or partially completed plans, drawings, information, and other property that, if the contract had been completed, would be required to be furnished to the Government.

(7) Complete performance of the work not terminated.

(8) Take any action that may be necessary, or that the Contracting Officer may direct, for the protection and preservation of the property related to this contract that is in the possession of the Contractor and in which the Government has or may acquire an interest.

(9) Use its best efforts to sell, as directed or authorized by the Contracting Officer, any property of the types referred to in subparagraph (b)(6) of this clause; *provided,* however, that the Contractor (i) is not required to extend credit to any purchaser and (ii) may acquire the property under the conditions prescribed by, and at prices approved by, the Contracting Officer. The proceeds of any transfer or disposition will be applied to reduce any payments to be made by the Government under this contract, credited to the price or cost of the work or paid in any other manner directed by the Contracting Officer.... [16]

The **genesis of the termination-for-convenience clause** dates back to the end of the Civil War when the cessation of hostilities placed the government in the position of remaining contracted for supplies and equipment that were no longer needed. At that time, the general purpose of the clause was to permit the government to stop contract performance when a major change in circumstances obviated the need for further performance. Since the clause first appeared in federal contracts, a number of federal court and board decisions have broadened its use to the point of permitting the government to terminate a contract for practically any reason, providing that the government acts in good faith. More recently, several federal court and board decisions have been more restrictive to prevent the contracting officer's **abuse of discretion** when invoking the clause. In most instances today, the clause is invoked for legitimate reasons, and abuse of discretion cases are relatively rare.

Further actions that the contractor should take when the clause is invoked are fully spelled out in succeeding paragraphs of the federal clause (not cited here). A procedure is established for the contractor to make a monetary claim to the government for an equitable adjustment to settle the contract fairly. Generally speaking, such termination settlements reimburse the contractor for all costs incurred, including settlement costs with subcontractors and suppliers plus a reasonable profit thereon. Anticipated profit on the unperformed terminated work is not allowed.

Termination-for-convenience clauses in other contracts may or may not follow the line of the federal clause. A prudent contractor should be particularly interested in the provisions in these clauses governing how the contract will be settled in a termination-for-convenience situation.

---

[16]F.A.R. 52.24902 48 C.F.R. 52.249-2 (Nov. 1996).

CONCLUSION

Closely related to delays, suspensions of work, and terminations are the subjects of liquidated damages, *force majeure,* and time extensions. These topics are discussed in the next chapter.

QUESTIONS AND PROBLEMS

1. Discuss the popular view and the judicial view of the meaning of the words "time is of the essence" in a construction contract, subcontract, or purchase order.

2. What is the prudent view of time-is-of-the-essence language in a contract with respect to the following:
   a. Your contractual commitments to others; and
   b. Others' contractual commitments to you.

3. Explain two differences between a "delay" and a "suspension" of work.

4. In what two ways does delay to a construction contract increase costs for both the contractor and owner?

5. Explain the difference between an excusable delay and a compensable delay. State some common examples of excusable delay.

6. Explain the principal provisions of the federal contract suspension of work clause.

7. Explain the principal provisions of a typical no-damages-for-delay clause.

8. Are no-damages-for-delay clauses universally enforceable?

9. What is the reasoning of courts that
   a. Refuse to enforce no-damages-for-delay clauses?
   b. Do enforce no-damages-for-delay clauses?

10. When the contract is silent on the subject of damages for delay, what course of action must a contractor follow to recover time and money lost caused by an owner's delay when the owner refuses to grant additional time and money?

11. Explain why a contractor is entitled to be paid for extra costs suffered because of an owner-caused delay when, in spite of the delay, the contractor finishes the contract on or before the contractually stipulated date. Under what circumstances is the contractor not entitled to be paid such costs when the contract is finished on or before the specified date?

12. What can a contractor do in advance to enhance the chances of recovering costs incurred because of owner-caused delays when the contractor plans to finish before the contractually specified date?

13. What are the four general root causes of delay discussed in this chapter?

14. Explain two reasons for the importance of prompt written notice to the owner when the contractor has been delayed. Does the necessity for prompt written notice occur only when the owner is delaying the contractor or for excusable delays as well?

15. Explain constructive notice. Does the fact that constructive notice may exist mean that the contractor should not also give prompt written notice?

16. Explain how a termination differs from a delay or suspension of work.

17. Name and explain the two types of terminations discussed in this chapter. Do they each require an enabling clause in the contract? Does the federal contract contain an enabling clause for each?

18. What was the original reason behind the termination-for-convenience clause in the federal contract?

19. Does current federal contract law allow the government the completely unfettered right to invoke the termination-for-convenience clause?

20. What should be the primary concern of the contractor concerning termination-for-convenience clauses in contracts other than the federal contract?

17

Liquidated Damages, *Force Majeure,* and Time Extensions

Key Words and Concepts

Liquidated damages provisions
Conceptual basis of liquidated damages
Liquidated damages provisions are a
    contract remedy
Judicial attitude to liquidated damages
    provisions
Bonus/penalty clauses
Force majeure

Common conditions of *force majeure*
Contract relief for *force majeure*
Time extensions
Importance of notice of claim
Contractor responsibility to prove
    entitlement
Owner's responsibility to act
No time extension until owner grants it

Suppose that you had hired a contractor to build a home for your family that was to be completed and ready for occupancy by a certain agreed date. Based on this expectation, you sold your previous home and were required to vacate by the agreed date that the new home was to be ready. If the contractor failed to complete the new home by that date, you would not only be greatly inconvenienced but might have to rent temporary accommodations until the new home was ready at totally unexpected additional expense. If an ongoing business property or product manufacturing facility had been involved instead, the inconvenience and monetary loss would be increased enormously.

When something like this occurs, who pays, and how much do they pay? If the delay was not the contractor's fault, what then? How is this situation handled contractually? These and related questions are answered in this chapter.

LIQUIDATED DAMAGES

Today, most large construction contracts contain **liquidated damages provisions** stating explicitly that, for each calendar day the contract work remains uncompleted after the final completion date stated in the contract, the contractor shall pay the owner a certain dollar amount stated in the contract. Sometimes a series of dollar amounts are stated, each applying if interim completion dates for separate parts of the contract work called *milestone completion dates* are not met, in addition to the provision applying to the final completion date. These specified payments are intended as reimbursement for the monetary loss suffered by the owner that was caused by the delay in completion. They are called *liquidated damages* because they are stated as fixed dollar amounts per day.

Conceptual Basis of Liquidated Damages

The **conceptual basis of liquidated damages** provisions is that, in many cases, the actual damages that the owner will suffer in the event of late completion are very difficult (if not impossible) to determine when the contract was signed. The owner and the contractor, therefore, agree on a fixed daily dollar amount or, if milestone completion dates are specified, fixed daily dollar amounts that are considered a reasonable measure of the extent to which the owner could be damaged by late completion. In practice, the contractor usually has no input into the determination of the daily dollar amount(s). In the public sector and in much private work, the determination is unilaterally made by the owner, and the contract documents are advertised for bids on a "take-it-or-leave-it" basis.

Liquidated Damages Provisions Are a Contract Remedy

Under common law contract principles, a breach of the contract by one party that damages the other entitles the nonbreaching party to the actual monetary damages suffered. Unexcused failure of the contractor to meet the contractually specified completion date clearly is a breach of contract. In the absence of liquidated damages provisions in the contract, the owner would have to itemize the actual damages and present them to the contractor in order to be made whole. If the contractor failed to pay, the owner's recourse would be to either withhold the amount from money otherwise payable to the contractor or sue, prove the extent of the actual damages, and obtain a judgment compelling the contractor to pay. The liquidated damages provisions relieve the owner from this burden. Their effect is to substitute a contract remedy for a common law breach remedy.

Liquidated Damages Are Not a Penalty

It is important that both parties to the contract realize that **liquidated damages** are a contractually **specified remedy** to make the owner whole in the event of late completion. They cannot be properly assessed as a penalty to punish the contractor for some act that displeases the owner or, when not properly due, as pressure to coerce the contractor into a course of action favorable to the owner. In cases of disputed liquidated damages assessments, the courts will not support punitive or coercive motives on the part of the owner.

For instance, the Iowa Supreme Court ruled in 1991 that liquidated damages clauses in three highway contracts were unenforceable penalties. The contractor had entered into three simultaneous contracts for highway resurfacing that each required completion within 40 days and called for liquidated damages of $400 per day. The contractor finished two of the contracts behind schedule. A county department had withheld a total of $32,400 in liquidated damages. The contractor filed suit to recover the withheld money, alleging that the imposition of liquidated damages was punitive in nature. The court held that a project owner must be able to show how the daily rate was determined in order to enforce a liquidated damages clause. In this case, the county disregarded their own construction manual, which called for a sliding daily rate based on the total contract price. The three contracts ranged from a contract price of $37,957 to $251,696, yet the county assessed a daily rate of $400 in each case. Further, at the trial, one of the county's engineers testified, "We wanted the liquidated damages amount to be sufficient to make the contractor aware that we need that project completed." In the court's view, this testimony added to the impression that the liquidated damages assessment was intended as a penalty rather than reflecting the level of damages that conceivably could have been suffered from late completion. In ruling for the contractor, the Iowa Supreme Court said:

> No witness was called to justify the suggested liquidated damages amount contained in the DOT manual schedule. The county engineer did not conduct studies or present any other data suggesting that the defendants anticipated that the government entities and the public could sustain damages equivalent to the $400 per day liquidated damages amount contained in each of the three contracts. . . . Therefore, we conclude that the $400 per day liquidated damages clause is an unreasonable amount and therefore a penalty that should not be enforced.[1]

---

[1] *Rohlin Construction Co., Inc. v. City of Hinton,* 476 N.W.2d 78 (Iowa 1991).

Judicial Attitude Toward Liquidated Damages Provisions

The contractor in the previously related case was fortunate. The current **judicial attitude toward liquidated damages** is to enforce such provisions in the event of unexcused late completion. The owner does not have to prove the amount of damages or that *any* damages resulted as a consequence of late completion. For every unexcused day of late completion, the owner is generally due the liquidated amount stated in the contract. However, there are exceptions. In addition to overturning improper assessments made for punitive or coercive purposes, courts may overturn liquidated damages assessments if the daily amount stated in the contract does not bear a reasonable relationship to the amount that the owner could be thought to be damaged. The standard of reasonableness is based on whether the daily amount is a reasonable estimate of the extent to which the owner might be damaged by late completion, in light of the level of knowledge possessed by the owner and contractor when the contract was signed.

A typical judicial holding along these lines is exemplified by a 1985 decision of the Corps of Engineers Board of Contract Appeals. A contract for the construction of rest area facilities allowed 90 days for performance and called for liquidated damages of $143 per day for late completion. The contractor was very late in completing the work, and the government assessed liquidated damages of $18,447 against a total contract amount of $29,189. In supporting the contractor's appeal of this relatively large liquidated damages assessment, the Board of Contract Appeals said:

> The Board concludes that the liquidated damages provision in this contract was not based on any reasonable forecast of probable damages that might follow a breach, and therefore that the liquidated damages provision will not be enforced.[2]

Even though payment is sometimes evaded as just explained, contractors are well advised in planning the performance of their contract work to believe that liquidated damages provisions will be enforced.

Bonus/Penalty Clauses

Can the liquidated damages provisions be applied in reverse if the contractor finishes early? If the owner is damaged for every day's late completion, is there a like benefit from every day's early completion? Not necessarily. The owner may not have planned on the use of the completed facility until the specified contract completion date and may be unprepared to occupy and use it in the event of early delivery. There are other reasons as well why early completion might not benefit the owner. Therefore, the typical liquidated damages clause cannot be applied in reverse for early completion. However, contracts sometimes contain a **bonus/penalty clause** that does provide the contractor a monetary benefit for early

---

[2]*Appeal of Great Western Utility Corp.,* ENGBCA No. 4934 (Apr. 5, 1985).

completion as well as providing for payment to the owner in the event of late completion. Usually, the daily rate for early completion will be less than the rate for late completion. Bonus/penalty clauses are relatively rare in the public sector although quite common in private work.

FORCE MAJEURE

In a contractual sense, *force majeure* means a condition beyond a party's control. An owner-caused delay would be a condition of *force majeure* from the standpoint of the contractor, even though the delay was within the control of the owner. On the other hand, inclement weather or a flood are conditions of *force majeure* from the standpoint of both parties.

Common Conditions of *Force Majeure*

In addition to owner-caused delays, acts of God, war, riots, labor strikes, inability to obtain critical materials when all proper procurement actions have been taken, and other similar situations are **common conditions of** *force majeure.* It should be noted that mere failure of a prime contractor's subcontractors or material suppliers to perform in a manner that meets the time requirements of the prime contract seldom constitutes a condition of *force majeure,* since both are under the control of the prime contractor. For a subcontractor or material supplier delay to be considered *force majeure,* it is necessary for the prime contractor to prove that the inability of the subcontractor or material supplier to perform is caused by conditions not only beyond their control but beyond the control of the prime contractor as well. This is usually a heavy burden of proof.

Contract Relief for Conditions of *Force Majeure*

Since such conditions are not the contractor's fault, the **contract relief for conditions of** *force majeure* normally is an **extension of contract time** to avoid the unfair assessment of liquidated damages. The resulting delay is contractually considered excusable. If the contract does not contain an enforceable no-damages-for-delay clause and the condition was caused by the owner, the delay is also compensable, entitling the contractor to both a time extension and additional payment.

TIME EXTENSIONS

Even though extensions of contract time for conditions of *force majeure* are promised by the contract, they are far from automatic. The contractor must follow prescribed contract procedures and must prove entitlement to assure that contractually justified time extensions will be forthcoming.

Importance of Notice of Claim

Most contracts contain a provision that the contractor claiming entitlement to a time extension must file **notice of claim** within a stated number of calendar days after the event giving rise to the claim or waive the right to relief. Although sometimes the owner has constructive notice of the cause of the delay for which the contractor is entitled to a time extension, the importance of the contractor filing time extension claims within the contractually prescribed time cannot be overemphasized.

The owner has no duty to grant a time extension if the contractor has not requested one. Therefore, when the contractor has been delayed, an immediate request for a time extension should be submitted in writing. The initial notice should be followed by a written claim for the number of days that the completion of the contract has been delayed. The claim should be filed at the earliest possible time following the end of the delay so that the total extent of the delay can be determined. This is normally shortly after the conclusion of the delay.

The importance of notice is dramatically illustrated in the following 1991 decision of the Alabama Supreme Court who reversed a trial court decision in favor of a contractor who had been assessed $85,500 in liquidated damages on a contract for site preparation and road construction for a residential subdivision. The contract called for liquidated damages of $300 per day for late completion and provided that time extensions for delay beyond the control and without the fault of the contractor would be granted, provided that written requests for time extensions were submitted to the owner's engineer within 20 days of commencement of the delay. The contract also contained a no-damages-for-delay clause, so the only remedy for delay was an extension of time. The contractor completed the contract 285 days behind schedule but contested the liquidated damages assessment on the grounds that the delay had been caused by the interference of the owner's separate utility contractor and therefore was excusable. A trial court agreed and remitted the liquidated damages to the contractor.

On appeal, the Supreme Court of Alabama reversed, stating that the contractor was aware of the requirement to submit a written request within 20 days of the event giving rise to a request for an extension of time and had, in fact, complied with that procedure on one occasion when receiving a 45-day extension of time for a separate cause. Holding that the contractor had waived any right to extensions of time, the Supreme Court stated:

> The Cove Creek contract provided that time was of the essence and then went on to specify liquidated damages for delay. The contract also contained a provision for extensions, and APAC availed itself of that provision on at least one occasion and received a 45 day extension because of delays caused by R & M. We hold that APAC's delays were not excusable and that it is bound by the contract and subject to the liquidated damages provisions.[3]

---

[3]*Cove Creek Development Corp. v. APAC-Alabama, Inc.,* 588 So.2d 458 (Ala. 1991).

Contractor Responsibility to Prove Entitlement

In any type of claim situation, whether for time, additional contract payment, or both, the contractor-claimant bears the **legal burden to prove entitlement** under the terms of the contract to whatever is being claimed. For this reason, the contractor must support a time extension claim by showing that delaying events beyond his or her control have consumed part of the time allotted by the contract for performance of the contract work—in other words, by showing that the delaying events have extended contract completion. This is usually done by supporting the claim with a *critical path method* (CPM) schedule analysis indicating the extent of the overall delay to the project.

Owner's Responsibility and Contractor Time-Extension Requests

Contractors bear the heavy contractual burden of performing the required contract work within the contract time period. They also are contractually entitled to the benefit of having the contract time extended due to the impact of an excusable or compensable delay within a reasonable time after the delay ends so that they can properly and efficiently plan the remaining contract work. To secure this right, it is incumbent upon the contractor at the conclusion of each significant delay to make a CPM schedule analysis and to request a discrete number of days' time extension in accordance with the result of the analysis, which should also be submitted to the owner in support of the contractor's claim. The majority of courts today support this approach, as well as holding that if an owner receives a time extension claim properly supported in this manner, the **owner has a duty to grant the time extension** in a timely manner rather than waiting until the end-of-project performance before granting it. Failure of the owner to grant a properly supported request for an extension of contract time or failure to grant it in a timely manner is a breach of the contract.

Granting of Time Extensions

The contractor may not safely assume that a time extension will be granted simply because it has been properly claimed and the contractor believes it to be due. A time extension can only be granted by a formal change to the contract executed by the owner. Regardless of the merits of the contractor's claim, the contract date is not extended until and unless the owner has formally notified the contractor by a written change to the contract that the contract has been extended by a stated number of calendar days to the new date stated. An oral intimation that the contract will be extended or may be extended if the contractor "needs it later" to avoid being assessed liquidated damages is not sufficient or contractually proper. Once the owner has had sufficient time to act following receipt of the contractor's claim for a time extension and a change to the contract has not been initiated, the contractor must necessarily assume that the claim has been denied.

If the owner fails to act on a properly supported contractor time extension claim or denies it directly, the contractor's proper course of action is clear. First, a notice should be filed in writing protesting the denial or lack of timely action as the case may be, and, second, the contractor should take all possible and reasonable action to meet the unextended contract completion date. By failing to prosecute the work in a manner that assures project completion by the then-existing completion date, the contractor is exposed to a breach of contract determination by the owner that could result in the contract being terminated for default. Although a court may eventually declare the default termination to be improper, the long legal battle that would ensue is an expensive burden. The contractor's proper contractual position after protesting in writing is to attempt to meet the unextended contract completion date and pursue a separate remedy under the doctrine of constructive acceleration, which is discussed in Chapter 19.

CONCLUSION

This chapter discussed the general concepts of liquidated damages, *force majeure,* and contract time extensions. Contractor time extension claims, owner entitlement to liquidated damages, and contractor claims for monetary damages for compensable delays are closely related issues and must normally be determined by a structured CPM schedule analysis. The following chapter explains how the owner's and contractor's respective liabilities and entitlements are sorted out in practice by this method.

QUESTIONS AND PROBLEMS

1. Is an owner's right to assess and collect liquidated damages an express or an implied right under a construction contract? Who ordinarily determines the daily amount? What is the general attitude of courts concerning the determination of this amount?

2. Can liquidated damages provisions be properly used as a means of intimidation or coercion? Can they be properly assessed as a penalty?

3. Under typical contract provisions, can liquidated damages be applied in reverse for early completion? What are the provisions of a bonus/penalty clause?

4. What is a condition of *force majeure?* From the contractor's standpoint, can such a condition be caused by the owner? Why is the mere failure of a material supplier or a subcontractor to perform often not a condition of *force majeure?* What relief does a contractor usually receive for costs incurred because of delays caused by an act of God? Same question when the delay is caused by an act of the owner?

5. When a delay has occurred because of an act of God or some other cause beyond the contractor's control, does the owner have the duty automatically to grant an extension of time? If not, what triggers the owner's duty to act?

6. When an owner does grant an extension of time, how is this act accomplished contractually?

7. What are two separate aspects of an owner's duty when the contractor presents a properly supported and justified claim for an extension of time during contract performance? Is the owner's duty met by granting the extension of time after the contract work is completed if the contractor "needs" the extension of time to avoid the assessment of liquidated damages? Why is timeliness in the owner's granting a time extension an important factor from the contractor's standpoint?

8. What is the contractor's proper course of action when justified extensions of time have been properly claimed and the owner refuses to grant them and/or simply fails to act on them? Why? What is the contractor's proper contractual position in this situation?

18

Allocating Responsibility for Delays

Key Words and Concepts

Work activities
Dependency ties
As-built network
As-planned network
Schedule update network
Owner responsibility delays
Contractor responsibility delays
Discrete events
Burden of performance
Excusable delays
Incorporation of delays into network
Forward-looking analysis
Retrospective analysis
Intermediate impact analysis
Concurrent delay

Four principles governing delay impact
  analysis
Delay analysis for single-path projects
Delay analysis for multi-path (concurrent
  path) projects
Delay impact analysis for complex
  projects with several interconnected
  concurrent paths
Float time
Owner liability for delay damages
Contractor-caused delay
Contractor liability for liquidated damages
Contractor entitlement to an extension
  of time
Damages offset not necessarily day-for-day

This chapter explains the principles and procedure by which contractor liability for liquidated or actual damages and owner liability for monetary damages for owner-caused delay are determined in practice. Delays usually occur during performance of the typical contract, some within the control of the contractor, some caused by the owner or for which the owner is otherwise liable, and some that are beyond the control of either party, for which neither party is liable. All three commonly occur at various times, generally affecting only one part of the project, although some may affect the entire project.

When the owner and contractor disagree on questions of extensions of time, liquidated damages, or owner-caused delay damages, the first problem facing courts and other dispute resolution bodies is determining delay responsibility. Once the individual delays and the party responsible for them have been identified, the second problem is determining the consequences of the delay(s). This latter problem is usually solved by performance of a *critical path method* (CPM) schedule delay impact analysis. The principles and procedure for performing such an analysis follow.

PRELIMINARY POINTS AND DEFINITIONS

Construction contracts today commonly provide that the performance of the work be planned and monitored by the use of the critical path method. The contractor is required to submit a CPM network schedule that depicts the construction work activity sequence and the beginning and ending dates of all work activities as the contractor intends to perform them. Such an initial schedule is often referred to as the baseline schedule. As the work progresses, the contractor is usually required to update the baseline schedule periodically (monthly or quarterly), reflecting the actual beginning and ending dates for all completed work activities, the actual start and estimated completion dates for all activities in progress, and the anticipated start and end dates for all remaining work activities. Such schedules provide a convenient method by which the impact of delays can be determined. (If you are not familiar with the CPM scheduling method, refer to any of the numerous available texts on that subject for details.) In the following discussion, only general concepts will be presented to illustrate the methods of delay impact analysis.

As-Planned, As-Built, and Schedule Update Networks

A CPM network is a graphic depiction in which the various physical work items of the project are represented as a sequential arrangement of **work activities** joined together by **dependency ties.** The dependency ties indicate the sequence in which the activities must be performed as well as the requirement that immediately preceding activities must be completed prior to the start of following activities on the same path of work or to the start of following activities on parallel paths of work.

For instance, consider the simplified generic CPM network schedule illustrated by Figure 18–1 in which contract work activities are represented as time-

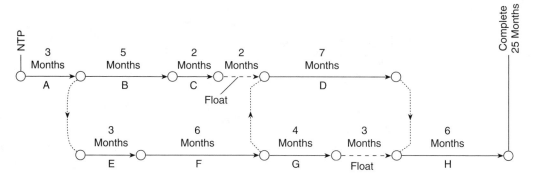

FIGURE 18–1 A generic CPM schedule network.

scaled solid arrows A, B, C, D, E, F, G, and H. The time duration of each in months is indicated directly above each work activity arrow.

Such a CPM network schedule implies that the following logic discipline be maintained:

■ Along each line of consecutive work activity arrows, each predecessor work activity must be completed before the successor work activity can commence.

■ The dependency ties that exist between separated work activity arrows are established by the dotted lines between the work activity arrows, either those included in a line of separated arrows such as between work activities C and D and between work activities G and H, or between work activity arrows on parallel lines such as between work activities A and E, F and D, and between work activities D and H.

■ The direction of the arrowhead included in dependency ties determines which of the connected work activities is the precedent activity and which is the successor activity that can not start until the completion of its predecessor. In Figure 18–1, work activity E can not start until work activity A has been completed, work activity D can not start until work activities C and F have been completed, and work activity H can not start until work activities D and G have been completed.

■ The time duration that the completion of work activities could be delayed without delaying the completion of the project is termed **float time.** In Figure 18–1, work activities B and C together have 2 months of float and work activity G has 3 months of float.

■ **Early start** and **early finish** dates are the earliest possible points in time that a work activity can start and finish, while **late start** and **late finish** dates are the latest points in time that a work activity can start and finish without delaying the completion of the project. For instance, the early and late start dates for work activity B would be 3 months and 5 months after NTP and 8 months and 10 months after NTP, respectively, while early and late start dates for work activity C would be 8 months and 10 months after NTP, and 10 months and 12 months after NTP, respectively. Similarly, early and late start dates for work activity G would be 12 and 15 months after NTP, and 16 and 19 months after NTP, respectively.

- The **critical path** is a path of work activities that contains no float and thus controls the completion date of the project. In Figure 18–1, the sequence of work activities A, E, F, D, and H is the critical path. Some networks may contain more than one critical path.

- Early and late start dates and early and late finish dates are the same points in time for work activities on the critical path (i.e., activities that contain no float).

When a network schedule such as Figure 18–1 is created before the commencement of project work as a planning tool, or is submitted to the owner by the contractor before contract work in compliance with project specification scheduling requirements, it is referred to as an **as-planned or baseline schedule network** reflecting the contractor's plan for the accomplishment of the work. As the work progresses, such a schedule is monitored by periodically updating it to reflect the completion status of the project at the points in time of the periodic updates. Such a network would be referred to as a **schedule update network**.

For instance, if the generic schedule network shown in Figure 18–1 had been submitted by a contractor as the as-planned or baseline schedule, the schedule update after seven months of contract performance might look as indicated in Figure 18–2. Such an update schedule reflects actual *as-built performance* up to the date of the update documented by project records and as-planned performance for the balance of the work to project completion. At the time of the update in this

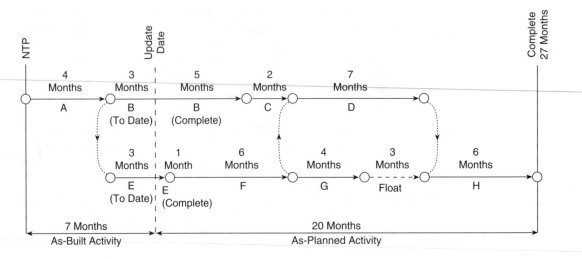

FIGURE 18–2   A generic CPM schedule update network seven months after NTP.

hypothetical illustration, activity A had been completed and activities B and E partially completed. The completion dates for activities B and E necessarily would have to be estimated based on experience to date while the balance of the work is shown in accordance with the baseline schedule indicating the contractor's belief that, in spite of a slow start, the balance of the work will be accomplished in accordance with the original plan. The updated schedule network shown in Figure 18–2 indicates that at the time of the update, the contractor was two months behind the baseline schedule. Subsequent periodic schedule updates as the work progressed would normally be carried out until the project was completed, each update regularly reflecting as-built performance up to the date of the update and as-planned performance thereafter to project completion.

A final update made at the point in time of project completion would reflect total as-built performance as documented in project records. Such an **as-built network** for the project represented by Figures 18–1 and 18–2 could well turn out as indicated in Figure 18–3. By improving performance in the completion of activity B and for all of activities D, F, and H, the contractor in this hypothetical example regained time and completed the project one month earlier than the 25-month completion time of the baseline schedule.

It should be noted that the hypothetical schedule networks shown in Figures 18–1, 18–2, and 18–3 are simple generic networks utilized here for purposes of illustration only. Actual project schedule networks are normally far more complex and contain many more work activities and dependency ties as well as numerous paths to project completion.

Owner Responsibility Delays

Delays or extensions of work activity performance exclusively caused by the owner or otherwise the contractual responsibility of the owner are compensable delays. These kind of delays entitle the contractor to additional payment for any costs incurred as a result of the delays. The contractor is also entitled to an extension of

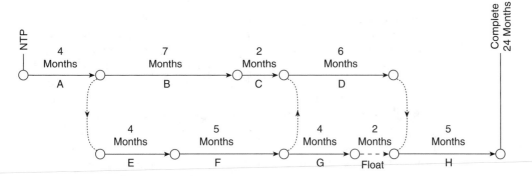

FIGURE 18–3   A generic CPM as-built schedule network.

contract performance time if the delays cause the overall project performance duration to be extended. For purposes of identification of this class of delay, the symbol "ORD" (**owner responsibility delay**) is used in the schedule networks that follow in this chapter.

Contractor Responsibility Delays

If the total time allowed for contract completion is exceeded, delays or extensions of work activity performance that are exclusively the fault of the contractor or otherwise the contractual responsibility of the contractor do not entitle the contractor to extra compensation or an extension of contract performance time and may result in the contractor becoming liable for the payment of liquidated damages. For purposes of the analysis in this chapter, this class of delay must be subdivided into two subclasses:

- The first subclass consists of delays that can be easily recognized as **discrete events** or happenings. Examples would be clearly identified contract breaches such as failure to make required submittals by contractually stipulated dates or any other identified delay caused by or the contractual responsibility of the contractor including subcontractors and suppliers. For purposes of identification in the networks that follow, the symbol "CRD" (**contractor responsibility delay**) will be used for this subclass of contractor responsibility delay.

- The second subclass arises from the contractor's failure to perform the actual work items of the contract at a rate sufficient to complete the contract on time. This subclass of contractor delay is not directly identified by a symbol on the network schedules that follow. The contractor's **burden of performance** is to complete all of the contract work in accordance with the requirements of the technical specifications within the time limits specified in the contract. To meet this burden, the contractor is free to choose the means, methods, techniques, sequences, and procedures of accomplishing the work. Contractor failure to meet the burden of performance, unless interfered with or delayed by others, may entitle the owner to liquidated damages—or actual provable damages in contracts that do not contain a liquidated damages provision. However, the contractor's failure to accomplish a given item of work (i.e., a *work activity*) within the time limits of an as-planned or intended project schedule does not in and of itself mean that the contractor has failed to meet the burden of performance or has incurred liability to pay damages. Unless the contract contains explicit language to the contrary, the contractor is free to make up for such lost time by performing later work activities at a rate faster than the as-planned or originally intended rate that may have been depicted on the as-planned schedule or on any other form of contractor-produced project schedule. Only when the required work of the entire contract has been completed, or the required work for a given milestone has been completed in the case of milestone completion date contracts, is it possible to determine whether the contractor has satisfactorily met the burden of performance.

Excusable Delays

Delays that are not the fault of either the owner or contractor are **excusable delays** (ED). If they result in the project duration being extended, EDs entitle the contractor to an extension of time only. The most common examples are *force majeure* conditions such as acts of God, war, riot, and so on.

Incorporation of Delays into the CPM Network for Delay Impact Analysis

The previously explained classes of delays or extension of work activity performance include:

- Owner responsibility delays (ORDs)
- Discrete event contractor delays (CRDs)
- Slow-work-performance contractor delays (not directly identified by a symbol)
- Excusable delays (EDs)

If the starting dates of particular project work activities shown on a schedule network have been delayed by ORDs, CRDs, or EDs, each delaying event can be identified, both as to the point in time at which it occurred (just before the start of the affected work activity) and as to its duration (the time duration of the delay). Also, some ORDs do not delay the start of a contractor work activity but rather take the form of extending the work activity to a longer duration than would have been the case without the delay. (An example of this kind of ORD would be the improper imposition by the owner's engineer of a requirement that was not included in the project specifications that increased the time required for a work activity to be performed.) In these cases, an estimate can be made for the additional time the work activity was improperly extended. This time duration can be identified as a ORD and extracted from the duration of the affected work activity. Such a delay would be arbitrarily shown in the network to have occurred at the end of the shortened work activity (just before the start of the following work activity), even though in actuality the delaying effect was uniformly experienced throughout the work activity.

By these procedures, all of the above described delay types that may have affected the contractor work performance activities represented in a CPM schedule network can be identified and depicted in the network as discrete delay activities, each with its own duration positioned in the network at the point in time at which it is considered to have occurred.

Identifying and depicting each of the various kinds of delays as discrete activities in the network *is the first step in CPM schedule delay impact analysis.*

Forward-Looking and Retrospective Impact Analysis

If known or anticipated delays are inserted as discrete activities in an as-planned schedule and a delay impact analysis is performed to determine their impact on job completion, the analysis is referred to as a **forward-looking delay impact analysis.** This method of analysis is similar to forward-pricing a monetary claim.

On the other hand, if all project delays are inserted into an as-built network after all project work has been completed, the analysis is a **retrospective delay impact analysis** (akin to retrospectively pricing a monetary claim).

Some contract delay analysts believe that the impacts of delays should be analyzed when they occur and appropriate time and cost adjustments made to the contract progressively as the project work proceeds. If this is done, each delay is inserted into the updated schedule in effect when the delay occurs and a **contemporaneous impact analysis** is performed on a part as-built, part as-planned schedule to determine the impact of that delay.

There are arguments for and against all three approaches to delay impact analysis that are beyond the intended scope of this book. However, the principles underlying all of them are essentially the same. Once the delays have been inserted into the CPM schedule, whichever one of the three approaches is used, the analytical procedure is similar. Therefore the principles and procedures that follow, which are illustrated by application to an as-built schedule, are equally applicable to any CPM delay impact analysis, whenever performed.

Consecutive and Concurrent Events

A series of events, whether work activities or delays inserted into a network, are said to be *consecutive* if they follow along the same path of the network one after the other. For instance, work activities A, B, C, and D, as well as work activities E, F, G, and H, in Figure 18–1 are consecutive activities. When the events occur on separate parallel paths of the network, they are said to be *concurrent* events. Concurrent events may or may not occur within the same time frame. The fact that they occur on separate paths to project completion is what makes them concurrent. In Figure 18–1, work activities B, C, and D are concurrent with work activities E, F, and G.

Four Principles Governing Delay Impact Analysis

As stated previously, the starting point in determining either the number of calendar days of liquidated damages due the owner, or the number of days of compensatory delay damages due the contractor in a complex delay analysis situation, is identifying each delay as an ORD, CRD, or ED delay and inserting each into the CPM network as a discrete activity where each occurred. Once this step has been accomplished, the concept of **concurrent delay** must be considered.

Concurrent delay means delay to project completion that results from a number of individual delays, one or more of them occurring on a particular path to project completion and the others occurring on concurrent or parallel paths. In this situation, each of the delays may or may not have a contributory effect on project completion. Because of this, consideration of the following **four principles** is necessary to allocate liability between owner and contractor:

- *First Principle:* An owner cannot properly assess liquidated damages (LD) for periods of time during which the owner was concurrently delaying the project. In other words, the contractor can properly be assessed liquidated damages for only that part of any delay to completion of the project that was exclusively caused by or was exclusively the contractual responsibility of the contractor.

- *Second Principle:* A contractor cannot properly be paid delay damages (DD) for periods of time when the contractor and/or excusable delays were concurrently delaying completion of the project. In other words, the contractor can be properly paid delay damages for only that part of the total project completion delay that was exclusively caused by, or was exclusively the contractual responsibility of, the owner.

The following cases illustrate the application of the first and second principles. In one case, the government delayed completion of a floodgate rehabilitation project by delivering faulty government-furnished equipment to the contractor. However, during the final months of work, the contractor fell behind schedule with the project's electrical work. The Engineer Board of Contractor Appeals found the two problems to be intertwined, each exacerbating the other, and refused to allow the government to withhold liquidated damages—but the board also denied the contractor recovery of delay damages.[1]

In another decision, the Veterans Administration Board of Contract Appeals similarly ruled that where government-cost and contractor-cost delays are so intertwined that they cannot be segregated, the government may not recover liquidated damages, and the contractor may not recover delay damages. In a contract for the demolition of various structures and construction of new buildings and facilities, the contractor's slow progress and need to perform rework activities delayed completion of a boiler plant. On the other hand, the Veterans Administration's slow response to a differing site condition and failure to coordinate the work of a separate contractor delayed completion of the paving and utility work. In total, the contract was completed 241 days behind schedule.

When the Veterans Administration withheld $282,452 in liquidated damages, the contractor filed a claim for a time extension and more than $1.6 million in delay damages. Both the government and contractor alleged that the other's delay had been on the CPM schedule's critical path, thus causing the late completion of the overall project. In rejecting both parties' as-built CPM schedules, the board stated:

> We find both parties have failed with regard to their attempts to establish that one or the other's delay was solely on some mythical critical path and, therefore, was the sole cause of the delay to the contract. The project did not consist solely of the boiler plant, nor did it consist solely of final paving and electrical services. . . . Given the intertwined causes of delay to the project, we leave the parties where we find them. Accordingly,

---

[1]*Appeal of Gulf Construction Group, Inc.,* ENGBCA No. 5961 (Oct. 13, 1993).

the government is not entitled to liquidated damages, nor is the contractor entitled to compensation for delay damages.[2]

However, case law has clearly established that when delays attributable to the owner and contractor can be separately identified and quantified, costs of compensable delay and liquidated damages can be recovered. In a 1986 decision, the Interior Board of Contract Appeals ruled that the contractor renovating a building at the U.S. Merchant Marine Academy could recover costs for delays that were identified as caused by the government. The project was plagued by a variety of delays, but the board determined that the contractor had properly segregated periods of contractor-caused delay and concurrent delay from periods of government-caused delay.[3]

Similarly, in a 1990 decision, the Postal Service Board of Contract Appeals held that when contractor-caused delays can be segregated from owner-caused delays, the contractor is entitled to recovery for the compensable portion of the delay. The contract called for substantial completion of a post office building and associated site improvements within 300 days of notice to proceed. The contracting officer complained repeatedly to the contractor about inadequate worker supply and slow progress. However, municipal officials then altered the required grades for paving and curb work, necessitating a change order from the Postal Service. The Postal Service was slow to issue the change order, bringing the contract work to a complete standstill. The project was completed well behind schedule. When both parties claimed that delay by the other had contributed to the late completion, the board agreed but said that fact did not preclude the contractor's recovery for owner-caused delay. When periods of owner-caused delays can be segregated from periods of contractor-caused delays and the resulting costs can be separately identified and documented, the contractor can recover for periods of delay solely caused by the owner.[4]

The next principle to be considered in dealing with concurrent delay establishes the basis for segregating the exclusive effect of owner-caused delays on overall project completion from the exclusive effect of contractor-caused delays.

- *Third Principle:* To determine the exclusive effect on overall project completion of any one class of delays that have been identified on an as-built schedule, or on the as-built portion of an updated schedule, it is necessary to collapse the schedule on which that class of delays has been identified by removing that class of delays and reconstituting the schedule as a *collapsed schedule*. The effect of the removed class of delays is the difference in the completion date of the collapsed schedule from the completion date of the original schedule.

A corollary application of this principle in reverse can be stated as follows when a forward-looking delay impact analysis is made on an as-planned schedule or on the as-planned portion of an updated schedule:

---

[2]*Appeal of Coffey Construction Co., Inc.,* VABCA No. 3361 (Feb. 11, 1993).

[3]*Appeal of Wickham Contracting Co., Inc.,* IBCA No. 1301-8-79 (Mar. 31, 1986).

[4]*Appeal of H. A. Kaufman Co.,* PSBCA No. 2616 (July 31, 1990).

■ To determine the exclusive effect on overall project completion of any one class of delays, it is necessary to insert that class of delays into an as-planned schedule or into the as-planned portion of an updated schedule to reconstitute the schedule as an *expanded schedule*. The effect of the inserted class of delays is the difference in completion date of the expanded schedule from the completion date of the original schedule.

The fourth and final principle governs the determination of the proper time period that the contract performance time should be extended.

■ *Fourth Principle:* The original contractually stipulated completion time plus the extension of time to which the contractor is entitled plus the contractor's liability for liquidated damages equals the as-built project completion time.

DELAY IMPACT ANLAYSIS FOR SINGLE-PATH PROJECTS

Actual construction projects rarely if ever occur with just one consecutive path of activities from notice to proceed (NTP) to completion. However, in order to start discussion of delay impact analysis with the simplest possible case, the single-path project situation will be considered first. Figure 18–4 represents a single-path, as-built schedule.

The typical questions to be answered by the analysis are:

■ What is the owner's liability for delay damages (if any)?

■ What is the contractor's liability for liquidated damages (if any)?

■ What is the contractor's entitlement to an extension of contract time (if any)?

By inspection, the project completion date is shortened by four months if the schedule is collapsed by removing the ORD. Thus, by application of the third principle

FIGURE 18–4 Single path, as-built schedule.

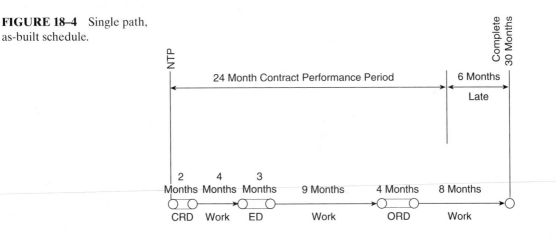

stated earlier, the effect or impact of the ORD is to increase project completion by four months for which the owner has delay damage liability to the contractor.

Similarly, if the schedule is collapsed by removing both the ORD and the ED (leaving only contractor-controlled activities in the schedule), project completion is shortened by seven months, and the project will be completed 23 months after NTP, meeting contract completion requirements. Thus, the contractor has met the burden of performance and has no liability for liquidated (or actual) damages. By application of the fourth principle, the contractor's entitlement to an extension of time is determined as follows:

a. Original completion time + extension of time + liability for liquidated damages = total as-built completion time.

b. 24 months + extension of time + 0 = 30 months.

c. Extension of time = 30 months – 24 months = 6 months.

Now, assume that the contractually stipulated completion date is 20 months (instead of 24 months), resulting in the situation depicted by Figure 18–5.

The owner's liability for delay damages does not change, remaining at four months determined, as before, by shortening the schedule when the ORD is removed. However, when both the ORD and the ED are removed, leaving only contractor-controlled activities, the schedule will collapse to a total of 23 months from NTP. If neither the ORD or ED had occurred, the contractor still would not have completed the work within the contractually stipulated performance period. Completion would have been three months late. Therefore, the contractor is subject to payment of liquidated or actual damages for the three months that actual performance extended beyond the time allowed.

Note that both subclasses of contractor delays were present in the preceding example. Even if the two-month CRD (a discrete identifiable delay) had not occurred, the contractor would still have been one month late—that is, would have failed to perform the three work activities at progress rates sufficient to meet contract time requirements.

Although perhaps overly simplistic, this example illustrates the application of the proper principles and thought processes to arrive at correct conclusions. Discussion of more complex situations follow.

FIGURE 18–5 Single path, as-built schedule.

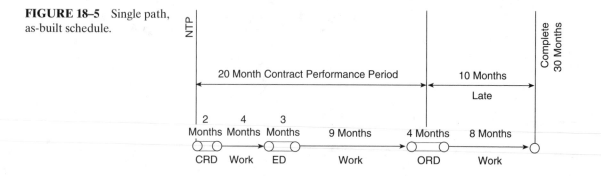

DELAY IMPACT ANALYSIS FOR MULTI-PATH (CONCURRENT PATH) PROJECTS

In the preceding discussion for the second single-path project, when all ORD and ED activities were removed and the schedule collapsed, the remaining project duration consisted of activities that were entirely within the control of the contractor. In that case, since this duration exceeded the contractually stipulated project completion period, contractor-controlled delays existed, and the contractor had liquidated or actual damages liability.

In the general case, contractor-controlled delay can consist of discrete identifiable delays (CRDs), failures to complete physical work activities at a pace sufficient to meet contract time requirements, or a combination of both. Almost all construction projects are multi-path projects in which a number of separate concurrent paths of consecutive activities extend from NTP to project completion. When all ORD and ED activities are removed from a network schedule for such a project, the collapsed schedule will represent what the project duration "would have been" if the ORD and ED activities had not occurred. All remaining activities, whether CRD activities or work activities, are entirely under the control of the contractor. Under these circumstances, it might seem as if any remaining time overrun past the contractually stipulated completion date will result in liquidated or actual damages liability. This may not be true, however, because in accordance with the first principle stated earlier, the project overrun must also have been caused exclusively by the contractor—that is, there must not have been any concurrent delay to project completion that was caused by or was the responsibility of the owner or was the result of an excusable event (ED). To ensure that this condition is met prior to determining that the contractor has liability, an additional step in delay analysis is required.

Consider the multi-path project with an as-built schedule shown in Figure 18–6.

By removing the ORD activities, the as-built schedule will collapse as shown in Figure 18–7. Based on the second principle, the owner's liability for payment of delay

FIGURE 18–6 Multi-path, as-built schedule.

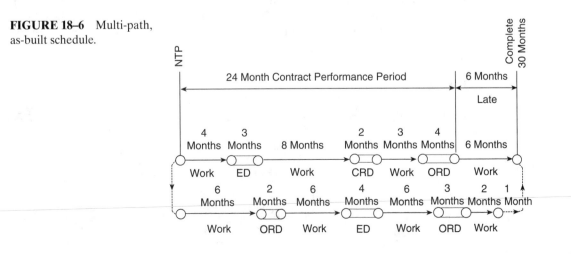

FIGURE 18–7 Collapsed schedule with ORD delays removed.

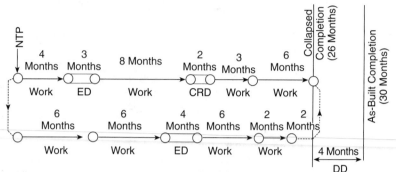

damages to the contractor is four months. This delay to the project completion was exclusively caused by or was otherwise the contractual responsibility of the owner.

The next step in analysis is to remove the ED activities, collapsing the network further as shown in Figure 18–8. The collapsed schedule now represents a "would have been" schedule, consisting entirely of contractor-controlled activities. This schedule would have been achieved if none of the ORD or ED events had occurred. Since, by this schedule, the project is completed in 23 months (one month earlier than the contractually stipulated time), the contractor has no liability for liquidated or actual damages.

If the contractually stipulated completion period for the as-built performance shown by Figure 18–6 was 20 months rather than 24 months, all analytical steps previously taken through production of the collapsed network shown in Figure 18–8 would be the same. It is now clear that the contractor would not have met the burden of performance required by the time requirements of the contract. As Figure 18–8 shows, on the upper path, the contractor was three months late (consisting of a two-month discrete identifiable delay and one-month combined slippage in the required time performance of the four work activities on the path). On the lower path, the contractor met the burden of performance exactly by completing all activities on that path in 20 months. Even though three months late on the upper path, the contractor did not incur three months' liability because of the first principle, stated earlier. For the contractor to incur liability for delay, the

FIGURE 18–8 Collapsed schedule with ORD and ED delays removed.

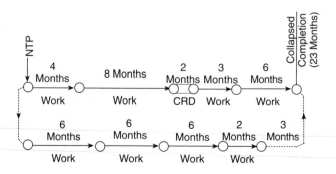

delay to the project must be exclusively caused by or the contractual responsibility of the contractor.

The three-month delay on the upper path of Figure 18–8, although caused by the contractor, did not exclusively delay the project by three months. The delay to the completion of the project that was exclusively caused by the contractor was one month only. The reasoning is as follows:

a. By inspection, as-built completion on the upper path occurred 30 months after NTP.

b. If the three months of contractor delay on the upper path had not occurred, the as-built completion on the path would shorten to 27 months after NTP.

c. There are no contractor-controlled delays on the lower path.

d. If the upper path had been shortened to 27 months after NTP, total project completion would have been determined by the length of the lower path and would have occurred 29 months after NTP.

e. Therefore, the impact of all contractor-controlled delays on total project completion was 30 months less 29 months, or one month. Project completion was exclusively extended by contractor-controlled delays by only one month.

The final step in the analysis is determining the extension of time due the contractor. The reasoning follows:

a. Original contractually stipulated completion + extension of time to which contractor is entitled + contractor's liability for liquidated damages = as-built completion time.

b. For the case of original contractually stipulated completion time of 24 months:

$$24 \text{ months} + \text{extension of time} + (0) = 30 \text{ months}$$
$$\text{Extension of time} = 30 \text{ months} - 24 \text{ months} - (0) = 6 \text{ months}$$

c. For the case of original contractually stipulated completion time of 20 months:

$$20 \text{ months} + \text{extension of time} + 1 \text{ month} = 30 \text{ months}$$
$$\text{Extension of time} = 30 \text{ months} - 20 \text{ months} - 1 \text{ month} = 9 \text{ months}$$

DELAY IMPACT ANALYSIS FOR COMPLEX PROJECTS WITH SEVERAL INTERCONNECTED CONCURRENT PATHS

The typical construction project consists of a number of *concurrent paths of activities where dependency ties exist between activities on separate paths.* Such projects can be analyzed by similar procedures to those previously explained. Refer to Figures 18–9, 18–10, and 18–11.

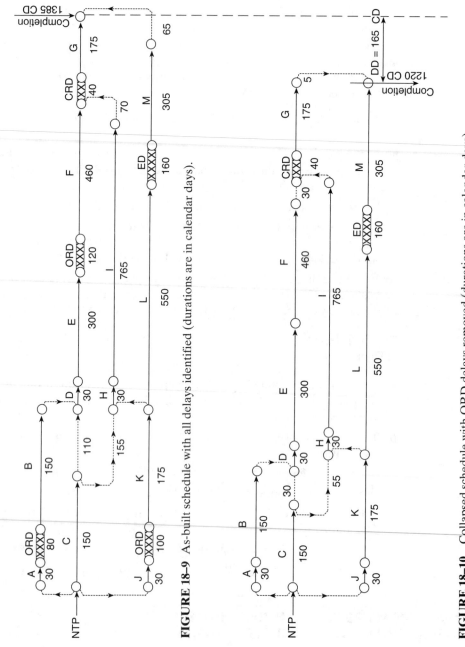

FIGURE 18-9 As-built schedule with all delays identified (durations are in calendar days).

FIGURE 18-10 Collapsed schedule with ORD delays removed (durations are in calendar days).

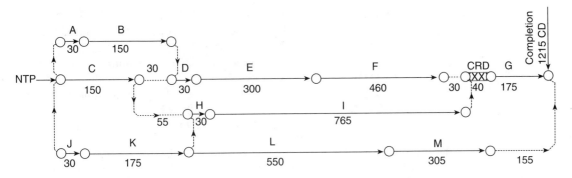

FIGURE 18–11 Collapsed schedule with ORD and ED delays removed (durations are in calendar days).

The starting point is the representation of the as-built performance of the project constructed from project records, which results in Figure 18–9. All delays (ORD, CRD, and ED delays) are identified as activities on Figure 18–9. The dotted line durations of 110 CD, 155 CD, 70 CD, and 65 CD respectively, are *float time*, the length of time that the completion of the preceding activity can be delayed without delaying the completion of the project. The as-built completion time was 1385 calendar days (CD), whereas the contractually stipulated completion time was 1100 CD.

Owner Liability for Delay Damages

The first step in analysis is to remove all ORD activities from Figure 18–9, collapsing the schedule to the network shown in Figure 18–10. Note that all interpath dependency ties are maintained. Also, when collapsing the schedule, all activities are shown with the earliest possible start times (the "early" start times). Total project completion time reduces from 1385 CD to 1220 CD, establishing the **owner's liability for delay damages** equal to 1385 CD – 1220 CD, or 165 CD.

Has the Contractor Met the Burden of Performance?

The second step is to remove all ED activities from Figure 18–10, collapsing the schedule to the network shown on Figure 18–11. (Again note that all interpath dependency ties are maintained.) The completion time of Figure 18–11, which contains only contractor-controlled activities reduces to 1215 CD.

The third step is determining whether the contractor has performed the actual work activities at a pace sufficient to meet the contract time requirements (the burden of performance by the contractor). This must be done separately for all of the possible paths leading to completion of the project. Thus

Path ABDEFG: $30 + 150 + 30 + 300 + 460 + 40 + 175 = 1185$ CD
$1185 – 1100 = 85$ CD longer than required time

Path CDEFG:	$150 + 30 + 300 + 460 + 40 + 175 = 1155$ CD
	$1155 - 1100 = 55$ CD longer than required time
Path CHIG:	$150 + 30 + 765 + 40 + 175 = 1160$ CD
	$1160 - 1100 = 60$ CD longer than required time
Path JKHIG:	$30 + 175 + 30 + 765 + 40 + 175 = 1215$
	$1215 - 1100 = 115$ CD longer than required time
Path JKLM:	$30 + 175 + 550 + 305 = 1060$
	$1100 - 1060 = 40$ CD longer than required time

Note that the durations of any float are not considered in making these determinations.

Clearly, the contractor did not meet the burden of performance on any path except path JKLM. The extent of contractor-caused delay on each individual path was

Path ABDEFG	85 CD
Path CDEFG	55 CD
Path JKHIG	115 CD
Path JKLM	-0-

Contractor-Caused Delay to Project

The fourth step is determining the extent to which the contractor exclusively extended the completion date of the project, if any, by failing to meet the burden of performance. It is first necessary to determine to what extent the **contractor-caused delay** extended each of the paths to completion of the as-built schedule. This is done in accordance with the third principle by removing the exclusive contractor-caused delay from each individual path and noting the extent to which the path shortens. Working with Figure 18–9,

Path ABDEFG:	$30 + 80 + 150 + 30 + 300 + 120 + 460 + 40 + 175 - 85$
	$= 1300$ CD (without contractor delays)
Path CDEFG:	$150 + 30 + 300 + 120 + 460 + 40 + 175 - 55$
	$= 1220$ CD (without contractor delays)
Path CHIG:	$150 + 30 + 765 + 40 + 175 - 60$
	$= 1100$ CD (without contractor delays)
Path JKHIG:	$30 + 100 + 175 + 30 + 765 + 40 + 175 - 115$
	$= 1200$ CD (without contractor delays)
Path JKLM:	$30 + 100 + 175 + 550 + 160 + 305 - 0$
	$= 1320$ CD (without contractor delays)

Again, note that the duration of any float is not considered in making these determinations.

Contractor Liability for Liquidated Damages

As just illustrated, if there had been no contractor delays, the project would have been completed in 1320 CD, the longest of the five possible paths from which all contractor delays have been removed. Therefore, the extent of delay exclusively caused by the contractor is the actual project duration minus 1320 CD, or 1385 CD – 1320 CD = 65 CD. The **contractor's liability for liquidated damages** equals this number of calendar days.

Contractor Entitlement to Extension of Time

The final step is determining the **contractor's entitlement to an extension of time** that is consistent with the liability for liquidated damages. By application of the fourth principle,

    a. 1100 CD + extension of time + 65 CD = 1385 CD

    b. Extension of time = 1385 CD – 1100 CD – 65 CD = 220 CD

Summary of Delay Impact Analysis

Referring to Figure 18–9, the following is a summary of the delay impact analysis:

    Owner's liability for delay damages = 165 CD.

    Contractually stipulated completion date should be extended by 220 CD.

    Contractor's remaining liability for liquidated or actual damages = 65 CD.

Determining Damages Offset

In situations such as the preceding, the principle of offsetting the monetary value of damages applies. However, the monetary consequences of one day of delay caused to the other party may be considerably different for the owner and for the contractor. In other words, the contractor's actual provable costs caused by each calendar day that the project completion is extended may be very different from the contractually stated liquidated damages figure due the owner per day of delay or, in cases in which the owner is due actual damages, from the provable actual costs to the owner for each day completion is extended. Therefore, the *number of days delay may not be offset directly;* only the monetary consequences of the respective delays may be offset.

CONCLUSION

Determining which party to the contract is responsible for delays and the relief if any to which each is entitled in complex multiple-delay situations is elusive. However, if the various delays can be isolated and properly identified as either owner-caused, contractor-caused, or excusable, the proper allocation of rights to relief and liabilities can be determined by application of the principles outlined in this chapter. In complex cases, the use of computers greatly reduces the analytical labor required.

    An additional topic closely related to delay and extension of time is the concept of constructive acceleration, the subject of the next chapter.

QUESTIONS AND PROBLEMS

1. Explain the difference in as-planned, as-built, and intermediate CPM network schedules.

2. What are the three distinct classes of delays to construction that were discussed in this chapter? Which of the three could be said to be a neutral delay or a delay that is no one's fault?

3. What are the two subclasses of contractor-caused delays? Does the occurrence of either necessarily mean that the contractor will be liable for liquidated damages? Explain your answer.

4. What are forward-looking, retrospective, and contemporaneous delay impact analyses?

5. Explain concurrent and consecutive events and the difference between them. What is concurrent delay?

6. Explain the four principles discussed in this chapter that are useful to allocate properly liabilities and damages for delay between contractor and owner.

7. Explain why the contractor's liquidated (or actual) damages liability cannot be offset against the owner's liability for delay damages on a day-for-day basis when both are present.

8. Redraw to a convenient scale the as-built network shown in Figure 18–9, changing the CD durations of the various delays and work activities as follows. Maintain all dependency ties shown. Note that the location and duration of float intervals will change.

Work Activity	A	–	72
" "	B	–	125
" "	C	–	260
" "	D	–	Same as Figure 18-9
" "	E	–	275
" "	F	–	490
" "	G	–	190
" "	H	–	60
" "	I	–	800
" "	J	–	Same as Figure 18-9
" "	K	–	190
" "	L	–	520
" "	M	–	260
ORD between	A & B	–	50
" "	E & F	–	110
" "	J & K	–	175
CRD "	F & G	–	60
ED "	L & M	–	55

The contractually specified completion date remains 1100 CD.

   a. Determine the actual completion date.

   b. Determine the owner's liability for delay damages in CD.

   c. Determine the contractor's liability for liquidated damages in CD.

   d. If the contract completion date should have been extended by the owner, determine the number of CD after NTP to which it should have been extended. If the contract should not have been extended, indicate this.

9. Refer to the as-built network (see p. 284) constructed on the basis of job records. All delays have been identified and contractual responsibility for each determined as noted. Note that delay H is fixed in time and occurred between 130 CD and 138 CD after NTP. Delay H will therefore not shift to an earlier time frame when networks are collapsed. The contractually stipulated project completion date was 120 CD after notice to proceed.

   a. Determine the owner's liability for delay damages in CD.

   b. Determine the contractor's liability for delay damages in CD.

   c. If the contract completion date should have been extended by the owner, determine the number of CD after NTP to which it should have been extended. If the contract should not have been extended, indicate this.

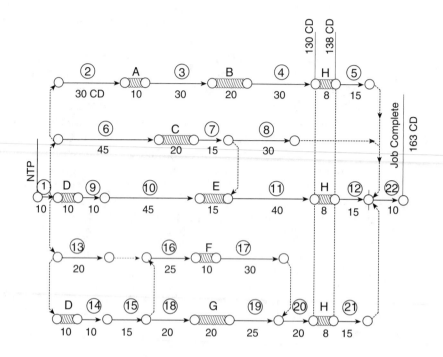

As-Built Network Including All Delays

Delay A – Contractor fails to man job
Delay B – Owner adds work to contract
Delay C – Contractor encounters a Type II differing site condition
Delay D – Flood stops work on part of job
Delay E – Owner adds work to contract
Delay F – Owner suspends work on part of project
Delay G – Owner adds work to contract
Delay H – Unusually severe weather shuts down entire job

Key:

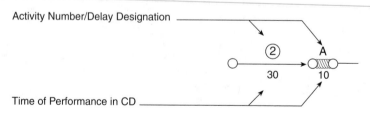

Activity Number/Delay Designation

Time of Performance in CD

19

Constructive Acceleration

Key Words and Concepts

Acceleration
Voluntary acceleration
Directed acceleration
Delay with time extension
Delay without time extension

Accelerated performance without delay
Constructive acceleration
Effect of owner's directive to accelerate
Contractor's proper contractual
  procedure

As discussed in Chapter 17, a contractor cannot assume with impunity that the contract completion date will necessarily be extended simply because a properly supported claim for a time extension has been filed with the owner. This is true even when the owner's project representatives have informally indicated their personal belief that an extension will be granted if it is later determined to be necessary for the contractor to avoid being assessed liquidated damages. The proper and prudent position for the contractor to take if the owner denies or simply fails to act on a properly supported claim for a time extension is to protest the lack of action or the denial in writing and then advise the owner that the denial or lack of action has placed them in a position where they are compelled to attempt to complete the contract by the original required date. Completion by this date when significant delays have been experienced or additional work has been added to the contract usually will entail incurring additional costs for overtime, shift work, and mobilization of additional crews, equipment, and material. A contractor, who has incurred such costs in meeting or attempting to meet the original completion date when an extension of time should have been granted by the owner, is entitled to recover these costs under the doctrine of constructive acceleration.

VOLUNTARY AND DIRECTED ACCELERATION

An understanding of the terms *acceleration, voluntary acceleration,* and *directed acceleration* in a contractual sense is necessary to understand the concept of constructive acceleration.

Acceleration and Voluntary Acceleration

Acceleration means completion of the contract work or part of the contract work at a more rapid rate than required by the contract. Ordinarily, the contractor has the right to work at a faster pace than the minimum needed to meet the contract completion date. This is an implied right under the contract. The contractor is usually the party bearing the financial risk of performance, and unless the contract expressly prohibits completion of the work before the contractually specified date, the contractor is free to speed up the work. Exceptions might include, for instance, a contract involving embankment construction where it was necessary to control the vertical soil load on substrata by requiring that the rate of embankment placement not exceed a stated maximum rate. Except in such situations, contractors sometimes voluntarily accelerate their performance to reduce time-related costs by finishing the project early or because they believe a faster pace is more cost effective for other reasons. Also, when unexcused delays have put the contractor behind schedule, voluntary acceleration of remaining work is the only way to regain schedule and avoid being declared in default, being assessed liquidated damages, or both. In any of these situations, **voluntary acceleration** on the part of the contractor has occurred.

Directed Acceleration

Acceleration may also be directed by the owner, if the contract so provides. The right of the owner to direct acceleration is not an implied right; it must be explicitly provided in the contract. The changes clause usually does provide that the owner may direct acceleration of all or part of the work. Completion of contract work at a pace that is faster than would ordinarily be required pursuant to a directive from the owner is called **directed acceleration.** As with any other change, an owner who directs acceleration in order to complete the project earlier than contractually required must pay the extra costs incurred by the contractor in complying with the directive.

CONSTRUCTIVE ACCELERATION

Constructive acceleration is a forced completion of the contract work in a shorter period than should have been allowed by the issue of proper contract time extensions. The normal scenario that triggers constructive acceleration is that either compensable or excusable delays are encountered by the contractor, for which properly supported claims for appropriate extensions of time are made to the owner. If the owner either denies the claims or simply fails to act, the contractor must conclude that the contract time remains unchanged and therefore make every reasonable effort to complete the work by the unextended date, usually incurring additional costs. Failure to make this effort places the contractor in a position in which the owner, shielded by a superior economic position, could contend, however improperly that the contractor is behind schedule and is breaching the contract and could declare the contractor in default. A contractor cannot passively afford to be placed in this position.

The absence of a change order granting a time extension within a reasonable time after submittal of a properly supported claim creates the constructive acceleration situation. It makes no difference if the owner eventually grants a time extension after the acceleration effort and extra costs have been expended. Constructive acceleration still will have occurred. In other words, even though time extensions may eventually be given, the failure of the owner to issue time extensions in a timely manner also triggers constructive acceleration.

Timely manner means within a reasonable period of time after submittal of the contractor's properly supported claim for a time extension. *Reasonable period of time* means sufficient time for the owner to evaluate the contractor's claim and determine if it has merit.

It makes no difference to a claim of constructive acceleration whether causal events giving rise to the claim are excusable or compensable, as long as they are not the contractor's fault and cause more time to be needed to complete the contract. Thus, the causal events could include a strike or inclement weather (excusable events) or an owner-caused delay or change in the work (compensable events).

A CONSTRUCTIVE ACCELERATION EXAMPLE

Figure 19–1 illustrates a constructive acceleration situation. In the original contract, the contractor had 24 months to complete the work. Three separate cases are discussed as follows.

Case I—Delay with Time Extension

Case 1 in Figure 19–1 illustrates a **delay with time extension.** After 12 months of contract performance at a normal pace (sufficient to finish all work within 24 months), the contractor is delayed for six months and is contractually entitled to an extension of time. The owner promptly issues a six-month time extension,

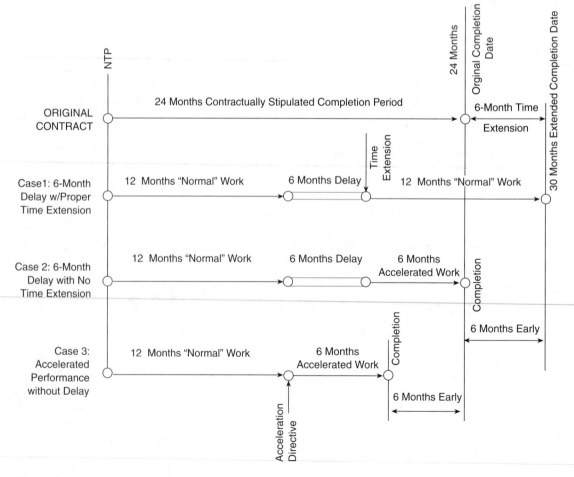

FIGURE 19–1 Constructive acceleration.

extending the original contract completion date from 24 months to 30 months. Having been granted this time extension, the contractor continues work at the normal pace for 12 additional months and completes the contract in 30 months, meeting the contract completion requirement. No acceleration has occurred. If the six-month delay was compensable, as opposed to being merely excusable, the contractor would be entitled to monetary damages equal to the extra time-related costs incurred as a result of the delay.

Case 2—Delay with No Time Extension

The second case in Figure 19–1 illustrates a **delay without a time extension.** It is the same as Case 1 until the end of the delay when, in contrast to Case 1, the owner denies or refuses to act on the contractor's claim for a six-month extension of time. Since the contractor does not have a time extension, the contractor works at an accelerated pace for six months at added expense and finishes the job in 24 months, the original completion date. In this situation, the contractor finishes the work in only 18 months of actual working time. The contractor also finishes the project six months earlier than the date to which completion should have been extended. This is a classic case of constructive acceleration. Because an extension of time to which the contractor was entitled was not granted by the owner, the contractor was forced to accelerate performance by six months even though the owner did not issue a formal directive to do so.

Case 3—Accelerated Performance Without Delay

In Case 3 in Figure 19–1, **accelerated performance without a delay** is illustrated. After 12 months of performance at the normal pace, even though there is no delay, the owner issues an acceleration directive to the contractor, who then works six months at an accelerated pace, completing the project in 18 months in accordance with the directive, six months earlier than the original completion date.

Insofar as the acceleration aspects are concerned, there is no practical difference between Case 2 and Case 3. Case 3 illustrates directed acceleration; Case 2, constructive acceleration. In both cases, the contractor is entitled to be paid for the costs of the acceleration effort. If the delay in Case 2 was compensable, the contractor is also entitled to recover the extra time-related costs incurred due to the delay.

It would make no difference if the owner in case 2, instead of failing to issue a time extension at all, waited until the completion of the project before issuing a six-month time extension. The contractor still has been constructively required to accelerate and is entitled to recover the extra costs incurred.

It is not necessary in the constructive acceleration situation to finish the contract by the original completion date as depicted by Case 2. Now consider Figure 19–2. In this case, although the contract work is not finished until three months after the original completion date, the contractor finishes three months earlier than the

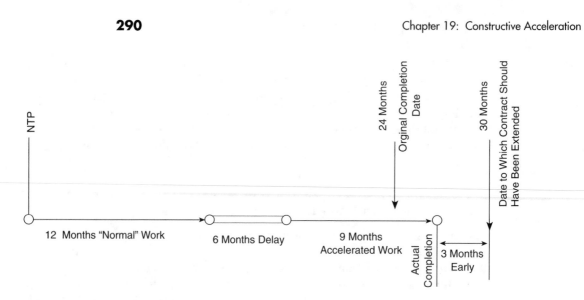

FIGURE 19–2   Acceleration with completion beyond original date.

date to which the contract should have been extended. This is also a valid constructive acceleration situation, and the contractor is entitled to the acceleration costs
exactly as in Cases 2 and 3.

PROVING CONSTRUCTIVE ACCELERATION

Constructive acceleration normally results in extra costs incurred in trying to meet
the unextended contract completion date. If the elements required for a valid constructive acceleration claim can be established, the contractor is entitled to recover
these costs. Four elements must be proved.

Entitlement to Time Extension

To prevail in a constructive acceleration claim, the contractor must first establish
entitlement to a time extension or time extensions by proving that performance was
delayed by some event or condition for which the contract promises that an extension of time will be granted. A properly documented claim for a time extension
must have been promptly submitted to the owner after the event or condition giving
rise to the claim in accordance with the notice provisions of the contract. For
instance, the Department of Agriculture Board of Contract Appeals denied a contractor's claim for constructive acceleration because they failed to establish their
entitlement to an extension of time.

On a contract to construct an earthen dam, the contractor had fallen behind
schedule and was directed by the contracting officer to bring the work back into
compliance with the progress schedule. After adding two scrapers to the equipment

spread and commencing to work ten-hour days, the contractor demanded compensation for the increased costs, alleging that the contracting officer had constructively accelerated the schedule. In denying the constructive acceleration claim, the board held that

> Acceleration is defined as a directive to increase efforts in order to complete performance on time, despite excusable delay. To prevail on an acceleration claim, a contractor must show excusable delay; notice to the government of the excusable delay, with a request for a contract extension; and the contractor must also prove that the costs claimed were actually incurred as a result of action specifically taken to accelerate performance.[1]

Similarly, the National Aeronautics and Space Administration (NASA) Board of Contract Appeals denied a contractor's claim for constructive acceleration because the contractor failed to furnish timely notice of the delay claimed and failed to submit evidence supporting their entitlement to an extension of time.[2]

In a California case, the General Services Board of Contract Appeals granted a contractor's claim for constructive acceleration costs because the government failed to grant a legitimate request for an extension of contract time in a timely manner. Heavy rains at the start of construction of a federal building made it impossible for the excavation subcontractor to proceed. The contracting officer did not grant an extension of time for this delay until 16 months after the completion of the excavation. The subcontractor was required to switch to a more expensive method of excavation to comply with the original schedule. In the words of the Board:

> As a defense to a claim of constructive acceleration, a belated time extension is worthless. . . . It had to have become clear to anyone who did not sleep through the entire two days that the soil at the site was saturated with moisture and could not be compacted as required. The Government could not, by continually insisting on documentation of what was already known, justify its refusal to grant a time extension.[3]

Failure of Owner to Issue Extension of Time

The owner must not have issued a time extension, or if one was issued, the owner must have failed to issue it within a reasonable period of time after receiving the contractor's properly documented claim.

Proof of Extra Costs

The contractor must prove that extra costs were incurred in attempting to finish the project by the unextended completion date.

---

[1] *Appeal of Donald R. Stewart & Associates,* AGBCA No. 89-222-1 (Jan. 16, 1992).

[2] *Appeal of Carney General Contractors, Inc.,* NASABCA No. 375-4: Sept. 1980.

[3] *Appeal of Continental Heller Corp.,* GSBCA No. 7140 (Mar. 23, 1984).

Completion Before Date to Which Contract Should Have Been Extended

The contractor must complete the project earlier than the date to which project completion would have been extended if the owner had issued the time extension in a timely manner. As noted previously, the actual completion date need not be as early as the original completion date as long as it is earlier than the date to which the contract should have been extended. For instance, the U.S. Court of Claims (now the United States Court of Federal Claims) determined that a contractor could recover acceleration costs on a contract that was completed 524 days after the original completion date.[4]

Effect of an Owner's Directive to Accelerate

Although not one of the four elements necessary to prove entitlement to damages, a fifth point is that the contractor does not have to have been explicitly directed by the owner to meet the original date in order to prove a valid case of constructive acceleration. However, if the contractor can show such explicit direction or pressure, the case becomes much stronger. What has occurred when an owner either refuses to act or denies a meritorious request for an extension of time is that the owner has breached a contractual duty. The breach is further compounded if the owner then improperly orders or otherwise pressures the contractor to finish the work by the original date. In the last case cited, the court concluded that an acceleration order need not be couched in mandatory terms. The contracting officer had issued extensive correspondence citing the original completion date and pressuring the contractor to step up progress. The contractor did not know until the end of the project how long an extension of time would be granted, and the court felt that, with the threat of liquidated damages hanging over the contractor's head, the contracting officer's letters improperly pressured the contractor to accelerate the work beyond the rate required if the contract had been properly extended.[5]

CONTRACTOR'S PROPER CONTRACTUAL PROCEDURE

The **proper contractual procedure for the contractor** in a constructive acceleration situation includes the following:

- First, promptly file a properly supported claim for an extension of time for a definite number of days, as soon as possible after each excusable or compensable causal event causing delay. When appropriate, such requests should be supported by the type of as-built, forward-looking CPM network analysis discussed in Chapter 18.

---

[4]*Norair Engineering Corp v. United States,* U.S. Claims Court No. 259-80C (Dec. 2, 1981).
[5]*Ibid.*

- Second, if a change order granting the claimed time extension is not received within a reasonable period of time, the contractor should protest in writing and advise the owner in writing that operations are being accelerated in an effort to meet the original unextended contract completion date.

- Third, as a follow-up to the preceding point, the owner should be advised in writing as soon as practical the details of the acceleration effort, the estimated additional daily costs, and the contractor's expectation of payment for these costs. The contractor must then ensure that the project will be completed before the date to which the contract should have been extended.

- Finally, the contractor must carefully document all acceleration costs actually incurred to be able to prove conclusively the expenditures in an eventual constructive acceleration claim to the owner.

CONCLUSION

This chapter on constructive acceleration concluded a related group of chapters dealing with problems associated with the time allowed for contract performance and the impact of delay on performance.

The final four chapters focus on the generalized rules by which contracts are interpreted, the importance of job documentation and records in the construction industry, construction contract claims, and a discussion of the means by which contract disputes are settled.

QUESTIONS AND PROBLEMS

1. What is acceleration, voluntary acceleration, and directed acceleration? Why might a contractor want to accelerate voluntarily? Does the contractor normally have the contractual right to do so? Is the owner's right to direct acceleration of contract work an implied right of a construction contract?

2. What is constructive acceleration? How does it come about? When contractors are contractually due an extension of time and their claim is either ignored or not acted on by the owner, what motivates them to attempt to complete the project by the original specified completion date?

3. Is it necessary in the constructive acceleration situation for the contractor to complete the project by the original contractually specified completion date? What is necessary?

4. After the contractor has accelerated construction because the owner refused to grant an extension of time, is the contractor's claim for the costs of acceleration defeated if the owner eventually relents and issues an extension of time such that, had it been issued in a timely manner, there would have been no need for the acceleration?

5. What are the four elements that a contractor must prove to establish a valid claim for constructive acceleration?

6. What are the four procedural steps that a prudent contractor should take in the constructive acceleration situation?

7. Refer to Figure 18–11 in Chapter 18. Assume that this network schedule was the as-planned schedule submitted by the contractor to the owner at the beginning of the project. Assume further that activity J represented a contractually stipulated period after NTP within which the owner was required to turn over the area for one of the tunnel portals to the contractor. Assume further that the 40-calendar-day CRD was not present in the network and that the network completion date was thereby 1175 calendar days after NTP. Finally, assume that the contractually specified completion date was also 1175 CD after NTP.

    The owner did not turn over the tunnel portal until 130 calendar days after NTP. At the end of this delay, the contractor filed a properly documented written claim for an extension of time. At that point, none of the durations of the other activities in the network were expected to change, and the contractor's extension of time request documented the number of days claimed on the basis of a forward-looking analysis starting from the as-planned schedule. The owner refused to grant an extension of time, so the contractor accelerated the performance at considerable extra cost of activities K and I.

    By what number of calendar days after NTP must the contractor finish the contract to be entitled to the acceleration costs under the doctrine of constructive acceleration?

8. Under the circumstances of question 7, the contractor was able to prove that the time-related costs of each day's delay in project completion were $2,375. To what figure in dollars (if any) is the contractor entitled, in addition to the costs of constructive acceleration?

20

Common Rules of Contract Interpretation

Key Words and Concepts

Contract must not be redrafted
Determination of the intent of the parties
Manifestations of intent
Express contract terms
Course of performance
Course of dealing
Separately negotiated terms
Customs and trade practices
Contract must be read as a whole

Interpretation giving lawful and
    reasonable meaning to all other
    provisions preferred
Express terms govern over all else
Relative importance of the various
    manifestations of intent
Parole evidence rule
Doctrine of *contra proferentem*

Previous chapters dealt with various important provisions of construction-related contracts and how courts interpreted and applied these provisions. The interpretation of a contract is a legal matter that lies in the province of judges and arbitrators, not the parties to the contracts themselves. However, it is important that these parties possess at least a rudimentary understanding of the rules of contract interpretation. This chapter explains and discusses some of the more common rules.

The resolution of many construction contract disputes turns on what the terms and provisions of the contract really mean. When disputes arise, courts, arbitrators, or other dispute resolution bodies determine the correct meaning of the contract and apply it to the situation of each particular case. They approach their task with the following mindset:

1. The contract must be interpreted as it is. The **contract must not be redrafted** to reflect what the reviewing body believes "it should have said."

2. The reviewing body tries to **determine the intent of the parties** when they entered into the contract. In other words, they try to find what the parties were trying to accomplish when they wrote the language of the contract.

3. In the search for that intent, the reviewers look for "tracks," or **manifestations of intent,** that may lead them to an understanding of what the parties were thinking when they entered into the contract.

MANIFESTATIONS OF INTENT

Some common manifestations of intent include the following:

Express Contract Terms

Perhaps nothing can express the intent of a party to be bound by a contract provision more clearly than signing a contract prominently containing that express provision. By signing a contract, the parties indicate their intention to be bound by each provision in the contract. If the provision is express and clear, there is no need to look further. However, if the contract is silent or the expressly stated provisions are badly drafted and unclear, it is necessary to search for other manifestations of intent.

Course of Performance

Course of performance means the sequence of events during the contract from its beginning up to some particular point in time. The actions and attitudes of the parties during the period prior to the occurrence of a dispute reveal how each party to the contract understood the contract's meaning and how each responded to the causal events leading to the dispute. For example, an owner's practice of previously paying for changes in the work based on oral direction indicates that the owner intended the contract to operate that way as opposed to a situation in which the owner paid for changed work only if a signed change order had been issued. Similarly, a contractor who does not put the owner on notice at the time of a breach of contract by the owner is sending a clear message that the contractor did not think a breach had occurred or, if it had, that it was not an important breach.

Course of Dealing

A third manifestation of intent is **course of dealing.** This means how the parties have previously dealt with each other, prior to entering into the current contract. Past actions and attitudes indicate what the parties are likely to have intended in a new contract that on its face is unclear.

Separately Negotiated Terms

If a contract contains **separately negotiated terms** or provisions as opposed to standard "boilerplate" language, those terms are taken as a very strong manifestation of intent. Separately negotiated terms mean those that were obviously drafted for that particular contract. The inclusion of such provisions clearly shows that the parties intended them to apply. Otherwise, why would they have taken the trouble to draft the special language? On the other hand, boilerplate language could be present and frequently is—simply because it was lifted or carried over from other contracts used in the past. One or both of the parties may not have realized that the language was there and thus failed to insist that it be altered or deleted. This can happen when preprinted contract forms are used or when a previously used specification or other provision is carelessly included in the new contract documents without careful scrutiny.

Customs and Trade Practices

A fifth manifestation of intent is an express or implied reference to the **customs and trade practices** of the industry. Customs and trade practices are sometimes determinate in resolving unclear contract meaning, particularly when the contract expressly provides that normal trade practices are intended to apply. Even when normal trade practices are not specifically mentioned, there is an implied presumption that they were meant to apply. Parties to the contract are generally expected to interact according to the customs and trade practices of the industry in the absence of express indications to the contrary.

GENERALIZED RULES OF CONTRACT INTERPRETATION

The preceding manifestations of intent are involved in the following generalized rules of contract interpretation.

The Contract Must Be Read As a Whole

First, and most important, **the contract must be read as a whole,** not as a series of isolated parts. It must also be read with an attempt to give reasonable meaning to each provision. No provision in the contract can be arbitrarily regarded as meaningless. Otherwise, why would the parties have included that provision in the contract?

An excellent example of the application of this rule is afforded by the action of the Supreme Court of Montana in reversing a trial court decision arising from the construction of a housing project for the Montana Housing Authority. A conflict developed between the utility subcontractor and the mechanical subcontractor over who was responsible for installation and hookup work within five feet of the building lines. A lower court had ruled that the utility subcontractor must perform this work based on the court's interpretation of the technical specifications that required the utility contractor to complete its work "in every respect complete and ready for immediate and continued use."

The Supreme Court of Montana reversed the lower court, based on their review of all of the contract documents. Another clause stated that the work of the utility subcontractor terminated at a point five feet from building foundations where the utility lines were required to be plugged or capped. A further clause indicated that the plumbing subcontractor's duties continued to a point five feet outside the building foundation. Reading the contract as a whole, the court concluded that it was not the utility contractor's obligation to bring the lines within the five-foot limit of the buildings. The court said:

> When read together, these contractual provisions indicate Palm Tree (utility subcontractor) was not required to make the water and sewer service lines connections. The whole of the contract is to be taken together so as to give effect to every part if reasonably practicable, each clause helping to interpret the other.[1]

This case illustrates the principle that an interpretation that gives lawful and reasonable meaning to all the other provisions of the contract will prevail over an interpretation that does not. In other words, each provision will be read so that it will not conflict or be inconsistent with other provisions when this is reasonably possible.

Similarly, the Supreme Court of Arkansas settled an argument whether undercutting was required in certain work areas of a shopping center project but not required in other areas of the same project by considering *all* of the contract documents including an engineer's soil report deemed to be incorporated into the contract by reference. The court concluded that undercutting was required in all areas of the project. That interpretation was the only one that permitted harmonizing the various parts of the contract documents. In the court's words:

> In seeking to harmonize different clauses of a contract, we should not give effect to one to the exclusion of another, even though they seem conflicting or contradictory, nor

---

[1]*Bender v. Rookhuizen,* 685 P.2d 343 (Mont. 1984).

adopt an interpretation which neutralizes a provision if the various clauses can be reconciled. The object is to ascertain the intention of the parties, not from particular words or phrases, but from the entire context of the agreement.[2]

Determine the Relative Importance of the Manifestations of Intent

If irreconcilable conflicts or ambiguities remain after reading the contract as a whole, the various manifestations of intent should then be examined to see if they shed light on what the parties intended. In doing that, the **relative importance of the various manifestations** are usually weighted as follows:

- Express contract terms are more important than course of performance, course of dealing, or the customs and trade practices of the industry.
- Course of performance is more important than course of dealing or the customs and trade practices of the industry.
- Course of dealing will take precedence over the customs and trade practices of the industry.
- Separately negotiated or added terms will take precedence over boilerplate language.

Although applicable primarily to purchase order agreements, clear articulation of the preceding principles is set forth in Article 2-208 of the Uniform Commercial Code, subparagraph (2) which states:

> The expressed terms of the agreement and any such course of performance, as well as any course of dealing and usage of trade, shall be construed whenever reasonable as consistent with each other; but when such construction is unreasonable, expressed terms shall control course of performance and course of performance shall control both course of dealing and usage of trade.

Even though customs and trade practices of the industry are at the bottom in the previous list of precedences, they are not unimportant. They cannot be used to override clear express language in the contract, but when a contract is ambiguous, consideration of customs and trade practices often removes the ambiguity. Words and terms will be given their ordinary and customary meaning. In particular, technical terms and usages will be given meaning according to the customs and trade practices of the industry.

For instance, a New York general contractor was held to have breached the contract when they withheld money retained from a subcontractor until final approval and acceptance of the prime contract, when the subcontract contained express language stating, "Any balance due the subcontractor shall be paid within 30 days . . . after his work is finally approved and accepted by the Architect and/or

---

[2]*Rad-Razorback Limited Partnership v. Coney,* 713 S.W.2d 462 (Ark. 1986).

Engineer." The general contractor argued, "By trade custom and usage, the general contractor always withholds money retained from the subcontractor pending final approval and acceptance of the total job."

Unimpressed by this argument, a New York court concluded, "There is no reason to resort to trade practices or evidence of custom for an interpretation when the contract is unambiguous" and that under such certain circumstances, the subcontract clause "may not be changed by an attempt to invoke trade custom."[3]

However, in a case in which a contract, on its face, was clearly ambiguous, another court relied on customs and trade practices of the industry to help determine the probable meaning of the ambiguous provision.[4]

PAROLE EVIDENCE RULE

Construction practitioners should be familiar with the **parole evidence rule.** Parole or extrinsic evidence is evidence of the intent of the parties other than the express provisions of the contract itself. Specific examples include the following:

- Previous oral or written understandings or agreements between the parties, such as records of the negotiations leading to contract formation. This category also includes letters and other written forms of communications.
- Course of performance and course of dealing.
- Customs and trade practices of the industry.

If an express contract provision is clear and prominent, it matters not how it got that way—courts will give it full force and effect and will not consider parole evidence.

Only when the contract is not clear does parole evidence become important. Then, courts will apply the tests just discussed to attempt to resolve the ambiguity by determining the intent of the parties.

The following cases illustrate these points. In the first, the Supreme Court of South Carolina would not permit the introduction of parole evidence consisting of an oral agreement that contradicted the terms of an unambiguous written contract. A general contractor on a HUD housing project had issued subcontracts for interior plumbing to a plumbing subcontractor and for utility work to a second subcontractor. The utility subcontract clearly stated that the subcontractor was to perform its work in conformity with the plans and specifications. The court found that the plans and specifications clearly placed the obligation to pay water and sewer tap fees on the utility subcontractor. The general contractor paid these fees and withheld that amount from monies otherwise due the utility subcontractor. A trial court permitted the introduction of parole evidence to the effect that an independent oral agreement between the general contractor and the utility subcontractor provided that the

---

[3]*Cable-Wiedemer, Inc. v. A. Friederich & Sons Co.,* 336 N.Y.S.2d 139 (Cnty. Ct. 1972).

[4]*Hardware Specialties, Inc. v. Mishara Constr. Co., Inc.,* 311 N.E.2d 564 (Mass. App. 1974).

subcontractor would not be required to pay the fees. When the trial court found in favor of the subcontractor, the general contractor appealed, asserting that the lower court had violated the parole evidence rule in allowing the introduction of evidence relating to the independent agreement.

Agreeing with the general contractor, the Supreme Court reversed the trial court, stating:

> Where the terms of a written agreement are unambiguous, extrinsic evidence of statements made contemporaneously with or prior to its execution are inadmissible to contradict or vary the terms. . . .

> Under the written subcontractor agreement, Ward (utility subcontractor) was responsible for the tap fees. We hold the terms of the written contract were contradicted in direct violation of the parole evidence rule.[5]

On the other hand, the Supreme Court of Nevada permitted the introduction of parole evidence to determine the true intent of the parties when they found that the contract was ambiguous. The subcontract for the installation of a roof on a new warehouse resulted in a dispute when the owner withheld payment from the general contractor, alleging that the installed roof did not comply with the contract specifications. A trial court ruled for the general contractor, who had sued to recover the withheld payments. The owner appealed, claiming that Johns-Manville roofing specifications were required by the contract, but that the contractor had installed the roofing in accordance with Bird specifications, in violation of the contract. The owner conceded that both specifications were considered prior to execution of the contract but that only the Johns-Manville specifications were integrated into the final agreement and that evidence submitted by the contractor relating to the Bird specifications violated the parole evidence rule.

After review of the trial record, the Supreme Court found that, although the contract referenced the roofing specifications, nowhere in the document was it stated which set of specifications were intended. The contract was, therefore, ambiguous. For this reason, the court held that the lower court properly admitted parole evidence to determine the intent of the parties. The lower court decision in favor of the general contractor was affirmed.[6]

DOCTRINE OF *CONTRA PROFERENTEM*

When a contract provision is ambiguous and all of the preceding steps, including consideration of parole evidence, fail to resolve the ambiguity, the **doctrine of *contra proferentem*** will control. This rule requires that the meaning of an ambiguous contract provision be construed against the drafter. The drafter is the party that had

---

[5]*Southern States Supply Co., Inc. v. Commercial Industrial Contractors, Inc.,* 329 S.E.2d 738 (S.C. 1985).
[6]*Trans Western Leasing Corp. v. Corrao Constr. Co., Inc.,* 652 P.2d 1181 (Nev. 1982).

the opportunity to make the provision clear, and the drafter bears the burden of failure to do so.

The rule cannot be successfully invoked simply because one party does not agree with the other party's interpretation of a particular contract provision. The provision in question must be determined to be ambiguous—that is, the provision must be susceptible to more than one reasonable meaning before it can be construed against the party that drafted it.

As long as the claimant's interpretation is reasonable and does not conflict with other provisions of the contract, it does not matter that the drafter also has a reasonable interpretation of the provision. After all, the word *ambiguous* means "subject to more than one reasonable meaning." Therefore, the meaning of the provision will be construed against the drafter by acceptance of the claimant's interpretation, even though the drafter's interpretation is also reasonable.

In arguments concerning contract ambiguity, owners frequently take the position that they wrote the specifications, know what they meant to say, and therefore their interpretation of the specifications controls. Courts have little sympathy for this argument. In one case, the U.S. Court of Claims (now the United States Court of Federal Claims) said:

> A government contractor can not properly be required to exercise clairvoyance in determining its contractual responsibilities. The crucial question is "What plaintiff (non-drafting party) would have understood as a reasonable construction contractor," not what the drafter of the contract terms subjectively intended.[7]

Similarly, the U.S. Court of Appeals said that when dealing with the question of contract ambiguity, a court should

> ... place itself into the shoes of a reasonable and prudent contractor and decide how a contractor would act in claimant's situation.[8]

When the court finds that the contract is ambiguous, the following cases illustrate the usual outcome.

In resolving an argument over payment for reinforcing steel accessories, the Engineer Board of Contract Appeals found the contract drafted by a mass transit district to be ambiguous in a way that was too subtle to create a duty for bidders to inquire. The transit district contended that payment should be made only for the weight of reinforcing steel detailed on the drawings, whereas the contractor argued that the specifications required that payment be made for accessories and welding rods as well. In finding for the contractor, the board concluded that the contract was ambiguous, but not so obvious that it imposed a duty on the contractor to inquire into its intended meaning at the time of bid. The contractor was paid for the weight of the accessories and welding rods.[9]

---

[7]*Corvetta Constr. Co. v. United States*, 461 F.2d 1330 (Ct. Cl. 1972).

[8]*P. J. Maffei Bldg. Wrecking Corp. v. United States*, 732 F.2d 913 (Fed. Cir. 1984).

[9]*Appeal of George Hyman Construction Co.*, ENGBCA No. 4506 (Sept. 29, 1981).

Similarly, the Court of Appeal of Louisiana found that a payment provision drafted by the State of Louisiana Department of Transportation and Development for the laying of drain conduit was ambiguous on whether the unit bid price for drain conduit included the work of placing and compacting backfill around the conduit. The contractor contended that backfill was to be separately paid, whereas the state's chief engineer contended that backfilling the conduit was included in the unit price for laying the conduit. The court found that the contract was ambiguous and that the ambiguity was latent, thus excusing the contractor from inquiring at the time of bid. The contractor received separate payment for the backfill.[10]

The controlling principle is well defined by the words of the U.S. Court of Claims (now the United States Court of Federal Claims) in one of the leading cases on this point:

> When the Government draws specifications which are fairly susceptible of a certain construction and a contractor actually and reasonably so constitutes them, justice and equity require that construction be adopted. Where one of the parties to a contract draws a document and uses therein language which is susceptible to more than one meaning, and the intention of the parties does not otherwise appear, that meaning will be given to the document which is more favorable to the party who did not draw it. This rule is specially applicable to Government contracts when the contractor has nothing to say as to its provisions.[11]

In each of these cases, it is important to note that the court found the contract to be ambiguous and that the ambiguity was latent, excusing the contractor from the duty to inquire about the intended meaning at the time of bid. If the court found that the contract was not ambiguous or that, even though ambiguous, the ambiguity could be cleared up by consideration of parole evidence, the disputed language would be given the meaning that the court determined to have been intended. If the court found that the disputed language was ambiguous but that the ambiguity was so obvious that the contractor should have inquired as to the intended meaning at the time of bid, the contractor's claim that the disputed language be construed in its favor would fail.

CONCLUSION

The interpretation of a contract is a legal matter that in cases of dispute is not decided by laypersons. This chapter gave a brief overview of how judges and arbitrators approach the difficult problem of interpreting the meaning of a contract. Understanding these highlights makes the conduct of proper contractual relations easier for all participants in the construction process.

---

[10]*Johnson Brothers Corp. v. State of Louisiana,* 556 So.2d 154 (La. App. 1990).

[11]*Peter Kiewit Sons, et al. v. United States,* 109 Ct. Cl. 390 (1947).

QUESTIONS AND PROBLEMS

1. What are the three things explained in the introduction to this chapter that courts and others do to determine the meaning of disputed contract provisions?

2. What are five manifestations of intent discussed in this chapter? What do the terms "course of performance" and "course of dealing" mean?

3. What is meant by "reading the contract as a whole"? Can some provisions of the contract be regarded as meaningless?

4. Explain the order of importance of the following four manifestations of intent:

   a. Course of dealing
   b. Customs and trade practices
   c. Express terms
   d. Course of performance

5. What is the relative importance of separately negotiated terms and boiler-plate language?

6. What is parole evidence? What is the parole evidence rule?

7. What is the doctrine of *contra proferentem?* Under what narrow circumstances will it be applied by a court? Is it negated when the drafter's interpretation of a disputed contract provision is just as reasonable as the claimant's? Why not?

8. The preprinted standard terms and conditions on the back of a purchase order for the supply of transit mix concrete to a project provided that payment for materials delivered would be made within ten days of the buyer's receipt of payment from the project owner and that there would be no pay until the buyer had received payment from the owner. The face of the purchase order in one of the blank spaces under the section entitled "Additional Provisions" contained a typed-in statement that read: "Payment for all concrete delivered in the month will be made to Seller by the end of the following month." Work started, and the contractor-buyer refused to pay the supplier-seller until the tenth day after receiving payment from the owner, which usually occurred 30 to 45 days later than the end of the month following delivery. The supplier protested each payment and, on completion of the work, sued the contractor for interest on the late payments, alleging breach of contract and citing the typed-in payment statement. The contractor contended that the typed-in statement was never intended to supersede the standard terms and conditions and the contractor only agreed to it because it was expected that the owner would pay early enough to permit payment to the supplier by the end of the following month.

   What would the court's likely decision be? Explain your answer in terms of the rules for contract interpretation discussed in this chapter.

9. A certain contract contained the following clause:

> Contractor shall execute and return the contract along with all required insurance policies and contract bonds within 10 calendar days of its delivery to contractor by owner. Notice to proceed shall be issued by owner within 15 calendar days of receipt of the executed contract, insurance policies, and bonds from the contractor. The work of the contract including punch list work and final cleanup of the site shall be completed within 210 calendar days from the date of notice to proceed.

A separate clause provided for the assessment of $1,000 per calendar day in liquidated damages for each day that the contract work remained uncompleted beyond 210 calendar days from the notice to proceed (NTP).

The contractor completed the contract 295 calendar days after NTP, and $85,000 in liquidated damages was withheld from the final contract payment. The contractor sued for the $85,000 alleged to have been wrongfully withheld. The contractor claimed that they had been advised by an owner's representative prior to the bid opening that the schedule was flexible and that "it would be all right" if the contractor did not make the required completion date and that there would be no liquidated damages assessed.

a. Would the contractor's suit be successful? Why or why not?
b. If the court conducted a trial, would it be likely that the contractor would be allowed to testify about the claimed pre-bid understanding? Why or why not?
c. With respect to question b., if the contractor had a written note from the owner's representative confirming what the contractor was told pre-bid, would the chances of success be enhanced? Would the contractor be allowed to introduce the note as evidence at the trial? Why or why not?

10. A clause in the technical specifications of a contract for the construction of a 3,500,000 CY embankment reads as follows:

> Fill material shall be spread in six-inch lifts and compacted by a maximum of four passes of a Caterpillar 825C compactor. The minimum compacted density shall be 95% modified Proctor density.

When compaction tests were taken during contract performance, it was found that six to nine passes of the 825C compactor were required to obtain 95% modified Proctor density. The engineer directed the contractor to compact the embankment to 95% modified Proctor density. After filing a letter of protest and notice of claim for the additional compaction costs, the contractor complied and made the additional passes. Following project completion, the contractor sued for the extra costs, alleging a constructive change. The contractor testified in court that they thought the specification provision meant that no more than four passes would be required and that the sentence about the required density being 95% modified Proctor was included because it was thought that this density would be achieved with less than four passes. An engineer, testifying on behalf of the owner, said that he had written the specification and knew what it meant, which was that the 95% modified Proctor density must be met and that the sentence about the four passes was included because it was expected that the 95% density would be achieved with no more than four passes.

What would the court's likely decision be? Explain your answer in terms of the rules for contract interpretation discussed in this chapter.

21

Documentation and Records

Key Words and Concepts

The "put-it-in-writing" rule
Definition of documentation
The value of good documentation
Hearsay
Job records exception to hearsay rule
Conditions for introduction of job records
Letters of transmittal/submittal

Letters of dispute or protest
Confirmations and meeting minutes
Routine job records
Contractual notices, orders, or directives
Personal diaries
Job document matrix

Previous chapters have been replete with references to the importance of well-kept job records in preserving the contractual rights of all parties to the construction process. Another name for well-kept job records is "good documentation," the subject of this chapter.

DOCUMENTATION

Good documentation on a construction project does not just happen. It is the result of careful preplanning and a concerted effort at all levels of the field organization. It also requires constant application of the "put-it-in-writing" rule.

"Put-It-in-Writing" Rule

The **"put-it-in-writing" rule** is one of the cardinal rules of good contract administration, if not *the* cardinal rule. It is much easier to state than to implement. Self-discipline and strong work habits are required to detail in writing the thousands of daily occurrences on an active construction job, even though you may know that the potential value of such writings far outweighs the effort required to produce them.

Events should be recorded at or shortly after they occur, not at some later time. Anyone with construction experience knows how intense daily activity can become and how difficult it is to take the time to make a written record of something that has just occurred. Often, this is just not possible at the moment, but it ordinarily can be done at the end of the day or at least by the end of the following day. Even records prepared within a week of the event are more valuable than no records at all. One useful technique is to dictate into a hand-held recorder kept constantly nearby, replacing the tape at the start of each new day. The information from the previous day's tape can be transcribed by an office associate or stenographer into a daily job diary, a permanent written record. Once transcribed, the tape can be reused on the third day. Such daily records are detailed and extremely valuable for later reference. Writings prepared later than a week or more after the event have little or no value as a job record. By this time, they are more "recollections" than records.

The writer vividly recalls the usefulness of this type of recordkeeping on a tunnel project executed by his company in the mid-1970s. The project consisted of two parallel soft-ground, shield-driven tunnels under compressed air for a subway project in Baltimore. The schedule required two headings to be driven simultaneously, three shifts per day, five days per week. Each of the three shifts was supervised by a "walker"—a tunnel superintendent—who reported to the general tunnel superintendent. The general tunnel superintendent's home was in southeastern Washington, D.C., a 75-minute drive from the jobsite. His practice was to arrive at the job early in the morning prior to the end of the graveyard shift so that he could visit each heading during that shift and talk to the graveyard walker. He remained on the job throughout the day shift and stayed long enough into the swing shift to observe conditions in both headings and to talk to the swing shift walker. For this reason, the general tunnel superintendent was intimately familiar with the details of the work in each of the two headings for each of the three shifts of the day. He then dictated the events of the day into a hand-held recorder while waiting in traffic between Baltimore and Washington on his trip home, completing the dictation on the reverse trip from Washington to Baltimore early the next morning. On reaching the jobsite, the cassette for the previous day's activities was given to the project secretary in exchange for a clean cassette. The secretary typed the dictation each day and returned the copy to the general tunnel superintendent who edited the typed record, making any necessary corrections.

A major differing site condition was encountered during the project, which resulted in a claim for additional compensation and contract time that was litigated before the Maryland Board of Contract Appeals. During the three-week hearing, both the Transit Authority and the contractor almost totally relied on the contractor's job records, including the daily reports resulting from the general tunnel superintendent's dictation. Although the language in these reports was sometimes quite colorful, the reports proved invaluable in securing a successful board ruling.

What Is Documentation?

Written work products that are mere recitations or summaries written long after events occur are often incorrectly represented as documentation. Such written work products may be useful as effective tools of persuasion in a dispute resolution proceeding, but they are *not* documentation. Contemporaneous written records of the facts themselves *are* documentation, but the recitations and summaries are not.

Written opinions of persons who were not present at the events in question also do not constitute documentation, no matter how experienced and knowledgeable the persons may be. Such expert opinions are important and useful in successfully resolving disputes and may be heavily relied upon by courts and arbitrators, but they are not documentation.

Documentation consists of the writings or records of persons who were present at events, written at the time or shortly after the time of the event. In many instances, it may be the only evidence in existence that reveals what actually occurred.

Value of Good Documentation

Good documentation is invaluable in resolving misunderstandings before they escalate into disputes. One party to a misunderstanding may have an incomplete or incorrect picture of the facts of an event or occurrence on the project. Good documentation of the true facts in the possession of the other party is very effective in clearing up the misunderstanding, thus avoiding a potential dispute before it starts.

If a dispute does arise that cannot be resolved short of litigation or arbitration, the party that can produce carefully prepared authentic job records supporting its position usually will prevail. The litigation or arbitration usually occurs some time after the completion of the project involved. The actual participants in events, such as the engineers, foremen, and superintendents who were assigned to the project are often not available to testify because they have been transferred to other work, have left the employ of a party to the contract, or even, in some instances, have died. The existing job records, properly prepared by these persons, usually may be introduced and accepted as valid evidence of what actually occurred on the project without the necessity of the person who created the records appearing in court and personally testifying.

The home office principals of the parties involved, such as owners and company officers, usually are more readily available to testify, and they may be knowledgeable about what occurred on the job because their subordinates orally reported events to them at the time. However, they are not permitted to testify about what occurred or did not occur on the job because they were not there; and oral statements made to them by their subordinates are **hearsay.** Hearsay is a communication that is secondhand. The person "knows" some fact only because someone else told it to them, not because the person was present at events and knows the fact to be true on the basis of firsthand knowledge. Since these persons are not allowed to testify, the presentation in court of good documentation of events may be the only way to prove what actually occurred.

Exceptions to the Hearsay Rule

Although hearsay generally may not be admitted as evidence in court, there are certain exceptions. One such exception important to the construction industry is that, subject to certain rules, **construction job records (which are hearsay in written form) are usually permitted to be introduced and accepted as evidence.** The federal rules for acceptance of job records as evidence are quite broad, with the result that the records will be admitted if they can be authenticated as genuine. Some state jurisdictions are more restrictive, but properly authenticated job records will generally be admitted.

Conditions for Introduction of Job Records

In most cases, satisfaction of the following **conditions permit the introduction of job records** as evidence in court:

- It must be established that the persons who prepared or originated the records were actually present at the events covered and were in a position to have accurate knowledge. For instance, no one could reasonably argue that a crew foreman's signed and dated time card was not prepared by a person who was present on the job and who had accurate knowledge.

- The records must have been prepared in the normal course of business— that is, it must be shown that the records are of a type that would normally be prepared under the circumstances existing at the time of preparation. For instance, foreman's time cards, project daily progress reports, and accident reports are all clearly the type of documents routinely prepared in the normal course of the business of construction companies. Other examples are daily diaries, weekly and monthly cost reports, force account records, tax returns, material delivery tickets, records of work quantities measured for payment, and so on.

- The records must have been prepared at the time of events, or reasonably soon thereafter.
- There must be no suggestion or intimation that the records were prepared for the specific purpose of use in litigation. Such a suggestion impugns the objectivity and believability of the records.

TYPICAL JOB RECORDS

By way of example, the following is a discussion of 20 typical construction job record documents. Each document is intended to serve specific purposes. To be certain that these purposes are served, each must be carefully drafted and must contain certain necessary elements. The specific job records are:

1. Letters of transmittal
2. Letters of submittal
3. Notice of claim for constructive change
4. Notice of claim for constructive suspension
5. Notice of claimed delay
6. Request for time extension
7. Notice of acceleration
8. Notice of differing site conditions
9. Letter requesting information/interpretations
10. Letter disputing instructions/interpretations
11. Letter advising proceeding under protest
12. Confirmations of instructions or agreements
13. Minutes of meetings
14. Project daily reports
15. Force account time and materials records
16. Cross-sections and other records of work performed
17. Foremen's daily time cards
18. Material delivery tickets
19. Contractual notices—that is, NTPs, notice to correct deficiencies, notices of suspension, termination, and so on
20. Personal diaries

For discussion purposes, it is useful to consider these types of documents in a series of six closely related groups.

Letters of Transmittal and Submittal

The first group consists of **letters of transmittal and letters of submittal** (documents 1 and 2). Both are similar in that each is a cover document for some other document of importance, such as a contract, purchase order, subcontract, drawings, schedules, and the like. Each of these documents has two aims: to establish a record of precisely what was transmitted or submitted and a record of the date that the transmittal or submittal was made. It is not difficult to understand the importance of both of these pieces of information with regard to the liability question if, for example, a series of concrete footings, poured according to superseded construction drawings, had to be demolished and repoured. Were the footings wrongly poured because the owner's engineer failed to transmit the revised drawings to the contractor? Or was it because of poor drawing control by the contractor, who left the revised drawings rolled up in the corner of the job trailer and poured the footings according to the original drawings? The letter of transmittal of the revised drawings, if properly drafted, will settle this question.

Letters of submittal differ from letters of transmittal in one important way. Letters of transmittal do not imply or state that an approval is required or sought, whereas letters of submittal do indicate a request for approval. Both usually require an acknowledgement of receipt. Letters of transmittal are typically used to send drawings, specifications, prime contracts, purchase orders, subcontracts, change orders, certificates of insurance and similar documents, whereas letters of submittal are used to send material samples, shop drawings, proposed CPM schedules, proposed methods or procedures for carrying out the work, and the like. Preprinted forms for both letters of transmittal and letters of submittal are in common use today.

Letters of Notice

The second group consists of the typical contractor notices required by the "red flag" clauses of most construction contracts. All of these (documents 3 through 8) contain the same two basic elements as the first group—that is, they describe or identify an event or subject to which the notice pertains, and they establish a date of record that the notice was given. In addition, in each case, the contractor is taking a position. Therefore, each document should contain an additional element, stating the contractor's position and the basis for believing that the position is correct. In addition to the three preceding elements, the notices in this group should contain other elements, depending on the specific notice. For instance, the notice of acceleration (document 7) should make clear that the contractor is accelerating construction operations and expects to be paid the extra costs of the acceleration. Similarly, the claim for constructive change (document 3), the claim for constructive suspension (document 4), the claimed delay (document 5), an independent request for a time extension (document 6), and the notice of differing site conditions (document 8) should all make the contractor's position clear and that additional time and money are being requested.

Letters Requesting or Disputing Instructions or Letters of Protest

The third group consists of a **letter requesting information or instructions** (document 9), a **letter disputing or taking exception to instructions previously furnished by owner or engineer** (document 10), and a **letter advising that the contractor is proceeding under protest** (document 11). The two elements of identification and establishment of a date of record are required as for all the other documents. In addition, document 10, which disputes instructions or interpretations, should explain that a dispute exists and the reason that the instructions or interpretations have been disputed. The letter advising proceeding under protest (document 11) must make clear that a dispute exists, that the contractor is proceeding under protest, and that additional time and money are expected.

Confirmations and Meeting Minutes

The fourth group includes **confirmation of instructions or agreements** (document 12) and **minutes of meetings** (document 13). Both possess the two elements of identification and establishment of a date of record and, in addition, contain an element that confirms an understanding of a conversation, meeting, or instructions received. Such letters can relieve the recipient from the necessity of replying by indicating that if no advice to the contrary is received, the understandings stated in the letter or meeting minutes will be regarded as correct.

Routine Job Records

The fifth group—daily reports (document 14), force account records (document 15), cross-section data and other measurements of work performed (document 16), daily time cards (17), and material delivery tickets (18)—all share a common attribute. They are all forms of **routine job records** required to operate the project. Their purpose is to record facts about what has occurred. There are only two elements: recording facts and establishing the date that the facts were recorded.

Contractual Notices, Orders, or Directives

This class of project documents includes the more formal type of **notice, order, or directive,** required by the contract to be given by the owner or construction manager to the prime contractor, or by the prime contractor to subcontractors. Such things as notice of award of contract or subcontract, notices to proceed, stop orders, cure notices (order to remedy defaults), suspension of work or acceleration directives, and termination notices (document 19) are all included in this category. Although less frequent than other job documents, their importance is obvious. They should be drafted with great care and must contain some mechanism to establish the fact and date of delivery.

Personal Diaries

Many construction executives and managers maintain **personal diaries** (document 20) on a routine basis, entering facts about important meetings or events shortly after they occur when recollection is fresh. Such diaries are highly regarded as probative evidence in construction disputes, provided the entries are factual and not unduly editorialized.

The writer maintained this type of daily diary throughout his contracting career. These diaries repeatedly were effectively used in dispute resolution, including use as trial exhibits in court and in hearings before administrative boards. However, such diaries must be factual, inasmuch as they are subject to discovery during litigation. For this reason, some in the industry do not keep diaries because they regard them to be a two-edged sword. However, the writer's experience has been that the benefits to be gained in maintaining a detailed diary far outweigh the drawbacks. On one occasion, the writer's original diaries were subpoenaed by the federal government as evidence in a criminal trial involving other parties and were not returned for a number of years. These experiences should make clear the importance that courts, arbitrators, and other dispute resolution bodies place on this type of record.

Job Document Matrix

The relation of the various necessary elements just discussed to the documents themselves is represented diagrammatically by the **job document matrix** shown in Figure 21–1.

CONCLUSION

Most construction documentation, particularly correspondence, is generated during the "heat of battle" on active construction projects. There are usually two sides to every issue, and each person's view of the situation will be highly influenced by "where he or she sits in the stadium." The purpose in writing a letter to an opposite number should not be to vent one's spleen, but by being factual and professional, to convince the other of the correctness of one's position. Unfortunately, much actual construction correspondence overlooks this simple truth.

QUESTIONS AND PROBLEMS

1. What is the cardinal rule of good contract administration? At what point should the rule be exercised to result in good job documents?

Elements That Should Be Contained in the Document

Type of Job Document	Describe and/or Identify	Establish a Date of Record	State Basis of Belief	Notify that Dispute Exists	Notify Proceed Under Protest	Confirm an Understanding	Record a Fact	Instruct or Direct	Notify Extra Time Expected	Notify Extra Money Expected
1. Letters of Transmittal	●	●								
2. Letters of Submittal	●	●								
3. Notice of Claim for Constructive Change	●	●	●						●	●
4. Notice of Claim for Constructive Suspension	●	●	●						●	●
5. Notice of Claimed Delay	●	●	●						●	
6. Request for Time Extension	●	●							●	
7. Notice of Acceleration	●	●	●	●	●					●
8. Notice of Differing Site Conditions	●	●	●						●	●
9. Letter Requesting Informations/Interpretations	●	●								
10. Letter Disputing Instructions/Interpretations	●	●	●	●						
11. Letter Advising Proceeding Under Protest	●	●		●	●					●
12. Confirmations of Instructions or Agreements	●	●				●				
13. Minutes of Meetings	●	●				●				
14. Project Daily Report	●	●					●			
15. Force Account Time and Material Records	●	●					●			
16. Cross Sections and Other Records of Work Done	●	●					●			
17. Foreman's Daily Time Cards	●	●					●			
18. Material Delivery Tickets	●	●					●			
19. Letters to Subs/NTP/Correct Deficiencies/ Suspension/Termination	●	●						●		
20. Personal Diaries	●	●					●			

FIGURE 21–1 Job document matrix.

2. Does the term *documentation* include recitations or summaries of events written after the fact? Are later written opinions of qualified construction experts considered to be documentation?

3. Why are good job records useful in construction litigation?

4. Why are home office principals often not permitted to testify in court about events that occurred on the project?

5. What is *hearsay*? Does the hearsay rule usually apply to construction project records?

6. What are the four requirements that must be met before project records may be presented as evidence in court?

7. What is the difference between a letter of transmittal and a letter of submittal?

8. What ten separate elements of various project documents are discussed in this chapter?

9. What is the general purpose of construction correspondence dealing with disputed matters that is so often overlooked in practice?

22

Construction Contract Claims

Key Words and Concepts

Claim definition
Change in contract time
Written claim notice
Causal event
"Proximate" costs
Detailed claim submittal
Impact costs
Entitlement element
Extended indirect costs
Quantum element
Escalation costs
Failure to give notice
Severe weather costs
Waiver

Decreased efficiency of work
  performance
Constructive notice
Claim processing procedure
Industry published inefficiency factors
Time limits for owner's consideration
Excessive overtime
Change in contract price
Comparison with bid estimate
"Cost of the work"
"Measured mile" analysis
Contractor's fee
Comparison with other contracts

To some construction owners, A/Es, and CMs, "claim" is an unsavory word. They regard claims as hostile assaults on their management of the contract and contractors who file them as devious and unscrupulous. On the other hand, some contractors indiscriminately file claims whether they are contractually justified or not. In reality, filing a claim is the only contractually provided procedure by which either party to the contract can openly and fairly assert their position regarding contract time or money when disputes arise. Filing a claim is the first step in the contractually provided dispute resolution process.

This chapter highlights some of the more important aspects of this complicated subject.

THRESHOLD MATTERS

Nearly all claims originate with the contractor following the occurrence of a contract dispute. The Massachusetts Water Resources Authority contract for the construction of the Inter-Island Tunnel in Boston Harbor defined a **claim** as follows:

> A claim means a written demand or assertion by the Contractor seeking an adjustment in Contract Price and payment of monies so due, an extension or shortening in Contract Time, the adjustment or interpretation of Contract terms, or other relief arising under or relating to the Contract following denial of a submittal for change under Article 10....

By the above definition, a contractor's claim is triggered by the owner's denial of a contractor's proposal for a change in contract price or time. The claim is a response to the owner's denial, which now takes the form of a *demand* for a stated amount of money or time, which demand becomes subject to the dispute resolution provisions of the contract. The original **contractor's proposal** for an adjustment in contract price or time that triggers the owner's denial typically originates for one of the following reasons:

- The owner issues a formal change order or change notice adding contract work or making changes in original contract work, originally specified working conditions, or originally permitted construction methods. The occasion for the owner's issuing of the change order or change notice could be a desired scope change in the finished project or because acknowledged differing site conditions had been encountered by the contractor. In these situations, the contractor is required to propose a change in contract price, time, or both in response to the change order or change notice.

- The contractor, believing they have encountered differing site conditions, so notifies the owner and requests (proposes) that the owner issue a change order for an appropriate increase in contract price, time, or both.

- The contractor, believing that instructions received from the owner constitute a constructive change to the contract, so notifies the owner and requests (proposes) that the owner issue a change order for an appropriate increase in contract price, time, or both.

- Some causal event that the contractor believes is compensable or excusable has occurred and the contractor, after so notifying the owner, requests (proposes) that the owner issue a change order increasing the contract price, time, or both.

In order for a contractor's claim to be valid, it usually must be established by **written notice** submitted to the owner within a stated number of days after the occurrence of the event giving rise to the claim. For instance, the Massachusetts Water Resources Authority contract provides that

> For any claim under this article to be valid, it shall be based upon written notice delivered by the Contractor to the Authority promptly, but in no event later than twenty-one (21) days, after the occurrence of the event giving rise to the claim and <u>stating the general nature of the claim</u> (underline added for emphasis).

In the context of this type of contract provision, the "event giving rise to the claim" **(causal event)** could be the owner's denial and refusal to issue a change order in accordance with a contractor's cost/time proposal, or the occurrence of some event that the contractor believes is either compensable or excusable under the terms of the contract.

Once the written notice of claim has been delivered to the owner by the contractor, most contracts provide that the contractor's **detailed claim submittal,** supported by a CPM schedule analysis in cases involving a demand for additional contract time be submitted to the owner within a stated number of days following the notice. Some contracts require the detailed claim to be submitted within a stated number of days following the occurrence of the event that gave rise to the claim notice. For instance, the federal government contract proscribes that the contractor's detailed claim proposal be submitted within 30 days after the furnishing of a written claim notice while the Massachusetts Water Resources Authority contract proscribes that the detailed claim submittal be submitted within 60 days after the occurrence giving rise to the claim notice.

The contractor's detailed claim submittal must clearly establish that (1) the contractor is *entitled* by the terms of the contract to an adjustment in contract price, time, or both *of some amount* (the **entitlement element**), and (2) establish the amount of the claimed dollar change in contract price or claimed number of calendar days of contract time extension—the **quantum element**.

"RED FLAG" CONTRACT PROVISIONS

The above discussed matters pertain to contract claims in general. Some of the more specific provisions that contractors should be particularly alerted to include the following.

Notice Requirements

Perhaps the most important provision regarding claims is that requiring the giving of notice by the contractor that they are filing a claim. Most contracts provide explicitly that **failure to give notice** within the number of days specified in the contract after the event giving rise to the claim results in **waiver** of the contractor's right to file a claim. Contractors sometimes avoid waiver of their claim rights by showing that the owner was aware of the event giving rise to the claim and had **constructive notice** of the contractor's intention to seek monetary or contract time relief in respect to that event. This is particularly true for claims for an extension of contract time following an obvious excusable event such as a labor strike or a flood shutting down the entire project for a finite period of time. However, "dodging the bullet" in this manner is risky and should be avoided by strictly complying with the notice requirements stated in the contract.

The contractor should always follow up the initial notice of claim with a submittal explaining their detailed claim position, citing relevant contract language supporting entitlement to monetary, time relief, or both as well as detailed calculations establishing the dollar amount claimed, and, in cases where an extension of contract time is claimed, a CPM analysis supporting the number of calendar days of contract time extension claimed. The entitlement explanation can always be submitted promptly but, in many cases, costs and contract time associated with the claimed event may be ongoing and can not be finalized until the total impact of the event has been experienced, sometimes many months after the onset of the event. In these situations, it is common for the contractor to submit best estimates of the monetary and time quantum, subject to later correction when final actual figures are available.

Claim Processing Procedure

The contract usually proscribes the **procedure for processing the claim** once the contractor has properly submitted it. In some contracts, these procedures are relatively straightforward, resulting in reasonably prompt consideration of the claim by the owner's engineer or construction manager. The owner usually awaits the recommendation of their engineer or construction manager before communicating their position on the claim back to the contractor, either accepting it, denying it, or accepting in part and denying in part. The contractor then must either accept the owner's decision or dispute it and invoke the dispute resolution procedures of the contract, usually within a stated number of days after receiving the decision. Other contracts have extremely complicated and time-consuming procedures for consideration of contractor claims, often resulting in no serious consideration of the claim until the end of the contract work. Since the contractor often can not invoke the dispute resolution procedures of the contract until they have received the owner's final decision with respect to the claim, complicated and time-consuming claim consideration procedures unfairly penalize contractors who may have legitimate claim positions and seriously impact their fiscal liquidity. For this reason, many contracts contain provisions setting strict **time limits for the owner's consideration of contractor**

claims. Failure of the owner to furnish a final decision on the claim within these time limits is considered tantamount to a denial of the claim, which frees the contractor to immediately invoke the dispute resolution provisions of the contract. Contracts containing such time limits are far preferable from the contractor's standpoint.

Proscribed Procedure for Determination of Adjustments of Contract Price and Time

If the claimed entitlement issue is resolved in the contractor's favor, the monetary adjustment to the contract price or the number of calendar days of contract time extension with respect to the claim must each be determined. With regard to the first determination, the **change in contract price**, most contracts provide the following methods, listed in order of preference:

- By use of lump sum prices or unit prices in the contract bid schedule that were applicable to the original contract work.
- By mutual acceptance of new lump sum prices or unit prices to be applied to the claim work.
- If the owner and contractor do not agree to one of the above methods, on the basis of actual costs of the claim work determined from mutually accepted job records, plus a fee to cover contractor's indirect claim costs and contractor's profit—the so-called **"cost of the work"** method.

Since by their nature claims are contentious, the owner and contractor seldom agree on one of the first two methods and contract price changes are usually determined on the basis of the third method—that is, on the basis of the "cost of the work" plus a **contractor's fee**.

The contract provisions defining the "cost of the work" are usually explicit and detailed. For instance, the Oakland County Drain Commission contract for the construction of a sewage retention treatment basin in Michigan included the following pertinent language:

25. BASIS FOR DETERMINING COST OF CHANGES IN THE WORK (CONTINUED)

"COST" is herein used shall be the actual and necessary costs incurred by the Contractor by reason of the change in the work for –

(1) labor

(2) materials

(3) equipment rental

(4) insurance premiums

   (1) Labor costs shall be the amount shown on the Contractor's payrolls with payroll taxes added when such taxes can be shown to have been incurred. In no case shall the rates charged for labor exceed the rate paid by the Contractor for the

same class of labor employed by him to perform work under the regular items of the Contract.

(2) Material costs shall be the net price paid for material delivered to the site of the work. If any material previously required is omitted by the written order of the Owner after it had been delivered to or partially worked on by the Contractor and consequently will not retain its full value for other uses, the Contractor shall be allowed the actual costs of the omitted material less a fair market value of the material as determined by the Owner.

(3) Equipment rental shall be the actual additional costs incurred for necessary equipment. Costs shall not be allowed in excess of usual rentals charged in the area for similar equipment of like size and condition; including the cost of necessary supplies and repairs for operating the equipment. No costs, however, shall be allowed for the use of the equipment on the site in connection with other work. If equipment not on the site is required for the change in the work only, the cost of transporting such equipment to and from the site shall be allowed.

The rental rate established for each piece Contractor owned equipment, including appendices and attachments to equipment used, will be determined by the Rental Rate Blue Book for Construction Equipment Volume 1, 2, or 3 as applicable; the edition which is current at the time the work was started will apply. The established hourly rental rate will be equal to the "Monthly" rate divided by 176, modified by the applicable rate adjustment factor and the map adjustment factor, plus the "Estimated Operating Costs per Hour."

For equipment not listed in the Rental Rate Blue Book, Volume 1, 2, or 3, the rental rate will be determined by using the rate listed for a similar piece of equipment or by proportioning a rate listed so that the capacity, size, horsepower, and age are properly considered.

In the event the machinery and equipment actually on the project site is idle for reasons beyond the control of the Contractor, the rental rate of the Contractor-owned equipment will be the "Monthly" rate divided by 176, modified by the applicable rate adjustment factor and the map adjustment factor, and then multiplied by 50%.

No payment will be allowed for operating costs. This section applies to only machinery and equipment necessary for performance of the work in question.

(4) Insurance premiums shall be limited to those based on labor payroll and to the types of insurance required by the Contract. The amount allowed shall be limited to the net costs incurred as determined from the labor payroll covering the work. The Contractor shall, upon request of the Owner, submit verification of the applicable insurance rates and the premium computations.

(5) "Plus" as herein used is defined as a percentage to be added to the items of "Cost" to cover superintendents, use of ordinary tools, bonds, overhead expense, and profit. The percentage shall not exceed 15% on work done entirely by the Contractor and shall not exceed an aggregate total of 25% on work done by a Subcontractor.

(6) "SPECIFIED MAXIUM LIMIT OF COSTS" is the amount stated in the written order of the Owner authorizing the change in the work. The amount to be

allowed the Contractor shall be the "cost", and "plus" the percentage or the specified maximum, whichever is the lessor amount.

This contract goes on to provide:

B. The Contractor shall keep complete, active, daily records of the net actual cost of changes in the work and shall present such information at the end of each working day as verified by the inspector, in such form and at such times as the Owner may direct.

C. If the Owner and Contractor can not reach mutual agreement in establishing the cost of changed work, the method of establishing said costs shall be on a cost plus basis.

The cited above Oakland County Drain Commission contract provision pertains to determining contract price changes for claims that do not involve an extension of contract time. This contract also provides for a change of contract time in a separate article stating in pertinent part:

26. CHANGE OF CONTRACT TIME (CONTINUED)

B. The Contract Time may be extended in an amount equal to time lost due to substantial delay of a type or of a cause that could not reasonably have been foreseen or anticipated by the Contractor, and that is beyond the control of the Contractor or its Subcontractor, if the Contractor timely and properly asserts a claim pursuant to this section. Delays that may give rise to an extension of time, if such delays are substantial and otherwise come within the preceding sentence, include those caused by negligent acts or omissions by Owner or others excluding Contractor or its agents or its Subcontractors performing additional work as contemplated by Section 9, or caused by fires, floods, labor disputes not involving a dispute between Contractor or its subcontractors and their own employees, epidemics, or other "Act of God," as that term is commonly understood.

The Massachusetts Water Resource Authority (MWRA) Inter-Island Tunnel contract contains language to a similar effect with regard to contract claims that do not involve an extension of contract time, but in its provisions regarding changes in contract time, the MWRA contract distinguishes between time extensions due to causes which are excusable only and those that are compensable as far as extended contract costs are concerned.

With regard to extensions of contract time for *excusable* causes, this contract provides:

11.12 CRITERIA FOR DETERMINING ADJUSTMENTS IN CONTRACT TIME

The Criteria to be used to determine an adjustment in Contract Time necessitated by changes ordered or negotiated pursuant to these General Conditions, or work covered by a submittal or a claim, are limited to the following:

11.12.1. An adjustment in Contract Time will be based solely upon net increases in the time required for the performance or completion of parts of the Work controlling achievement of the corresponding Contract Time(s) (Critical Path). However, even if the time required or the performance for the completion of the controlling parts of the Work is extended, an extension in Contract Time will not be granted until all of the available Total Float is consumed and performance or completion of the controlling work necessarily extends beyond the Contract Time.[1]

11.12.2. The Authority may elect, at its sole discretion, to grant an extension in Contract Time, without the Contractor's request, because of delays meeting the requirements set forth below.

11.12.3. An extension in Contract Time will not be granted unless the Contractor can demonstrate through an analysis of the Progress Schedule that the increases in the time to perform or to complete the Work, or specified part of the Work, beyond the corresponding Contract Time(s) arise from unforeseeable causes beyond the control and without the fault or negligence of both the Contractor and his Subcontractors, suppliers, or other persons or organizations, and if such causes in fact lead to performance or completion of the Work, or specified part in question, beyond the corresponding Contract Time, despite the Contractor's reasonable and diligent actions to guard against those effects. Examples of such causes include: (1) Acts of Gods or of the public enemy; (2) Acts of the Government or of another Public Entity in its sovereign capacity; (3) Acts of another contractor in performance of a contract with the Authority; (4) Fires, floods, epidemics, quarantine restrictions; (5) sinkholes, archeological finds; (6) freight embargoes; (7) unusually severe weather; (8) a case of an emergency; (9) delays as itemized in this paragraph, to Subcontractors or Suppliers or other persons or organizations at any tier arising from unforeseeable causes beyond the control and without fault or negligence of either the Contractor or any such Subcontractors, Suppliers or other persons or organizations.

11.12.4. It is the intent of the Contract Documents that an extension in Contract Time, if any granted, shall be the Contractor's sole and exclusive remedy for any delay, disruption, interference, or hindrance and associated costs, however caused, resulting from causes contemplated in this paragraph but not included under paragraph 11.13.

11.12.5. The provisions of this paragraph 11.12. shall govern and are applicable to Contractor requests, submittals or claims for acceleration in lieu of the alternate extension in Contract Time.

The MWRA contract then continues with article 11.13, dealing with **changes in contract time** due to *compensable* causes as follows:

11.13 CHANGES IN CONTRACT TIME MAY BE COMBINED WITH CHANGES IN CONTRACT PRICE:

It is the intent of the Contract Documents that an extension in Contract Time shall be combined with an appropriate increase in Contract Price to provide the Contractor with full remedy for any delay, disruption, interference, extension or hindrance caused by: Acts of the Authority in its contractual capacity in connection with changes in the Work, differing physical conditions or differing reference points; a case of an emergency, of uncovering work, or a suspension of work not excluded by another provision

---

[1]In the context of this contract language, "Total Float" has the meaning of "float" as defined in Chapter 18.

of the Contract Documents. However, no adjustment in Contract Price under this paragraph shall be provided: (1) to the extent that performance would have been so extended by any other cause, including fault or negligence of the Contractor, or his Subcontractors, Suppliers, or other persons or organizations; (2) for which an adjustment is provided or excluded under any other provision of the Contract Documents; (3) for acceleration costs in lieu of extension costs to the extent that the acceleration costs exceed those of the alternate extension in Contract Time; or (4) if delays merely prevent the Contractor's achievement of completion of the Work, or part in question, ahead of the corresponding Contract Time(s). The Contractor shall be entitled to a Contract Price increase due to these delays, disruptions, extensions, interferences or hindrances only when delays extend the Work or specified part of the Work, beyond the applicable Contract Time(s) including any authorized adjustments.

Finally, the MWRA contract continues with article 11.14 placing a limitation on the costs allowed due to an extension in contract time:

11.14 COST OF THE WORK INVOLVED—EXTENSION IN CONTRACT TIME:

When determining the cost of the work involved to complement an extension in Contract Time, amounts shall be allowed only if related solely to the extension in Contract Time, . . . "

As can be seen from the above, contract provisions governing changes to contract price and time are apt to be complicated. In the following sections of this chapter dealing with methods of proving the price and time quantum elements, the contract provisions of the type illustrated above must be strictly observed.

METHODS OF PROVING PRICE AND TIME QUANTUM

Two separate general claim scenarios can each generate cost and time impacts. In the first scenario, some new element of work not present in the original contract is required to be accomplished either as a result of an owner directive or due to the contractor encountering differing site conditions. If the contract price and time change is to be forward priced by agreement between the owner and contractor, the quantum analysis is nothing more than making a cost and time estimate for performance of the added work by the same general methods as used for the original total project cost and time estimate. Alternately, if the price and time changes are to be determined retrospectively, it is only necessary to maintain mutually agreed accurate job records detailing the elements of contractually allowable cost and time adjustments previously discussed in this chapter.

In this first claim scenario, costs may consist of the **"proximate" costs** directly associated with the added work itself, incurred at the time and location where the work was added and the consequential or **"impact costs,"** which consist of (1) time-related costs such as increased **indirect costs** due to the extension of the contract period, **escalation costs** on unchanged work that is pushed into a period of increased labor rates or material prices, excess costs resulting from pushing original work into periods of **severe weather** that otherwise would have been avoided; and (2) the adverse effect of the added work on the **efficiency of performance of related original contract work**.[2]

The second general claim scenario is one where the *original contract work is made more difficult* as the result of (1) an owner directive changing the details of the original work itself, changing the conditions under which the original work must be constructed, or restricting the construction methods or equipment that is permitted to be employed for the original work; and (2) situations where the original work is made intrinsically more difficult for the above reasons due to the contractor encountering differing site conditions.

In this second claim scenario, proving time and price quantum always involves evaluation of *a decrease in efficiency of performing work originally included in the contract*. Several different methods utilized by contractors to prove decreased efficiency of original work performance are discussed and illustrated in the following sections.

Use of Industry Published Factors

The National Association of Electrical Contractors and others have conducted studies and **published factors** claimed to quantify the loss of efficiency in performing unchanged work due to stacking of trades, frequent crew movements with associated starts and stops, frequent requirements for prolonged overtime, the necessity of going through a learning curve more times than would otherwise would be necessary, and the general effect on morale due to continual changes and delays. Similarly, the Business Roundtable has published data illustrating the loss of efficiency when **excessive overtime** is worked on an extended basis.[3] Generally speaking, this method of proving decreased work efficiency of performance is met with skepticism by owners, courts, and arbitrators because of a lack of proof that the same conditions applying to the underlying studies were present in the claim situation involved.

Comparison with Contractor's and Engineer's Bid Estimates

Typically, the contract bid price is based on the contractor's cost and time estimate prepared at the time of bid. Also, the owner's engineer usually makes a parallel estimate indicating their assessment of a reasonable bid price under the competitive conditions existing at the time of bid. Either or both of these estimates provide a useful standard for measuring the adverse impact of causal events not contemplated at time of bid on the performance of unchanged original contract work.

In one case in the writer's experience, both the contractor's bid estimate and the engineer's estimate for a TBM-excavated tunnel in rock, which had been impacted by excess water inflows not expected at the time of bid, were available

---

[2]These two general types of impact costs are the same as those discussed under price and time adjustments for contract changes in Chapter 14.

[3]The effect of this published data is discussed in connection with the pricing of contract changes in Chapter 14.

to establish a reasonably expected rate of advance under the water inflow conditions indicated by the contract documents. In this case, the advance rate was also heavily dependent upon the tunnel excavation temporary support assumptions in each estimate. When the engineer's estimate was adjusted to reflect the same temporary support assumptions as the contractor's estimate, the adjusted engineer's estimate advance rate was 121.8 ft. per day. The actual advance rate in the contractor's estimate was 123.9 ft. per day. Alternately, when the contractor's bid estimate was adjusted to reflect the same temporary support assumptions as the engineer's estimate, the adjusted contractor's estimate advance rate was 95.5 ft. per day. The actual advance rate in the engineer's estimate was 95.1 ft. per day. It would be difficult to argue in this case that these estimates did not provide a reasonable figure for the tunnel advance rate that could be expected under as-bid water inflow conditions.

Measured Mile Analysis

The most reliable methodology to prove impact of an adverse causal event on the efficiency of original unchanged work performance is to compare work performance in an impacted area of the project with the performance of identical work in an area of the project that was not impacted by the causal event—that is, the so-called **"measured mile" analysis**. The following two examples, taken from the writer's claim evaluation experience, illustrate the use of this method.

During pile-driving work for steel bearing piling supporting an outfall sewer, the contractor alleged a loss of productivity caused by excessive owner directed changes, extra work, and owner-caused delays experienced during pile-driving operations. The contractor had based their claim on a productivity of 11 piles per day, which they stated was their "as-built" production for pile-driving work where the alleged interferences were not encountered. However, a study of as-built driving performance unimpacted by the claimed causal events revealed a production of 159 piles in 16.33 days for an average of 9.74 piles per day. The contractor's actual productivity in driving 434 piles that was impacted by the claimed causal events was 434 piles in 63.0 workdays for an average of 6.89 piles per day. The extra pile-driving time on account of the claimed interferences therefore was:

Actual time required	=	63.0 workdays
Time required at 9.74 piles per day	=	44.6 workdays
Additional time required	=	18.4 workdays

In another example from the same project, the contractor claimed that productivity losses in the Stage 2 phase in the construction of a bypass conduit from the productivity achieved during the Stage 1 phase were incurred due to delays caused by owner-directed strengthening of the Stage 2 conduit, differing site conditions caused by leakage from the existing outfall sewer, and numerous other directed changes in the work. The contractor also claimed that owner-caused delays pushed the Stage 2 work into severe winter weather.

According to the contractor's claim, the following actual work quantities and man-hours (mh) required to accomplish them represented the as-built bypass conduit Stage 2 construction for which reimbursement for lost productivity was sought:

Excavation	2419 cy	786 mh	0.325 mh/cy
Form and strip	6733 sfca[4]	2729 mh	0.405 mh/sfca
Place concrete	357 cy	440 mh	1.232 mh/cy
Backfill	1141 cy	276 mh	0.242 mh/cy

The as-built Stage 1 figures taken as the "measured mile" were:

Excavation	3040 cy	740 mh	0.243 mh/cy
Form and strip	8355 sfca	1398 mh	0.167 mh/sfca
Place concrete	458 cy	254 mh	0.555 mh/cy
Backfill	1842 cy	257 mh	0.140 mh/cy

Two adjustments to the Stage 2 as-built mh were found to be necessary to reflect replacing a failed sheet pile wall during excavation due to contractor error and reflecting an estimated 15% increase in general complexity of Stage 2 work over Stage 1 work. The adjustments to the actual Stage 2 mh are shown in Figure 22–1. Based on Figure 22–1, the productivity losses for Stage 2 construction, including the effect of performing Stage 2 in the winter relative to Stage 1 construction were calculated as shown in Figure 22–2.

In both the above examples, the productivity loss can easily be converted into dollars and cents. In carrying out this step, the contractual provisions governing labor and equipment hourly costs and the application of percentage markups for indirect costs and profit discussed in the previous sections of this chapter must be strictly observed. For instance, in the first of the above examples the parties had agreed that the daily labor costs including all applicable fringes and taxes for the pile driving crew were $2,443 per day. They further agreed that the crew equipment

---

[4]sfca = square feet of contact area

Activity	Reported mh	mh for Replacing Sheet Pile Wall	mh for Increased Complexity	Net mh
Excavation	786 mh	108 mh	88 mh	590 mh
Form and Strip	2729 mh	—	356 mh	2373 mh
Place Concrete	440 mh	—	57 mh	383 mh
Backfill	276 mh	—	36 mh	240 mh

FIGURE 22–1 Adjustments to Stage 2 mh.

Activity	Quantity	Net mh	Adjusted Productivity Factor	Stage 1 Productivity Factor	Loss in Productivity Factor	Productivity Loss in mh
Excavation	2419 cy	590	0.244 mh/cy	0.243 mh/cy	—	—
Form and Strip	6733 sfca	2373	0.352 mh/sfca	0.167 mh/sfca	0.158 mh/sfca	1246
Place Concrete	357 cy	383	1.073 mh/cy	0.555 mh/cy	0.518 mh/cy	185
Backfill	1141 cy	240	0.210 mh/cy	0.140 mh/cy	0.070 mh/cy	80
Total Impact						1511

FIGURE 22–2 Calculation of productivity loss in Stage 2 construction.

costs totaled $1,800 per day according to the equipment hourly rates proscribed by the contract provisions. The pile-driving work was performed by a subcontractor and the contract proscribed the following percentage markups for the subcontractor and prime contractor:

Subcontract markup on labor @ 15% and on equipment @ 10% for indirect costs and profit.

Additional allowance for subcontractor small tools and supplies @ 2% of the labor total.

Prime contractor markup @ 5% of subcontractor labor and equipment total for prime contractor indirect cost and profit.

Additional prime contractor allowance for bond @ 0.68%

Additional prime contractor allowance for insurance @ 1.2%

On this basis, the claim quantum was computed as follows:

Subcontractor labor 18.4 days	@ $243/day	=	$44,951
Subcontractor equipment 18.4 days	@ $1,800/day	=	$33,120
Subcontractor subtotal		=	$78,071
Subcontractor markup on labor	@ 15%	=	$6,743
Subcontractor markup on equipment	@ 10%	=	$3,312
Subcontractor subtotal		=	$88,126
Subcontractor small tools and supplies	@ 2% of labor	=	$899
Subcontractor total		=	$89,025
Prime contractor's markup	@ 5% of $78,071	=	$3,904
Prime contractor subtotal		=	$92,929
Prime contractor allowance for bond	@ 0.68%	=	$632
Prime contractor allowance for insurance	@ 1.2%	=	$1,115
Total claim amount		=	$94,676

Comparison with Similar Cost Experience on Other Contracts

Sometimes the entire contract work is adversely impacted by a series of intertwined causal events that significantly affect the efficiency of performance of original unchanged contract work. Such was the writer's experience in the early 1980s during the performance of structural concrete work for the underground Peachtree Station constructed in downtown Atlanta for the Metropolitan Atlanta Rapid Transit Authority (MARTA). In this case, the entire surface and underground structural concrete operation was adversely impacted due to the following causations:

- Excessive number of changes both by formal change notice and constructive changes.

- Changes directed at the "eleventh hour" preventing their incorporation into the work in a timely and organized manner.

- Numerous errors, omissions, and conflicts found in the drawings and specifications as the work was performed.

- Lack of engineering information and/or direction and eleventh-hour provision of same.

- Directed acceleration of the work requiring stacking of crews and overtime work.

- Change in sequence of performance of the underground cavern structural work.

- Impacts associated with interference of other MARTA contractors who were allowed into the main cavern work area concurrently with the structural concrete operations.

Since the entire surface and underground work area was adversely impacted, there was no "measured mile" that could be used to compare work item productivities to prove the claimed decrease in efficiency of performance. However, our heavy engineering construction division performing the concrete work had completed eight other rapid transit projects involving similar work operations and was concurrently completing a similar deep-mined station for the Washington Metropolitan Area Transit Authority (WMATA) in Bethesda, Maryland. All of these projects had been set up and operated in a virtually identical manner and the labor productivity cost records for each of them was structured in an identical format making it possible to directly compare actual construction performance for similar work items. Great similarity existed between many of the MARTA work items and comparable work items on six of the other projects for which our computer bank contained the work-item productivity records. None of the previously constructed projects departed from the norm in factors adverse to contractor work performance.

Figure 22–3 shows the comparison made for 27 separate MARTA concrete work items to our average "normal" performance for similar work items from the other company projects. For each work item, the work-item description is listed as well as the as-built MARTA quantity and unit of measure, the MARTA mh factor per unit of work accomplished, the MARTA mh total, the normal project mh factor, and the normal project mh total. The MARTA project required 309,100 mh for the 27 separate work items, which would have required only 254,960 mh according to our experience on the other projects. The excess MARTA mh equal to $309,100 - 254,960 = 54,140$ exceeded our experience on comparable projects by 21.23%. Following an extensive review of our records, MARTA accepted our offer of proof and issued a change order that compensated us for the claimed inefficiency.

CONCLUSION

This chapter has reviewed the conceptual basis of construction contract claims, typical contract provisions delineating procedural requirements for their filing and processing, and the methods of proof traditionally offered by contractors seeking to establish the associated contract price and time quantum.

Work Item No.	Work Item Description	As-Built Quantity	Unit of Measure	MARTA Performance mh Factor	mh Total	Normal Performance mh Factor	mh Total
1	Outside Concrete – S.O.G.[1]	1897	cy	1.222/cy	2,318	0.414/cy	785
2	" - Walls	4060	cy	1.599/cy	6492	0.816/cy	3313
3	" - Suppt. Slab	1097	cy	1.493/cy	1638	0.578/cy	634
4	E&S Outside S.O.G. Bulkheads	1936	cy	0.644/cy	1247	0.458/cy	887
5	" Wall & S'Slab "	4138	cy	0.490/cy	2028	0.459/cy	1899
6	" Single Face Walls	18205	sfca	0.666/sfca	12125	0.222/sfca	5862
7	" Double Face Walls	68503	sfca	0.335/sfca	23056	0.248/sfca	17068
8	" Suppt. Slabs	16503	sfca	0.434/sfca	7162	0.172/sfca	2839
9	Erect/Dismantle Outside Shoring	263396	cf	0.015/cf	3951	0.009/cf	2371
10	Underground S.O.G. Concrete	5668	cy	1.469/cy	8326	1.079/cy	6116
11	" Wall "	11707	cy	1.844/cy	21588	5.015/cy	58711
12	" Suppt. Slab "	2237	cy	2.063/cy	4615	1.880/cy	4206
13	Tunnel Invert Concrete	2902	cy	1.38/cy	4008	1.149/cy	3334
14	" Arch	4911	cy	0.953/cy	4729	0.804/cy	3929
15	E&S U/G Double Face Walls	72279	sfca	0.433/sfca	31297	0.268/sfca	19371
16	" U/G Single Face Walls	95157	sfca	0.652/sfca	62042	0.492/sfca	46817
17	" U/G Invert Bulkheads	5891	sfca	0.795/sfca	4683	0.848/sfca	4996
18	" U/G Wall	10222	sfca	0.898/sfca	9179	0.467/sfca	4774
19	" U/G Slab "	16821	sfca	1.098/sfca	18469	0.820/sfca	13793
20	" U/G Hung Forms	15436	sfca	0.319/sfca	4924	0.280/sfca	4322
21	" U/G Invert Edges	2690	sfca	0.812/sfca	2184	0.326/sfca	877
22	" U/G Arch Forms (Wood)	28771	sfca	0.723/sfca	20801	0.667/sfca	19190
23	Erect/Dismantle U/G Shoring	925354	cf	0.027/cf	24986	0.014/cf	12955
24	E&S Tunnel Invert Forms	2807	sfca	1.276/sfca	3582	1.589/sfca	4660
25	E&S Arch	50130	sfca	0.109/sfca	5464	0.057/sfca	2857
26	E&S Bulkheads	8580	sfca	1.000/sfca	8580	0.777/sfca	6667
27	Unload/Handle Reinf. Steel	2829	ton	3.332/ton	9426	0.681/ton	1927

Total mh 309100   254960
Excess mh 54140

$$\% \text{ Inefficiency} = \frac{\text{Excess mh}}{\text{Normal mh}} \times 100 = \frac{54140}{254960} \times 100 = 21.23\%$$

(1) Slab on Grade

FIGURE 22–3   Structural concrete with performance inefficiency factor developed by comparison to average work performance in eight similar projects.

If the owner rejects a claim, the contractor must abandon it or contest the owner's rejection through the dispute resolution provisions in the contract. The following final chapter in this book reviews the methods of contract dispute resolution practiced in the United States today.

QUESTIONS AND PROBLEMS

1. What triggers the filing of a contractor's claim?

2. What are the four basic reasons why contractors submit proposals for a change in contract price or time before the filing of a claim that were discussed in this chapter?

3. What two examples of "the event giving rise to the claim" were given in this chapter?

4. What two separate elements of a claim must be established by the contractor's detailed claim submittal?

5. What is the most important contract provision regarding contractor claims discussed in this chapter?

6. What is the usual consequence of a contractor's failure to conform to the claim notice provisions in construction contracts? What is "constructive notice"? Should contractors rely on the legal sufficiency of constructive notice?

7. Discuss the importance of the claim processing procedure provisions in construction contracts from the contractor's standpoint.

8. In the case of construction contracts that proscribe strict time limits for the issue of the owner's decision on a properly submitted contract claim, what is the usual consequence of an owner's failure to issue a decision within the proscribed time limits?

9. What general methods for the determination of changes in contract price, when entitlement has been recognized on a contract claim, are provided by most construction contracts? Of the three methods, which is usually employed?

10. According to the Oakland County Drain Commission contract, what four elements make up the "cost of the work"? What is the maximum fee to be paid to a prime contractor for overhead and profit in addition to the cost of the work when their own forces perform the work of the claim? What is the maximum fee in the aggregate for the prime contractor and subcontractor when the work of the claim is performed by a subcontractor?

11. How does the MWRA contract differ from the Oakland County Drain Commission Contract with respect to extensions in contract time?

12. Discuss the two general claim scenarios presented in this chapter, pointing out how they differ and the kinds of claim costs generated by each.

13. Discuss the four methods for proving the level of decreased efficiency of original contract work performance due to claim causations presented in this chapter? Which is generally the most persuasive? Which is the least persuasive?

23

Dispute Resolution

Key Words and Concepts

Lawsuits involving important federal
   questions
Diversity cases
Federal district courts
United States Court of Federal Claims
United States Courts of Appeal for the
   Federal Circuit
United States Supreme Court
State trial courts
State courts of appeal
State supreme courts
Venue
Bench trials
Jury trials
Discovery
Depositions

Fact witness/expert witness
Transcript
Plaintiff/respondent
Cross-examination
Findings-of-fact
Conclusions-of-law
Right of appeal
Hearings before boards of contract appeals
Arbitration
AAA arbitration
Party arbitration
Single arbitration
Alternative dispute resolution
Mediation
Mini-trials
Disputes review boards

When contracting parties cannot settle disputes themselves, the disagreement must be resolved by other means. The farther from the job level that the dispute reaches, the more likely it is to become highly adversarial, time consuming, and expensive. For instance, settling disputes by the decision of a court following a lawsuit can lead to costs that are on the order of magnitude of the most favorable judgment that can be obtained. These costs include legal representation, various consultants, expert witnesses, and so on, as well as the drain on a company's organization. Key personnel are often tied up for extended periods preparing for trial and for actual court appearances, keeping them away from their normal revenue-producing duties.

For these reasons, *alternative dispute resolution* (ADR) procedures are common today. When the parties in the dispute are genuinely committed to the process, these methods can be very effective, as well as far less time consuming and expensive.

The disputes resolution clause in a contract determines the particular method of settlement to be used for that particular contract. If a particular method is mandated, it must be used unless the parties mutually agree to change it.

COURTS OF LAW

If a dispute resolution method has not been mandated by the disputes resolution clause of the contract, a dissatisfied contractor is free to file a lawsuit in a court-of-law in the state or federal system.

Lawsuits in the Federal Court System

Unless the contract provides otherwise, **lawsuits involving an important federal question** will be tried in the **federal district court** for the geographical area in which the dispute arose. **Diversity cases**—those in which the parties are residents of different states—are also tried in federal district court. Appeals from a contracting officer's decision on a federal contract may be heard by one of the government administrative boards of contract appeals or, at the contractor's option, may be heard by the **United States Court of Federal Claims** (formerly the U.S. Court of Claims), a federal court established for the purpose of trying cases involving claims against the federal government. Decisions of the federal district courts and the United States Court of Federal Claims can be appealed to one of the **United States Courts of Appeal for the Federal Circuit,** the particular court depending on the geographical area.

Decisions of the Courts of Appeal for the Federal Circuit can be appealed to the **United States Supreme Court.** If the Supreme Court agrees to take the case, the appeal will be heard. The decision of the Supreme Court is final and binding.

Lawsuits in the State Court System

Lawsuits other than those involving important federal questions or diversity are tried in the first level of the state court system of the various states. The name of the first-level court, or **state trial court,** varies depending on the particular state.

Like the federal system, there are a number of first-level trial courts based on geographical area.

Decisions of the trial courts are appealable to the **state courts of appeal** and decisions of the courts of appeal are appealable to the **state supreme court,** whose decisions are appealable to the United States Supreme Court.

Determination of Venue

Venue means the court in which the lawsuit is tried. Its determination is a legal matter, often itself requiring the decision of a court. However, in some cases, there may be a choice. In these instances, the choice of venue will be made by the attorneys representing the party filing the lawsuit.

Features of Court Trials of Lawsuits

The trial of a construction case lawsuit in a court of law is a civil proceeding as opposed to a criminal trial. The features of such trials include the following:

- The trial may be conducted by a judge sitting without a jury—a **bench trial**—or, on demand of either party, the trial may be held before a jury. In both cases, the purpose of the trial is to determine the facts, to which the law is then applied, resulting in the decision of the court. In a bench trial, the judge first determines the facts and then applies the law to arrive at the decision. In the case of a **jury trial,** the jury's function is to determine the facts. Then the judge carefully "instructs" the jurors what the law is in that particular case and how they must apply the law to the facts to arrive at a correct decision. In both cases, the judge conducts the entire proceeding and maintains the order and decorum of the court.

- Court trials are very formal. The judge maintains complete control, and his or her procedural decisions (rulings) are final insofar as the trial is concerned, although they may be appealed. Every word that is spoken is recorded verbatim by a court reporter.

- The judge controls the quantity and type of exhibits and testimony that go into the trial record as evidence. There are strict rules defining what is admissible and what is not. See for instance, the parole evidence rule and hearsay rule discussed in Chapters 20 and 21, respectively.

- The process of **discovery** prior to the trial will be afforded both sides. Discovery gives each side the right to examine and make copies of all pertinent files and documents possessed by the other side. Certain types of documents claimed to be privileged may be excluded by the judge from the discovery process. Included among these are communications between the parties and their attorneys and all attorney work-products.

- As part of the discovery process, each side also has the right to take the **deposition** of employees of the other side and whomever the other side intends to call as a witness at the trial, either as a **fact witness,** a person who has been involved in the project and has firsthand factual knowledge or as an **expert witness,** an expert in the field of the lawsuit who offers an opinion based on his or her knowledge and experience. At the deposition, the witness must truthfully answer all questions asked. A fact witness will speak from his or her own knowledge of the facts in the case, whereas an expert witness must reveal all opinions held and the basis for them. A verbatim record of the questions and answers is recorded by a court reporter who prepares a **transcript** that may be used by attorneys for either side when questioning that witness on the stand at the trial.

- At the trial itself, each side is allowed to present its case starting with the **plaintiff,** the party who instituted the lawsuit followed by the **respondent,** the party being sued, who presents a rebuttal. The plaintiff then responds to the rebuttal with a surrebuttal at which point the trial usually ends, although the judge may permit another round of presentations. During each presentation, each side introduces trial exhibits in the form of various documents, explanatory charts, and so on, and each of the side's witnesses offer oral testimony under oath.

- At the end of each witness's testimony, the opposing attorney has the right to conduct a **cross-examination** of the witness. The purpose of cross-examination is to give the opposing attorney every reasonable opportunity to discredit or impugn the testimony of the witness. Cross-examination of an opponent's witnesses is one of the fundamental rights of a litigant in our legal system.

- In the case of bench trials, the judge may issue written **findings-of-fact** and **conclusions-of-law** along with the decision of the court, although this is not common in the lower courts, where the trial initially occurs. The appellate courts usually issue findings-of-fact and conclusions-of-law. These writings state the facts that the court found to be true and the principles of law that the court applied to these facts to arrive at the decision. The collective body of these writings constitute what has previously been described as case law, which will then be cited by judges and lawyers in future cases. No findings-of-fact and conclusions-of-law are issued in jury trials, only the jury's decision, which is announced immediately following the jury's deliberation at the conclusion of the trial. In bench trials, many months may elapse, sometimes even years, between the conclusion of the trial and the decision.

- Finally, a most important feature of court trials is the **right of appeal**—that is, the decisions of the trial court can be appealed by either party to an appellate court. If the appellate court agrees to hear the appeal, it reviews the trial court's decision, either affirming it, overturning it, or affirming in part and overturning in part. The appellate court's decision can then be appealed to the state or federal supreme court, as the case may be.

HEARINGS BEFORE THE FEDERAL BOARDS OF CONTRACT APPEALS

The federal boards of contract appeals have been established by the various agencies of the federal government to hear and render decisions on contract disputes arising from construction contracts administered by the particular agency. Typical federal boards include the Armed Forces Board of Contract Appeals, the Corps of Engineers Board of Contract Appeals, the Department of Transportation Contract Appeals Board, and many others. At least one state, Maryland, has established a state board of contract appeals. These boards consist of judges experienced in construction contract law who are appointed by the agency concerned. A contractor dissatisfied with the final decision of the contracting officer of a federal agency on a matter arising from a federal contract may appeal that decision either directly to the United States Court of Federal Claims or to the administrative board of the agency involved.

Hearings before the federal boards of contract appeals are conducted in a manner similar to court trials, except that the proceedings will always be conducted by a sitting judge. There is no jury. Following the hearing, the board will issue a written decision supported by findings-of-fact and conclusions-of-law. As with bench trials in courts of law, many months or even years may elapse prior to the board's issuing its decision. The decisions of the federal boards of contract appeals may be appealed to the United States Court of Federal Claims.

ARBITRATION

Arbitration is a third method of dispute resolution. It is generally faster and less expensive than court trials or hearings before administrative boards. Even so, arbitration of large, complicated cases can still be time consuming and expensive. The arbitrators, who are usually working professionals, cannot sit continuously for complicated cases, so the hearings are often fragmented, extending the time required. One arbitration in which the writer appeared as an expert witness was conducted intermittently over a period of 18 months. Most arbitration proceedings are not that long. Occasionally, however, they can last even longer.

Arbitration of a contract dispute cannot be compelled unless the contract expressly requires it. The right to arbitration is not an implied right. However, if the contract does require it, courts compel arbitration of the dispute on the demand of either party. The following cases are typical of the extensive case law on this point.

In a federal case involving a contract for construction of a sewer, the United States Court of Appeals required a city to arbitrate a differing site condition claim in spite of the city's argument that the contract provided that the engineer's decision would be final. The contract stated:

> All claims of the Owner or the Contractor shall be presented to the Engineer for his decision, which shall be final except in cases where time and/or financial considerations

are involved, and in such cases shall be submitted to arbitration if not solved by mutual agreement between the Owner and the Contractor.

When the contractor submitted a differing site condition claim for ground water that had not been anticipated, the city refused to arbitrate, alleging that the engineer had final authority in these matters and the arbitration clause did not extend to disputes of this nature. Although the court criticized the language used in the arbitration clause, it applied federal law requiring that arbitration clauses be generously construed and resolved in favor of arbitration. In the words of the court:

> Obviously, financial considerations are the heart of the instant contractor's claim. Though we entertain some doubt whether the agreement was intended to cover the instant claim, we must enforce federal policy and come down in favor of arbitration.[1]

In another case, a project owner opposed arbitration, arguing that the demand for arbitration was not a dispute "arising out of, or relating to, the Contract Documents," because the disputed issue involved work not authorized by the contract or by written change order. The original contract was for a stipulated sum of $592,000 and stated that, although change orders would be necessary, the total contract price was in no event to exceed $700,000. However, the contract also contained a broad form arbitration clause.

The court found that since the contract documents provided that the contract included change orders pertaining to "all items necessary for the proper execution and completion of the Work," a dispute involving a claim for extra work necessary for completion of the project was subject to the arbitration clause. The court stressed that, in ordering arbitration, it was not establishing owner liability in excess of $700,000. Rather, the court said, the contractor's entitlement, if any, as well as the effect of such entitlement on the contract price ceiling, would have to be determined by the arbitrators.[2]

The following three principal systems of arbitration are commonly used today for construction cases. Normally, the contract states that one or the other of these systems is to be used. If the contract does not state this, the parties must agree on one of the systems.

AAA Arbitration Under Construction Industry Rules

One system is arbitration under the auspices of the **American Arbitration Association (AAA)** in accordance with the construction industry rules. In this system, each party reviews a list of potential arbitrators furnished by the AAA. Persons on the list are knowledgeable professionals who have been screened and prequalified by the AAA and who have agreed to serve as arbitrators. Each party may strike from the list anyone who is not satisfactory to them. Three persons who are acceptable to both parties—that is, persons remaining on the list who have not been struck by one

---

[1] *Ruby-Collins, Inc. v. City of Huntsville*, 748 F.2d 573 (11th Cir. 1984).

[2] *Sisters of St. John the Baptist v. Phillips R. Geraghty Constructor, Inc.*, 494 N.E.2d 102 (N.Y. 1986).

party or the other—are then selected by the AAA to form a panel to hear the case, one of whom is usually an attorney and who serves as chairperson. Arbitrators must disclose any material facts about themselves that could be perceived as affecting their ability to render an impartial decision, such as prior acquaintance or business dealings with any of the parties. A party may demand replacement of an arbitrator who they feel may not render a fair decision based on such disclosure. For smaller cases, the procedure is the same except that the board consists of a single person who usually is an attorney.

Party Arbitration System

A second system is the **party arbitration** system. Each party unilaterally selects a knowledgeable professional to serve as an arbitrator on the board. These two persons then select a third member of the board who functions as chairperson. In this system, the first two members sometimes act as party advocates as well as arbitrators, whereas the third member must always be strictly impartial. If the first two members are unable to agree on the third member, a court can be petitioned to appoint the third member.

Single Arbitrator System

The third system is one in which the parties agree on a **single arbitrator** to constitute the board. Such a person often is a retired judge experienced in construction cases who agrees to serve as arbitrator and hear the case.

Features of Arbitration Proceedings

The following features distinguish arbitration proceedings from court trials and hearings before administrative boards:

- Arbitration generally is far less formal. Arbitrators have broad powers to set the rules on such matters as discovery and procedural matters for the conduct of the hearing. Arbitrators usually allow discovery, but they are not compelled to do so.
- Arbitration panels are far more flexible than courts on the rules of evidence. Generally, these rules are considerably relaxed in arbitration.
- Following the hearing, which is generally conducted in a manner similar to a court trial, the panel will issue its decision. The time period between the conclusion of the hearing and the decision is generally fairly short, far less than in a court trial. Usually, only a conclusory decision is issued with no supporting findings-of-fact or conclusions-of-law.
- Finally, and most importantly, there is generally no viable appeal to an arbitration decision. Only in cases where it can be proved that the arbitrators exercised bad faith or refused to permit the introduction of evidence or that

an arbitrator failed to disclose information that might have prevented rendering an impartial decision is a successful appeal to a court possible.

Examples of case law on this subject include vacation of the award due to the arbitrator's refusal to hear relevant testimony[3] and vacation of the award because one of the arbitrators failed to disclose ongoing business dealings with one of the parties to the arbitration.[4]

ALTERNATIVE DISPUTE RESOLUTION

In recent years, **alternate dispute resolution** (ADR) procedures have increasingly been used. These methods include the following:

Mediation

In **mediation,** the parties engage a respected, knowledgeable neutral person to serve as a mediator. This person investigates the facts of the dispute, meets with the parties jointly and separately, and listens to their arguments. The mediator then proposes a settlement, sometimes as a written report and sometimes orally. The mediator's recommendation is not binding. Ordinarily, the mediator's recommendations are not admissible as evidence in a later court trial if either party pursues the matter in a lawsuit.

Mini-Trials

Another procedure, called a **mini-trial**, is also used. In this case, the parties arrange for a hearing to be conducted somewhat like a court trial. There is no judge or jury. Instead, two senior persons with settlement authority hear the evidence, one from each party. They do not participate in the presentation of the respective cases other than to ask questions. Following the conclusion of the hearing, these two individuals have each become personally knowledgeable about the strengths and weaknesses of each side's arguments. They then confer privately and attempt to arrive at a settlement through negotiation. This system has the advantage of speed and a less adversarial atmosphere. A number of major disputes have been settled in this manner.

Disputes Review Boards

Another form of alternate dispute resolution that is increasingly used is a contractually provided contract **disputes review board** (DRB). In this instance, the construction contract between the parties expressly provides for the creation of a three-member board. As soon as the contract has been signed, each party selects a knowledgeable person to serve as member of the board. These two persons then select a third member, who normally acts as chairperson. Once each party has

---

[3]*Manchester Township Board of Education v. Thomas P. Carney, Inc.*, 489 A.2d 682 (N.J. Super. A.D. 1985).

[4]*Barcon Associates, Inc. v. Tri-County Asphalt Corp.*, 411 A.2d 709 (N.J. App. Div. 1980).

selected a member of the board, the two selected members have no further contact with those parties, instead becoming fully independent. All contact between the board and the parties to the contract is conducted through the chairperson.

Board members are required to act impartially and are subject to the same type of conflict-of-interest disclosure requirements as arbitrators are. The board members are furnished copies of the project plans and specifications and periodically visit the project jobsite to become familiar with the project as it progresses. If the parties are unable to resolve contract disputes as they occur, either party may refer the dispute to the board. The board then holds a hearing, listens to the arguments of both parties, and promptly furnishes a written recommendation for the resolution of the dispute that contains a detailed explanation of the reasoning supporting the recommendation. The recommendation is not binding, but along with the supporting reasoning, it is usually admissible as evidence in any later court trial. Such boards are now widely used, and in most cases the parties have been able to resolve the dispute promptly with the aid of the board's recommendations. This form of dispute resolution has the obvious advantage of great speed. Disputes are resolved quickly and inexpensively once they have been presented to the board. The continuous availability of the board, which has been kept in close touch with the project as it progresses, is a unique feature that is not present in any of the other methods of dispute resolution available to the industry today.

Model specifications to be included in the contract for the appointment and operation of disputes review boards first appeared in a publication of the American Society of Civil Engineers.[5] This was followed by a second ASCE publication[6] and, more recently, by *Construction Dispute Review Board Manual*.[7]

CONCLUSION

Dispute avoidance far outweighs the merits of any of the dispute resolution methods discussed in this chapter. Disputes will be greatly minimized, or will not occur at all, if each party to the contract fully understands both their responsibilities and their rights under the contract and truly endeavors to honor the contract. Only when one or both parties fail to do this does dispute resolution become necessary.

QUESTIONS AND PROBLEMS

1. What two general kinds of cases will be litigated in the federal district courts as opposed to the state courts of the state where the work was performed?

---

[5]*Avoiding and Resolving Disputes in Underground Construction* (New York: American Society of Civil Engineers, 1989).

[6]*Avoiding and Resolving Disputes During Construction* (New York: American Society of Civil Engineers, 1991).

[7]*Construction Dispute Review Board Manual* (New York: McGraw-Hill Companies, Inc., 1996).

Which two avenues for dispute resolution are available to a contractor for resolution of disputes arising from a federal contract?

2. What is the difference between a bench trial and a jury trial? In a bench trial, who determines the facts? Who applies the law? In a jury trial, who determines the facts? Who applies the law? Do the judge's instructions to the jury deal with the facts or the law?

3. In court trials, who controls the procedure? Who rules on the admissibility of evidence? Are court trials subject to appeal?

4. What is discovery? What are privileged documents? What is a deposition, and what is its purpose? What does the term *fact witness* mean? What is the difference between a fact witness and an expert witness?

5. What do the terms *plaintiff* and *respondent* mean? Which presents its case first? What is the function or purpose of trial exhibits, oral testimony, and cross-examination?

6. What are findings-of-fact and conclusions-of-law? Who issues them? With what type of court proceeding are they usually associated? What is their relationship to case law?

7. Do hearings before the various administrative boards of contract appeals differ materially from court trials? Is there a jury? Will there be findings-of-fact and conclusions-of-law issued with the decisions of such boards? Are the decisions of the federal boards of contract appeals themselves appealable? To whom?

8. What is arbitration? Under what circumstances can arbitration be compelled in construction cases? Is the choice of arbitration an implied right of either party to the contract? What are the three different systems of arbitration used for construction cases discussed in this chapter?

9. Explain the party arbitrator system. How many panel members are there? How are they selected? Is a party arbitrator necessarily impartial and neutral? How is the chairperson selected?

10. What are the four features of arbitration proceedings that were discussed in this chapter?

11. Under what limited circumstances may an arbitration decision be appealed or overturned?

12. What three ADR procedures were discussed in this chapter? Is mediation binding? In a mini-trial, who makes the final decision for settlement of the dispute? What are two principal advantages of the mini-trial?

13. What principal feature of the disputes review board approach to dispute resolution is not present in mediation, court trials, hearings?

Bibliography

Collier, K. *Managing Construction—The Contractual Viewpoint*. Albany, NY: Delmar Publishers, 1994.

Cushman, R. F., and Butler, S. D. *Construction Change Order Claims*. New York: John Wiley & Sons, 1994.

Cushman, R. F., and Taub, K. S. *Design-Build Contracting Handbook*. New York: John Wiley & Sons, 1992.

Fisk, E. R. *Construction Project Administration*, 3rd ed. New York: John Wiley & Sons, 1988.

Hinze, J. *Construction Contracts*. New York: McGraw-Hill, 1993.

Jervis, B. M., and Levin, P. *Construction Law Principles and Practice*. New York: McGraw-Hill, 1988.

Richter, I., and Mitchell, R. S. *Handbook of Construction Law and Claims*. Reston, VA: Reston Publishing Company, 1982.

Rubin, R. A., Guy, S. D., Maevis, A. C., and Fairweather, V. *Construction Claims Analysis, Presentation, Defense*. New York: Van Nostrand Reinhold Company, 1983.

Samuels, B. M. *Construction Law*. Upper Saddle River, NJ: Prentice Hall, 1996.

Schwartzkopf, W., McNamara, J. J., and Hoffar, J. F. *Calculating Construction Damages*. New York: John Wiley & Sons, 1992.

Simon, M. S., Esq. *Construction Claims and Liability*. Princeton, NJ: John Wiley & Sons, 1989.

Sweeney, N. J., Kellerher, T. J., Beck, P.E., and Hafer, R. F. *Common Sense Construction Law*. New York: John Wiley & Sons, 1997.

Sweet, J. *Legal Aspects of Architecture, Engineering, and the Construction Process*, 4th ed. St. Paul, MN: West Publishing Company, 1989.

Sweet, J. *Sweet on Construction Industry Contracts: Major AIA Documents*. New York: John Wiley & Sons, 1987.

Wickwire, J. M., Driscoll, T. J., and Hurlbut, S. B. *Construction Scheduling: Preparation, Liability, and Claims*. New York: John Wiley & Sons, 1991.

Index